About the Author

Emily Anne Croom is an active researcher, teacher, and lecturer in genealogy. She holds a master's degree in history and contributes articles to several genealogy periodicals, including *Family Tree Magazine*. In addition to several privately printed family histories, her other works include the widely acclaimed *Genealogist's Companion and Sourcebook*, and the popular *Sleuth Book for Genealogists*. Emily is also the co-author of *A Genealogist's Guide to Discovering Your African-American Ancestors*. She resides in Bellaire, Texas.

The Essential Guide to Unpuzzling Your Past. © 2003 by Emily Anne Croom. Manufactured in the United States of America. All rights reserved. No part of this book may be reproduced in any form or by any electronic or mechanical means including information storage and retrieval systems without permission in writing from the publisher, except by a reviewer, who may quote brief passages in a review, or by the purchaser, who may copy blank forms for personal use. Published by Betterway Books, an imprint of F&W Publications, Inc., 4700 East Galbraith Road, Cincinnati, Ohio 45236. (800) 289-0963.

Other fine Betterway Books are available from your local bookstore or on our Web site at http://www.familytreemagazine.com. To subscribe to Family Tree Magazine Update, a free e-mail newsletter with helpful tips and resources for genealogists, go to http://newsletters.fwpublications.com.

1-55870-701-8

07 06 05 04 03   5 4 3 2 1

Part I
Unpuzzling Your Past. © 2001 by Emily Anne Croom, 4th edition
Editor: Sharon DeBartolo Carmack, CG
Production editor: Brad Crawford
Production coordinator: Mark Griffin
Interior designer: Sandy Conopeotis Kent
Icon designer: Cindy Beckmeyer

The map appearing on pages 83 and 254 was supplied by the Gaylord Stickle Company, 2715 Bissonnet, Suite 205, Houston, Texas 77005.

Part II
The Unpuzzling Your Past Workbook. Copyright © 1996 by Emily Anne Croom.
Edited by Argie J. Manolis
Cover photography by Pamela Monfort Braun, Bronze Photography

The map appearing on pages 37, 309 and 311 has been supplied by the Gaylord Stickle Company, 2715 Bissonnet, Suite 205, Houston, TX 77005.

Part 1

Unpuzzling Your Past

Icons Used in This Book

Case Study

Examples of this book's advice at work

Oral History

Techniques for getting family stories

CD Source

Databases and other information available on CD-ROM

Printed Source

Directories, books, pamphlets, and other paper archives

Citing Sources

Reminders and methods for documenting information

Quotes

Useful words direct from the experts

For More Info

Where to turn for more in-depth coverage

Reminder

"Don't-Forget" items to keep in mind

Hidden Treasures

Family papers and home sources

Research Tip

Ways to make research more efficient

Idea Generator

Techniques and prods for further thinking

See Also

Where in this book to find related information

Important

Information and tips you can't overlook

Sources

Where to go for information, supplies, etc.

Internet Source

Where on the Web to find what you need

Step By Step

Walkthroughs of important procedures

Library/Archive Source

Repositories that might have the information you need

Technique

How to conduct research, solve problems, and get answers

Microfilm Source

Information available on microfilm

Timesaver

Shaving minutes and hours off the clock

Money Saver

Getting the most out of research dollars

Tip

Ways to make research more efficient

Notes

Thoughts, ideas, and related insights

Warning

Stop before you make a mistake

Table of Contents At a Glance

Table of Contents

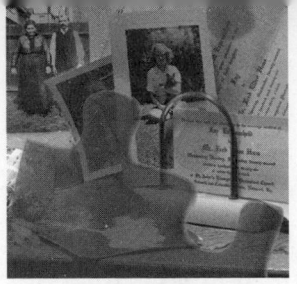

Foreword

Genealogy is akin to assembling a jigsaw puzzle about ancestors, one generation at a time. This fascinating hobby quite naturally begins at home and expands to research in public records of many kinds.

Genealogy and family history go hand in hand. The goal is not to accumulate more ancestral names than anyone else in town but to learn and preserve whatever you can about the ancestors you identify—their lives and cultures, their places in the history happening around them. Benefits include new friendships made among other researchers, boundless personal growth and education, and something worthwhile to keep you enthusiastic and busy for a lifetime.

The purpose of *Unpuzzling Your Past* is to give readers the information and tools necessary to learn to research wisely and achieve the best possible results. Thus, the book focuses on (1) answering basic how-to questions, (2) encouraging the use of family and public records, (3) promoting sound research methods, and (4) illustrating the process with pertinent research examples. Whether you use *Unpuzzling Your Past* as a researcher, student, or teacher, enjoy yourself and have fun working your own special puzzle.

Useful for researchers at any level of experience, *The Unpuzzling Your Past Workbook* combines well with this book, and readers are encouraged to use the two volumes together. *The Genealogist's Companion & Sourcebook* goes beyond the basics to focus on finding and using both common and less familiar U.S. public sources. *The Sleuth Book for Genealogists*, with lively advice and encouragement from literary detectives, addresses research methods and genealogical problem solving. Two of its strengths are its detailed guide to documentation and interesting case studies.

In this fourth edition, I extend my appreciation to my readers, students, and ancestors who keep me thinking and learning; to fellow genealogist Gay E. Carter, reference librarian at the University of Houston-Clear Lake; and to my husband, Robert T. Shelby.

A Note to Teachers

This book includes tools and ideas adaptable for classroom projects from elementary school to adult continuing education classes. As a young schoolteacher, I learned the value of working through any assignment I planned for my students before assigning it to them. Thus, I encourage all teachers who plan a family history project for students to do it themselves first.

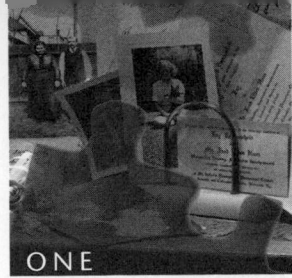

ONE

In the Beginning

H ave you wanted to work on your family history but don't know how to begin? Do you have elderly relatives you have never talked with about your family history? Have you done some information gathering on the Internet or among relatives but not tapped historical and genealogical records? Are you a teacher wanting to help your students begin to study their families and heritage? If you answered yes to any of these questions, this book is for you.

CAN YOU NAME YOUR GREAT-GRANDPARENTS?

That's the question that launched my search for family history in the seventh grade. I thought I could answer easily, but I couldn't. With great confidence I named four individuals. When I stopped, the librarian jolted me into reality: "But you have eight great-grandparents. You have two parents, who each had two parents. That's four grandparents, right? They each had two parents, and that gives you eight great-grandparents." Alas, I had to admit that my father's side of the family was one giant blank. Those people were hiding somewhere, and I knew I had to find them.

My dad knew one older relative, an uncle in Tennessee. I wrote to him, and we corresponded until his death. From him I got some answers, some erroneous traditions, and a bunch of cousins. I was on my way! After college and several visits to Tennessee, I knew something about three of the four missing great-grandparents. Pitser was a Methodist farmer who also owned a mill and got up at three in the morning to go to work. Mary Catherine, his wife, hated housework, so she raised peacocks and lambs while her daughter kept house. Isaac was a farmer who had asthma and at least thirteen kids by two wives; he did not require my grandfather to go to school but allowed him to hunt and fish before he was old enough to share in the farm work. By the time my research began, it was too late to find anyone who had known the fourth missing great-grandparent, Ann. After years of research, I finally identified her parents and brother but, unfortunately, still know little about her as an individual.

ANCESTORS AND GENERATIONS

The search now continues beyond the eight great-grandparents. It reaches as far back as there are records available. Neither you nor I will ever verify lineages back to Adam and Eve or Julius Caesar or, in most cases, much beyond the seventeenth century. Don't worry about that. We have plenty of challenges and adventures ahead to confirm our lineages to the seventeenth century. **The goal is to connect each generation to the previous one in such a way that you know you are claiming the correct ancestors on your family tree.**

Important

Think about it: Each generation going back doubles the number of ancestors you have—two parents, four grandparents, eight great-grandparents, sixteen great-great-grandparents, etc. Each couple represents the joining of two families, lineages, or ancestral "lines." The female lines are as important in genealogy as the male lines, and it sometimes takes more effort to identify the women and their parents. **Remember, half your ancestors were women.**

Reminder

All your ancestral lines back to 1650 could involve as many as eight to twelve generations of ancestors before you. If eight generations separate you from 1650, you could have had 256 ancestors living then. A gap of twelve generations could mean you had more than 4,000 ancestors living in 1650. Many people find that some ancestors appear more than once on their charts. You too may descend from brothers or sisters who lived generations ago.

Each line will have a different number of generations reaching back to 1650. One line may take only eight generations to get to 1650 because the parents in each generation were older when your ancestor was born. For example, my Croom line reaches 1650 in only eight generations before me because the average age of the father in each generation was just under thirty-seven years. Another line takes ten generations to reach 1650 because the average age of the parent in each generation was about thirty-one years.

In genealogy we often estimate a generation as about twenty-two to twenty-five years for men and about eighteen to twenty-three years for women. This estimate suggests the age of the parents when their *first* child was born. When an ancestor was the fifth or tenth child in a family, or when the parents were in a second marriage, the parents could have been considerably older than these estimates suggest. As an experiment, I listed ten of my lines that reach back to the late seventeenth or early eighteenth centuries and calculated an average age of all the parents at just under thirty-two years. The three youngest mothers were nineteen when my next ancestor was born; the oldest father was seventy-one!

WHY THE JIGSAW PUZZLE?

Agatha Christie's detective Hercule Poirot explained his methods much as a genealogist could:

> It is a little like your puzzle, Madame. One assembles the pieces. . . . and every strange-shaped little piece must be fitted into its own place. . . . And sometimes it is like that piece of your puzzle just now. One arranges very methodically the pieces of the puzzle—one sorts the colours—and then perhaps a piece of one colour that should fit in with—say, the fur rug, fits in instead in a black cat's tail.
>
> —*from* Evil Under the Sun

Quotes

The process of genealogy is indeed similar to working a jigsaw puzzle. In genealogy, **we begin with what we know and work backward in time.** In working jigsaw puzzles, "what we know" is the easily recognized straight-edged pieces of a jigsaw puzzle. We piece them together first to form the frame and then work with the other pieces to find where they belong. The excitement and satisfaction increase as more pieces fit into place.

Tip

In genealogy, the straight-edged pieces are the most recent names, dates, places, relationships, and stories that you know or can find easily for yourself, your siblings, your parents and their siblings, your grandparents and their siblings. Once these are recorded, you have a framework from which to look for more and in which to fit new pieces that you find. Some pieces of the puzzle fall into place more quickly and easily than others. Working backward in time, or toward the middle of the puzzle, the genealogist completes many sections of the puzzle but will never finish the whole. There will always be one more wife to identify or one more generation to verify.

ORGANIZE EARLY AND OFTEN

Probably three times as many genealogical organizing systems exist as there are genealogists, for many change their systems along the way. There is no right or wrong way to organize, but there are better and worse ways. The worse ways include spiral notebooks and storage space on the dining room table. The better ways are numerous, usually involving three-ring binders, file folders, or a combination of the two. These tools imply storage in bookcases and/or filing cabinets and boxes. Your system will depend on your budget, your filing time, your storage space apart from the dining room table, whether you can maintain the system you choose, and the way you think—i.e., how you can find your information quickly. Don't feel bad if you change your system after a while. You need whatever works best for you.

For More Info

For further discussion and ideas, see Sharon DeBartolo Carmack's *Organizing Your Family History Search*.

Considerations on Filing Systems

Most filing systems organize by surname or individual's name first, then by location, and then often by type of record. Begin with your surname or maiden name as one notebook or filing division. Perhaps at first your notes will fit into one binder, with dividers for the states where your ancestors lived. As your material increases, you can separate it into a different binder or filing section for each state, divided by counties if necessary and helpful.

Another approach is to organize by generation. Some genealogists prefer a binder or file folder for each person, or each ancestral couple, with all the notes and documents pertaining to them stored in their binder or folder. I personally prefer binders that contain all my notes on the generations that lived in the same county or same state. I don't want (1) the expense of making three copies of documents that contain information on three brothers or (2) to spend time filing the copies in three folders when I return from research. When I study my notes, I want to see the interaction of family members and generations without having to pull a number of folders and then sort and refile papers.

Research Tip

Frequently, ancestors migrated and lived in family groups. Elliott Coleman moved from Virginia to west Tennessee in 1845 because an aunt and family friends lived there. Later, three younger brothers joined him. The search for the brothers centered in one county, which held records on all four. Because they witnessed each other's documents, subscribed to the same newspaper, attended the same church and civic functions, and conducted business in the same town, their descendants have many records to read and abstract. Keeping the notes together in a notebook labeled "Coleman-West Tennessee" gives a good family picture. After all, Elliott was not an isolated individual but the oldest brother of a family group.

Subdivisions for Filing

For ease of finding specific notes quickly, it is helpful to divide each state, county, or generational file or notebook into sections based on the kinds of records in which the ancestors appear. Wait until you find a record before making a divider for that category, for not all ancestors appear in all the record groups. For example, if your ancestors never lived in federal land states, you probably will not find them in federal land records and would not need a divider for that record group. Customize each binder or file for the family whose story it holds.

Consider the following divisions for a notebook or family file:

1. Family group sheets, five-generation charts, chronologies, and other charts. If several nuclear families, such as four brothers, lived in the same county, consider a separate divider for each brother's family.
2. Research plans.
3. State and county maps.
4. Census records. If the family was large and you accumulate many census records, it is helpful to divide the records further: censuses 1790–1840, censuses 1850–1880, and censuses 1900 forward, or any other division that helps you find your notes quickly.
5. Birth and death records, tombstone inscriptions, family Bible records (one divider or three).
6. County and state land records.
7. Federal land records.
8. Tax records.
9. Marriage records.
10. Military records.

11. Court records.
12. Immigration and naturalization records.
13. Wills and probate records.
14. Local records, including school, church, and organization records and newspaper abstracts.
15. Local, county, state, and social history.
16. Miscellaneous or other records.
17. Correspondence with other researchers and family members.

What do you do about the wives' maiden names? Once you identify a maiden name, you can add a division in the husband's file or notebook for preliminary research on the wife's family. When you identify her parents by name, you probably would create a new binder or file for them because they represent two new ancestral lines, and their research may go in different directions from their daughter's.

CHOOSE A FOCUS ANCESTOR

Each generation adds a wife-mother and a husband-father, as well as their mothers and fathers and grandparents, and so on. At first, you may want to work on the two generations closest to you (parents, grandparents, and their siblings) to get a feel for what information is available and which lines may be the easiest or hardest to research. Especially if several of these families lived in the same county, it makes sense to gather information on each family as you research marriages, cemeteries, censuses, and vital records.

However, as you begin to research great-grandparents and beyond, you may discover that the ancestors are swimming around in your head and you cannot keep all the names and relationships straight. This phenomenon is common in genealogy and can make a researcher feel overwhelmed or frustrated. **Researchers who spread their efforts thin by trying to work on too many ancestors at once usually do not tackle and solve the tough questions.** They often spin their wheels without making much progress. The remedy often is (1) keeping good charts (chapter two) in organized binders or folders and (2) narrowing the search.

Warning

Choose one or two ancestors or couples on which to concentrate. The others are not going anywhere; they will be there for you to research at a later date. By focusing on one or two, you can stay better organized and research smarter.

TAKING NOTES

Below are tips for taking notes as you research, whether in interviews, libraries, cemeteries, or electronic databases. Figure 1.1, on page 8, illustrates the process.

1. Dedicate each page of notes to one surname or family only. Write the family name at the top of the page so that it can be filed in the proper notebook or folder.

2. If one document pertains to two of your surnames, such as an ancestor

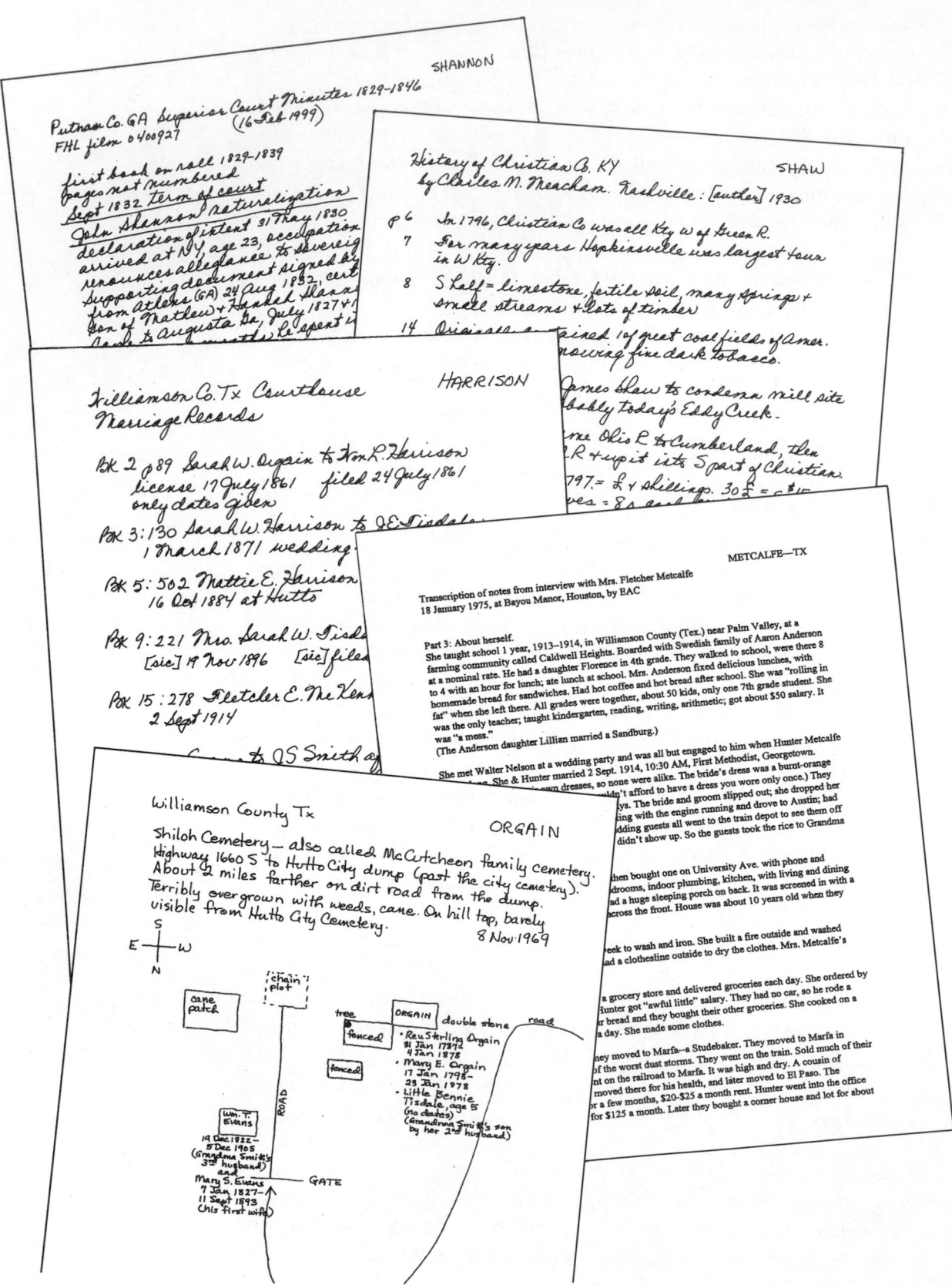

Figure 1.1 Examples of note taking

and his father-in-law, make a photocopy or carbon copy of your notes or make two photocopies of the document, one copy for each notebook or file. If you take your notes on a computer, print out a copy for each file.

3. At the top of the page of notes, before you write down information you have found, record the name of your source and enough identifying information that you can write a complete footnote. (See chapter three.) Note the medium you used—microfilm, CD-ROM, original document, online database—if your identifying information does not already indicate that.

4. It is also helpful to write on your notes the date you create them, the facility (library, courthouse, cemetery, etc.), and call numbers, when applicable. In genealogy, we sometimes need to find the sources again.

5. As you take notes, record volume and page number for each piece of information.

COMPUTERS?

What about using computers instead of notebooks and folders? First, you can "do genealogy" quite effectively without a computer. Second, even if you use a computer to take and store research notes from a library, you will need an organized way of recording, filing, and studying the information and photocopies you gather elsewhere—interviews, courthouses, cemeteries, and correspondence.

Many genealogists do not have the time or inclination to transfer all their notes from paper into a computer. Besides, many find it easier to study and evaluate data on people of the same surname or from the same county with the notes on paper spread out around them. For example, you may find multiple marriage records and cemetery inscriptions in one county for people of your surname. Are they related to each other? Are they related to you? Do all records in the name of Gouldsberry Greenapple refer to one person? You may not know at the time you write down the information. You need to keep this information together until you know which individuals fit into which families. Then you can link them in the computer.

THINGS TO DO NOW

1. Make a list of your grandparents, using full names.
2. How many of your great-grandparents can you name? Make a list.
3. Decide whether you want to try three-ring binders or file folders or a combination for your organizing efforts. Talk to other genealogists. Think about what will work for you. Write down your organizing ideas and choices.
4. Organize for research on at least one family name. Remember that with eight great-grandparents, you have at least eight families to choose from.
5. Read on to begin one of the most fascinating, rewarding, never-ending, adventure-filled, and addictive hobbies available anywhere.

Idea Generator

TWO

Charting Your Course

See Also

Appendix D, starting on page 246, contains blank forms.

Three kinds of charts are important worksheets as you put together your family history puzzle: the five-generation chart, the family group sheet, and the chronological profile. Properly used, they will show you at a glance what you already know at any point in your search. You can maintain a working set of these charts as you gather new information and keep a master set for information already verified and documented.

The one feature these three charts have in common is the most basic information on each person—**vital statistics**. To save space, we often use standard abbreviations on charts. Vital statistics include

- birth date and place (abbreviation: b—born)
- marriage date and place (abbreviation: m—married)
- divorce date and place, if applicable (abbreviation: div—divorced)
- death date and place and burial place (abbreviation: d—died, bur—burial/buried)

In other respects, these three charts are different in scope and content. The five-generation chart outlines one person and four generations of ancestors. The family group sheet lists three generations of a nuclear family—parents, children, and grandparents—with details on the parents and children. The chronological profile focuses on one ancestor, listing all the events you discover for that person's life. Although the three charts serve different functions, together they are extremely valuable tools for recording and studying your family's history.

FIVE-GENERATION CHART

The multigeneration chart (usually three, four, or five generations) is a road map of you and your ancestors—your family tree. The version in this book provides a reference for any person and four generations of ancestors. (See Figures 2.2 and 2.3, pages 13 and 14.) In each set of parents, the father's name goes on the top line. Reading from left to right, the chart has five columns. Consider the chart that begins with you.

- First column (the box), for your vital information.
- Second column (with two lines), for your parents.
- Third column (with four lines), for your four grandparents.
- Fourth column (with eight lines), for your great-grandparents.
- Fifth column (with sixteen lines), for names of great-great-grandparents. You can continue each of those sixteen ancestors on additional charts to carry their ancestry back as far as you can find information.

Most genealogy software can print out a similar chart for your linked individuals. **It is wise not to link them in your software until you have verified the accuracy of the information.** The form in this book gives you charts to work with as you do that checking. One of the great detectives of literature, Agatha Christie's Miss Marple, was fond of saying, "I make it a rule to take nothing that is told to me as true, unless it is *checked*" (from *Sleeping Murder*).

Important

To be thorough, you can footnote each piece of information for each person and list the sources on the back. To save time and space, the footnote numbers can refer to specific sources—family Bibles, census records, tombstones, etc. For example, footnote number one may refer to a specific family Bible. Cite it on the back of the chart; your copy of the record is in your file folder or notebook on that family. This one Bible may be the source (and the footnote) for ten different pieces of information on your chart.

Some researchers number or code the pages or documents in their folders or notebooks and use these numbers as source numbers on the charts. One problem with this method is that when you share the chart with others and they see the footnote or document numbers, they have no notes to correspond to the numbers. Thus, they have no way of knowing where the information originated or evaluating it.

If you have all these statistics documented on accompanying family group sheets (see the discussion below), you may choose not to duplicate your effort on the five-generation chart. In this case, you can note at the bottom of the chart "Documentation on accompanying family group sheets."

Some genealogists prefer to keep all their five-generation charts together in a separate binder for reference. Others choose to keep a chart in each notebook or family folder to identify the ancestors in that particular file. You may want to do both, keeping your working copy in the binder that goes with you to research and storing permanent copies with proven information safely at home.

Ahnentafel Numbers

Ahnentafel is a German word meaning "ancestor table." The system is easy to use and gives each ancestor an identification number. Some genealogists like to use these numbers to organize their files or notebooks, for each ancestor's number is permanent. It does not change as you identify new ancestors.

In this system, fathers are even numbers and mothers are odd numbers. To find a father's number, double the child's number. You are #1, so your father

For More Info

Paternal comes from the Latin *pater*, "father." *Maternal* is from the Latin *mater*, "mother." Paternal ancestors are your father's side of the family. Maternal ancestors are your mother's side. Ahnentafel charts and other useful forms are included in Croom's *Unpuzzling Your Past Workbook*.

is #2 and his father is #4. To find a mother's number, add one to the father's number. You are #1; your mother is #3. Her father is #6 (3 × 2) and her mother is #7. Figure 2.1, below, shows an easy-to-use ahnentafel chart that can accommodate you and five generations of ancestors. You can expand the chart to include all the ancestors you identify.

The five-generation charts in Figures 2.2 and 2.3, pages 13–14, show the use of ahnentafel numbers, beginning with you as #1. Figure 2.2 is a five-generation chart numbered from 1 to 31, for you and four generations of ancestors.

As you work back in time, any ancestor can begin a new five-generation chart. That is why the five-generation chart in this book has blanks for you to

Ahnentafel Table for No. 1 _____

Double a person's number to find the father. Double the number and add 1 to find the mother.

Paternal Line	Maternal Line
Parents	
2	3
Grandparents	
4	6
5	7
Great-Grandparents	
8	12
9	13
10	14
11	15
Great-Great-Grandparents	
16	24
17	25
18	26
19	27
20	28
21	29
22	30
23	31
Great-Great-Great-Grandparents	
32	48
33	49
34	50
35	51
36	52
37	53
38	54
39	55
40	56
41	57
42	58
43	59
44	60
45	61
46	62
47	63

Figure 2.1 *Reprinted from* Unpuzzling Your Past Workbook

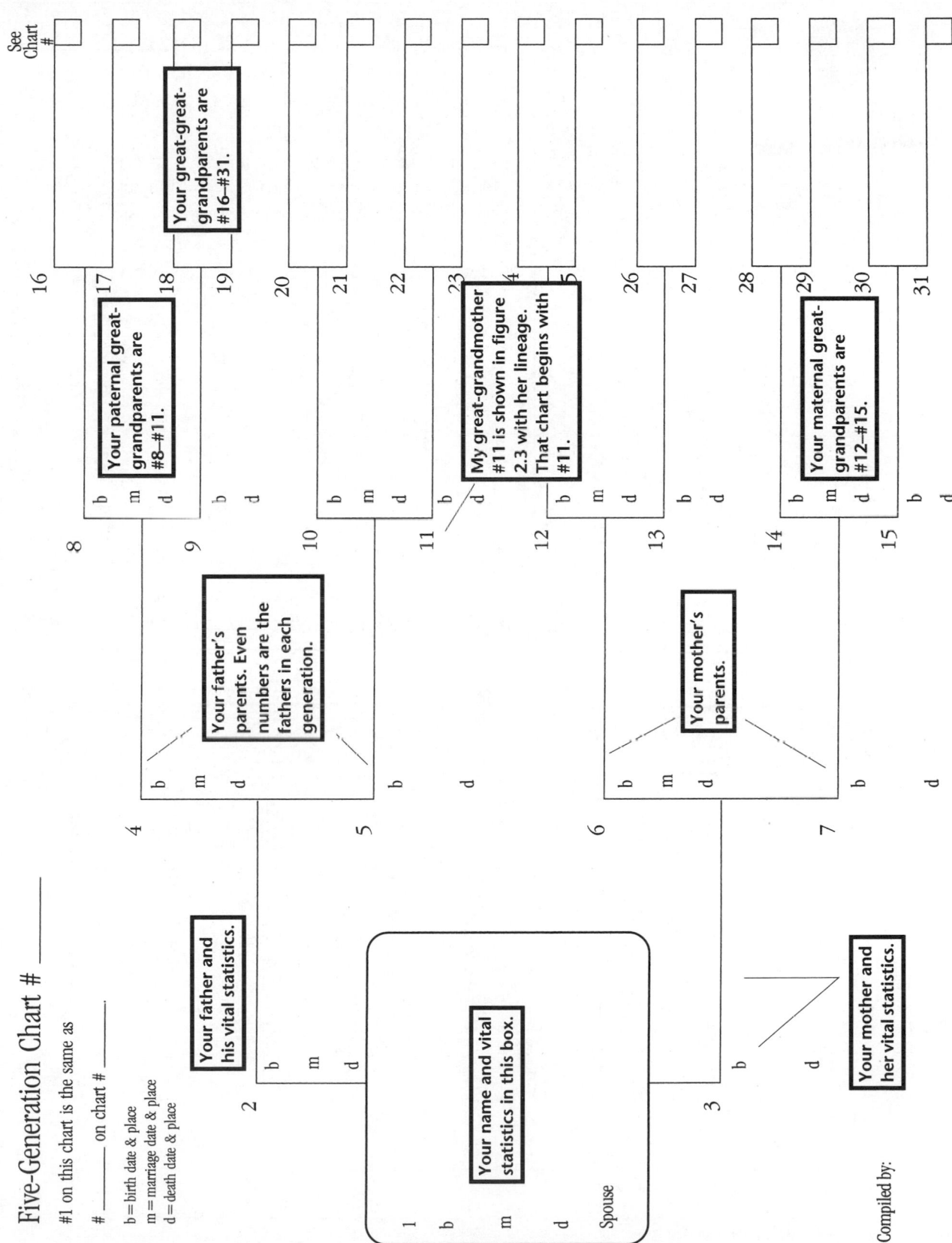

Figure 2.2 Five-Generation Chart for Numbers 1-31. *Reprinted from* Unpuzzling Your Past Workbook

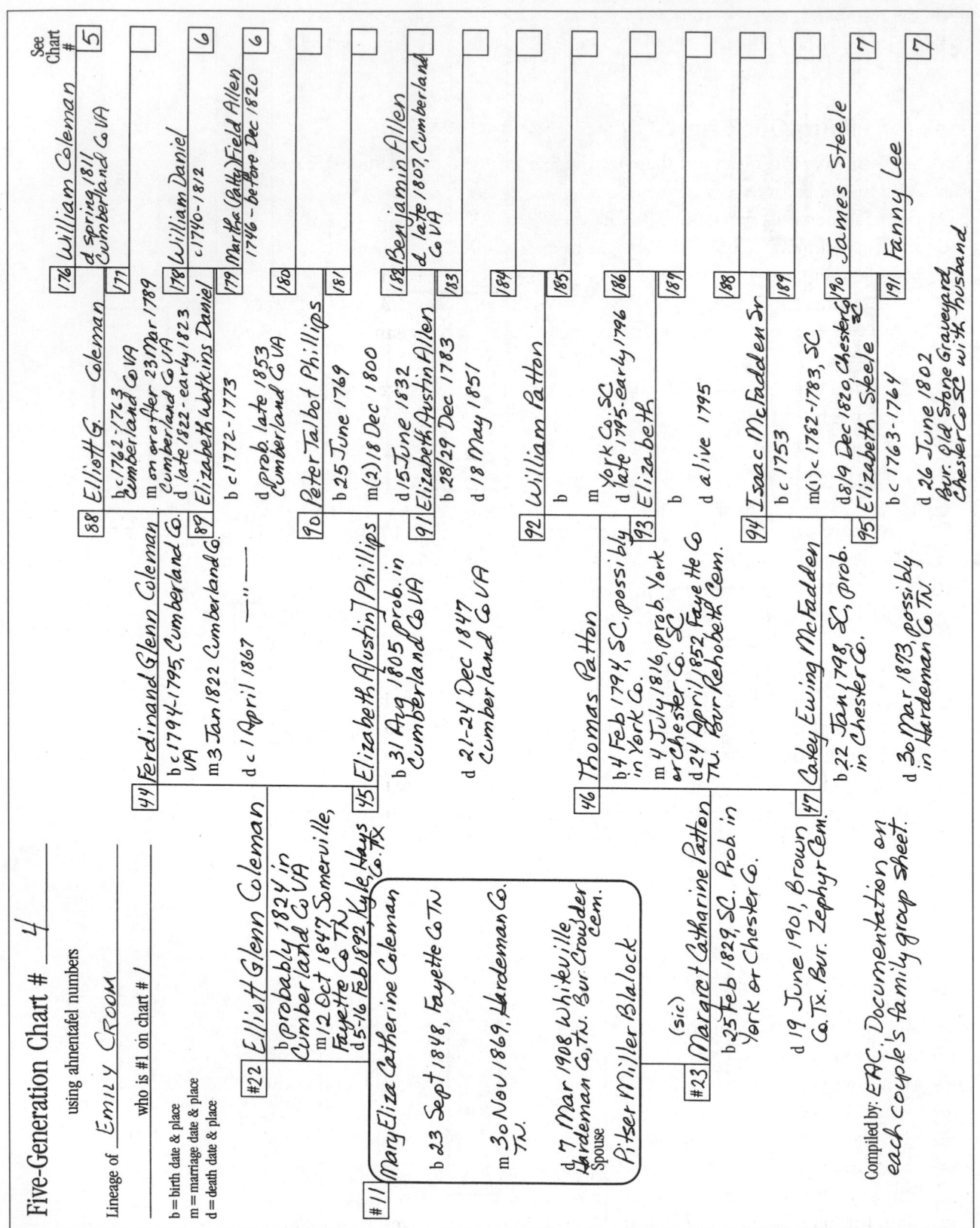

Figure 2.3 Ahnentafel Five-Generation Chart

fill in the number of each person. The example in Figure 2.3, on page 14, shows the ancestry of Mary Eliza Catherine Coleman, who is #11, a paternal great-grandmother of #1.

Tips for Filling Out Charts

Tip

Here are some tips for filling out these multigeneration charts and family group sheets (discussed below):

1. Use each person's full name when it is known.
2. Show a nickname in quotation marks or parentheses after the given name.
3. List each female by her maiden name (surname before marriage).
4. When estimating a date from facts, as shown in Figures 2.3 and 2.4, use *about* or *c* (or *ca*), an abbreviation for the Latin *circa*, meaning "about." The letters *b c* before a date mean "born about."
5. When you have evidence but cannot determine an exact date or place, use qualifiers: b *by* 1764, m *after* 20 Jan 1823, d *before* 20 May 1735; b *prob[ably]* in SC.
6. When you do not have a piece of information or data on which to make an estimate, leave the space blank.
7. If you have evidence for a date, place, or name but have not yet proved it, write on your working copy what you think is true and add a question mark to indicate the uncertainty.
8. If you have conflicting pieces of evidence for a date and have not yet determined which is correct, list both on your working copy of the chart: 1828/1829. State your evidence on the back of the page.
9. If you have narrowed down a range of dates for an event, list the range to show that the event took place between the given dates: 5–16 February 1892. State your evidence on the back.
10. When you have the space and the inclination, you can name the children or add other notes, such as military service or cemetery name, to a person's entry.
11. If you do not have evidence or confirmation of the facts, leave the space blank.

FAMILY GROUP SHEET

The family group sheet is a most useful chart for keeping together the genealogical information on each nuclear family. The version used in this book is unique in that it allows you to list your documentation as you go. This way, you know where you got each piece of data: a middle initial, a mother's maiden name, a marriage date, or the fact that each child was indeed a child of these parents. You can record as many sources as are applicable to any piece of information.

In this way, the chart answers such questions as these: Why did I put that death date for her? Where did I find the two children who never appeared on a census record? Why did I say he was born in Georgia when the other siblings were born in Mississippi?

Citing Sources

Writing on the chart your sources for each piece of information is very important to having a credible and quality product for yourself and for sharing. When you send the chart to others, they too will know exactly where you got the information. To avoid a common mistake that many genealogists make, and save yourself time, **record the sources on each group sheet when you start it; then add the source each time you add information.** Then, when someone asks you to share a particular group sheet, you won't have to take a week of vacation to find the information and get it in shape to share. You will have been smart enough to do this documenting all along.

You need a family group sheet for each nuclear family you study:

- yourself as a parent
- yourself as a child with your parents and siblings
- each of your parents as a child with parents and siblings
- each aunt and uncle with their children
- cousins with their spouses and children
- each grandparent as a child with parents and siblings
- each great-grandparent as a child with parents and siblings
- each nuclear family you study in each generation as you reach back in time
- siblings of each ancestor you study in each generation

Figure 2.4 is a family group sheet for a nineteenth-century family. Notice that it took twenty-two sources to document the parents and their children because there were no family Bibles, birth and death certificates, or tombstones, and few other records gave direct statements of the information. The data was gathered in true puzzle fashion and pieced together. Some entries remain estimates and may never be more specific. The source page documents each piece of information in the form of footnotes.

The facts on a family group sheet probably are not everything you know about the family. Your research notes may contain information on education, occupation, daily life, land ownership, military service, etc. The focus of this chart, however, is the confirmation of names, relationships, and vital statistics of the nuclear family.

Using the Family Group Sheet Advantageously

Because we research the cluster of friends, siblings, cousins, and neighbors among whom an ancestor lived and worked, we need to keep track of them as well. The family group sheets on the people in the cluster provide not only a place to record information systematically but also a ready reference to it. By studying the charts of a group of brothers and sisters with their spouses and children, you may find naming patterns that may be clues to former generations and maiden names. Birthplace patterns may suggest former residences where you can research. You may also discover discrepancies that necessitate additional research.

For example, if tombstones for two sisters give birth dates only six months apart, you have a dilemma: Which date is correct? You may never notice the

Family Group Sheet of the _Thomas Robertson_ Family

	Source #		Source #
Thomas Roberson Full name of husband (This is how he signed his name.)	1, 3, 10, 12	Birth date c 1807–1809	10, 11
		Birth place	
His father		Death date c 30 June – 1 July 1842	12
		Death place _Putnam County GA_	12
His mother with maiden name		Burial place	

	Source #		Source #
Elizabeth C. _Arnold_ Full maiden name of wife	1, 3, 10	Birth date c 1808–1809	7, 10
Arnold	2	Birth place _Georgia_	7, 14
Her father		Death date _1857–1868_	15, 16, 17, 21
Elizabeth Allen Her mother with maiden name _dau. of James Allen_	2 2	Death place _probably Caddo Parish LA_ Burial place	

Other Spouses _She m 2nd Isaac Croom Sr, Caddo Parish LA, bond dated 22 June 1846. By Isaac, she had dau Louisiana, in Aug. 1848. Louisiana m J H Harris._ Source #s 4, 7, 15, 17	Marriage date, place, etc. _18 Aug. 1833, Putnam County GA._ Source #s 3

Children of this marriage	Birth date & place	Death date, place, & burial place	Marriage date, place & spouse
1. _Ann Maria Robertson_ Source #s 19, 22	c 1835–1836 probably in Putnam Co. GA #7,8	c 1873–1879 probably in Madison Co TN #13, 20	Isaac Croom Jr 15 Sept 1856 Caddo Parish LA #5
2. possible daughter, name unknown, under 5 in 1840 Source #s 10	c 1837–1840 #10	before 1850? #7	no record found
3. possible daughter, name unknown, under 5 in 1840 Source #s 10	c 1837–1840 #10	before 1850? #7	no record found
4. _Thomas James Robertson_ Source #s 7, 9, 18	c 1841–1842 probably in Putnam Co. GA #7,9	after 1871 possibly in Arkansas #18	M. A. Gerrald 28 Dec 1865 Caddo Parish LA #6
  Source #s			
  Source #s			

Figure 2.4 Example of a Family Group Sheet

Source #	Sources (Documentation)
1	Putnam County, GA, probate file 42A, estate of James Allen, writ to sheriff 6 Jan 1837, frames 212–213, FHL microfilm 1832253; the writ shows that James A. Arnold, Thomas Roberson, and his wife, Elizabeth C., were entitled to property under the will of Allen; this shows Thomas and Elizabeth as husband/wife and confirms her maiden name as Arnold. The only way she (by law, her husband in her name) and James A. Arnold were entitled to property from the estate was that they were brother and sister and children of Allen's daughter Elizabeth Arnold as named in his will.
2	Ibid., will of James Allen, frame 210, naming his daughter Elizabeth Arnold.
3	Putnam County, GA, Marriage Book D:206, FHL microfilm 394053, Robertson–Arnold.
4	Caddo Parish, LA, Marriage Bk 1:143 (bond), Croom [Sr.]–Robinson, Parish Clerk's office, Courthouse, Shreveport.
5	Ibid., Bk 1:484 (bond), Bk 2:10, Croom, Jr.–Robertson, date on minister's return.
6	Ibid., Bk 2:367, Robertson–Gerrald.
7	U.S. Census of 1850, Caddo Parish, LA, roll 230, p. 358, family 54, household of Isaac Croom [Sr.] with Elizabeth (41), Ann (14), James (8), these three born in GA; and Louisiana (2).
8	U.S. Census of 1860, Madison County, TN, roll 1263, p. 196, fam. 1872, household of Isaac Croom [Jr.] with Ann, age 24, suggested as his wife.
9	U.S. Census of 1860, Caddo Parish, LA, roll 409, p. 13, fam. 87, with T.J. Robberson (18, b GA).
10	U.S. Census of 1840, Putnam County, GA, roll 49, p. 176, household of Thomas Robinson (age 30–40), female 30–40, 3 females under 5, where Ann would fit.
11	Putnam County, GA, tax digest, 1830, District 309, FHL microfilm 401837, with Thomas as a defaulter, suggesting he was already 21; no 1829 list survives, FHL film 401836, for the 1820s. Thomas was not on the Putnam County 1828 list; either he was not yet 21 then or was living elsewhere.
12	Putnam County, GA, probate file 101R (1842), estate of Thomas Robertson, frames 029 & 036 showing 2 bills that narrow the death date, FHL film 1851587; notes in file show his signature.
13	Ann was not in 1880 census with rest of family: U.S. Census of 1880, Madison County, TN, roll 1270, e.d. 103, sheet 24, fam. 206, household of Isaac Croom [Jr.]; youngest daughter, age 7, born c 1873 (indicating her mother was alive c 1873); Ann not in 1880 mortality schedule.
14	U.S. Census of 1880, Caddo Parish, LA, roll 449, e.d. 14, sheet 2, fam. 19, household of J.H. Harris; U.S. Census of 1900, Caddo Parish, LA, roll 559, e.d. 29, sheet 3, fam. 62, household of J.H. Harris, both censuses reporting wife's mother born in GA; wife was Louisiana Croom.
15	Caddo Parish, LA, Conveyance Bk P:975, deed of gift, Apr 1868, Isaac Croom [Sr.] to daughter Louisiana Harris, wife of John H. Harris, Parish Clerk's office, Courthouse, Shreveport, suggesting Elizabeth had died.
16	Ibid., Bk L:194, 5 Nov 1857, Isaac's wife Elizabeth C. Croom relinquished her right to land, indicating she was alive.
17	Ibid., Bk S:721, Isaac Croom [Sr.] of Panola County, TX, to John H. Harris, Oct 1871, selling land, Croom's undivided half interest held in common with heirs of Elizabeth C. Croom, indicating Elizabeth had died.
18	Ibid., Bk S:855, Dec 1871, Thomas J. Robertson of Lafayette County, AR, selling his interest in the estate of his mother Elizabeth C. Croom, deceased, and his stepfather Isaac Croom [Sr.], confirming his relationship to Elizabeth.
19	Ibid., Bk 51:690–693, Bk 57:163, showing Ann's surviving children involved with Ann's interest in the estate of Elizabeth C. and Isaac Croom [Sr.], confirming Ann as Elizabeth's daughter.
20	U.S. Census of 1900, Marshall County, MS, roll 820, e.d. 66, sheet 9, household of O.P. Armour, showing wife Elizabeth C., born in July 1873, indicating her mother, Ann Croom, was alive then.
21	Panola County, TX, Marriage Bk C:22, Isaac Croom [Sr.] to Mary Jones, Nov 1868, County Clerk's office, Courthouse, Carthage, indicating Elizabeth had died.
22	Madison County, TN, Deed Bk 97:182, sale of land of Isaac Croom [Jr.] by his heirs per court decree, 1891, Office of Register of Deeds, Courthouse, Jackson; Madison County, TN, Probate Court Minute Bk 18: 582 (list of heirs), County Clerk's office, Courthouse; combined with censuses, these confirm his children and thus Ann's.

Figure 2.4 Reverse side of Family Group Sheet

problem unless you fill out and study the family group sheet for the nuclear family. Once you realize the problem, you need to use other sources to determine the actual dates. You may find that your ancestor's tombstone was engraved incorrectly. **The family group sheets help you study such details more thoroughly and thus more accurately by bringing the data together.**

If you keep these charts handy, you can readily add information to them. I like to keep the appropriate family group sheets in the first section of each notebook. If you have a large number, you may want to divide the charts into several sections. For example, if you are researching three siblings who lived in the same county, you could create a separate notebook subdivision for each sibling, with the pertinent group sheets and other charts.

Try sending copies of five-generation charts or family group sheets to relatives when you ask for information, along with a letter explaining your project. It is often easier for them to fill in blanks in a chart you have started than to create a chart from scratch. Thus, you may have better luck in getting a reply. This is a sample letter that could accompany a family group sheet:

> Dear Aunt Jane,
> I am finally working on Grandma Martin's side of the family. I'm enclosing a family group sheet of her children. I've filled in what I could, and you see I have lots of blanks. Would you please fill in whatever you can and return the chart to me? I'd appreciate any information: names, approximate dates, places, even notes on how many children each sibling had. Can you tell me where you found the information if it is not from personal knowledge? (I know that you knew some of these folks personally.) Also do you know *where* Grandma and Grandpa Martin married? Thanks a million!
> Love, Mary Jane

CHRONOLOGICAL PROFILE

In your research, you will collect information from many sources. It is essential to have a way of capsuling what you have learned about your ancestors, especially the ones you choose for concentrated, focused study. On a chronological profile, you can see at a glance, in the order they occurred, the events you have identified in the life of one ancestor. Although your notes will contain more complete data and documentation for each event, it is beneficial to put the documentation on the chart as well, even in capsuled form.

At first, the chronology may contain only basic events: the birth, marriage, and death of the profiled ancestor or ancestral couple. As you gather other information from family and public records, add to the chart such biographical items as the following:

1. births, marriages, and/or deaths of all known children in the family
2. home or business addresses; moves from one to another
3. residence in the census years: 1930, 1920, 1910, etc.
4. education, occupation, military service, religious milestones

5. real estate transactions, court appearances, jury service, listing on tax rolls

6. deaths of the parents, siblings, and spouse

Perspective

Tip

The profile is a valuable tool for thinking about what you have found and planning the next step. **As you think about your data, the chart helps keep the events in perspective and helps you catch discrepancies in your information.** When you list events in order and fill in the known or estimated age of the ancestor at the time of the event, you can tell whether your record is logical. Events such as the following warn a genealogist of a problem:

- A man married before his bride was born or married at age eleven.
- A man fathered a child at age eight. A mother had a child at age sixty-nine.
- A mother had two children in one year, seven months apart.
- A man volunteered for military service at age six.

If such occurrences appear on your chronology, you know you need to sort the facts from the fiction. Perhaps you copied a record incorrectly; perhaps the source itself was in error. You may be confusing two people of the same name. Regardless of the reason for the discrepancy, it becomes your task to resolve the issue. Without the chronology, you may not realize you have a problem.

Review and Planning

Reminder

The chronology provides a quick review of what you know and what you lack. **The holes in your information are important in deciding what to do next.** Here are examples:

- Does the chronology show large gaps of years between events? Can you find out what was happening in the ancestor's life or community during those years?
- Does it identify events in the ancestor's life only during adulthood or only after marriage? You may need to learn of earlier events and siblings in order to identify the ancestor's parents.
- Does it show the birth of the first child a number of years after the marriage occurred? Could this suggest earlier children who are not yet identified or an error in one of the dates?
- Does it list only three of six children known to be part of the family? Who were the others?
- Does it lack vital statistics or parents' names?

Use the profile to help you generate questions for research. For example, if your chart shows a marriage when the groom was forty-six years old, you would wonder whether he had a previous marriage. Plan to look for such a record and for census records that were taken between his coming of age (twenty-one) and his marriage at forty-six.

Figure 2.5 illustrates a chronological profile, showing what the researcher had found, or had not found, so far on the subject's life.

A Chronological Profile
Working Chronological Profile of Thomas King, 1844–1891

Date	Age	Event	Documentation
1844–June 20		Thomas King born. His grandson A.T. King said he was born in England. Census records of his only son give as the birthplace Germany (1900), Texas (1910), England (1920).	*Tombstone, Washington Cemetery, Houston, TX, gives date. Censuses 1900, 1910, 1920, Harris County, TX, (see notebook); interview with A.T. King, 1971.*
1870 census (June 1)	25	His future wife, Emilie Preuss, and Wilhelm Rock in household of Paul and Clara Prusler. Thomas King not found.	*1870 Census, Travis County, TX, p. 308.*
1872–Aug. 17		Amelia Preuss married William Rock.	*Travis County, TX, Marriage Book 3:200, microfilm.*
1873	29	No mention of Thomas King in Houston.	*Houston city directory.*
1874, 1875		William Rock on Travis County tax roll.	*Travis County, TX, tax rolls, 1874–1875, microfilm.*
1877–1879	33–35	No mention of Thomas King in Houston.	*Houston city directories.*
1880 census (June 1)	35	Thomas King not yet found. Amelia Rock, widowed or divorced, and 3 Rock children in house of Catherine Smith and sons, 160 Washington St., Houston.	*1880 Census, Houston, Harris County, TX, e.d. 72, p. 13.*
1880–Dec 3	36	Thomas King married Amelia Rock.	*Harris County, TX, Marriage Book H:391, #10278.*
1880–1881	36–37	Thomas King, carpenter, H&TC railroad shops, no home address given.	*Houston city directory.*
1884–1885	40–41	Thomas King, residence, south side of Union St., between White and Henderson Streets in Houston.	*Houston city directory*
1885–June 20	41	Only son, Alfred, born.	*Tombstone, Forest Park Lawndale, Houston, TX.*
1891–Dec 16	47	Thomas King died.	*Tombstone, Washington Cemetery, Houston, TX.*

Figure 2.5

THINGS TO DO NOW

1. Create an ahnentafel chart with yourself as number one. List all the ancestors you can identify at this time. Blank charts appear in *The Unpuzzling Your Past Workbook*.
2. Begin a pedigree chart with yourself as number one. Also begin one for your spouse.
3. Begin family group sheets for yourself and your spouse, for both sets of parents, and so forth, as outlined earlier in this chapter.
4. Make an effort to contact at least one cousin or other relative to help fill in information on other parts of your extended family.

Idea Generator

5. Create chronological profiles for your parents and grandparents. Fill these in as you gather information from family members, and document the source of each event.

6. Choose a focus ancestor or ancestral couple and create a chronological profile. Fill it in as you gather information, and document the source of each event.

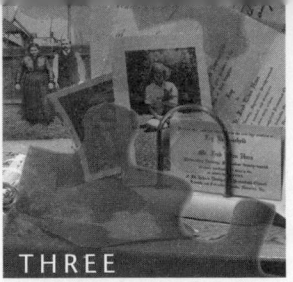

THREE

Strategies for Winning in Genealogy

G ames have rules, and successful game players, like detectives, have strategies for winning. The successful genealogist, being both puzzle solver and detective, develops and uses strategies that get the best results. The genealogy puzzle is made up of pieces found in many places through research. Remember, the goal of the search is to discover ancestors and to connect each generation to the previous one in such a way that you know you are claiming the correct names, dates, places, and relationships for your ancestors.

A widespread pastime these days is visiting surname Web sites and using electronic databases to look for ancestors. Many a site posts queries saying, "Beginner needs help." The message often requests parents or lineages for a particular ancestor. Some people post such messages on eight or ten sites, apparently representing all the ancestral lines they know.

We need to understand that "surfing" and querying surname databases on the Internet or CD-ROMs in libraries is not research. It is surveying what other people have submitted. These Web sites and database submissions contain both correct and incorrect information. Unless they are well documented, you cannot know if they are accurate. Thus, following up on such "finds" and documenting your efforts are essential for you to have a valid and first-rate genealogy.

The surname and county Web sites are often great places to meet other researchers working on the same families. However, many of the "help" queries get no replies. The reasons are numerous, but the lack of answers does not always mean a dead end. It does mean the seeker needs to research, working back to earlier generations until someone recognizes a connection. If you have researched wisely before you find other individuals working on the same line, you have knowledge (1) with which to judge what they tell you, (2) to share with them, and (3) to use in working back in time with them.

With this book as a guide, research need not be scary. It can be exhilarating and satisfying in many ways. Helping novices learn to research wisely in order

Important

to achieve the best possible results is the focus of this book. Thus, what are the special rules and strategies of genealogy and the research that uncovers the puzzle pieces?

1. BE SYSTEMATIC

The following tips are important to success. They are discussed throughout the book.

1. Decide what specifics you are looking for; establish short-term and long-term research goals.
2. Plan and organize each segment of your search before you begin it.
3. Concentrate on one or two ancestors at a time.
4. Read or learn in workshops about (a) records that might help your search and (b) researching in your specific ancestral location.
5. Research backward in time one generation at a time. Proceed from the known to the unknown, beginning with yourself.
6. If you are lucky enough to identify your immigrant ancestors and want to research them in their homelands, first learn everything you can about them in their adopted country, including the generations between you and them, before you attempt research in foreign records.
7. Remember to look for information within the family and in local, county, state, and federal records.
8. Look at enough records that you and others who look at your work can say with confidence that you have correct information.
9. Use tools such as five-generation charts, family group sheets, chronological profiles, census forms, and maps.
10. To facilitate research and study, keep all information about one family together.
11. Write at the top of each page of notes the surname or section to which they pertain; file notes in the proper folder or notebook section.
12. Maintain whatever organizing and filing system you devise.
13. Study your findings to determine whether you have achieved your research goal(s).
14. Plan the next step.

2. BE RESOURCEFUL

Plan to investigate many sources. You may need several documents to determine a correct date, place, name, or relationship. (See Figure 2.4, page 17, and chapter seventeen.) **Firsthand accounts and documents closest in time to the events they report are often the most reliable and desirable.**

Not all of the following sources will be available for each ancestor, but the genealogist strives to find as many sources as possible. Examples of firsthand or contemporary records include

1. a grandmother telling about her life and her parents and grandparents, whom she knew

For More Info

For more on research strategies and methods, tips for scaling brick walls, case studies using "cluster genealogy," and detailed information on citing your sources, see Croom's *Sleuth Book for Genealogists.*

Research Tip

2. accounts (oral or written) from relatives, neighbors, friends, or associates about family members they knew, interaction with them, and events they experienced together

3. contemporary letters, diaries, or memoirs describing life in the ancestral community when your ancestors lived there

4. family papers such as certificates, yearbooks, scrapbooks, passports, school records, and some Bible records

5. newspaper clippings from the time of the event (considered firsthand if written by a participant in the event)

6. church records of baptisms, confirmations, membership, weddings, burials, and church business

7. fraternal or labor organization membership applications and records

8. original wills and other documents in a probate file

9. original marriage licenses

10. public records such as tax rolls, deed records, census records, military pension applications, death information on death certificates, birth information on most birth certificates, court records, federal land entry files, naturalization papers, Social Security applications, World War I draft registrations

3. BE THOROUGH

A good historian will try to learn who, what, when, where, how, why, and with what results. The family historian wants to know where and how as much as who and when. Perhaps you are lucky enough to talk to several people who knew your great-grandmother. Each one may provide something different in your effort to "know" her. One talks about the pecan pie she always took to church suppers and gives you her recipe. Another remembers her needlework talents and shows you a quilt she made. A neighbor describes her house and remembers her sitting in her rocking chair on the front porch knitting. A fourth may tell of her love of picnics and something funny that happened on a picnic at the beach. Your puzzle needs all of these parts to be as complete as you can make it.

In short,

• Approach your subject from different angles.

• Write down as much information as you can find, using multiple sources.

• Work on each generation in order; don't skip one in an effort to reach back quickly.

• Evaluate all your information carefully, considering the reliability of your sources.

Many researchers have early successes; this sweet taste of victory keeps us in the game. Sooner or later, however, all of us run into brick walls. You must decide for yourself how hard you want to work for answers and how much you are willing to travel or spend in the effort. For many of us, the challenge and excitement of getting over a brick wall keep us researching.

The following example illustrates being resourceful and thorough in an interview situation. The same principles apply to research in public documents.

For a client, we were trying to identify Uncle George's wife. The interviewees were of the client's parents' generation, talking about his grandparents' generation. Thus, we used the names most familiar to the interviewees.

Sister said that Uncle George's wife was Aunt Tella but could not remember her real name. A cousin knew George's wife as Aunt Stella. Hearing both names, these two relatives remembered that Tella and Stella were both short for Costella, but neither could remember Aunt Tella/Stella's maiden name.

The 1880 census showed her given name as Euphima, but no relative present remembered anyone by that name. Did George marry twice, first to Euphima and then to Costella? No one remembered, and the county marriage records and the family Bible, both of which might have answered the question, were lost in fires years ago.

What about other aunts and uncles and their spouses? Everyone agreed that Uncle Walter married Sally Campbell and Papa married Emma Campbell. Two Campbell girls? Were they sisters? Then it clicked. Mama (Emma Campbell) always said she and Aunt Tella were sisters. That made Aunt Tella a Campbell too. Three sisters married three brothers? They were not sure. The 1870 census of Mama's family listed a person in Aunt Tella's spot as "E.C." Was that Euphima Costella Campbell? Seeing this, someone remembered, "Oh, yes, that *was* her name."

A new question had arisen in answering the original one: What about the third girl, Sally, who married Uncle Walter? The marriage record identifies her as a Campbell. Costella and Mama had a sister Sarah, or Sally. However, if their sister Sally had married Walter, she would have been twenty-five years older than her husband. Again we asked, "Were Aunt Sally and Mama related?" The response was noncommittal.

Approach it from a different angle: "Did you know any of Aunt Sally's relatives?" *"Aunt Sally's mother was called Aunt Cindy."* OK, this solved part of the dilemma. Mama's mother was Emily, not Cindy, so Aunt Sally was not Mama's sister. The new question was "What Campbell family *was* she part of?" Additional searching and asking would be necessary to answer this question and raise still others.

Technique

4. BE A CLUSTER GENEALOGIST

As shown in the example above, a valuable strategy for genealogists is to study each ancestor as part of a cluster of friends, relatives, and neighbors. By gathering information on this cluster, you often learn more about your own family, for ancestors did not live in a vacuum. They witnessed deeds and wills for family members or close friends. They were bondsmen for the marriages of brothers, sisters, cousins, or close friends. They moved or went to war with classmates, fellow church members, lodge brothers, or relatives. Elderly parents often migrated with one or more of their grown children. Uncles and nephews joined together to move their families to newly opened land. They lived next door to or across the road from other family members, including in-laws or married sisters, and thus appear close to each other in the census records and some tax rolls, even when their surnames were not the same.

Consider three examples:

1. W. M. McAlpin of Mississippi testified on George M. Shelby's Texas Confederate pension application that George had indeed served when and where he said he had, for they were together. McAlpin was married to George's first cousin, Emeline Shelby.
2. The 1900 census listed Annie Oldham and her husband, Lafayette Oldham, next to John and Jane Shelby in Robertson County, Texas. Annie Oldham turned out to be John Shelby's sister. The census record did not reveal this, but land records later did.
3. The Alfred Moore who was in business with Sterling Orgain when they petitioned Congress in the 1820s was also Orgain's brother-in-law.

Your picture of the family is more complete when you work on the cluster. Even in the interview example on page 26, you often learn more by interviewing several people who knew the ancestors you are investigating than by talking with only one person. **Even more important, by studying the cluster, you may find evidence or confirmation of names, dates, relationships, and life experiences you could not have found by working only on one individual.** If the road from A to B has been washed out, you may have to detour to C and D to reach B. In genealogy, you may have to study C and D in order to verify that A and B were related.

Research Tip

5. BE CONSIDERATE

You have heard the saying that one rotten apple spoils the whole barrel. Family history researchers who forget their manners or damage public records give all of us a bad name. We must remember that sometimes the people we need most in our research are not genealogists, and thus we must deal with them in a way that allows them to help us.

In interviewing, you will get more cooperation when you are on time, tactful, polite, to the point, and appreciative—and when you don't stay too long. Often forty-five minutes to an hour is long enough. A few short visits or telephone calls may be more effective than one long, tiring visit.

In libraries and public buildings, observe their rules as well as common courtesies. When you visit a county courthouse to look at public records, introduce yourself to the clerk and ask for the location of the particular volumes or documents you are interested in. It is sometimes helpful, but not necessary, to explain that you are working on family history. Do not go into detail about your search. The employees are not usually research experts or genealogists and are not being paid to listen to a visitor's family history.

If you have questions about using a particular type of record, ask for help. It may be beneficial to ask the clerk for the name of a local historian, genealogist, or society to contact in your search. Respect the old and aging records you may be privileged to handle. Never, ever, write on them, tear out pages, or handle fragile records in a way that could carelessly damage them. Some offices and agencies have closed records "because you genealogists are tearing them up." Whether or not genealogists are at fault, that is the perception that some officials have.

6. BE A CAUTIOUS DETECTIVE

We cannot automatically believe what we read in print, hear from relatives, or receive from other researchers and submitters. Ask yourself, What documentation confirms or supports what they say? With documentation from original records, you are in a position to evaluate the facts and draw conclusions yourself. You are the detective in the case and surely don't want to contaminate the results of careful research with material of undetermined origin or accuracy.

If you find a published family history, a county history with your ancestor's biographical sketch, or an Internet site with names of five generations that may be your ancestors, you still have much to do. Genealogists, like detectives, try to determine the best possible information: the right people in the right places at the right times. We must not jump to conclusions but must be ready to question and scrutinize what we hear or read. **We must realize that any kind of record or database can contain mistakes, and insufficient or inaccurate information can lead to incorrect conclusions.**

Warning

But I Found All My Ancestors on the Internet . . .

At this time, you cannot find all your ancestors on the Internet. The Internet, CD-ROMs, books, and articles are tools that provide genealogists with clues. Some clues are better than others. Some contain truth, and some do not. Some contain documentation of where the information originated, but many do not. Clues are not the same as genealogical facts. Clues are pieces of information that may or may not lead you to facts.

For example, you find three mentions of an ancestral name on the Internet or another database. One says the ancestor was born in 1867 in Missouri and gives parents' names. The second gives her birth information as 1871 in Kentucky and names the same father but a different mother. The third says only that she was born in 1871 in Missouri. They cannot all be correct; maybe none is correct. Perhaps the data actually mixes the facts for two or three individuals as if they were one. All you really have is someone by the same name as your ancestor and a clue that someone by that name may have been born about 1867–1871 in either Kentucky or Missouri, or somewhere else. How do you know she is *your* ancestor? It becomes your task to look at records such as censuses, family Bibles, tombstones, newspaper obituaries, and death certificates to try to determine the correct birth date, birthplace, and parents for the person who really is your ancestor.

In other words, to be successful in identifying your ancestors, you must research—carefully and thoughtfully. Look at many kinds of sources—original and microfilmed documents and records published on paper, in electronic data-bases, or online. Think about what you find to determine (1) whether it is logical and likely and (2) whether it fits with or contradicts other information you have found. Keep track of your sources so that you know where you got each piece of information. Be prepared to defend your conclusions and your lineages with reliable data from legitimate records. Saying "I got it on the Internet" or "It was in that big blue book" is not appropriate or sufficient support.

Furthermore, **no source contains all your ancestors.** Part of the fun, the challenge, the excitement, and the satisfaction is finding ancestors in all kinds of places from newspapers and church records to censuses and military pension records. As upcoming chapters explain, you have access to thousands of sources through family, cemeteries, libraries, courthouses, interlibrary loan, rental libraries, and the Internet. All require cautious use.

Reminder

Is the Record Contemporary With the Event?

Researchers usually find the best information by getting as close as possible to the event they are studying—a marriage record for a marriage date or a birth certificate for a birth date and place. If these original documents are not available, genealogists must look elsewhere—with caution.

For example, in filling out his father's death certificate, Alfred furnished for public record his father's birth date and place. This was not firsthand birth information, for Alfred was not present at his father's birth. This was, at best, secondhand information, possibly from his father or his paternal grandmother. It was thirdhand information if his mother told him, for she got it secondhand. It was also possible that he and his father never discussed the birthplace and Alfred made an assumption, knowing that his father had lived in that town during childhood.

However, research uncovered the father's church confirmation record, which gave a different town of birth. This discrepancy led to a search for documents in which the father himself had named his birthplace.

See Also

See page 170 for more about Social Security records.

Because Alfred's father was born in 1885 in a state that was not yet recording births, no birth certificate was available, and no baptism record has surfaced. However, he was employed in 1936, when Social Security began, and his death certificate gave his Social Security number. The Social Security number led to his Social Security application. That document and his Masonic Lodge membership record confirmed his birthplace. Their information agreed with the church record, not the death certificate. These were three independently created documents for which the father himself had named his birthplace, and all three agreed. The father would have had no reason to lie about his birthplace in these three documents. Because they were as close as possible to a contemporary document, the researcher concluded they were probably correct.

People ask, "Why go to all that trouble to get all those records?" That "trouble" helps us get the best possible answers. Perpetuating incorrect information or not knowing what is correct weakens our family histories and harms genealogy as a discipline.

Sometimes, we tend to accept the first piece of information we find, such as

Alfred's statement of his father's birthplace. However, cautious, thorough genealogists will be alert for, or actively seek, other sources to confirm such details in order to know they have the best available data in their family histories.

Transcriptions and Abstracts

Another situation in genealogy that calls for caution is reviewing *copies* of records, including those online. **Handwritten or typed copies of originals can contain errors, so it is wise to consult the original whenever possible.** Microfilm, photocopies, and digital images of originals normally are good substitutes when the original is not available.

Transcribed and abstracted records are often available when originals are not, and thus they are valuable sources. However, human error is possible in copying and abstracting as well as in typing or typesetting and printing. The possibility for error rises when researchers read the handwriting of a century or two ago or when they are not familiar with the names, places, or other words used in the documents. In addition, some abstracts leave out details essential to your particular use of the document. Therefore, when you find important information about an ancestor in a transcription or an abstract, try to get a copy of the original record.

Case in point: The search for Isaac Croom's first marriage record began in a library with a typed abstract of the county's marriage book. It gave the name of the bride: Elizabeth Steer. A follow-up look at the microfilm of the county marriage record showed clearly that her name was not Steer, but Sturdevant. The court clerk had divided the name in the original because it could not fit on one line. (See Figure 3.1, below.) The transcriber had written only the first syllable, and that, incorrectly. Since the original marriage book is missing from the county courthouse, the microfilm is the closest researchers can get to the original.

For accuracy and detail, it is helpful to photocopy records and to photograph

Research Tip

Notes

A **transcription** is a complete handwritten or typed copy of an original record; it is not a photocopy. An **abstract** is a summary of essential details in a document, not the full text.

N° 211

Marriage License was this day Issued to
Isaac Croom Jr to mary Elizabeth Stur
devant this 22nd day of July 1840
James D McClellan clerk

Figure 3.1

tombstones and houses if the information is likely to be questioned, may be destroyed, or is of major importance in your family history.

7. BE PASSIONATE ABOUT ACCURACY

As you research in documents, published sources, or electronic databases, you must be concerned with reliability and accuracy. Who wants to spend time and money collecting misinformation or claiming the wrong ancestors?

One friend is working to clear up an accuracy question in her family. A cousin who sent her a family group sheet happily announced that she had found the long-sought-after parents and siblings for their common ancestor, George. For its documentation, the chart listed two incomplete, unverifiable references—either nonexistent or so poorly cited that finding them is impossible. As my friend compared the chart with her ongoing research, she realized few similarities existed between the two: the name George, the surname, the name Samuel as a possible brother, a close (but not the same) birth year, and North Carolina as George's birthplace. The cousin apparently picked up the information from a published source or electronic database and made a giant leap of faith. However, the results of real research, concentrating on the known ancestor, suggest that these Georges are two individuals from entirely different families.

Although some of these points have been suggested above, review them as you research to consider the quality of your source.

1. How contemporary is the source to the ancestral event? The closer to the event, the better.
2. Is it firsthand information, or has it experienced a number of retellings? The more removed it is from an eyewitness version, the more likely it is to contain errors.
3. Was the informant, if identified, in a position to know correct facts? Family tradition five generations after an event is more likely to contain inaccuracies than an account by someone of the first generation.
4. If your source is published on paper or in electronic form, does it specify the original source of the information? If not, do not accept it as fact until you find and approve a reliable original source. If so, get a copy of the original to check for reliability and accuracy.
5. Can you find more than one legitimate source that helps answer your question? Do several reliable, contemporary sources suggest the same answer? We want to be able to answer yes to both questions.
6. Have you found any differing information? If not, perhaps you indeed have found a correct answer. If so, you need to do more research and/or account for the discrepancies.

8. BE SMART: DOCUMENT YOUR FACTS

Write down your sources of information: who told you or where you read it. This process is called **documentation**. Besides accumulating data, the genealogist seeks to test and verify facts. People will ask, "How do you *know* Great-Grandpa was from North Carolina? Papa always said he was from Alabama."

What documents or sources can you show that verify, or even suggest, his North Carolina origin? Your list of facts from legitimate sources gives your research validity and credibility. Remember, your goal is to confirm the parents and children in each generation as you work back in time so that you know you claim the correct ancestors and their correct history.

To document your notes, title the page with a heading that contains the source information, as in Figure 1.1, page 8. The process is a simple one if you ask yourself, **Specifically, where can I find this exact information again if (when) I need it?**

Citing Sources

- For an interview, write down your name as interviewer, the name of the person you are interviewing, the location of the interview, and the date.

- For published books and articles, list the author or compiler, title, publication information, and volume and page numbers you used. If you photocopy the title page of books where you have found information, be aware that title pages do not always contain all the bibliographic information you need. You may have to look at other pages or the library's catalog to find when or where the book was published or by whom.

- When copying data from family Bibles, newspapers, cemeteries, or public records, write down when and where you copied the information and exactly where the information can be found if needed again, including applicable page numbers for each record or piece of information. Include the publication information for the Bible.

- If using a medium other than the original form, cite what you use—CD-ROM, microfilm, etc. We generally consider census records to be on microfilm unless otherwise cited. (See examples below.)

Below are sample citations for some kinds of records genealogists use. Citations for books and articles are standardized across most subject areas, such as history, genealogy, and literature. Citing genealogical records is not so uniform. Some people prefer to begin a footnote (or endnote) with a name, such as the name of the ancestor mentioned in the document or the person who created the document. Other researchers prefer to begin the citation with the name or type of document. Other elements in the citation include the date of the record, the form you used (county record book, photocopy, microfilm, etc.), and where the document can be found again. Regardless of the order of the elements, researchers need to choose a format or style that makes sense to them and use it regularly and consistently.

Sample Footnote Citations in Genealogy

Citing Sources

Article: Emily Croom, "Setting the Record Straight about Isaac McFadden, Sr.," *The Bulletin* (Chester District Genealogical Society, Richburg, South Carolina) 20 (December 1996): 131. [*20* is the volume number; *131* is the page number of the information cited.]

Bible Record: Birth registry for Fletcher Elizabeth Metcalfe, Dr. Francis Asbury Mood family registry, *Holy Bible, . . . with a perpetual genealogical Family Register*, new edition (Nashville: Southern Methodist Publishing House, 1859),

p. 28 of the registry, in the Special Collections of the A. Frank Smith Jr. Library Center, Southwestern University, Georgetown, Texas, photocopy in author's possession.

Birth Record: Henry Turner Coleman birth record, Mills County, Texas, Birth Record Book 8:284, County Clerk's office, Courthouse, Goldthwaite.

Book: David Ludlum, *Early American Winters 1604–1820* (Boston: American Meteorological Society, 1966), 201, sketch of Winthrop Sargent and his work.

Census Record: U.S. Census of 1880, Williamson County, Texas, National Archives microfilm T6, roll 1333, enumeration district 162, sheet 53, family 459, household of J.E. Tisdale. [Citing the microfilm M or T number for census records is optional; the rest is necessary.]

Census Record on CD-ROM: U.S. Census of 1870, Pontotoc County, Mississippi, Township Nine, roll 746, p. 271A, family 39, household of William Farrar, Family Quest Archives CD-ROM M593-746 (Bountiful, Utah: Heritage Quest, 1998).

Courthouse Record (Deed Record): Caddo Parish, Louisiana, Conveyance Book S:721, Isaac Croom to John H. Harris, October 1871, Parish Clerk's office, Courthouse, Shreveport. [S is the volume; 721 is the page number. This or a similar format could be used for any courthouse record.]

Death Certificate: Sarah Shelby death certificate, #37030, Texas Department of Health, Bureau of Vital Statistics, Austin, copy in compiler's possession.

Family Story: Story told to author by Sue Logan (Mood) McMichael several times, including at a family dinner in Houston, Texas, Mother's Day, 1985.

Interview: Interview with Mary Katherine Earney, 20 September 1993, Houston, Texas, at Judy and Fred King's residence, audiotape in compiler's possession.

Letter or E-Mail: Letter to author from Emily (Cooper) Blalock, Bentonville, Arkansas, 9 July 1973.

Microfilm Record: Putnam County, Georgia, Marriage Book D:206, Robertson-Arnold marriage, Family History Library (FHL) microfilm 394053.

Newspaper Article: Obituary of Jesse Blalock, *Bolivar (Tennessee) Bulletin*, 12 December 1890, p. 3.

Newspaper Clipping: Obituary of John Fletcher McKennon, undated clipping from unidentified [possibly Maury County, Tennessee] newspaper shortly after his death, photocopy in compiler's possession.

Online Source: Nice Blaydes entry, *1798 Direct Tax, List 2a, Berkeley Parish, Spotsylvania County, Virginia*, online, Gary Stanton, comp., 21 July 1996, accessed 13 March 1999, <http://www.mwc.edu/~gstanton/hispinfo/1798l2a.htm>. [Note: This information now appears at <http://departments.mwc.edu/hipr/www/1798l2a.htm>.]

THINGS TO DO NOW

1. List relatives to contact for interviews by telephone or in person. Gather current addresses (postal and/or e-mail) and telephone numbers.

Idea Generator

2. Begin identifying (and copying if they do not belong to you) documents within the family that might contain information on your parents, grandparents, or great-grandparents, especially documents that place them in a given place at a given time or answer any of the name, date, place, or relationship questions that genealogists ask.

3. If you have such records in your possession, investigate putting them into archival (acid-free) sheet protectors, resealable plastic bags, or storage boxes to protect them from critters, air, and light. Acid in non-archival containers can damage or destroy records, photographs, cloth, and other keepsakes.

4. Practice writing citations for some of the family papers in your possession, including birth and death certificates, family Bibles, letters, etc.

FOUR

What's in a Name?

Names present special challenges and opportunities to the genealogist. Challenges include variant spellings and anglicized versions or translations of foreign names. From given names and middle names, genealogists sometimes get clues to ancestors. In addition, researchers need to know common nicknames and standard abbreviations for given names that they will find in the ancestral records.

SPELLING VARIATIONS

Expect your family name to be spelled different ways in public documents. The census taker recorded what he heard, or thought he heard. The clerk copied into the deed book what he thought he read in the original. It does not matter what the family called themselves, how they spelled their name, or how your family spells its name now. Expect a variety of spellings, as in these examples:

Meyer(s), Meir(s), Mayor(s), Myer(s), Mears
Robertson, Rob(b)erson, Robinson, Robison, Robeson
McCollister, McCalloster, McAlister, McAlster, McOllaster, McAlisdar
Harrel(l), Harold, Harwell, Harle, Harrille

You as the researcher need to be aware of this phenomenon and study records accordingly. Remember that not all ancestors could read and write and, therefore, spell their names for a clerk. To research wisely, consider these tips:

1. Don't assume it is not your family because the name is spelled differently from what you expect.
2. Make a list of the ways your ancestral surnames might have been spelled in the records. Try saying the name the way it could have been said in Massachusetts, Georgia, Texas, or wherever the family lived. Regional pronunciation may have affected the spelling, as in Hanner for Hanna (a surname) or Hannah (a first name).

3. Consult your list of variations when you use indexes. Look up all the variations, especially once you have found your family with variant spellings in the records. You may need to read the entire alphabetical section of the index looking for additional variations.

4. Some variations in indexes, abstracts, and transcriptions are the result of accidents, as when Thomas is indexed as Thomsa.

5. Be alert to spelling variations of given names, as in Catherine, Catharin, Kathryn, etc.

ANGLICIZED, TRANSLATED, AND CHANGED NAMES

Notes

Surnames can change over the years. A French immigrant named Pierre de la Chapelle may have found his name Americanized to Peter Chapel. The German immigrant Johann Peter Muth became Peter Mood. Zimmerman may have been translated to Carpenter, and the French LeBlanc may have become White.

Such changes can reflect the way the family pronounced their name or the attempt of a clerk to approximate what he heard and make it manageable for the English-speaking community. In this way, an Irishman named Sean Maurice could have become John Morris. A Welshman named David ap Howell might have become David Powell. The German Koster may have been altered to Custer.

From the reverse point of view, a family named Chapel may or may not have a French origin. **We must not assume a national origin for our surnames or our ancestors until research gives us specific and valid clues.**

Reminder

Name Changes

Before the Civil War, a number of state legislatures legalized name changes. Evidence of these proceedings is usually found in the legislative records in the state archives or in the state laws, called session laws, which you can view at law libraries and many university libraries. For example, in 1856 Julius Valentine Cook of Fayette County, Texas, became Richard Valentine Cook by action of the Texas legislature. In 1848, a Philadelphia native and resident of Bexar County, Texas, Ralph William Peacock, prevailed upon the same legislature to change his name to John Bowen to comply with the wishes of a will by which he would inherit property in Jamaica (Gammel's Laws of Texas, Vol. 4:352 and Vol. 3:146). As the nineteenth century progressed, individuals could obtain name changes in various state courts as well.

When people moved to a new location, they sometimes assumed new names or reverted to maiden names with or without legal action. An entry from the 1890 special census of Union veterans and widows suggests an assumed name. In Beaverhead County, Montana, lived a Kansas infantry veteran named "Henry Wills, alias Charles Wright." This find could be a researcher's dream or nightmare, but we never know what interesting tidbits await us in public sources until we try them.

When African-American ancestors became free, they chose their surnames. They chose, individually or as a family, a name from one of these:

- their former owner
- their mother's or father's former owner
- a famous American, such as Washington or Jackson
- a person who befriended them
- a name they liked

Sometimes siblings selected different surnames. Some probably changed names along the way as did some white ancestors.

Native American ancestors, too, may have experienced name changes, not only within their tribal culture but as they moved into non-Indian communities. If they had a non-Indian father, they often used the father's surname. Others used an English translation of an Indian name.

CLUES IN NAMES

Naming practices vary from place to place and generation to generation. However, certain consistencies have existed for nearly four centuries in the area we now call the United States. Children were, and still are, often named for parents, grandparents, and other relatives.

Namesakes

For generations, given names have come from surnames, such as Allen, Cameron, Clyde, Davis, Dudley, Elliott, Glenn, Keith, Lloyd, Spencer, and many others. This practice gave these nineteenth-century Southerners interesting name combinations: Green Cash, Ransom Cash, Pleasant Pigg, Wiley Crook, Hardy Flowers, Eaton Cotton, Green P. Rice, and DeForest Menace. **When an ancestor has a surname as a given name, think *clue*.** Was it the mother's maiden name? A grandmother's maiden name? Another relative's given name? Only research can answer these questions.

Tip

For example, Benjamin Allen Phillips (1801) was named for his grandfather Benjamin Allen. Emily Cooper (1882) was named for her father's deceased first wife, Emily (Blalock) Cooper. Emily Cooper Blalock (1874) was named for the same deceased lady, in this case, her father's sister. On the other hand, Pitser Miller Blalock (1848) was named for a neighbor not thought to be a relative.

Naming Patterns

Various genealogists have suggested a pattern to naming practices of the eighteenth and early nineteenth centuries in England and Wales, which may give clues for studying families of the American colonies and the United States.

Eldest son—often named for the father's father
Second son—for the mother's father
Third son—for the father
Fourth son—for the father's eldest brother
Eldest daughter—for the mother's mother

Second daughter—for the father's mother

Third daughter—for the mother

Fourth daughter—for the mother's eldest sister

In the United States, this pattern may be considered a possibility but not a rule. Some families did name eldest sons for paternal grandfathers, but the naming of children for relatives generally followed no particular pattern or order. Families also named eldest sons for relatives on both sides of the family or for no one in particular.

Each of the following was an eldest child. Hunter Orgain Metcalfe (1887) was given his maternal grandmother's maiden name, Orgain. Samuel Black Brelsford (1829) was named for his maternal grandfather, Samuel Black. Edward Philpot Blalock (1837) was named for his father's foster brother, Edward Philpot. Mary Eliza Catherine Coleman (1848) received a name from each grandmother.

Be alert to recurring given names or middle names in a family, especially over several generations. The middle name Steele in the Isaac McFadden family of Chester County, South Carolina, was used for one of his children and several of his grandchildren and great-grandchildren. The name turned out to be the maiden name of Isaac's first wife, Elizabeth Steele. The other recurring middle name in that family was Ewing, the middle name of two of Isaac's children and several descendants. Perhaps it is a clue to someone else's maiden name. Studying the extended family cluster helps you identify such repetition of names and may identify the reason.

Important

Given Names

The genealogist becomes aware of other naming practices. Of course, a daughter was, and still is, sometimes given a feminine form of her father's name: Josephine (Joseph), Georgianna (George), Pauline (Paul), or Philippa (Philip). Almanzon Huston had a daughter named Almazona.

Some children were, and are, indeed named for relatives. However, others carry the names of famous Americans or prominent local personalities. In the early years of the republic, some families showed their patriotic feelings by naming daughters or sons Liberty, Justice, or America. Other nineteenth-century families gave daughters the same names as states and cities: Arizona, Carolina, Georgia, Indiana, Louisiana, Missouri, Philadelphia, Tennessee, and Virginia. Nineteenth-century census records revealed these interesting names: Florida Ferry, Arkansas Neighbors, French Fort, Egypt Land, Vienna Wood, and Australia Shepherd.

These people from the eighteenth and nineteenth centuries had a title for a given name: Major Topping, Admiral Croom, Squire Blalock, Pharaoh Lee, Doctor Godwin, Lieutenant Campbell, and Patsy Empress Jones.

Every culture and era seem to have names whose origins are obscure. They may be nicknames, made-up names, combinations of other names, names of characters in literature of the period, or place names. Parents may have simply liked the sound of a name or wanted to choose something different. Sometimes the names researchers find in records are the result of phonetic spelling. Some may be corruptions of other names or attempts to keep names in a family within a particular pattern, such as names in alphabetical order or names beginning with the same initials. These are some of the numerous such names found in this country from 1750 to the present: Benoba, Bivy, Bozoila, Callie, Dicy, Dovie, Fena, Floice, Hattie, Jincey, Kitsey, Laney, Levicy, Lottie, Lovie, Luvenia, Mittie, Nicey, Olan, Olean, Ora, Ottie, Ozora, Parilee, Parizade, Periby (Pheribah, Pheriby, Fereby), Perlissa, Rebia, and Sinah.

NICKNAMES AND ABBREVIATIONS

Nicknames by which individuals were known to their contemporaries are sometimes found in place of "real" names in documents. Some dictionaries can help you determine the given name from a nickname. Here are common first names with their usual nicknames:

Ann(e)	Annie, Nan, Nannie, Nina, Nancy
Catherine (Katherine)	Catey, Katie, Cathy, Kathy, Kate, Kat, Katy, Kay, Kitty, Kit
Dorothy	Dottie, Dot, Dollie, Dora, Dory
Eleanor	Ella, Ellie, Nell, Nellie, Nelly, Nora
Elizabeth	Beth, Eliza, Liz, Liza, Lizzie, Lisa, Lise, Elsie, Betty, Betsy, Bitsy, Bess, Bessie, Libby
Frances	Fran, Frankie, Fannie
Margaret	Maggie, Peg, Peggy, Meg, Midge, Madge, Daisy, Maisie, Meta, Greta
Martha	Marty, Martie, Mattie, Patty, Patsy
Mary	Mamie, Molly, Mollie, May, Maisie, Polly, Minnie, Moll
Sarah	Sallie, Sal, Sadie
Henry	Hank, Harry, Hal, Hen
James	Jamie, Jim, Jimmy, Jem
John, Jonathan	Johnny, Johnnie, Jack, Jackie, Jock
Richard	Dick, Rick, Ricky, Rich, Richy
Robert	Rob, Bob, Robby, Robbie, Bobby, Dobbin, Robin
Theodore/Theodorick	Ted, Tad, Teddy, Theo, The, Dode, Dory
William	Will, Bill, Willy, Billy

Some nicknames are used as actual given names or may substitute for more than one given name, as in these examples:

Bell(e)	Arabella, Anabelle, Isabel
Cindy	Lucinda, Cynthia
Delia, Dee	Cordelia, Adelia, Ledelia, and others
Dora, Dory	Theodora, Eudora, Dorothy
Ed, Eddie	Edgar, Edmund, Edward, Edwin, Edwina
Frank, Frankie	Frances, Francis, Franklin, Francine

Hettie	Esther, Henrietta, Hester
Jenny	Jane, Virginia, Janet, Jeannette, Jennet, Jennifer
Lina, Lena	Eveline, Emeline, Carolina, Angelina, Selina, Helena
Lucy	Lucretia, Lucia, Lucille, Lucinda
Millie	Amelia, Mildred, Millicent
Nell, Nellie	Ellen, Helen, Eleanor
Nora	Honora, Honoria, Leonora, Eleanor
Patty	Patricia, Patience, Martha, Matilda
Sam(my)	Samuel, Samson, Samantha
Stella	Costella, Estelle

For additional lists of nicknames, consult name books, dictionaries, and Barbara J. Evans's book *A to Zax: A Comprehensive Dictionary for Genealogists & Historians.*

Clerks copying documents by hand often abbreviated or contracted names, as in these common examples. Record the name as you find it. Figure 4.1, on page 41, shows examples in the handwriting of the eighteenth and nineteenth centuries.

Alexander	Alex^r	Joseph or Josiah	Jos, Jos:
Charles	Chas	Nathaniel	Nathl
Christopher	Xo^{pher}, Xtoph	Richard	Richd, Rich^d
Daniel	Danl, Danl	Robert	Robt
George	Geo, Geo:	Samuel	Saml, Saml
James	Jas, Ja:, Ja^s	Thomas	Thos, Tho:, Thos
Jonathan, John	Jno	William	Wm, Willm, W^m

FADS AND ERAS

In the United States, each era seems to have had favorite names in addition to the standard ones which have been used for centuries. The "period" names may be related to the attitudes, events, or personalities of the generation, even in subtle ways. Perhaps they were simply fads that gave way to new patterns after several decades. Being aware of these patterns could give you clues to the period when your ancestor lived.

Virtue Names

Many girls and some boys of the latter seventeenth century and the eighteenth century, especially among New England Puritans, were named for virtues: Amity, Charity, Civility, Constance or Constant, Faith, Grace, Honour, Hope or Hopeful, Mercy, Obedience, Patience, Piety, Pleasant, Prudence, Reason, Rejoice, Temperance, Thankful, and Truth.

Another group of names may have suggested experiences or feelings of the parents: Anguish, Comfort, Desire, Mourning, Seaborn, and Sorrow. A number of Southern men had the given names Merit and Sterling, which could come from surnames as well as valued traits.

Thos S Richards

Geo Davidson

Wm Byrom, J[ustice of the] P[eace]

Wm Roberts

Jas W Richards

Robt Ridley/Dec[ease]d

Jas Sherman

Chas W Hunt

Ja: Home Secr[etar]y

Ferd[inand] G Coleman

Stime, Jno E

Eliz[abeth] W Coleman

Arch:ᵇ Home Secr[etar]y

Figure 4.1 Abbreviations of given names

Double Names

In the late seventeenth century, Germans poured into Pennsylvania, bringing with them their custom of giving children two names. Some families even kept the first name the same for all the sons, for example, and varied only the middle name: Johann Peter, Johann Friedrich, Johann Sebastian, and Johann Georg. As these families and their descendants moved throughout the colonies, other ethnic groups picked up this double naming custom. By the mid-nineteenth century, the practice was widespread.

As we have seen, the idea allowed parents to name children after grandparents and perpetuate a surname from previous generations at the same time. Patty *Field* Allen, Hiram *Hawkins* Brelsford, Ferdinand *Glenn* Coleman, George *Rogers* Clark, and many others carried surnames as their middle names and give genealogists at least a clue to another set of roots.

Biblical Influence

Especially between 1650 and 1860, many children received biblical names, some of which have been favorites for centuries. Popular female names included

Elizabeth, Hannah (Anna, Anne), Julia, Judith, Mahala, Martha, Mary, Priscilla, Rachel, Rebecca, Ruth, Sarah, and Susanna. Some families used biblical names less familiar to us: Ascenath, Dorcas, Jemima, Jerusha, Keturah, Kezia, Orpah, Phebe (Phoebe), and Zilpah.

Favorite male names from the Old Testament included Benjamin, Daniel, David, Elijah, Ezekiel, Hiram, Isaac, Jacob, Jedediah, Jeremiah, Jesse, Joel, Joseph, Joshua, Josiah, Lemuel, Levi, Malachi, Moses, Nathaniel, Samuel, Seth, Simeon, and Zachariah. New Testament names, of course, included Matthew, Mark, Luke, John, James, Simon, Peter, Thomas, and Rufus. Families also gave boys biblical names less familiar to us, including Abiel, Enoch, Esau, Hezekiah, Jubal, Laban, Mahlon, Obed, Salathiel, and Zebulon.

Classical Revival

The study of Latin and Greek had long been part of the "classical" school curriculum. However, from the mid-eighteenth century to about the mid-nineteenth century, Europe, and therefore the United States, experienced a revival of classical architecture, language, and cultural influences, which carried over into naming practices. Below are some of the Latin and Greek names and derivatives from that classical revival period. Today, some are considered quite usual. Others were unique even then, as was that of a Georgia girl named Semiramis Lucetta Artemesis McClendon.

Aurelius	Fabia	Lucius	Phyllis	Sibyl
Artemis	Guglielmo	Lucia	Philena	Sophronia
Artemesia	Gulielmus	Marcellus	Portia	Theophilus
Caesar	Horatio	Marcella	Penelope	Theodocia
Cassius	Honoria	Marcus	Parmelia	Tessa
Cassia	Hortense	Nonna	Philadelphia	Urbanus
Claudia	Julius	Ophelia	Quentin	Valentine
Clementine	Junius	Octavius	Rhoda	Virginious
Chloe	Justin	Octavia	Septimus	Virgil
Fortunatus	Justina	Pericles	Sylvanus	Xene
Florian	Latinus	Pompey	Sylvia	Zeta
Fabius	Lydia	Primus	Stephanie	Zenobia
Fabian	Lucian	Parmen(i)us	Sophia	Zephyr

Twentieth-Century United States

Many late-nineteenth- and early-twentieth-century daughters, especially in the South, received the names of flowers and gems: Daisy, Lily, Pansy, Rose, Violet, Ruby, Jewel, Opal, and Pearl. Three girls of the early twentieth century had these names: Lillie White, Rosey Brown, and Pansy Violet Flower.

In the late nineteenth and early twentieth centuries, more children than in previous or later generations seemed to be named Bessie, Bertha, Clara, Edna, Elvira, Ethel, Evelyn, Florence, Gladys, Gertrude, Gussie, Helen, Ida, Lillian, Lula, Malvina, Maude, Mildred, Nora, Thelma, Velma, Verna, Albert, Alvin, Claude, Elmer, Ernest, Grover, Herbert, Marvin, Maurice, Maynard, and Oscar.

Likewise, the mid-twentieth century (about 1920 to 1960) saw a set of names that were not so common in earlier or later years: Barbara, Bonnie, Brenda, Carol, Carolyn, Cynthia, Deborah, Diane, Donna, Gay(e), Janet, Jean, Jill, Joan, Joyce, Karen, Kay, Linda, Marilyn, Nancy, Patricia, Sandra, Sharon, Shirley, Carl, Dean, Dennis, Gary, Jerry, Kenneth, Larry, Mark, Ron(ny), and Terry.

Finding popularity from the 1960s forward have been names that often have no ethnic, historical, or genealogical relationship to the family using them. Some derive from surnames, and some are used for both boys and girls: Alexandra, Allison, Ashley, Barrett, Brandon, Brian, Brittany, Cody, Dara, Darin, Derek, Eric, Erica, Erin, Hailey, Heather, Jason, Jennifer, Jordan, Justin, Kelly, Kendall, Kendra, Kevin, Kimberly, Kristen, Kyle, Lauren, Lindsey, Lisa, Megan, Melissa, Meredith, Michelle, Nicole, Nicholas, Paige, Ryan, Scott, Shawn (Sean), Stacey, Tammy, Taylor, Tiffany, Tracy, Trevor, Trey, Tyler, and Whitney.

In addition, the last quarter of the twentieth century saw a renaissance of such biblical names as Adam, Andrew, Benjamin, Daniel, Hannah, Jeremy, Joshua, Matthew, Michael, Rachel, Rebecca, and Zachary.

Through all these eras, certain names remained popular: Anne, Anna, Catherine, David, Elizabeth, Emily, George, Henry, James, John, Joseph, Margaret, Martha, Mary, Richard, Robert, Samuel, Sarah, Susan, Thomas, and William.

CAUTIONS FOR GENEALOGISTS

Rather common names such as James Davis, Thomas Williams, or George Carter may appear in the records of many localities. In any one place, how many Jameses, Thomases, or Georges were there? Maybe several at the same time. Which records belonged to which man? We must use land records, family groupings, signatures, names of neighbors, and other sources to try to sort them out. We cannot assume they were related. **Nor can we assume a person is our ancestor just because the name is the same.**

Estate names or other descriptive appellations sometimes help to identify men in the records. Peter Bland "of Jordan's Point" is distinguishable from other Peter Blands. One James Turley drew an eye after his name to separate himself from other James Turleys in the area. He is referred to now, as perhaps he was then, as James One Eye. Perhaps this designation tells us something about his physical appearance.

Warning

Sometimes men added "Jr." (or "Jun.") or "Sr." (or "Sen.") after their names to distinguish themselves from a father, son, or other relative of the same name. For example, three men from Madison County, Tennessee, in the mid-nineteenth century had the name Isaac Croom. The senior Isaac was the uncle of the other two. The younger nephew used his middle initial, N, and the other occasionally added "Jr." to his name. Isaac Jr. was distinguishing himself from his uncle rather than his father, who was Charles.

In previous centuries, men frequently lost wives to disease, childbirth, and accidents. Especially if they had young children to raise, men needed to marry again. It was not uncommon for the second wife to have the same name as the first wife, Elizabeth and Mary being common examples. This situation can trap genealogists, who may count only one wife, especially if the two wives were of similar ages. One clue to a second marriage would be a gap of years between the births of children in the family. If the second wife was older than the first, the age discrepancy—as found in subsequent census records, for example— would also be a clue. Thorough research often will reveal the second marriage.

Researchers also find families in which a child was given the name of a sibling who had died, sometimes to carry on a family name. When widows or widowers remarried, they sometimes named children for the husband's first wife or the wife's first husband.

Researching

Technique

We cannot always solve discrepancies and problems of names and relationships. However, we can form educated guesses. **To tackle such research dilemmas, consider these techniques:**

1. Read case studies that show how other researchers solved similar problems. These can be found in a number of genealogical books such as *The Sleuth Book for Genealogists*, and journal articles, such as those in the *National Genealogical Society Quarterly*.
2. Use sources as near to the ancestral event as possible.
3. Gather and document as much information as possible on the same-name individuals.
4. Sort your information and use only the most reliable. Do land, tax, military, probate, newspaper, or other records distinguish the activities of same-name people? What patterns or clues can you find to distinguish same-name people: names of spouses and children, locations of land or residences, occupations, witnesses to documents, signatures or marks?
5. Evaluate your facts thoroughly and objectively.
6. Write down your conclusions along with the supporting facts.

THINGS TO DO NOW

Idea Generator

1. Ask members of the family how they got their names or for whom they were named. Identify relatives who have family names from previous generations.
2. Identify given names or middle names in your family that occur in several generations. Do you know or can you find out the origin of these names in the family?
3. On your charts, identify people by their "real" names, with nicknames in parentheses or quotation marks.
4. Identify relatives whose names fit into the period naming patterns discussed in this chapter.
5. Begin to list or highlight names on your charts that may contain clues to ancestors.

FIVE

Begin Solving the Puzzle With Interviews

R elatively speaking, we have plenty of time to search for the distant past, but preserving the more recent past, the last eighty to one hundred years, should take place while the best sources are available: the family members and friends who experienced those years, knew the great-grandparents, and can relate a treasury of family stories and describe the family homes, weddings, and holiday celebrations. I knew only one of my great-grandparents, and it never occurred to me to sit down and talk with her—until it was too late.

Most families, extended to include cousins, have members who remember clearly events of fifty to eighty years ago. They knew other family members whose lives and stories reached back into the nineteenth century. **No amount of library research can duplicate or replace what these people can tell.** If you are the elder generation in your family, you have an opportunity and perhaps a genealogical obligation to share this information with the younger generations.

My generation lived what younger people consider rather ancient history. They find it hard to believe that we existed without television, air-conditioning, computers, microwave ovens, and cellular phones, just as my generation wonders about what life was like before cars, radios, telephones, or electricity. We ought to record, as part of our family history, our recollections of and reactions to what happened around us.

If they are to have meaning, family history and genealogy cannot be separated from the community's history and culture. Therefore, to give a family history perspective and interest, we must eventually try to put the family into the society and culture in which it lived and worked. Chapters five through eight help researchers gather this kind of information, especially for the more recent past.

Oral History

AT ANY BEGINNING

The logical way to begin anything new is to start with what you know. In working a jigsaw puzzle, it is easy to begin with the outside edges because they

Tip

are straight and are easily identified. Similarly, in genealogy, begin with what you know best—yourself—and work backward in time.

The best source to use to begin filling in the rest of the "straight-edged" pieces of your puzzle is your family: your parents, siblings, children, grandparents, aunts, uncles, and cousins. With their answers in writing, you have a springboard from which to gather other information. If you are lucky enough to have living grandparents and older relatives, you have a gold mine at your fingertips. They generally love to talk, especially when you are interested enough to listen carefully and ask questions. Some of their stories may seem totally unrelated, but record, either in writing or on tape, as much as you can. You never know when you may want or need this information.

INTERVIEWING FOR VITAL INFORMATION

Regardless of any other information you seek, such as family stories and facts about the family's role in the community, try first to gather this basic information for *each generation* as you work back in time:

1. names of parents and their siblings
2. names of their parents and grandparents
3. names of spouse(s) and children for each person
4. vital statistics (dates and places of birth, marriage, death) for each person

Preparing for an Interview

As an interviewer, make a list of questions in advance, and give your informant either the questions or an idea of what you want to cover before you begin. Of course, you are not limited to these questions. Ask any others that occur to you as the interview progresses. Make your questions short and to the point, and ask one question at a time. The following attempt to start an interview is wordy and confusing:

> Now, Aunt Ellie, I'd like to get a little background as to your birth and childhood, your full name at birth, when and where you were born, your parents' names, and something about your brothers and sisters, as to their names and whether they were older or younger than you if you can't remember their birth dates, some of your early education and childhood experiences, especially as they relate to what it was like to grow up on a farm.

Whew! A much better attempt is to begin simply: "OK, Aunt Ellie, let's begin at the beginning. When and where were you born?" She may give you all the rest of the information you might have asked for, without your asking. If she leaves something out, or if you get confused or lost, ask for clarification. You may have to ask other questions to help her with an answer or to keep her on track. It may be helpful to summarize periodically to make a graceful transition into a new subject, to stimulate any further memories, to return to the subject you want to pursue, or to be certain that you understand what she is really saying.

Consider these tips in preparing your questions:

- Encourage more than yes or no answers. Ask for explanations and details.
- Seek more than names, dates, and genealogical facts. Although you often must begin with these, you also want to find out *how*, *why* or *why not*, *to what extent*, and *with what results or effects*. You want stories about people, occupations, daily life, and the effects of historical events.
- Try to avoid the question, "Do you remember . . . ? Word your questions to trigger memories and elicit feelings, reactions, and descriptions.

Tip

In preparing for a successful interview, consider the following suggestions:

1. You may want to make an audio or video recording of your interview, even if you are taking notes. Taping gives you a backup record of the event and an important memento.
2. While your interviewee is speaking, be an attentive listener, but think ahead at the same time. Eye contact, enthusiasm, appropriate facial expressions, and natural reactions encourage and reassure your informant.
3. If the interviewee seems to be getting tired, confused, or involved too deeply in a topic that you consider completely off the subject, you may want to initiate a short break.
4. The session is not a forum for expressing your own opinions or winning a convert to your views. You need your interviewee's statements, even if you disagree.

In order to be a good genealogist, one must also be a historian. In order to make the most of your interview session, you must have done enough advance preparation to know what questions to ask or not to ask. Be sure that your questions relate to the topic or historical period under consideration. For example, you would not want to ask people about their experiences in the Great Depression (1930s) if they were born after 1940. Your interviewee may mention an event, person, or tradition that is new to you or that you neglected to include in your outline of questions. Be alert and learn to catch such jewels when they are tossed your way. They may be more important in the long run than your prepared questions. Feel free to divert the conversation away from your list to expand and develop these new topics.

Tip

Vital Questions to Ask

Perhaps you decide to talk with your grandmother. You are armed with your charts, paper, pencil, and a list of questions. Title your notes and include the date and place of the interview. A logical place to begin is "Where were you born?" If your grandmother is like mine, she will answer quickly, but it took me years of asking to find out *when*.

Then gather information about her childhood family and her husband, especially if he is deceased. Ask her to spell given names or surnames that may be out of the ordinary or spelled uniquely.

- What is her full name? Who were her parents?
- Who were her brothers and sisters? When and where were they born, and

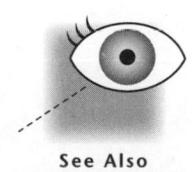

See Also

For historical questions you can use in interviews, see chapter eight.

whom did they marry? Are they still living? Get their addresses.
- How did she and Granddaddy meet? When and where did they get married?
- What was/is Granddaddy's full name? When and where was he born? Who were his parents? When and where did he die?

You can move in any of several directions next. You can inquire about your aunts and uncles. Ask her for the birth dates of her children (your aunts and uncles). Even a year filled in is helpful. Encourage her by letting her know that you appreciate any piece of information, even if it is incomplete. Whom did each of your aunts and uncles marry? Does she remember when and where they married? Together, can you list your cousins? Get their addresses from her and write to your cousins directly to ask for any missing information and verify what you already have. Telephone and e-mail are also good communication options.

Once your grandmother has shared her own vital statistics and family outline with you, ask her what she remembers of her parents. Did she know her grandparents or any of her great-grandparents? Ask for the same information about each generation:

1. full names and maiden names
2. dates and places of birth, marriage, and death
3. parents' names
4. siblings' names, their spouses' and children's names
5. cousins' names
6. where these relatives lived and where they are buried
7. addresses for living relatives

If your grandmother cannot remember exact dates, use a general reference point to help both of you: Did your grandfather die before World War II? Was Aunt Sue born before you were? Did Grandma and Grandpa get married when the family was living in Leesville? Any piece of information may help you pinpoint the date you are seeking.

For example, she may tell you about the house burning down. When was that? Well, she was about eight, so it was about 1930. Yes, her grandpa was still living with them then. So you conclude that her grandfather died after 1930. Aunt Annie may remember that Grandpa died before her wedding, which was in 1945. So you begin to narrow the gap. Their grandpa died between 1930 and 1945.

Lists of brothers and sisters are not vital statistics, but they are vital pieces of information. The only information we could ever get out of one grandfather was a partial list of his twelve brothers and sisters and his parents' first names. The list was little to go on, especially after we lost the paper. However, we remembered the names of his parents and two sisters. When I began researching, I found several men by the father's name but only one with daughters named Clarkey and Theodocia. The sisters' names led me to the correct family.

Once you have picked your grandmother's brain, perhaps over several visits,

Reminder

contact aunts and uncles, great-aunts and great-uncles, your parents' cousins, and older friends of the family. Ask them about the names and vital statistics in their parts of the family and about the ancestors you have in common. Write down whatever they tell you, even if it is sketchy.

Sometimes you will find differences of opinion on names or dates. Two aunts may give different death dates for their grandpa. Two cousins may give different names for Cousin Sallie's husband. Write both in your notes. Later, when you establish the correct date or name, explain the answer in those notes. In the meantime, you don't know which to accept and which to discount. Keep them both. Identify each page of notes with the name of the person who provided the information and when and where the visit took place. If it was a telephone conversation, say so in your notes.

If You Are the Elder Generation

What if you are part of the elder generation in your immediate family as you begin this puzzle? The process is the same, and the material you need to gather is the same. The difference is that you may have a limited number of siblings, cousins, or older relatives with whom to consult. However, you can write down what you remember about your childhood family, your grandparents, and other relatives you knew or heard about when you were growing up. Get your children, nieces and nephews, and children of cousins to fill in their family group sheets. You still may be able to contact first, second, or third cousins who have information in family papers. You may have an advantage over younger researchers because (1) you knew relatives and ancestors whose lives extended farther back in time and (2) you may have family mementos and papers that can help furnish some of the information you need for your charts.

Considering Touchy Subjects

How should you handle sensitive subjects? Very carefully. These may include subjects of divorce, death of a spouse or child, a child whose parentage is uncertain, or relatives who have been in prison or mental institutions. If these questions must be brought up because of their importance to the overall picture, hold them until you and your interviewee are comfortable talking and sharing with each other.

Be alert to the reaction of your interviewee to this kind of subject. If he or she is willing to talk, you may get valuable information. If it seems to be an emotionally upsetting topic, be prepared to drop it for the time being. Every family has "closets" they prefer not to open for airing. We need to be sensitive to their feelings and wishes and may need to find our information in other ways.

You must decide for yourself how far to intrude into someone's private territory. Family history must be truthful, but some relatives prefer to leave some chapters closed, at least for the present. For example, two cousins brought me up to date on their brothers but asked that I not include in a family history the fact that one was currently in prison and the other was in a mental hospital. On the other hand, several relatives did not mind furnishing the names and

See Also

See the relationship chart on page 239 for degrees of cousin relationships. You and your first cousin have at least one, often two, of the same grandparents. You and your second cousin have at least one, often two, of the same great-grandparents but different grandparents.

birth dates of their first (and later divorced) spouses because the children would someday want that information about their other parent. One cousin requested that I list his family in the history but with no dates of birth or marriage. He gave me the dates but asked that I not print them, and I honored his request.

Some genealogists feel that these facts are part of the family history and should always be included in compiled histories. They argue, for example, that if a divorce happened, the marriage and the divorce should be reported. On the other hand, if the couple had no children and the relative affected by these events requests that they not be publicized, I personally prefer to honor the request. The events did not change the genealogy of the family; omitting them from a family book simply excludes an apparently unfortunate experience from the life history of one individual. Besides, if I accept confidential information and then make it public, I will have betrayed a trust, and I choose not to do that.

Occasionally genealogists learn about a family member born out of wedlock and raised by other relatives as their child or placed for adoption outside the family. Some families will tell the truth about such facts, and some will not. We cannot force people to tell what they want to keep secret. However, when it affects your own genealogy—yourself, a parent, or a grandparent—you have a need to know. By continued contact with the family members who know the truth, you may be able to convince them that what happened in the past does affect you and that you attach no stigma, fault, or blame to what they can tell you—you simply need the truth. Some researchers get the information, and others do not.

Interviews by Mail

When you cannot talk with the relatives in person or on the telephone, write to them via mail or e-mail. To increase their cooperation, make their job easy. Explain your project and ask for their help. If you are corresponding by mail, enclose a self-addressed, stamped envelope (SASE) and a page of typed or neatly hand-printed questions with space left for their answers. They can simply fill in the blanks and return the page to you.

Title the page with a heading such as that shown in Figure 5.1, page 51: "Emily Croom to Emily Blalock, 9 July 1973." When the relative returns the page, file it in the appropriate family notebook or file, perhaps under "Correspondence." From the answers, add to your charts and use the interview letter as your source.

Reassure these correspondents that you appreciate any information they can give. No one can remember everything, and you'd rather they give you bits and pieces and leave some blanks than make up something to fill in!

If you are seeking information on two different ancestral surnames, send a separate question page on each family. Each one will fit nicely into the appropriate notebook or folder. **Filing systematically can be just as important as gathering the information.**

If you do not receive an answer within several weeks, try calling. People are busy and cannot always take the time to respond thoroughly and immediately.

Timesaver

Emily Croom to Emily Blalock, 9 July 1973:

Dear Aunt Emily,

Here are a few more questions...please...
1. When grandpa Pitser Blalock married Emma Bishop, she had 2 daughters. What were their names?

She had three daughters — Lucy Nell (who was married and living in Memphis when they married), Egene and Alberta.

2. I found Emma and Sim Bishop in the 1880 census with a 3-month-old son named Robert. Did he die young or move away? I had never heard of him before.

Robert died before Emma married Pitser. I do not remember his age when he died but I did hear her speak of him and I know he died before he reached adulthood.

3. Do you have any idea what Emma's maiden name was?

No, if I ever knew I have forgotten.

4. I found a county court order of 1867 binding 6 black children to Jesse Blalock. Do you have an idea of why this was done? It didn't say they were orphans.

No, I do not know. I have never heard this story.

5. When did Emma Bishop Blalock die?

I do not know the exact date of her death. I know that she was living when Lowe died in 1940. It seems to me that she died in the early or middle forties, though. However, we were not notified at the time of her death and heard it sometime later.

Figure 5.1 Sample interview letter

However, on the telephone, you may be able to get some answers without taking up a great deal of their time. Remember that their time is as valuable as yours.

Mistakes to Avoid

Warning

You have a better chance of getting answers to mail inquiries if you (1) make responding easy, (2) do not ask too much at once, and (3) ask for specific information on specific people. Once I received a letter that asked me to share what I had on the Allen family. As you might imagine, Allen is a common name found in every part of the country. The letter did not clarify which Allen family or when and where the one in question lived. In addition, the writer said he was also working on "these families if you have anything on them." He then listed no fewer than forty surnames! Nor did he include an SASE. As I recall, I did not answer the letter.

If you choose to write a second time as a reminder that you would very much like an answer to your inquiry, resist the urge to write a letter like one I received during an extremely busy season: "I cannot believe any genealogist would not respond to another immediately. I wrote you two weeks ago with an SASE and haven't heard from you yet. I've never had another genealogist act this way, and I don't understand why you have not responded." My immediate desire was to throw both letters in the trash. My next impulse was to send back her SASE with a note: "Cannot help you." (No, I don't remember what I did; I just remember that letter.)

CONDUCTING AND TAPING AN INTERVIEW

You may want to record an audiotape or videotape of your interview in addition to taking notes. Here are some suggestions for a successful taping session:

1. Whether taping on audiotape or videotape, include both the interview questions and the answers on the recording.

2. When recording the interview on audiotape, use the best quality recorder available to you and a good quality tape. Usually a sixty-minute audiotape is sufficient, although to be safe, bring an extra tape along. A battery-operated tape recorder may not be able to pull a longer tape with good results. Take extra batteries or use an AC/DC adapter and cord.

3. When using a video recorder or digital video camera, it is helpful to involve a third person to operate the equipment. If a third person controls the camera, you are free to concentrate on the interview, and the quality of the resulting video may be better. An operator can control the zoom lens, pan the scene, and control the movement of the camera. If you as the interviewer must also try to hold the camera still or keep an eye on the viewer to judge what you are taping, you cannot concentrate thoroughly on the interview.

4. If you videotape the interview yourself, place the camera on a tripod or stand and let it run unobtrusively in the background. Some digital video cameras have remote control devices that can be helpful during an interview.

5. Assure your interviewee that this will be an informal visit. Both of you need to relax and be comfortable. Feel free to laugh and have fun. Be ready

and willing to stop the recorder or camera in case of fatigue or to discuss something off the record. Create an atmosphere conducive to thinking and taping by turning off televisions or other noisy appliances and by sending pets and young children elsewhere.

6. When audio taping, place the microphone between you and the interviewee in such a way that both voices will record well. Place the tape recorder on a stationary object, such as a table, rather than in someone's lap, to minimize noises made if that person shifts positions or rattles paper. If you run the video camera, be aware that your voice will be closer to the microphone and will be louder on the resulting tape unless you lower your voice.

7. Test your equipment and the voices before you begin. View and listen to the sample to confirm that all is working and voices are loud enough and clear. Label the tape before you begin.

8. **Identify on the recording each person involved in the session and the date and place of the interview.** If more than two are present, have each person introduce himself or herself to put a voice with the name for easier identification in the future, especially on audiotapes. Include yourself in these introductions.

9. You will get a better recording if each participant remembers

(a) to speak slowly and loudly enough to be clearly understood.

(b) that dropping one's voice (trailing off) at the ends of phrases will mean losing what is said. The longer the interview, the more the voices tend to drop in volume and clarity toward the end.

(c) that more than one person speaking at a time means a garbled, confused section of tape in which no one is clearly understood. When it is possible, it is advantageous to limit the session to you and one interviewee.

10. It is helpful to spell aloud any proper names mentioned, especially unusual ones or any that could be misunderstood on tape. Beginning and final consonants are easy to lose on a tape. For example, is the nickname Card or Carg? Bud, Pug, or Pup? Confusion can occur with regional or foreign accents and speech that is rapid or trails off at the ends of words and phrases.

11. It is helpful to leave the audiotape visible in the tape recorder so you can tell when the tape is running out. Or note the time when you begin so that you can determine when the tape may be full. If possible, finish one topic before turning the audiotape, and begin the new side with a new topic.

12. Don't let the tape control the interview. Pauses for thinking or reflecting are often valuable to the conversation; you do not have to fill every moment of tape time with sound.

13. Remember that many people are nervous around tape recorders and video cameras and do not like to hear their own voices played back. Do what you can to allay these fears and, at the same time, to make yourself and the recorder less important than the interviewee and what he or she is saying.

14. Be sure that you and the interviewee have the same understanding about how the tape is to be used. If necessary, write out an explanation for both to sign that gives the purpose and intended uses of the tape.

15. Be aware that audiotapes and videotapes do not last forever, nor does

Important

Tip

Idea Generator

our memory. **Therefore, consider transcribing the interview while it is fresh on your mind.** With special equipment, digital videos can be transferred to VHS tapes. Fortunately, technology makes it possible to transfer both audio and video recordings to compact discs for a more permanent record.

After the interview, thank your interviewee, perhaps take pictures to commemorate the occasion, and leave the way open for another session at a later date.

If you have videotaping equipment available, you may want to record family gatherings and group interviews. Both videotapes and audiotapes become valuable for their content and the memories.

THINGS TO DO NOW

1. Make a checklist of relatives you could interview; include addresses, telephone numbers, and e-mail addresses when possible.
2. Begin listing questions to ask each contact person. (See also chapter seven.)
3. Begin contacting these people by mail, e-mail, or telephone to discuss your project, ask for input, and schedule interviews.
4. Plan to send at least one interview letter and one family group sheet. One method may work for you better than another, and they can serve different purposes.
5. If you are an elder in your family, use the interview process on yourself, siblings, and cousins. Your experiences and memories can be valuable to younger generations.

SIX

Hand-Me-Downs: Family Traditions

O ral tradition is the stories passed down from generation to generation by word of mouth. This tradition is stronger in some families than in others, but genealogists can use whatever they find. Family stories sometimes grow with the age or imagination of the teller, but there is often truth in them. Some of the details may get lost or altered, but basic truths often remain. Frequently, the genealogist must use these stories as clues rather than as absolute facts. Nevertheless, they are part of the family history. Genealogists can gather this tradition in interviews and at family gatherings.

ORAL TRADITION IN FAMILY HISTORY

Many oral traditions tell of the origin of the American family: Four brothers came to Texas from Prussia to escape military service; three sisters came from Ireland during the Great Potato Famine. The stories of origin often blur with age: "Mama used to tell me about a couple who eloped and came from Scotland." Somewhere, sometime, this couple may be identified. In the meantime, one task of the genealogist is to preserve oral tradition by recording it on tape or paper.

Many families pass on stories of Civil War experiences: the slave who saved the family home, the wife who ran the farm, the day church services were interrupted by the approach of the enemy, or the enemy who found a scared six-year-old hiding in the woods and saw him safely home. In all families, it is important for those who knew the Civil War generation to record whatever stories or memories they can. After all, how many families today have stories about their Revolutionary War ancestors? Wouldn't we like to know more about the people of that generation in our own family? **It is up to us to preserve the memory of the generations we can help record, however small that memory may be.**

My Civil War ancestor Susan lived in Columbia, South Carolina, when the

Important

55

Union army marched through and burned the city. Susan was among many who fled from burning homes. She carried the baby and instructed her three-year-old to hold tightly to her skirt. In her other arm, she hoped to carry a little bag of family silver, handmade by her father-in-law and his father, who had been fine silversmiths.

As her little family struggled on foot toward the insane asylum to find refuge for the night, they were approached by a Yankee soldier who asked if he could help. She knew she had to give him either the baby or the silver because she could not manage both. She regretfully handed him the bag of silver and resigned herself to the loss of a valuable family collection.

Miraculously, some time later, the enemy soldier or his family returned the bag of silver to her! Throughout the years of great sectional bitterness that followed the war, Susan continually reminded her family that there was at least one honest Yankee in the world. The two families even corresponded for some years. Unfortunately, by the time my grandmother told me the story, those who knew the identity of the Yankee soldier were gone.

Almost every family survived some disaster and still relates the story: the Drought, the Storm, the Flood, the Epidemic, or the Fire. One such story appears in unrelated families: the fire in which everything was lost except the piano. The move westward provided many experiences now preserved in oral tradition: selling the family heirlooms because they could not be moved, trying to carry the piano in the wagon, surviving Indian raids, or losing loved ones along the way.

African-American family traditions sometimes include memories of slave ancestors. In one family's tradition, the great-great-grandfather was a field hand, and his wife was a house servant; they lived in Louisiana near Shreveport. He ran away once, was found the next day, and was whipped. On occasion, public records, such as newspapers, censuses, and deeds, bear out the details of such traditions. This kind of story, though a sensitive issue for some, can prove very important in establishing the family's ancestry another generation or two back in time. One would hope that the older generation, who may prefer to forget such stories, would nevertheless pass them down to the younger family members interested in learning more about their ancestors.

In all families, the relatives who actually knew the Civil War generation are becoming fewer in number as the years pass. It is important to talk with these family members while we can.

Clues for the Genealogist

As 1900 gets further and further from us, it behooves the younger generations of all ethnic groups to preserve whatever memories do survive about their ancestors at the turn of the twentieth century, even if the memories and traditions do not include anything about slavery, freedom, "the War," or immigration. Even names, relationships, and places of residence can be very helpful to the researcher. If "Cousin Hattie was always with Mama's family at Christmas," ask who Cousin Hattie was. How was she related and on which side of the family? We must ask and begin to find out. She may or may not be an important link in your research.

How can you find out about her or other such relatives?

- If Mama is living, ask her about Cousin Hattie, how they were related, and the identity of other relatives in Cousin Hattie's family. Who were Cousin Hattie's parents?
- If Cousin Hattie is living, try to talk with her.
- If Cousin Hattie had children, try to contact them.
- Ask Mama's brothers or sisters about Cousin Hattie.
- Ask anyone who knew Mama and/or Cousin Hattie about them and how they were related.
- Ask for specific information about Cousin Hattie: birth date or age at a given time, marriage, children, death date.
- Get all the information you can about Cousin Hattie within your family and hers in preparation for researching in public records.

Sometimes, oral traditions are sketchy recollections about a particular person, such as Cousin Hattie, or a specific family. Yet, **sometimes these one-fact memories hold important clues for the genealogist.** Several case studies in *The Sleuth Book for Genealogists* began with scant remembrances and limited facts about the ancestor on whom research focused. In the African-American case study, family memory of a nephew-aunt relationship was significant in the search for an ancestor's parents. The alert genealogist will recognize and record such detail in interviews or discussions with family members. One of these may be the key to the research problem.

Oral traditions also give family statistics: Great-Grandpa was one of six boys and had six sisters—twelve children altogether. That was the tradition, yet cousins' combined efforts could name only ten. Census and probate records verified these. That left two girls' names missing. Finally, a distant cousin provided copies of old family letters, including a reference to "sister Luta sleeping in the crib" and another mention of "little Willie" recovering from the measles. Then Cousin Bea remembered that she had heard about a little girl named Willie. The dates of the letters and the census records approximated the dates of the lives of these two little girls who apparently died in early childhood. The oral tradition of twelve children had checked out.

In some cases, genealogists can document and confirm these family traditions. We can reestablish the facts and return missing details to the story through newspapers, letters, public records, and interviews. However, when the records or the people who knew the truth are not available, we must accept some tradition as just that.

For example, the father of those twelve children was one of fourteen children, eleven of whose names appear in the records. Tradition says that three of the children were boys who died in infancy. Their dates of birth and death and names, if they were named, do not appear in any searched records. The tradition is considered correct because several branches of the family have handed down the same story, but it probably cannot be verified.

Warning

Traditions That Refuse to Die

In almost every family, somebody claims kinship with somebody famous.

1. "Great-Grandmother was a first cousin of Robert E. Lee." In truth, Great-Grandmother was born a North Carolina Lea, not related to the Virginia Lees.

2. "We are descendants of the Presidents Harrison." The fact that Great-Grandpa Harrison had relatives who lived near Washington, DC, when one of the Harrisons was president does not even suggest kinship. Very often these tales are simply wishful thinking. Seldom are they useful. Here, the tradition was nonsense.

3. One Texas family tradition said that "Grandma was a close relative of Sam Houston." In this case, the tradition had come down through several branches of the family and persisted in spite of the facts. After years of hearing Aunt Sally's claim of kinship with Sam Houston, her niece and I intensified the research. Her Grandma Cummings's maiden name was Huston, sometimes spelled Houston, but her father was Almanzon, not Sam.

As the niece presented our discoveries at the next family reunion, Aunt Sally did not contradict her niece's findings but added, as if to be helpful, that they were descendants of one of Sam Houston's sisters. However absurd that sounded, Aunt Sally was confident of its accuracy.

For the next reunion, we prepared a biography and genealogy of Sam Houston's family to compare the families of the two men who were similar in age. The facts clearly showed that Aunt Sally's story was not true. Then, Aunt Sally "remembered" that their Almanzon Huston was one of Sam Houston's brothers or father's brothers, and that was the gospel truth.

The next summer, her niece was ready with facts about the two men and their fathers to show that they were not brothers or close cousins. Even Sam's grandfather's four brothers are not possible links. Aunt Sally remained undaunted in her belief of close kinship with the popular Texas figure, and she was not alone. Other relatives of her generation agreed with her, whatever her story was at the moment, and several old newspaper clippings carried the tradition that Sam and Almanzon were cousins.

So far, no facts link the two as kin. However, they did know each other. Almanzon had been Sam's quartermaster general in the Texas War for Independence. Perhaps they called each other "cousin" because they had the same last name.

Genealogists can record such traditions in case evidence later justifies their further consideration. However, it is probably best to ignore the repetition of these kinds of stories and concentrate on learning more about the known and verified ancestors.

CUSTOMS AS TRADITIONS

Another meaning of the word *tradition* is a set of customs that are repeated year after year, sometimes generation after generation. These traditions, too, are part of the family history and are fun to collect. In some families, the birthday person has the honor of choosing the menu for the evening meal or where the family will dine out. One family hands down an antique quilt to the Sarah in the next generation. It has the embroidered signatures of related Sarahs dating back some two hundred years.

Expressions and sayings can be traditions as well. When we children asked my grandmother her age, she always said she was 107. We knew she wasn't, but that was always her answer. Recently, I found a letter to me from her mother (my great-grandmother), at age seventy-nine, saying, "It really is a grief to me that I cannot see you often and know you better But when one gets to the age of one hundred and seven the bus lines, the railroads, the airplanes all refuse to take them as passangers [*sic*]. Too much risk. . . . See? what I am up against." So that's where my grandmother got it! How many generations before her used it? Isn't it up to me, now, to continue that tradition?

Holidays are full of traditions. One grandmother always served boiled custard as a Christmas treat. For three generations, my family's holiday dinners have often ended with a group of four to seven folks, ages eight to eighty, sitting in a circle on the floor playing wild games of multiple solitaire, where all can play on everyone's aces. I wonder what my nineteenth-century Methodist preacher ancestors would say! They allowed no card playing in their families— at least none that they knew about.

Of course, holidays are often a time for family reunions and gatherings that continue these traditions. For the genealogist, these occasions are golden opportunities to ask questions, share and gather information, write down or tape stories, take photographs, get autographs, and show the progress on the family history.

THINGS TO DO NOW

1. What family stories do you know about your grandparents or great-grandparents? What would you like your children to know about these ancestors, your parents, and yourself? Begin writing down or taping some of your own memories about these people.
2. What oral traditions does your family have from the Civil War? Slavery days? World War I? The Great Depression? World War II? Other historical periods or events?
3. What oral traditions have you heard about your immigrant ancestors or their origins?
4. Does your family have an oral tradition about being kin to someone famous? How can you begin to find out whether it is true?
5. Write down traditions and customs from your childhood family. Were any of these carried over from earlier generations? What new traditions have you started and carried on in your family?

Idea Generator

SEVEN

Life History: Beginning to End

As you piece together your family history, what information do you want? Vital statistics, to be sure, but **there is much more to family history than lists of names and dates.** For example, if you have a pet, it surely has a name. What did Dad call his dog when he was a boy? What are his memories of the dog? What did Great-Grandma call her cow? One family tells that when the post-Civil War generation moved from Mississippi to Texas, their wagon team was a pair of oxen named Broad and Dave.

Each answer or story may suggest new questions. As you listen, you will begin to wonder how and why they did certain things, what the house was like, and what subjects they studied in school. Ask.

You can ask hundreds of questions about each generation. The farther back you go, the fewer answers you receive. However, even a few answers will give you an idea of life in the family. Your questions may stretch over several visits and/or letters, and you may not get answers to them all. Some questions may produce unexpected responses: "Heavens, child, how old do you think I am!" or "Good grief, yes!" or "For crying out loud! Do you think we lived like the Queen of England?" Well, we live and learn. That is why we ask questions.

For the benefit of your children and grandchildren, start with yourself and make notes on your life history. Ask your parents and aunts and uncles about their childhood, schooling, teen years, and early married life. If you are lucky enough to have grandparents or their siblings available, ask them the same questions about their lives. Even family friends can tell us interesting things about our parents and grandparents. For proper identification and documentation, label your notes with your name, the name of the interviewee, the date and place of the interview, and the topic or period covered.

Keep in mind that the questions in your interviews serve several purposes:

- to extend the information on your charts
- to give you clues for further research
- to gather life history of the family, especially your focus ancestor

Any information that contributes to these purposes is desirable. Some pieces of information are more important than others. Some are more interesting.

COLLECTING FAMILY STORIES

Most families have preserved stories that add life to the family history. These concern daily life; snatches of childhood memories; poignant or humorous events; and descriptions of places, things, and people.

For example, these incidents were serious to those involved but humorous to us today. Maggie was five in 1872 when it was strictly improper for a lady, whether five or fifty, to speak of the body and its parts. Maggie learned a limerick from her devilish older brother and made the mistake of sharing it with her mother. Mama, being concerned about decency and feeling the need to teach Maggie a lesson about such things, washed the little girl's mouth out with soap. Of course, Maggie never forgot the limerick and handed it down to her grandchildren and beyond. The limerick was

> There was a young lady named Mabel,
> Who loved to dance on the table,
> She blushed very red
> When the gentleman said,
> "Oh, look at the legs on the table."

Sue was about seven in the early 1900s when the bishop came for Sunday dinner. Imagine the disgrace the child suffered when, at a lull in the conversation, she addressed the guest, "You wanta hear me drink like a horse?"

The following sections of this chapter are interview questions you can ask yourself or relatives in an attempt to understand their lives and preserve memory of the family's collective past. Add other questions pertinent to your family.

INTERVIEW QUESTIONS: CHILDHOOD

1. What kind of relationship did you have with your siblings? What stands out about them in your memory of childhood?
2. What is your earliest memory of your house or residence, your family, your town, events in the news?
3. Who were your playmates or pets? Which games, toys, celebrations, and playmates were your favorites? How important were movies, television, radio, or bicycles in your childhood?
4. Where was your house or residence? If in a city, what address(es)? What county and state? Is the house still standing? What did it look like? How many rooms did it have? Describe the house and furnishings: one or two stories, frame or brick, paint colors, porch, garage, yard, outbuildings, fireplaces, kind of floor and wall coverings. If the family moved during your childhood, describe each residence. Do you have pictures of the house(s)?

Oral History

See Also

Review tips for asking questions on page 47.

5. How easily or often did you get into mischief? Why? What punishments did you incur? Were your parents strict? What rules did you have to follow?

6. What are your most vivid memories of childhood?

7. Which relatives do you remember, and what stands out in your mind about them? What trips did you take to visit relatives? How did you travel?

8. What chores were your responsibility? Did you get an allowance? How did you get your spending money? What did you do with it? What was the financial condition of the family?

9. How did you celebrate birthdays, Thanksgiving, Fourth of July, Christmas, or other holidays? Did you observe Halloween? How?

10. What were family customs for weekends, Sundays or Sabbaths, summer days?

11. What major events do you recall: fires, storms, moving, etc.?

12. How far was school from your house? How did you get to school? During what hours were you in school? When did school start in the fall and end for the summer? What subjects did you like best or least? Were you able to attend school regularly? What do you remember about your teachers? Does any teacher stand out in your mind as having a significant influence on you? How good were your grades? Did you feel pressure to make good grades? How did you spend recess? What memories stand out in your mind about elementary school, junior high or middle school?

13. What did you do in the summer or when you were not in school: trips, sports, scouting, camping, working, helping parents, visiting relatives?

14. Did you study or participate in music, art, dancing? What hobbies or sports did you pursue? Did you enjoy games, reading, making things?

15. During childhood, what were your favorite foods, clothes, sports, stories, movies, heroes, people?

16. What part did church and religious activities play in your early years, both at home and away from home?

17. What were your dreams or plans for the future? Which have become reality?

18. What experience did you have with death as a child or a teen? What funeral or burial customs were followed in the family or community?

19. What neighborhood gatherings—social or working—do you recall?

20. What lessons did you learn as a child or teen that have helped you in later life?

INTERVIEW QUESTIONS: TEEN YEARS

1. What high school(s) did you attend? Where? How long? Did you graduate? How large was the school? In what clubs or sports did you participate? Did you enter competitions or contests? (Explain.) What were some of the school rules? What was the dress code, either stated or implied? How did you get to school? How far was it from home? What did you do for lunch?

2. What were your favorite or least favorite subjects? Which courses helped you most?

3. What do you recall about teachers and classmates? Is there someone from these years who had great influence on you?

4. Did you go to college? Where? How did you choose your college? How did you finance your education?

5. What kinds of parties did you attend? Where did you go on dates? When did you start dating? What rules governed dating in your family? What did you enjoy most for recreation?

6. What clothes were in style when you were in high school? Did you make any of your own clothes?

7. Did you enjoy music, dancing, art, reading, or other hobbies? Who in the family sang or played musical instruments? Were you in the school band?

8. What unusual or special events do you recall?

9. Did you have a job? Doing what? How much money did you earn? How did you use your earnings?

10. What rules governed your teenage activities? Were you allowed to do these: play cards, date without a chaperone, stay out past dark, go to movies, dance, eat with adults, drive the family car? Were you required to go to church on Wednesday nights as well as Sunday? Were you expected to stand when adults entered the room? What was considered appropriate Sunday or Sabbath conduct? What were considered proper manners and proper dress?

11. Did you participate in any service projects or volunteer work? (Explain.)

INTERVIEW QUESTIONS: ADULTHOOD

1. When and where did you get married? Describe the wedding, clothes, attendants, parties, gifts, etc. What wedding customs prevailed in your community at the time?

2. What can you tell me about your courtship and dating? How did you meet your spouse?

3. When and where were your children born? What stands out in your mind about each one as a small child or as a teenager?

4. Where have you lived? Tell me about each house or residence.

5. What rules did you set for your children?

6. What jobs have you held as an adult? What jobs has your spouse held? How have wages and salaries changed since you first worked?

7. What trips have you taken? Which have you enjoyed most?

8. In what religious, civic, club, political, or service (volunteer) activities have you participated?

9. What is your political affiliation? Has it changed over the years?

10. What is your religious affiliation?

11. Do you enjoy music, art, gardening, handicrafts, needlework (knitting, crochet, embroidery, needlepoint, quilting, etc.), sewing, carpentry, etc.? Which members of the family do (or did) which of these activities?

12. How does the family celebrate Thanksgiving, Fourth of July, Christmas, or other holidays? What other holidays do you celebrate? How? What other traditions have you established in your family?
13. What kinds of cars have you had? When did you get your first car? Do you remember how much the cars or gasoline cost?
14. Do you enjoy cooking? What are your favorite recipes? Do you have recipes from your mother or grandmother?
15. What do you consider your special talents or abilities? What do you do best? What do you enjoy doing the most?
16. Do you have grandchildren? Who?
17. Do you enjoy entertaining? Do you entertain friends, relatives, business associates? What kind of entertaining do you do?
18. What are your favorite family stories?

WHAT WERE THEY LIKE?

One of the most interesting aspects of the family history puzzle is discovering some of the physical features and personality traits that made up the family. You can probably answer these questions yourself for the relatives you know. In an effort to learn something about individuals who are no longer living, ask to see photographs of them and ask these questions of the people who knew them.

Personal Appearance

1. Was he or she tall, average height, or short; thin, average size, stocky, or fat?
2. What color skin, hair, and eyes did he or she have?
3. What feature of his or hers stands out in your mind?
4. Was he or she healthy? Sickly? In what way?
5. Which men in the family were bald or had a beard or mustache?
6. What physical features or tendencies showed up in more than one member of the family, such as flat feet or a "drooping left eyelid"?

Habits and Personality

You can adapt the following questions to learn about individuals in present or previous generations. You may save time by using a number scale in answering some of the questions, such as 0 for *never*, 1 for *rarely*, 2 for *sometimes*, 3 for *frequently*. You can also use these questions in looking at the family collectively by asking "Who used to enjoy reading?" or "Whom do you remember as a worrier?"

1. How often did he or she (or who in the family used to) smoke, chew tobacco, drink, curse; travel, read; enjoy housekeeping, cooking; play tennis, golf, or other sports; ride a bicycle, skate, ski, etc.; raise animals or pets; like or raise cats; like or raise dogs; sleep late, rise early, stay up late, or go to bed early?

2. How often did he or she play cards (what games?), tell jokes, tease others,

play practical jokes, create nice surprises for others, entertain, correspond, visit friends, manipulate people?

3. To what extent or how often did he or she smile, frown, laugh, get mad, cry, complain, gossip, see the bright side, dwell on the past, experience failure or success, look to the future for happiness, enjoy today, have a one-track mind, start projects and not finish them, get things accomplished, work long hours, stay busy, work hard, make mountains out of molehills, imagine crises that were not really crises, organize well, worry, have a sense of humor, exhibit common sense?

4. Did he or she have a nickname? What?

5. If he or she had a few hours to pursue an activity for pleasure, what would the activity be?

6. What were his or her special talents or abilities?

7. To what extent was he or she (or who in the family was) a worrier, a loner, a hypochondriac, the life of the party, a good conversationalist, a willing worker, a perfectionist, a spendthrift, a stern disciplinarian, a good storyteller, a leader, a follower, a manager?

8. To what extent was he or she demanding of self, demanding of others, hard (easy) to please, hard (easy) to work with, neat (sloppy) in habit and dress, absentminded, scatterbrained, literal minded, argumentative, clever, ingenious, logical, lazy, ambitious, industrious, energetic, diligent, consistent, flexible, responsible, efficient, artistic, musical, creative, dramatic?

9. To what extent was he or she possessive, sharing, affectionate, generous, warmhearted, kind, stingy, miserly, critical, jealous, blunt, outspoken, soft spoken, clever with words, silly, open minded, narrow minded, forthright, easily angered, talkative, outgoing, understanding, empathetic, sympathetic, henpecked, bossy, hard (easy) to get along with, hard (easy) to talk to, shy, quiet, considerate, courteous, radiant, concerned about others, concerned about what others thought, aloof, confident, intuitive?

10. To what extent was he or she moody, even-tempered, grumpy, gruff, self-centered, eccentric (explain), lonely, finicky (explain), stubborn, suspicious, philosophical, religious, strong in faith, jolly, serious, lighthearted, cruel, nervous, relaxed, carefree, thrifty, hurried, stern, angry, happy, courageous, cheerful, egotistical, humble, honest, sensitive, temperate, temperamental, modest?

11. How did he or she feel about pregnancy, working women, housekeeping, hobbies, yard work, gardening, travel, death, sewing, spending money, daughters going to college, daughters getting married, single women living alone, women staying single, provisions for older members of the family?

12. Do any of these traits or habits stand out when you think of him or her?

FAMILY MEDICAL HISTORY

As science learns more about genetic, hereditary, and environmental factors in health and disease, it becomes increasingly important for us to record family medical history. Study of the cluster of blood-related siblings and cousins in each generation is particularly pertinent in this effort, for patterns of health history or disease within a family may help determine your own level of risk.

Certainly, not all physical, emotional, or mental illnesses are inherited or run in families. Each person's cultural and physical environment, lifestyle, health, and personal habits—such as diet, smoking, or alcohol consumption—can influence the onset or prevention of many diseases, whether or not they are prevalent in the family history.

Gathering family medical history involves recording such personal factors in addition to cause of death, chronic conditions, and major illnesses or conditions for each of these relatives. It is also important to learn at what age an individual developed a given disease or condition and how it affected that person.

The following is a partial list of diseases and conditions that are known or thought to have hereditary factors, some to a greater degree than others. Can you identify any family members who have been affected by them?

allergies	diabetes	mental retardation
Alzheimer's disease	epilepsy	multiple sclerosis
arthritis	fragile X syndrome	muscular dystrophy
attention deficit disorder	glaucoma	osteoporosis
blindness	heart disease	Parkinson's disease
cancer	hemophilia	physical disabilities
cataracts	high blood pressure	physical malformations
cystic fibrosis	Huntington's disease	sickle-cell anemia
deafness	learning disabilities	stroke

If any of these, or other conditions, exist within the family history, the relatives of the present and future generations may be able to learn their risk levels from medical professionals and take steps to prevent or make early detection and seek treatment of potential problems.

THINGS TO DO NOW

Idea Generator

1. Gather letters or stories about yourself in infancy and childhood: firsts, growth, funny incidents, curiosity, likes and dislikes, vocabulary, habits, diseases, accidents.
2. Record your memories of your brothers and sisters during childhood. Go through the questions about childhood, teen years, and adulthood and answer them for yourself, on paper or on tape. Answer the personality and habit questions about yourself.
3. Try answering the personality and habit questions about your parents and grandparents. Have siblings or cousins answer the same questions about your parents and grandparents. Compare the answers.
4. If your parents, grandparents, or great-grandparents are living, interview them about their childhood, teen years, and adulthood. If they are not living but their siblings are, interview them while you can and ask about your ancestor in the process.

5. If you are a grandparent, answer these questions for yourself and to the extent you can for your parents. Preserve your record for your grandchildren.
6. Begin gathering medical history on yourself and your siblings, your parents, your grandparents and their siblings, your cousins, and your blood-related aunts and uncles.

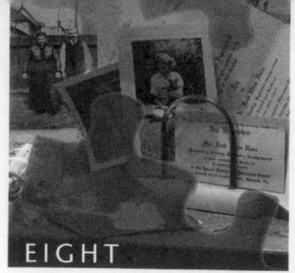

EIGHT

History as the Family Lived It

Reminder

See Also

Review tips for asking questions on page 47.

C ollecting family history also means trying to fit the family into the history of the community, county, state, and nation. You can find the political, economic, and social history of these areas in books and contemporary newspapers, but only family members can share their personal reactions to the public events. For whom did *they* vote? What prices did *they* pay? What jobs did *they* hold? When did *they* first get electricity, a telephone, a car, a radio, a television, air-conditioning, or a computer?

Some of the questions in this chapter deal with events discussed in history textbooks. Yet not all people living during the period were aware of or affected by these events. Some did not consider them important. **To keep history in perspective, we must balance textbook history with what ordinary people thought and experienced.**

The following questions are divided roughly into decades. Some public events, well-known people, and customs are included in the appropriate time periods. The questions are aimed at finding out about the family in each period. If family members are no longer available to interview, family friends and neighbors may be able to give you insight into your family's experiences during a particular period. Add other questions as you think of them. Figure 8.1, page 71, is a sample interview dealing with a family in the 1930s.

As you discuss a particular period with an interviewee, use the following questions to learn about the era and the family at that time. Or use them as a guide to retelling your own experiences for your descendants. Some of the questions duplicate questions in chapter seven because the answers vary in different generations or pertain to specific developments during a given decade.

An example of these different generational perspectives is a conversation between a young mother and her grandmother, about 1950. Grandma asked, "If you could have only one of your modern conveniences, which would you choose to keep?" After some thought, the granddaughter answered, "I don't think I could do without the refrigerator." Grandma laughed. "You don't know luxuries from conveniences. I'd pick running water every time."

FAMILY LIFE IN ANY GENERATION AFTER 1900

1. Where did the family live? Did the family move during this period? How frequently? Where?

2. How did the family earn a living? Did any women of the family work outside the home? In what job(s)? What provisions were made for child care when mothers worked outside the home?

3. If you lived on a farm, what crops and animals did you raise? Which ones were raised for sale and which for food? Did you have a garden and/or orchard?

4. Can you describe your house(s)? When did the family get indoor plumbing, running water, or electricity for the first time? Did each residence have these conveniences? What kind of stove, heating, and lighting did you have? Which outbuildings?

5. When did you get your first car? What kind? New or used?

6. Were the children of the family in school? What do you remember of school subjects, rules, activities, hours, sports, clothes, holidays, homework, pep squads (cheering sections, cheerleaders, etc.), bands and drill teams, extracurricular activities, etc.?

7. What part did religious, school, or family gatherings play in your life? What religious and school activities did you participate in?

8. If you lived in a town or city, did you have such improvements as paved streets, streetlights, sidewalks, parks? Describe.

9. How would you classify your economic status at this time? On what do you base this decision? Did your economic status change? How? Why? When?

10. To what extent were you aware of urban and industrial problems of this period?

11. What were the rules, restrictions, and etiquette governing your household?

12. Did the family make any of its own clothes? What hairstyles did family members have? Did the females of the family wear cosmetics, jewelry?

13. What part did mail-order catalogs play in your life? Which catalogs did you use?

14. What recollections from this period stand out vividly in your mind?

15. In what ways did the family celebrate weddings? What wedding customs were common in the period and the community?

16. What household chores were assigned to various members of the family? Whose job was it to wash or iron clothes, wash dishes, chop wood, keep house, take care of the yard and/or garden, prepare meals?

17. Do you have letters, diaries, or stories to share about events during the period, such as fires, drought, storms, floods, disease, weddings, funerals, or special achievements?

18. When did the family get its first telephone? If you were old enough to remember such an event, what was your reaction upon hearing or using a telephone for the first time?

19. How did you or the family wash clothes before you had a washing machine? How did you stay cool in the summer? How did you get groceries?

20. What was it like to travel during the period? What funny or interesting experiences did you have while traveling?

21. What did the family do for recreation? Did the family have a radio, phonograph, television? What games did the family play—adults or children?

22. What provisions were made for the older family members?

23. Did you hear of any special New Year's celebrations in the family when 1899 gave way to 1900?

24. Do you know any Civil War stories that have been handed down in the family?

25. Do you know how the family celebrated the end of World War I or World War II?

1920s

1. To what extent were you aware of the "Roaring Twenties" at the time? Were you aware of Prohibition? Did the family favor it at the time? To what extent do you feel it worked or did not work? Did the family obey it? Why or why not?

2. What electrical appliances or household conveniences did the family acquire for the first time during this decade? What was the first electrical appliance the family had? What kind of cookstove did the family have? How did the family heat the residence? Did the family have a car?

3. How did the family buy groceries? Were groceries delivered? Did the family shop at different stores for different food items? To what extent did you feel your family was part of the general prosperity of the decade?

4. What did the family do for recreation? What part did radio, movies, or sports play in the life of the family? What was your reaction to hearing a radio for the first time? Was there any family restriction on moviegoing? Where were movies shown? How much was admission?

5. What do you feel were the greatest changes of the decade? What invention or development do you feel caused the greatest change for the family, the community, the country in general?

6. What provisions were made for the older family members?

THE GREAT DEPRESSION AND THE 1930s

1. To what extent did the Depression change your habits, way of life, schooling, plans? Did you "feel" the Depression? Did you observe a difference

HOW THIS INTERVIEW FORM CAME ABOUT

As a teacher, I used the form on page 71 and one for World War II. Each student conducted two Depression interviews and two for the war years. In class we compared results to find patterns, trends, and interesting personal stories.

DEPRESSION 1930's   Interviewer *Emily Croom*   Date *May 1970*

Name *Mrs. H. O. Metcalfe*

Age group during most of the 1930's (circle one)   Child (Adult) Teenager

Family Size (family with which you were living in the 30's) ___4___

Residence in the 1930's *Marfa, Texas*   urban rural (small town)

Educational level in the 30's (circle the appropriate) high school student/(graduate)
   other *husband - college graduate*   college student/graduate

If you were a student during the 30's, how did the depression affect your education?
   Were you able to continue?* ___ How did you finance your education (scholarships,
   jobs, parents, etc.)? Did you or your friends drop out temporarily? permanently?
   *daughter in college did continue - financed her education with
   scholarships, summer & school-year jobs, & help from parents.*

For each job you held, what were the wages and hours? Please list chronologically.
   Job   Location   Days/week   Hours/day   Wages or Salary
1. *Housewife*   *Marfa*
2. *Husband lawyer*   "   *as necessary -*   *varied*
3.   *(self-employed)*
4. *He always said people fight more & get into disputes more*
5.   *in bad times than in good so lawyers did okay - were kept*
      busy.

What jobs did other members of your family hold?   *Many hobos
husband - lawyer & U.S. Commissioner   *came by & we fed
                    the family   *them too. Everybody
                                          in town did.

Were you self-supporting? *was* Did you help support your family? ___
   Did you have trouble finding a job when it was necessary to change? ___
   How were you able to find another?
also attended reviews, polo games, etc at the   *Mr. Raetzsch owned Palace movie*
army post, frequently went down to "meet   *theater & we went to movies some-*
the train." Followed the fire truck.   *about 10-15¢ admission. Didn't*
                                          get good radio reception except out on
What did you do for recreation or entertainment? *road to stock yard - so we went there.*
little dinner parties, bridge parties, young people had
ice cream parties & tennis & baseball & basketball.

Did your family raise, (make), can, preserve any of its own food? *yes* If so, what?

   bread, desserts   Canned peaches & other fruit. Made preserves.
Which food items were most difficult to obtain? easiest to obtain?
   Could get what we were accustomed to having before.
Which commodities (clothes, appliances, tools, toys, etc.) were most difficult to
obtain? easiest to obtain? What luxury items did you have to sacrifice?
   appliances - scarce   did without luxuries anyway
   money - scarce [note: daughter says she was excellent manager]
Was your family a "do-it-yourself" group to save money? *Yes* What did you make?
   Sewing most of the clothes for the 2 girls & myself.
Did you or your family own a car? *yes* More than one? *no* What make? *c 1925 Chevy*
   Do you remember the price of gasoline, or of the car? *No but 5¢/gallon on the*
                    (about 15¢-20¢/gallon) *army post in town*
Were you able to buy on credit? *yes - nearly everything - groceries,*
   cleaning, gasoline, drug store. Paid on first of each month.
Did you travel? *yes - summer* By what means? *car mostly*
   Were the trips mostly for business or pleasure? (Comments are welcome.)
   to visit relatives in San Antonio.

How have your experiences during the depression influenced your attitudes of the
   present? *Made us appreciate the value of money more.*

Figure 8.1

in the way the Depression affected people living in cities and people living in the country or small towns?

2. Did the family move during this decade? Why? How frequently? Where? What household conveniences did you have or lack: electricity, telephone, indoor plumbing, others?

3. Which family members had jobs? Doing what? Were they paid in cash, goods, or scrip? How much was rent? Was it difficult for the family to find housing or jobs?

4. At the time, what did you or the family think of Presidents Hoover and Franklin Roosevelt? Have you changed your opinions since then? Whom did the family support for president in 1928 (Hoover or Smith), 1932 (Hoover or Roosevelt), 1936 (Roosevelt or Landon)? Why? How effective were Hoover and Roosevelt as presidents?

5. Did any family member work for one of the New Deal agencies, such as the CCC (Civilian Conservation Corps), the WPA (Works Progress Administration), or the PWA (Public Works Administration)? If so, who? Which agency? Doing what? How long? Where?

6. Did the family raise, hunt, can, or preserve any of its own food? If so, what? What food items did you find to be scarce or plentiful? Did you live on a farm, in a small town, or in a city? Did you observe or experience any difference in the availability of food in rural and urban areas?

7. Did you experience the "Dust Bowl" that damaged so much of the middle of the country?

8. What sacrifices did you or your parents make during the Depression? Why?

9. Did the family have a car? What make or model? How much did it cost? How much did gasoline cost? Did you or the family limit driving? Did you or the family have to give up the car during the Depression? If you did not have a car, on what kind of transportation did you rely?

10. Did you or the family have money in a bank before or during the Depression? If so, did you lose any of it because of the Depression? Did you or the family lose money in the stock market crash?

11. Did the family make any of its own clothes during the Depression? If so, what?

12. Did you hear Orson Welles's "War of the Worlds" on radio on 30 October 1938? What did you think of it at the time? Did you fall for it? Why or why not? How did other family members react?

13. What was it like to go to silent movies? What was your reaction to your first talkie or your first color movie? Explain.

14. How have your experiences during the Depression affected your attitudes of the present?

15. What further recollections and stories can you share about your experiences during the 1930s?

WORLD WAR II AND THE 1940s

1. Did you or other family members participate in World War II? If so, who,

where, when, in what capacity, and in which service? What stories can you share about these experiences? Did the family lose members in the war? Explain.

2. What did you think of President Franklin Roosevelt at the time? Did you or the family support him at election time, even the third and fourth times? How did you feel about his third and fourth elections? Have you changed your opinion since then? How effective was he as president in the 1940s?

3. At the time, what did you think of President Harry Truman? Winston Churchill? Other political or military figures?

4. How did the war affect your plans or life? Did you have to leave school or change your way of life very much?

5. Who in your family had jobs in war industry? In what job did you or they work? Where? How many hours a day or days a week? How did you or they get to work? Was it easy to find a job or change jobs?

6. How did you feel about rationing? Did you know people who cheated or otherwise did not cooperate? What items were the hardest to get? What items were not so scarce? Did you or the family raise, can, or preserve any of your own food? What sacrifices did you make? What items did you miss most?

7. What were typical prices of rent, gasoline, food items? How difficult was it to find housing? Do you remember what wages anyone in the family earned?

8. Did you travel? For business or pleasure? How did you travel? Was it difficult to get tickets or space on public transportation? Did you have a car? Did you have difficulty getting gasoline, tires, or parts?

9. What part did radio, movies, or sports play in your life during the 1940s? Who were your favorite personalities? What were your favorite movies or programs?

10. What were you doing when you heard about the Pearl Harbor attack? What was your reaction? Do you think we would have entered the war without the Pearl Harbor attack? What was the effect of the news on your community?

11. What did you think at the time when you heard about the dropping of the atomic bomb? In your opinion, how necessary was it? How necessary was the second bomb? Have you changed your opinion since then?

12. What were you doing when you heard about President Roosevelt's death? What was your or your family's reaction?

13. Do you have and can you share any letters, diaries, or mementos from the period?

14. What pleasant or funny family stories can you share from the 1940s?

1950s AND 1960s

1. Where did you live? Did you or your family rent or own your residence? If you owned it, how much did it cost? If you rented, how much was rent? How was this home different from one(s) you lived in before? Was the residence new? Were you part of the new suburbs growing up all over the country?

2. During these decades, many women went to work outside the home. Was this the case in your family? Explain.

3. Which conveniences did you or your family get for the first time in the 1950s: washing machine, clothes dryer, dishwasher, electric or gas cookstove, air-conditioning, other? If not in the 1950s, when?

4. Did your recreational activities change in the 1950s or 1960s from what they had been earlier? (Explain.) Did you go to drive-in movies? How frequently did you eat at restaurants or fast-food establishments? Which were your favorite places to eat?

5. What rules of etiquette or dating prevailed in the family in the 1950s or 1960s?

6. When did your family get a television? What rules or restrictions governed its use? What were your favorite radio or television programs? Did television surpass radio as a major medium of information and entertainment for you during this period? Did you watch President Eisenhower's inaugurations or Queen Elizabeth's coronation on television?

7. Did you have favorite popular music stars? Did you or others in the family buy Elvis Presley records?

8. What fads or fashions did you enjoy in the 1950s and/or 1960s? Were there fads, fashions, or aspects of popular culture you avoided? Did you or someone in the family have a hula hoop (1958 and after)? Did you enjoy dancing? What kind?

9. Were any family members considered hippies or flower children in the 1960s?

10. When and why did you take your first airplane trip (even if before 1950)? What was your reaction to that experience?

11. How was your life affected or changed by the interstate highway construction (1956 and after) and other highway expansion projects? Did you travel more? How was your community affected?

12. Were you or family members in the military during the Korean War (1950–1953)? (Explain.) What was your reaction to the outbreak of the Korean War?

13. Did you watch any of these events on television? What was your reaction or that of your parents?
    - McCarthy hearings (1954)
    - first U.S. manned space flight (May 1961)
    - Cuban missile crisis (October 1962)
    - military buildup in Vietnam (1963 forward)
    - coverage of President Kennedy's death and funeral (November 1963)
    - coverage of Dr. Martin Luther King Jr.'s death or Robert Kennedy's death (1968)
    - Apollo 11 moon landing (20 July 1969)

14. Were you or any family members involved in antiwar, feminist, or civil rights demonstrations during the 1950s or 1960s? Who? Where? (Explain.)

15. Were you or any family members in the military during the war in Viet-

nam? Who? When? Where? Drafted or volunteered? What did you or the family think about that war at the time? Have you changed your opinion since then?

16. What firsts occurred in your life in the 1950s or 1960s?
17. What significant events in your life occurred in the 1950s or 1960s?
18. How would you characterize the 1950s and/or 1960s in the life of the country and in your personal life?
19. Looking back, what differences do you see between life in the 1940s and 1950s? Between life in the 1950s and 1960s? Between life in those two decades and the last part of the twentieth century?

1970s AND AFTER

1. Did you hear (or watch on television) President Nixon's resignation speech in 1974? What was your reaction?
2. Did school segregation or desegregation affect your family (1957 and after, largely 1970s)?
3. How did the family celebrate July 4, 1976, the United States bicentennial?
4. When and why did you or your family first get a computer? For what did you use it?
5. Did you have or when did you first get a tape recorder, boom box, VCR, CD player, mobile phone, pager, video camera, or microwave oven?
6. What memories stand out in your mind from the last quarter of the twentieth century?
7. Did you celebrate the new century and new millennium in 2000 or 2001 or both?
8. How would you characterize your life and that of your family in the last quarter of the twentieth century?
9. What inventions or developments do you feel caused the greatest changes in the family during this period?

THINGS TO DO NOW

1. If your parents and/or grandparents are living, interview one or more with the questions appropriate to their lives.
2. If your parents and/or grandparents are no longer living, answer as many questions as possible about their lives, stating that your answers are from your personal knowledge and memories of them.
3. If you are a parent or grandparent, begin writing answers to the questions that pertain to your life and family. Consider this effort a gift for your children and grandchildren.

Idea Generator

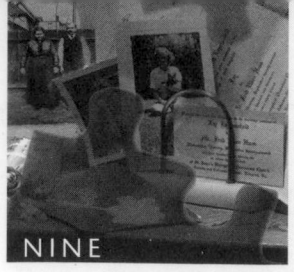

NINE

Family Sources and Beyond

G athering names, vital statistics, and other information from family sources—people and papers—is the logical way to begin one's genealogy search. The results will depend on the people available and the papers the family has saved. These sources vary greatly from family to family, but genealogists should continually seek them out.

The search for and use of family sources never really end, especially as your study broadens to great-grandparent lines and earlier generations. It is also an ideal way to pursue the cluster of an ancestor's relatives, friends, and neighbors. For example, learning the name of a cousin who once visited from Mississippi, the school an ancestor attended, or an organization to which he or she belonged may seem relatively trivial in the overall scheme of the family's history. However, the genealogist who follows up on such clues may not only learn more about the ancestor's life but also discover a genealogical gold mine: birth and death dates, a Bible record long thought lost, maiden names, evidence of children who lived and died between censuses, or names of a previous generation.

Use this chapter to

- identify many kinds of family mementos and records that aid genealogists
- begin determining those available in your family and extended family
- start planning for research beyond family sources

CHECKLIST OF FAMILY SOURCES

Notes

Relatives you already know are the first and most obvious source of family history information. They may be siblings, parents, grandparents, great-grandparents, cousins, aunts and uncles, great-aunts and great-uncles, nieces and nephews and their children, and in-laws. Contact these people, tell them of your project, ask for their help, and share what you are learning. They may contribute information or offer to participate in the search with you. (Chapters four through eight discussed interviews, oral history, and ways to enrich your collective family story.)

Longtime family friends and neighbors can occasionally add as much information about your family as relatives can.

Family Bibles and prayer books containing registers of births, marriages, and deaths may be available in several parts of the family. Check around for more than one. The most reliable of these sources is usually the record made at the time of the event. Look at the publication date of the Bible to determine whether the family entries predate or postdate publication. If the family dates predate the Bible's publication, it is clear that someone wrote these entries after the events themselves. In the course of time, people may remember facts incorrectly.

Family letters, diaries, memoirs, and autobiographical sketches are often excellent records of births, marriages, deaths, migrations, illnesses, education, daily life, church membership, and observations on contemporary events. On 27 August 1852, a letter from one brother to another commented, "Jane Hazlegrove and Mr. Wm Godsey were married last Wednesday week. They had a large wedding. we were all there. had fine dancing." The letter gives not only information from which to date the wedding but also a view of 1852 wedding customs in Virginia.

To his sister, Elliott Coleman wrote the names and weights of his children! His sister had never met his family, and he was describing everyone to her—and to us! He also expressed his opinion that "the plow should never have been brought west of the Colorado [River]." Written in one of the dry years of the 1880s, the letter is evidence of the problems that farmers, including Elliott, had in adjusting to the west Texas and larger Great Plains environment.

Such letters also furnish us with signatures and handwriting samples that may (1) tell us more about the writers themselves, (2) help distinguish handwriting in a family Bible, and (3) help sort out two or more relatives of the same name.

Scrapbooks often contain newspaper clippings, funeral cards, invitations, letters and postcards, speeches and essays, notes on family history, birth announcements, certificates and awards, photographs, graduation announcements and programs, diplomas, recital programs, and other mementos of important events in the person's life and family. They may yield vital statistics, family relationships, full names, information on distant cousins, and "spice" for your family history.

School and college yearbooks and other school publications usually contain photographs of students and faculty and give a good picture of school life, both academic and extracurricular. You may learn Grandpa's senior debate topic or discover that Grandma was elected Most Talented Freshman. If the family does not have copies, the institution's library often does.

Photographs often have identifying labels and clues. They may name relatives unknown to you. Pictures may also show the photographer's address, which could be a clue to the residence of the family in the pictures. People who moved away, whether across country or across the ocean, sometimes exchanged photos with family members who remained at home. These pictures could help you identify the place from which an immigrant came or the place to which part of

Notes

Based on the date of the letter, written on a Friday, "last Wednesday week" would have been August 18.

the family immigrated. Clothing and hairstyles, automobiles, buildings, or signs in the photos could help date them.

For more information on dating photographs, see

- *American Miniature Case Art.* Floyd Rinhart and Marion Rinhart. New York: A.S. Barnes & Co., 1969.
- *Uncovering Your Ancestry Through Family Photographs.* Maureen Taylor. Cincinnati: Betterway Books, 2000.
- *Who Wore What?: Women's Wear 1861–1865.* Juanita Leisch. Gettysburg, Pa.: Thomas Publications, 1995.

Family papers include a wide variety of items: deeds, land grants, military service discharge papers, wills, birth and death certificates, marriage licenses, oil and mineral leases, voter registration cards, records of naturalization or a family business, household accounts, school report cards and transcripts, old driver's licenses, membership cards from organizations, inventories made for insurance purposes, insurance papers, copies of income tax returns, and other documents. These papers may yield names, vital statistics, signatures of ancestors, or interesting biographical and socioeconomic data on the family. **See also chapter fourteen, especially the information on the *National Union Catalog of Manuscript Collections*, page 173.**

Living relatives whom you do not know when you begin your search can be valuable sources. Especially if you are an only child or only grandchild or the older generation in your family, you need to seek out second and third cousins and their families.

The following ideas may help you locate cousins and other relatives:

1. Relatives and longtime family friends may know current or past residences of extended family members. Use this information as clues in looking for them.

2. Family papers and letters may contain addresses, or at least town names, that may help locate any of the family still in that area.

3. Telephone directories, from your area or that of your ancestors, may give you names of people who have the same surname as the one you are researching. Contacting these may or may not lead you to relatives but may introduce you to helpful people.

4. Family association newsletters may help locate distant cousins. Family associations come and go, as do their newsletters. However, to learn of associations and publications for your surnames, you can consult

    a. each May-June issue of *Everton's Genealogical Helper* magazine,

    b. Elizabeth P. Bentley's *Directory of Family Associations*,

    c. the category index of Cyndi's List, <http://www.cyndislist.com>, under "Surnames, Family Associations & Family Newsletters,"

    d. *Ulrich's International Periodicals Directory* (New Providence, N.J.: R.R. Bowker, annual), in the alphabetical volume containing *G*, under "Genealogy and Heraldry," for local and family association publications.

5. Sometimes distant cousins can be found through surname and county Web sites. At this writing, several large Web sites allow you to post messages in an effort to find distant relatives:

See Also

See Also

Second cousins share a common great-grandparent; third cousins have a common great-great-grandparent. See the relationship chart on page 239.

http://www.genforum.com
http://www.surnameweb.com
http://www.usgenweb.org
http://www.rootsweb.com (click on "RootsWeb Surname List/RSL")

6. Contact the public library or genealogical society in the ancestor's community to learn whether they have vertical files on area families or, if the community is small, know of someone by your surname currently living there.

7. If the newspaper in the ancestral community has a genealogy column that accepts queries, send to the column a query with your name, address, and a brief statement: "I am seeking descendants of John and Mary (Rowe) Doe, who lived in Newtown between 1870 and 1900. Are descendants still in the area?" If they do not have a genealogy column and the community is relatively small, perhaps a newspaper ad will get your query into the community.

8. Some nationally circulated genealogy magazines, such as *Everton's Genealogical Helper*, accept queries. In a query, you can request information on an ancestor or contact with his or her descendants.

9. Genealogical societies often publish their membership roster with surnames that each member is searching. Joining a society in your ancestral county could get you a roster free or for a small fee.

10. Genealogical or historical society periodicals often contain queries about families from their area; members can often submit free queries. **Membership in a society in your research area is often money well spent.** To find out whether your ancestral county or area has such a society,

Money Saver

   a. inquire at the public library, via telephone or e-mail, for the name of a society and a contact person,
   b. browse through current periodicals at a large genealogy library to learn which titles come from your ancestral state,
   c. consult the genealogy section of *Ulrich's International Periodicals Directory*,
   d. look at a July-August issue (each year) of *Everton's Genealogical Helper*, which contains a directory of such societies, although the list may or may not include a current one for your research area,
   e. visit the Web site of the Federation of Genealogical Societies (FGS) at <http://www.fgs.org>,
   f. leave a query on a county Web site at <http://www.usgenweb.org>.

11. Old photographs sometimes identify the town where the photograph was made, and this may be the town where the family lived. By using such a photograph and writing to a local historian in the town, a distant cousin found me. Knowing that I was working on the family in question, the historian sent me the cousin's letter, and we corresponded until her death more than twenty years later.

12. Perhaps it was pure luck, but I once had success by sending a note with an SASE to the local postmaster of a small ancestral community asking if descendants of a particular family still lived in the area. I got a reply with the name and address of a second cousin who had moved from the community. She responded to my letter, and we corresponded for years.

13. If you visit a small ancestral community, ask around. You can sometimes

find out where descendants of the family went when they left town or whether some are still there.

14. Hereditary society membership rosters may help. If you have an ancestor who could qualify you for membership in such an organization, you may be able to obtain membership records of other relatives who have qualified by being descendants of the same ancestor. With current membership rosters or the help of the chapter from which the relative joined the society, you may be able to get in touch with these distant cousins. To know whether anyone from your ancestor's family has joined, check the society's ancestor or patriot index. These are two examples:

    a. *DAR Patriot Index*. Washington, D.C.: National Society, Daughters of the American Revolution, 1966–1974. 3 vols. Supplement, 1982.

    b. *1812 Ancestor Index*. Eleanor Stevens Galvin, comp. of vol. 1. Washington, D.C.: National Society, United States Daughters of 1812, 1970. Patricia Scruggs Trolinger, comp. of vol. 2. Marcelline, Mo.: Walsworth Publishing Co., 1992.

15. The *Hereditary Register of the United States of America*, published by Hereditary Register Publications of Phoenix, Arizona, gives addresses for the many hereditary societies, a list of family associations and their publications, and genealogical societies.

16. Published family or county histories that pertain to your families may contain the address of the author, editor, or publisher. Publishers will often forward a letter from you to the author or editor. Most county histories do not have space to include documentation, but they usually give the name of the submitter. Contact the editors to try to locate the submitter of your family's entry. Because these histories vary greatly in quality and reliability, use them with great caution, just as you would information from the Internet.

Caution: The widely advertised world books and family registries of one surname that solicit your money through the mail are not genealogies, usually do not include any of your specific family history, and usually are a waste of money, unless you want lists from telephone directories of people who bear your surname. **Remember that having the same name does not make two people related, and your relatives are not limited to those with the same surname.**

17. Finding people working on the same surname in the same research area can prove beneficial. Contact the public library genealogy department or the local genealogical society to learn whether they maintain such a list. Consult the *American Library Directory* in your local public or university library to identify libraries with genealogy collections and departments in your research area or your own vicinity.

Warning

Reminder

"SPICE" FROM FAMILY SOURCES

Your family history puzzle takes on depth and character in proportion to the amount of "spice" you add as you search. This spice comes in many forms.

Some families are fortunate enough to inherit antique furniture as part of their heritage. Others receive smaller personal belongings, such as books, crocheted work, teaspoons, and jewelry. Each of these items takes on new meaning as you learn of its past and its former owners. If these items belong to other family members, ask to photograph those you wish to include in your history.

One enjoyable project, full of family spice, was a booklet of recipes and food-related stories from five generations, prepared for the sixth generation. The stories came from letters, memories, and notes on recipe cards. What did grandparents or great-grandparents as children do for lunch during the school year? Why were Grandma's sugar cookies so special? What food traditions did each generation observe at holiday time? A large drop-line chart identified the relatives and spouses whose recipes or stories were included. It answered relationship and name questions: Who was Mamaw? Grammy? Ma?

A delightful story in the booklet came from a letter my grandmother wrote in 1969, reporting on my cousin's birthday party, held the day before her July 4 birthday.

> Yes, they had the [July 4] Carnival on the Court House lawn again this year . . . . Mary K had Ann's birthday party the night before and took 15 little girls swimming and Billy cooked hamburgers for them in the back yard. Can you believe it, but 2 of the little girls ate 4 hamburgers apiece and one came back and asked for another and I wouldn't give it to her. I've never seen such pigs. Then they all wanted seconds on the cake and Mary K told them that she didn't have seconds and one said, "I saw another cake there in the kitchen," but Mary K told her that it wasn't for her.

Photographs and Sketches

Photography offers a wide range of extras, from furniture and quilts to houses, from tombstones to living relatives. Photos can be waiting for you as unidentified faces in albums, tintypes in an old trunk, or water-stained sketches hidden behind later pictures in a frame. With the help and permission of older family members or owners of the pictures, label the photographs and have copies made. They make nice gifts and preserve an important part of family history.

When photographs are not available, you can create your own pictures by sketching such things as houses or household items. Descriptions of houses, inside or outside, can come from those who lived in them or visited them. With their careful observations and memories and your careful notations, together you can provide sketches or floor plans for future generations. An example is the floor plan of an ancestral house near Whiteville, Tennessee, which housed four generations of one family. The house no longer stands, but the sketch in Figure 9.1, page 82, provides one view of the ancestral home.

Mapping Ancestral Migrations

Another interesting addition to your history is a map showing the movement of your family. A dot can be used to show each place the family lived. Highway maps or atlases can help you find localities within each state, province, or

Notes

Words in brackets in quoted material indicate that the compiler or author added these to the original for clarification or explanation.

Floor Plan of the Blalock Home, Whiteville, Tennessee, 1839–1946

Figure 9.1 Ancestral floor plan

county. If you know when the family arrived at each location, write the year of arrival beside the dot.

After placing the dots on the map, connect them with a line. If you trace more than one family per map, use colored, dotted, or dashed lines to distinguish them clearly. In a legend or key, explain your marks and identify each date with the name of the city or county.

The example in Figure 9.2 is of the Croom and Coleman families who were united by marriage in 1900. As was the case with many families whose descendants later married each other, these two families lived in the same county in the eighteenth century, went separate ways, and ended up in the same county a century later.

Tip

Some genealogy software can generate similar maps.

Gaylord Stickle Company, Houston Texas

Croom family – – – – – –		Coleman family –·–·–·–·–
1719 Henrico Co, VA	1903 Fannin Co, TX	1741 Goochland-Cumberland Co, VA
1727 Goochland Co, VA	1905 Red River Co, TX	1845 Fayette Co, TN
1754 Johnston-Dobbs-Wayne Co, NC	1906 Mills Co, TX	1850 Hardeman Co, TN
1826 Madison Co, TN	1912 Angelina Co, TX	1872 Gonzales Co, TX
1895 Hardeman Co, TN	1926 Houston, TX	1881 Hays Co, TX
		1888 Mills Co, TX

Figure 9.2 Migrations of Croom and Coleman families united by marriage in 1900.

Handwriting and Signatures

More difficult to find but equally interesting are handwriting samples and signatures of your ancestors. Handwriting may be identified on many original documents, recipes, family Bibles, school report cards, driver's licenses, and other family or business papers. Clergymen and justices of the peace made it easier for descendants to find their signatures by signing and returning to the county courthouse the marriage licenses of couples whose wedding ceremonies they performed. If your ancestor was a census taker or court clerk, you may have many examples available.

Be aware, however, that the documents copied into the county record books—deeds, estate papers, marriage records—normally do not show the original signatures of the parties involved or the witnesses. The actual signatures were on the original documents; the record book contains copies in the clerk's handwriting. However, some court minute books have the signatures of the jury foremen, affirming the verdicts. In the case of a census taker, you may not be able to tell whether the microfilmed copy was written in his hand unless you look at the original record. Many originals exist in state archives or historical societies.

Handwriting samples often come from letters and diaries, as in the letter excerpts in Figure 9.3, page 85. These examples were written in 1855 and 1854, respectively.

Letters and Diaries

Hidden Treasures

Letters and diaries give you handwriting samples but also tell you about the people who wrote them and become a window on life in the period. Especially before 1900, even people with education often wrote with little punctuation and spelled erratically. As we sometimes do, they could think faster than they wrote, as shown by the omission of words or words they added as they proofread.

Nineteenth-century letters can say less in more words than we can imagine. Many seem to follow a standard recipe for letter writing: mention receipt of letters, apologize for delays in answering, inquire into the health of all members of the family, offer wishes for good health, and send love and greetings to everyone in the family. If they were not out of space by the end of the page, they shared a little of the "nuse" of the neighborhood: weddings, births, parties, courtships, and always illnesses and deaths.

If you are fortunate enough to read ancestral letters or diaries, try to find the persons behind the words. Ask yourself, Does the writer

- express opinions and values?
- share hopes, dreams, fears, disappointments, joy, or sorrows?
- disclose religious or political beliefs?
- gossip?
- give advice?
- mention enjoyment and pleasures, chores or duties?
- reveal personal habits or personality traits?

Catharin M. (Patton) and Elliot G. Coleman

*This leaves all well — hopeing
this may find and all the
family in the enjoyment of
the same blessing. I must close
write soon —*

*Your Affectionate
Son —
E. G. Coleman*

*Sister write soon we feel so lonely and distresed tell
Sister Mary that I just received a letter from her. and
will answer it soon give my love to all of the saints
and except a portion your self   no more.
   but remains ever the same
         your affectionate Sister untill death
            Catharin M. Coleman
               Adieu Sister Adieu*

Figure 9.3 Photos and handwriting samples.

Letters and diaries often reveal family information as well as customs and speech of the region or era. Look at each sentence for what it may reveal about the family, courtship and weddings, parties, childbirth, health and illness, death and funerals, work and play, weather, economic circumstances, travel and communication, and contemporary events.

This excerpt is from a letter that Elliott Coleman of Somerville, Tennessee, wrote on 2 February 1848 to his brother Archer Coleman in Buckingham County, Virginia. The letter is typical of the style and content of the period. Spelling and punctuation are original. Notice the evidence of two specific genealogical events: the recent death of their mother and the impending marriage of Aunt Susan (see also the 1849 excerpt on page 87). If no public records document such events, letters may furnish the only evidence of their occurrence. In what other ways does the letter give insight into Elliott's life and world?

Dear Brother,

Yours of date 15 of Jan reached us on the 31rst, you seem to be repenting that you had not writen to me before asking me to forgive you I will if you will not do so again I havent much nuse to communicate, but will answer all the letters I get as soon as I possibly can and ask the same of all my correspondents You stated in your letter you were at Fathers a few days before you wrote and they were all well, except Sister Lucy I am sorry to hear her health is bad. I am afraid she grieves too much after our dear and affectionate mother. I hope she is better off, as it is useless to grieve after her but endeavour to follow her—You wrote Aunt Susan was to be married to Wm Miller sometime during this month. If she has her choice I haven't a word to say but wish her all the happiness this world can afford You spoke of coming to this country I came in the summer I don't think it prudent for a person to leave their friends unless they can better themselves. If you will let me know what you are doing or in other words what wages you are getting and I can tell whether you can do better here than you can in Va Cotton is selling for a very low price from 5½ to 6 very little selling at present All that can are holding on until spring thinking it will be higher[.] . . . I delivered your message to Catherine she requested me to send her love to you in return for yours says you must write to her and she will answer. This leaves us well present my best love to all enquiring friends and relations and accept the same yourself. I must conclude as I haven't anything more to write adiue dear brother

I remain your devoted brother

E G Coleman

Following are excerpts from other nineteenth-century letters, illustrating the insight, history, and genealogy we gather from these special sources. Although these entries are from letters, diaries often contain similar items. (Spelling and punctuation are original.)

- "we had a tremendous fresh last Friday week it raind one hour as fast as I ever saw it rain . . . Elliott and Edward went to the creek the moon shown very bright they could not see a stalk of corn nor a plant of tobacco the best tobacco your Father had was washd away . . . Elliott is fixing to go to Tennessee he will start in about a month." (1845, Elliott's mother to a son)

- "Charles Parker has done a great a great [*sic*] deal better than any that knew him would have supposed. I dont think from what I can learn he has idled a day this year, he will make more than corn enough to supply him next year, and from eight to ten bales of cotton which will bring him fifty dollars per bale . . . so you may say he is doing well his wife helps him to pick his cotton you know she was above that in Va . . . Thare is a great contrast, in Mrs H and Parker Mrs P turns her hand to anything that comes while Mrs H does nothing but visit after making Wm clothes." (1846, gossip from Elliott to his mother)

- "Susan has the histericks very often . . . she is like all other ladies when near their giving birth to the first, swear they are going to die, so Lucy, when you get married dont you do so—but behave pretty; and stand it like a man, . . . all is right so far, and she has two mighty good fingerSmith's close by; . . . Dr. Jamerson lives in 1½ miles." (1849, Aunt Susan's husband to Elliott's sister)

Notes

Context suggests he used "fingerSmith's" to mean "midwives."

- "you have heard I recon that Sister Mary had broken up [housekeeping] and gone to Papa's to live. She had her sale the day before I got home and move to Fathers. She sold every thing except beds and chairs all her corn cows and horses except Dolly." (1852, brother to brother, after Mary's husband died)

- "Gallatin Woodson is courting Mary Calvin like thunder bucking up to her like a sick kitten to a hot brick . . . " (1853, brother to brother)

- "a few words about Ferdinand or—as he had to have your name in full all call him Nardy—he is a very fine looking boy can set alone—is very healthy" (1855, Elliott to his father about the baby, helps date the child's birth and confirm his and his grandfather's name)

- "I am not writing to you this evening because I have nothing else to do but because it is a pleasure to me to converse with you even in this way. . . . most young men think the girls like to be <u>flattered</u> but I had rather they would always be honest <u>with</u> me and not use too much flattery." (1875, young lady to her beau; underlining is hers; next excerpt is the same couple nineteen years later)

- "we have music about every night. John and son Robert plays on the violin and so does another man whom he has for wages and the cook is a widow and she plays the accordian. . . . I am going to try to quit using tobacco—but I can't tell the results yet I may quit or I may not. Mama I have not seen a woman dip any snuff since I have been here but there is a lot of it dipped in the neighborhood." (1894, husband in Texas to his wife in Mississippi)

- "My dear precious Maggie and her two little girls—What can I write you in this your hour of sore bereavement—I <u>know</u> my dear child it is the greatest trouble that can befall a wife and you know it too. . . . I was afraid to open the telegram but did so, and it told us of your dear precious Mr Mac's death on Monday eve 22 January—on Kittie's birthday and <u>now</u> they are together in Glory. My poor dear child, <u>how</u> I wish I could be with you . . . Kiss my darling little babies for me—dear children they don't know what a loss they have met." (1894, a widowed mother to her daughter whose young husband had just died; underlining is hers)

Numerous extras can add human interest and spice to your family history. Much depends on how much depth you want your history to show and how much effort and time you want to give to it. The results are always enlightening. These efforts, when shared within the family, help strengthen family ties, broaden understanding, and increase appreciation for your common heritage.

CHOOSING A RESEARCH FOCUS AND MAKING A PLAN

After gathering basic information from family sources and filling in your charts at least back to the early twentieth century, evaluate your information to see which pieces of the puzzle are missing. Decide which missing information you want to look for first. For example, you may want to

- complete the vital statistics for a particular ancestor
- identify a maiden name and parents for a great-grandmother
- find the birthplace of a great-grandfather
- learn all you can about a great-grandparent for whom you have only a name

Planning for Research

A journey into genealogy logically begins with available family sources. The next step is research in public records. Your choice of what to try first may depend on (1) information you glean within the family, (2) availability of research materials in your location, and (3) your ancestor's individual situation.

Research Tip

Whatever focus question or ancestor you choose, write down your research goals. A broad goal might be one of the bulleted items above. **In order to accomplish these goals, you often need to divide them into smaller research questions and gradually build the answer you seek.**

For example, you decide first to study a certain great-grandmother, your goal being to identify her parents. The research process involves these steps:

1. Make a chronological list of what you know about the ancestor and any known siblings, spouse(s), and children. Include dates and places for the events you identify and at least a brief citation of the source that gave you the information. Remember, if you identify the names of her brothers, you have her maiden name.

2. Study this information for the clues in it, such as an estimate of age on a given date (to estimate a birth date if you don't have one) or a place of death or burial (to look for a death record and tombstone). In this way, you are using the known to plan ways of finding the unknown. From this point on, you will use family sources and public sources together, for genealogists never really finish with either kind.

3. From the clues, decide where to look for information that may give you her maiden name or parents' names: marriage record, death record, tombstone, obituary for her and her husband, vital records for her children, and similar records of any known siblings. (See chapter fourteen.)

4. As you find (or don't find) these outlined records, evaluate what you have learned to plan the next steps, one at a time.

Depending on where you live, which research facilities are near you, and where your focus ancestor lived, you have several choices:

1. You can begin with the locality where your focus ancestor lived or died and research cemeteries, vital records, and newspapers. (See chapter twelve.) If you can't go to the locality in person, you can often access these sources by mail, on microfilm, or through interlibrary loan.

2. If you live near a research facility—a genealogy library, state archives or historical society, or National Archives regional branch—you may want to begin as many genealogists do—consulting the federal census records. (See chapter ten.) Appendix B is a list of National Archives regional branches. The *American Library Directory* in most public or college libraries can help you find a library in your area with a genealogy collection. Ask local genealogists where they go to research, or visit a Family History Center.

Jurisdictions

Whatever your next step, an almost endless supply of public sources awaits you. Family sources often give genealogists much of the information they seek, especially for the most recent generations. However, ancestors interacted with governmental bodies at four levels: local, county, state, and federal. All four of these jurisdictions maintain collections of old records, and any of them could have information on your ancestor. The next four chapters discuss records that genealogists typically use in these jurisdictions.

Local sources (chapter twelve) may include cemeteries, church records, newspapers, businesses, city tax records, and school records. In some places, county and city records overlap, or the city handles the kinds of records—land, marriage, birth and death—that the county handles in other areas. In most states, the county usually maintains marriage records, birth and death registrations, wills and probate files, deeds and other land records, voter registrations, and tax and court records (chapter eleven).

At the state level, especially in the state archives, researchers often find the earliest county and city records and records of citizens interacting with the state government departments: state land grants, tax records, legislative petitions, prison or mental hospital records, state censuses, and records from the Colonial and Confederate governments (chapter eleven).

Useful federal sources include the census, military service and pension records, immigration and naturalization papers, congressional documents, and public land records (chapters ten and thirteen). Libraries and archives of all kinds (private, city, county, state, university, and federal) often have research collections of great value for genealogists. Go for it, and have fun!

THINGS TO DO NOW

Idea Generator

1. Identify records, letters, scrapbooks, photograph albums, and other family papers that you, your parents, grandparents, or siblings have. Arrange to look at as many of these as possible.

2. Get photocopies of documents and mementos that have genealogical or

family history clues in them.

3. Label your photographs and any of your possessions from previous generations.

4. With other relatives, try to make a list of first, second, and third cousins.

5. Identify a genealogical society in your own area and in at least one ancestral county. Consider joining both.

6. Gather some spice, such as house pictures or floor plans, signatures, or recipes from earlier generations.

7. Choose a focus ancestor (or ancestral couple) and write down your research goal. Make a chronological list of what you know about the ancestor(s), and list your documentation for each item. Write questions that you think you will need to answer in order to work toward your goal. Revise or add to this as you read the remaining chapters.

TEN

Beyond the Family: Federal Census Records

Genealogists follow no particular pattern in deciding which records to research first, second, third, and so forth. Because each ancestor was different, each research case is unique. However, federal census records are often a good place to begin your use of public records. They are perhaps the most valuable of the federal records for the greatest number of genealogists. When many of us learn the names of "new" ancestors, we try to find them in census records as soon as possible, as if this makes them real people.

If you choose to begin with these censuses, you may amass enough information to go next to county records (chapter eleven) or local records (chapter twelve). The order depends on your access to records, the information you find early in your research, and your inclination of what to do next to get the best results.

The U.S. census is a list of families and individuals living in each state and territory. The government has thus counted the population every ten years since 1790 in order to apportion representation in the House of Representatives in Congress. Over the years, the government has asked more and more questions to learn demographic and economic information about the populace. Some of this data is particularly helpful to genealogists—especially ages, relationships, birthplaces, and birthplaces of parents.

UNDERSTANDING THE CENSUS

In order to use the census effectively, you need to understand certain things:

1. The records are closed as confidential information for seventy-two years before the public can use them for research.

2. Censuses are available to researchers on microfilm and as digital images on CD-ROM. At this writing, plans are in the works to make these images available on subscription sites such as <http://www.ancestry.com> and <http://

Internet Source

See a telephone directory or <http://www.familyse arch.org> (select "Family History Library System," then "Family History Centers") to locate Family History Centers. The list on the Web site may be incomplete for your area.

www.genealogydatabase.com>. Some digital images, abstracts, and transcriptions are online free of charge at <http://www.usgenweb.org> and various county genealogy Web pages. Abstracts and transcriptions for individual counties are also available in books, but it is better to use the microfilm or digital image of the original whenever possible. Many censuses are indexed.

3. The microfilm is available in many research and university libraries, and some libraries are acquiring the CD-ROMs. You can rent the microfilm from such places as the Family History Library in Salt Lake City (through its branch Family History Centers worldwide), and the National Archives Microfilm Rental Program. (See page 143, chapter twelve, for more information on these rental opportunities.)

The Family History Library is an institution of the Church of Jesus Christ of Latter-day Saints (LDS) in Salt Lake City, Utah. Members and nonmembers may use the main library and the hundreds of Family History Centers.

4. A catalog of National Archives census microfilm is available at research libraries, from many genealogy booksellers, from the National Archives, and online at <http://www.archives.gov/publications/genealogy_microfilm_cata logs.html#census>. The catalog is a state-by-state list of the counties and their microfilm roll numbers; the roll numbers apply to the CD-ROMs as well.

5. The microfilm and CD-ROMs are organized by state, then by county, then by communities, townships, precincts, wards, districts, or other subdivisions. Each roll or disc may contain several counties. In some cases, a large county or city may be split and appear on two or more rolls or discs. A list of the contents is often on the outside of the microfilm box and on the first frames of film. Seeing this list will help you know how far to scroll to find your county of interest. For the censuses of 1850 and after, the county name usually appears at the top of each page, and divider cards sometimes mark the beginning of each county on the film.

6. Some people are missing from each census for many reasons—inaccessibility of the residence, family not at home, bad weather, refusal to open the door, family in transit, the census taker not being aware of a house deep in the woods, language barriers, or a page being lost or skipped in the copying or filming process.

7. Some people are on the census but listed under a different name for some unknown reason. Some are listed twice.

8. Some census records no longer exist. They may be missing for a neighborhood, a county, or an entire state.

9. The information on ancestors varies from census to census. See the discussion below.

Census Day

Notes

Congress designated one day in each census year as census day. The enumeration began that day, and its report was to be correct as of that day. **Each household was to include all persons residing within the household on that day, regardless of when the census taker actually visited.** Persons who died after

CENSUS DAY 1790–1940	
1790, 1800, 1810	First Monday in August
1820	August 7 (first Monday)
1830, 1840, 1850, 1860, 1870, 1880, 1890, 1900	June 1
1910	April 15
1920	January 1
1930, 1940	April 1

census day but before the census taker came were to be listed because they were still alive on census day. Babies born after census day were to be omitted.

What Can the Census Give Me?

The censuses varied from decade to decade. The following is a sketch of what these records contain. Appendix C, pages 243–244, is a capsuled version of questions the censuses asked, and the extraction forms in Appendix D, pages 246–269, are full copies made from the original forms.

From 1790 through 1840, censuses named only the head of each household, and others in the household, slave and free, were grouped by age and sex. Beginning in 1850, census schedules named each individual in free households, with age, sex, race, occupation, birthplace (state or country), ability to read or write, schooling during the year, and infirmities such as blindness or deafness. Beginning in 1880, the censuses asked about relationships and for the birthplace of each person's parents. This information helps in the search for the preceding generation.

Finding someone's age in the census, of course, helps you estimate a birth date (see page 104). Comparing birthplaces within the family helps you study migrations and migration patterns and suggests where to look for further information.

Normally, the census listed first the head of household and spouse, then the rest of the nuclear family in descending age order, then others residing in the household, including stepchildren, in-laws, foster children, servants, employees who lived with the family, and boarders.

The slave census schedules of 1850 and 1860 are separate from the general population schedules. Many research libraries have them or you can rent them from the first two rental facilities listed in number 3 on page 92. The records contain the slave owner's name and the age and sex of each slave. The slaves were listed by number rather than by name in almost all cases.

Fire destroyed almost all of the 1890 census. Some fragments exist for Alabama, Georgia, Illinois, Minnesota, New Jersey, New York, North Carolina,

Tip

Although most of the 1890 census burned, check the microfilm index if your ancestors lived in Perry County, Alabama; Washington, DC; or McDonough County, Illinois.

For More Info

See *The Genealogist's Companion & Sourcebook,* chapter two, for a more comprehensive list of existing 1890 census fragments, census finding aids, and other aspects of researching census records.

Ohio, South Dakota, Texas, and the District of Columbia. An index is on microfilm. Fortunately for some researchers, censuses taken between 1880 and 1900 help bridge the gap created by the missing 1890 census and are available on microfilm:

- The first territorial census for Oklahoma, taken in 1890.
- Between 1880 and 1900, censuses taken by some states.
- 1885 federal censuses for Colorado, Florida, Nebraska, New Mexico Territory, and Dakota Territory.
- Part of the 1890 special census of Union Army veterans and widows—mostly for states alphabetically from Louisiana through Wyoming, Oklahoma and Indian Territory, and for naval stations and vessels. Fragments remain for California, Connecticut, Delaware, Florida, Idaho, Illinois, Indiana, Kansas, Kentucky, New York, and the District of Columbia.

A project at <http://www.ancestry.com/search/rectype/census/1890sub/main.htm> is building an 1890 database from many sources, especially city directories, to help make up for the loss of this crucial census. Substitutes cannot replace all the lost individual information but help locate people alive in a given place at a given time.

Several federal censuses asked for information pertinent to genealogy:

- From 1880 forward, the census asked for each person's relationship to the head of household—wife, son, daughter, brother-in-law, mother, etc. Extra people in households, in addition to the nuclear family, were often relatives, but the census does not always report them as such. Instead, they were sometimes listed as "boarder," "orphan," or "no relation."
- The 1900 census was the only one to include each person's month and year of birth. However, many of these birth dates are approximate; some are off by several years. Use them with caution.
- The 1900 and 1910 censuses asked for the number of children born to the mother, the number of her children still living, and how long each couple had been married. This information can help genealogists fill out family group sheets and estimate marriage dates.

READING CENSUS RECORDS EFFECTIVELY

Technique

To use the census,

1. Determine the state where your focus family lived in each census year, beginning with the most recently released and working backward in time.
2. Expect your family's name to be spelled in various ways, as discussed in chapter four.
3. Use indexes to help you place your family in a county or city; then read the census record itself on microfilm or CD-ROM. Published indexes are available by state in many research libraries for censuses of 1790 through 1870 and some for 1880. Some indexes appear in periodicals and on CD-ROM. A special index for the 1880 and later censuses is discussed below under "Soundex."

4. Record the following information for your documentation:
   - the year of the census
   - the roll number
   - the state and county
   - the page number of the family's listing, usually a stamped number in censuses 1790–1870
   - the enumeration district number and sheet number in censuses of 1880 and after
   - the name of the head of household
   - the family and dwelling numbers, given beside the head of household
   - the CD-ROM publication information and number, if you use the CD-ROM version
5. Record in your notes or on your census form
   - the beginning line number(s) of the family or person you are researching, especially if the film is difficult to read or several people by the same name existed
   - the date the census taker visited the family, if different from the official census day
   - the local community or subdivision where the family was enumerated
   - each member of the household, even those with different surnames
   - any and all information given about each member of the household
   - all names exactly as they appear in the record, even if misspelled
6. Add to your notes the Latin word *sic* (meaning "thus") in brackets beside misinformation or misspellings from the census to indicate that you copied exactly what was in the original. These problems usually occur in the columns for names, ages, and birthplaces, but they can occur in any column.

To use the census effectively in research, you need to
1. Look in indexes for your focus ancestor and other people by the same surname in the same county or in surrounding counties, especially if the surname is not a common one. However, people with the same surname in the same county may or may not be related.
2. Look in the indexes for variant spellings of your research surnames.
3. Read every available census for your focus ancestor and family. If you skip a census, you may miss valuable information. Usually, begin with the most recent census available for your focus ancestor and read backward in time one census at a time.
4. Understand that county boundaries sometimes changed between censuses. A family listed in two censuses in two different counties may not have moved; the county boundary may have been changed. Historical atlases of counties or states can help you determine boundary changes. Several reference books contain information on the creation of new counties and county boundary changes.
   - *Ancestry's Red Book: American State, County & Town Sources*. Alice Eichholz, ed. Shows county creation dates and parent counties, state by state.

- *The Handy Book for Genealogists*. George B. Everton Sr., ed. Shows county creation dates and parent counties, state by state.
- *Map Guide to the U.S. Federal Censuses, 1790–1920*. William Thorndale and William Dollarhide. Shows map of each state at the time of each census.
- *Atlas of Historical County Boundaries*. Available for many states from the Gale Group in Farmington Hills, Mich.

5. Know that the ages of young children were usually expressed in the number of months or days of age: "$5/12$" for five months or "$21/30$" for twenty-one days. Occasionally, older children's ages were also given this way—"$10^{3}/12$" for ten years, three months. (See Figure 10.1, page 101.)

6. Expect reported ages and name spellings to vary from one census to the next. It was not unusual for one person to be listed over five censuses as age 5, 14, 26, 35, and 47. A person could be listed as Susie, Susan, Susanna, S.E., or Sue in five censuses as well.

7. Understand that we cannot know who gave the information to the census taker in any given year. It could have been a child, one of the parents, a visiting grandmother, or even a boarder or neighbor.

8. Read several pages of the census on each side of your family to look for other families of the same surname or other families whose names you recognize as relatives.

9. Be aware that some census takers gave information in addition to what the forms asked for. Be alert for a census that may give you marriage dates for couples, middle names for everyone in the household, notes about orphans or heirs of a deceased head of household, relationships even when none were called for, or counties of birth instead of just state names.

10. Record information about home or farm ownership or the value of real estate. With this clue, plan to search land records for additional information.

11. Record information about schooling or the ability to read and write. Although some people could sign their names without being able to read and write, a signature or a mark sometimes helps the genealogist distinguish between two people with the same name.

12. Record information about birthplace of parents in censuses of 1880 forward.

13. Record information about immigration, naturalization, or citizenship. This data could help you research immigrant ancestors.

14. Note when any key information is missing: birthplace, occupation, relationship, value of real estate, etc.

15. Accept the alternative process: If you do not have access to an index or the family does not appear in an index, you need to read the entire county family by family. The process is sometimes long but can be rewarding and entertaining. Families in the census were sometimes missed in the indexing process or were indexed under a variation you would never imagine, such as the name Allen indexed as Allne.

16. Take some time to read an entire county or district, especially if a number of your related families lived there. You could find relatives unexpectedly.

17. Entertain yourself by reading the entire county to get acquainted with surnames, occupations, and other demographic information. Get a feel for the county: where most of the residents were born, from which foreign countries residents came, which given names were most popular, and which occupations were prevalent. Learn who was in jail, who the ministers and teachers were, what unusual occupations some people had, and who had really interesting names. Four of my favorite names from census records are Green Bird, Bright Bird, Preserved Fish, and Venus Staggers.

Most Common Surnames From the 1790 and 1990 Censuses

Figures available from the 1790 and 1990 censuses show an amazing similarity in the lists of the most common surnames. In the chart below, the 1790 list shows the number of people estimated to have that name. These figures in the government report do not include Delaware, Georgia, or New Jersey, whose 1790 censuses were lost.

1790 rankings*	1990 rankings*
1. Smith, 33,245 people	1. Smith
2. Brown, 19,185	2. Johnson
3. Johnson, 15,004	3. Williams
4. Jones, 14,300 and Davis, 14,300	4. Jones
	5. Brown
6. Clark, 13,766	6. Davis
7. Williams, 12,717	7. Miller
8. Miller, 12,694	8. Wilson
9. Wilson, 9,797	9. Moore
10. Moore, 9,701	10. Taylor
11. White, 9,523	14. White
12. Thompson, 9,390	17. Thompson
	18. Garcia
	19. Martinez
	21. Clark

*1790 rankings figured from information in *Surnames Listed in the 1790 United States Census* (reprint from a government document; South Prairie, Wash.: Researchers Bookshelf, Division of Heritage Quest, 1980s). 1990 rankings come from <http://www.census.gov/genealogy/names/dist .all.last> accessed 10 November 1999.

Many genealogists have ancestors by these and other common names. The message is that researching ancestors with common names, even unusual names that are common in a particular area, requires caution. We cannot assume that every mention of Methuselah P. Brown refers to one person. We must collect all the information we can and sort the facts to try to determine how many men by that name were in the area and which facts pertain to each one.

SUPPLEMENTAL SCHEDULES

Supplemental census schedules made between 1850 and 1880 still exist, for the most part. I call these the AIMS schedules: agriculture, industry, mortality, and social statistics.

The agriculture schedules report farmers' answers to questions on acreage, crops, livestock, and products. The manufacturing and industry schedules report on products, raw materials, employees and their wages, means of production, and income. These two schedules do not contain basic genealogical information but reveal interesting history. Sometimes, however, the listings of names can give you additional information, such as a first name where only initials appeared on the population schedule.

The social statistics, likewise, are not genealogical but historical, on such institutions as libraries, schools, churches, and newspapers in each community. They list categories rather than names: "four Methodist churches, two Presbyterian churches, two Primitive Baptist churches." The schedule gives additional information on wages for different classes of workers. Sometimes the census taker added notes about economic conditions in the county, including droughts or storms that had a negative effect on agriculture.

The mortality schedules *are* genealogical in nature. They report the names and ages of persons who died within the calendar year prior to the census, with the month and cause of death. Because these schedules include only persons whose families or doctors reported their deaths to the census takers, omissions occurred. Many of these mortality schedules have been published and microfilmed.

The supplemental schedules are available in a variety of places, predominantly major research libraries and the state library, archives, or historical society. You can rent them on microfilm from Family History Centers. *The Genealogist's Companion & Sourcebook* provides a comprehensive listing of known schedules.

SOUNDEX

The 1880, 1900, and 1920 federal censuses and parts of the 1910 and 1930 censuses are indexed by state using a code based on the sounds in surnames. This indexing system is called Soundex. It is most often available as microfilm of the cards on which basic census information was written. (See Figure 10.1, on page 101.) The Soundex is especially useful when you do not know specifically where the family was living in the census year. It will tell you their county and community and where you can find them on the census.

One drawback of the 1880 Soundex is that it includes only households with children age ten and under. If Great-Grandpa's children were already over age ten by 1880, you will not find him in the Soundex unless he lived with a family that included young children.

Important

| R AY | R000. R = initial letter. Strike A and Y. Add three zeros |
| R   000 | since there are no other letters to code. |

| SCHWENNEKER | S526. S = initial letter. Initial SC is treated the same as |
| S   5 2 6 | a double letter inside the word. Strike vowels, H, and W. Code NN once, and code K and R. |

| ROBERTSON | R163. R = initial letter. Strike vowels. Once you have |
| R 1 63. | a three-digit code, disregard the remaining consonants. |

Some census entries show the surname written incorrectly, spelled with *C* instead of *K*, minus the final syllable, spelled with an added final *e* or *s*, spelled phonetically instead of correctly, or misunderstood for another name entirely. If your research names can have several spellings (and most can), code the usual variations and look for them all in the Soundex or other index. Soundex codes that are almost the same, such as 450 and 452, are often grouped together as "mixed codes." Sometimes prefixes such as *von*, *van*, *de*, *de la*, and *le* are omitted in coding. Be aware that some names and their common variations will have different Soundex codes because of different initial consonants or subtle changes in spelling, as in the chart of examples below.

Examples of Soundex Problems

Names that are similar, with different initial letters:

Carson	C625	Riggins	R252	Ebert	E163
Garson	G625	Wiggins	W252	Hebert	H163

Names that are often confused with each other and have different codes:

Garner	G656	Larson	L625	Saddler	S346
Gardner	G635	Lawson	L250	Sandler	S534
Rich/Richey	R200	Robinson	R152	Carson	C625
Ridge/Ritchie	R320	Robertson	R163	Carlson	C642
Watters	W362	Harrell	H640	Finch	F520
Walter(s)	W436	Harold	H643	French	F652

When you determine the Soundex code that applies to your focus family and any variant spelling that may send you to a different code, you are ready to get the microfilm. You would choose for Gardner, for example, the 1920 Soundex for Kansas for G635 (year, state, code).

When you find the family on the Soundex microfilm, write down these references to find the family in the census itself:

- the county (you already know the state)
- enumeration district
- page (sheet)
- line number that begins the family's listing

You can also start your extraction of the information, as the household members, relationships, and ages are normally given on the Soundex cards. With this done, you can move to the census microfilm. **Reading the Soundex does not take the place of reading the census; the Soundex gives only partial information.**

Examples of Soundex entries for 1880 and 1920 are in Figure 10.1, below. All give names, ages, relationships, and birthplaces. Note that the cards in the figure illustrate these items:

- individuals living in households of a different surname
- children with ages expressed in years and months
- several birthplaces more specific than state or country
- immigration and citizenship information
- different surnames with the same Soundex code

Reminder

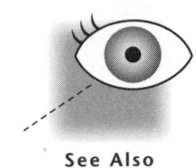

See Also

CHALLENGES OF CENSUS READING

Census reading can be fun and fascinating, yet it poses special challenges and cautions. To get the most from these records, researchers need to know about the potential pitfalls and understand ways of working with them.

See chapter thirteen, page 165, for explanation of the immigration/naturalization references in the Soundex cards and census records.

Figure 10.1 Soundex cards showing age, birthplace, citizenship, and other information.

See Also

See chapter sixteen for more on handwriting.

Handwriting

One challenge is handwriting. Some people write English as if it were Martian. Writers of a century or two ago adhered to a standard style more regularly than contemporary writers do, but they had a few quirks that trip us up if we are not careful. For example, the old style double *s* looked like *fs* or *p*. If the record seems to say that your ancestor "Jepe" was born in "Mip," he probably was Jesse, born in Mississippi, abbreviated "Miss."

One researcher puzzled over the occupation of her ancestor. The census seemed to say the young man's occupation was "apisling on farm." Knowing the "apis" stem referred to bees, the researcher thought he might have been beekeeping. At least, she was thinking and using knowledge to test a hypothesis, but she lacked key knowledge. The researcher was not aware of the old-style double *s*. In fact, the ancestor's occupation was "assisting on farm."

With practice, caution, and common sense, you can generally decide the writer's intentions. Try looking for the same word in the same handwriting elsewhere on the page or in the district for comparison. This often works better than comparing individual letters. If you cannot determine the name with a fair degree of certainty, get a photocopy of the record and keep it for future reference. Experience and other records may answer the question.

Examine and evaluate abbreviations of state names given for birthplaces. They are not always the same that we use today.

Figure 10.2, on page 103, is a page from the microfilmed 1860 census of Wright County, Missouri. Knowing its origin, you can decipher the county and state names at the top of the page and the Missouri birthplaces listed on the page. The other reported birthplaces are Kentucky and Tennessee.

Age and Birth Information

For age and birth date information, censuses can be very helpful but are not always accurate or specific. The 1790 federal census is of only general help in determining age; it shows simply that free heads of household were in that place and over age sixteen (usually) as of the first Monday of August 1790. It gives the number of free males (not specified as sons, or even relatives) in the household over sixteen or under sixteen. Females and slaves were not grouped by age at all.

The 1800–1840 censuses divided everyone into age groups. Only the head of household was named, but he or she was not always the oldest person in the family.

The 1820 census had a column for males between ages sixteen and eighteen. The next column was for males between sixteen and twenty-six. The males in the sixteen to eighteen age group are listed under both columns and should not be counted twice.

Beginning in 1850, the census reported each free person by name and age. This census is your earliest opportunity to find more specific information on age and birth in the federal census. Of course, not all families reported ages accurately, and sometimes a person was omitted.

See Also

Census forms in Appendix D show age brackets in censuses 1790–1840.

Figure 10.2 1860 census, Wright County, Missouri

An infant reported as "21/30," or twenty-one days old, could have been twenty-one days old as of the June 1 census day or as of the June 27 visit of the census taker. Even though we cannot know whether the family followed the census day rule, we can still narrow the birth date to between about May 10 and June 6. That's a more specific range than we get for many ancestors. (Census takers had instructions to list such infants as "0/12," meaning less than one month of age, but some enumerators were more specific.)

The 1870 and 1880 censuses asked for the month of birth for babies born within the census year, that is between 1 June 1869 and 1 June 1870 or between 1 June 1879 and 1 June 1880. This information may help you determine whether the family followed the census day rule, at least for the infant.

The 1900 census, as mentioned on page 94, specified the month and year of birth for all persons, though often inaccurately. The 1910 through 1930 censuses reverted to asking only for age, but were to give fractional ages for children under two: one year and three months as "1 3/12."

Working With Age and Birth Information

If your ancestor was a head of household and was listed as "over 45" as of 7 August 1820 (the official census day), subtract 45 from 1820 and you could suggest that, according to the census, he was born *by* 7 August 1775. That census gives you no more help in determining a birth date for the ancestor.

If the same ancestor was listed in the 1830 census as age "50–60," you could estimate his birth date a little more closely. Subtract 50 from 1830: 1780. Subtract 60 from 1830: 1770. You can suggest he was born between 1770 and 1780. Putting the two censuses (1820 and 1830) together, you could suggest a birth date between 1770 and 1775. Sometimes, that's the best estimate we can make.

Taking into account the official census day, you could estimate his birth a little more specifically. For the census, an ancestor was to report his age as of 1 June 1830, in other words, the age he became on the birthday before 1 June 1830—the birthday that fell between 1 June 1829 and 1 June 1830. If, for example, he was actually sixty years old for the 1830 census, then he turned sixty between 1 June 1829 and 1 June 1830. If you do not have an exact date, such as May 15, you have to allow for a full year of possibilities. To be accurate, therefore, you need to acknowledge that he could have turned sixty between 1 June 1829 and 1 June 1830 and thus could have been born in the last half of 1769 or the first half of 1770. Until you find other evidence of a specific birth date, you would need to record his birth as "about 1769–1770."

The census takers and families were supposed to follow the rule of census day—all information being correct as of that day. Unfortunately, we do not know to what extent they actually did. Therefore, we must speak of estimates, possibilities, and sometimes probabilities in drawing conclusions from census age and birth information. **We need other records to help pinpoint these facts more closely.**

Tip

Consider that the ancestor in the 1820 and 1830 censuses had three known sons, according to family tradition. Then you find three young males under ten in his 1820 census household and three males, aged fifteen to twenty, in his 1830 entry. You can suggest, but not be certain, that those three males were his sons. You would know that they were all born between 1810 and 1815 if their ages were accurately reported and recorded. At least you have something to work with as you look for their birth dates.

Estimating a Birth Year for Johnson Godwin

Case Study

You will find discrepancies in the ages of many ancestors in their census records. The chart on page 105, for a Johnson Godwin, shows that the 1850 census reported him as age fifty; the 1860 census, only eight years older. Why?

1. Different people could have given the information to the census takers.
2. The census taker could have written the age as he heard it, and he heard it incorrectly.
3. Many people rounded off their ages to the nearest 5 or 0. (If ages were reported this way, the census taker was to ask if it was accurate or rounded off, but we do not get that information.)

Using the Census to Find an Approximate Birth Year for Johnson Godwin			
Census Year	Age Given	You figure the suggested birth year	Birth Range
1830	30–40	1830 –30 = 1800, 1830– 40 = 1790	—b 1790–1800
1840	30–40	1840– 30 = 1810, 1840– 40 = 1800	—b 1800–1810
1850	50	1850– 50 = 1800	—b 1799–1800
1860	58	1860– 58 = 1802	—b 1801–1802
1870	67	1870– 67 = 1803	—b 1802–1803
1880	74	1880– 74 = 1806	—b 1805–1806

4. Not all the population had written records of birth (or death) dates or checked the ones they had when the census taker came. If the family was large, how many people could have remembered everyone's age correctly on any given day?

5. Some people felt it wasn't anyone else's business and weren't about to give correct information.

6. Sometimes the census taker may have guessed by looking.

According to the six censuses, Johnson Godwin's birth occurred between 1790 and 1806. The most consistent reports were the three indicating his birth about 1799 to 1800. These were made when he was younger, married, and head of household.

In 1860, he was head of household, his wife apparently had died, and three young adult children were still living at home. In 1870, he was living alone but near other relatives. The suggested birth dates of 1802 and 1803 from those two years are close to each other and not far from the 1800 date.

In 1880, Godwin was living with a daughter and her family. The age given in that census suggested an 1806 birth. This entry was the least similar to the others and possibly, the least accurate. Considering only these records and until more information is found, we can estimate Godwin's birth as "about late 1799–1803."

CENSUS CHECK FORM

The census check form, shown in Figure 10.3, on page 106, and full-size in Appendix D, is very useful in capsuling the information from each census record for one individual. I like to begin with the earliest census at the top of the page, but you could begin with the last one and read backward in time as you move down the page. The chart does not take the place of the census extraction forms, which give you space to record all information in the census. The census check form lets you see and study the bigger picture and compare your findings.

Even before you begin reading the census records, you can begin a census check form for your focus ancestor. Fill out as much of the top section as you can. Fill in the "Census Year" column for censuses for which you believe the ancestor was alive. Determine where your focus ancestor was, or probably was, at the time of the applicable census records. Pencil in the location(s) on the chart in the "State/Counties Searched" column and the ancestor's age at each census in the "Age" column. (Using pencil lets you make changes as necessary.) The "Age" column is meant to show the correct age, not necessarily the age given in the census. If the reported age is different, you can mention it in the "Notes" column or add it with some notation in the "Age" column. As you use the records, take advantage of the last column for recording your documentation, and keep your chart updated with your findings.

Keeping track of your census searches on such a chart can help you see at a glance where you have found or not found the family, plan where you could search next, and study new clues you have discovered. It may also save you from that irritating mistake of reading a census record, only to discover afterward that you had already read it!

Census Check on _____
Name

Birthdate/place _____ First Census _____

Father's Name _____ Mother's Name _____

Marriage date/place _____ Spouse _____

Death date/place _____ Burial place _____

Census Year	Age	State/Counties Searched	County Where Found & Notes	Film #, Roll #, E.D., Pg, etc.

Figure 10.3

THINGS TO DO NOW

Idea Generator

1. In a library or bookstore, look at the reference books mentioned in this chapter. Any or all of them would make helpful additions to your personal library.

2. Explain to a friend, or the cat, (a) when and why the federal census is taken, (b) the census day rules, (c) which years of the census give the names and birthplaces of household members, (d) which censuses report the relationship of each person to the head of household, and (e) when the next census will be opened to the public.

3. Practice the Soundex code by creating the code for your eight great-grandparent surnames or any ancestral surnames you know at this time.

4. Begin a census check form for your focus ancestor.

5. Find out if a library or institution near you has the microfilm or CD-ROM census schedules. Do they have the ones you need for your focus ancestor? If not, check Web sites for the state and county. If what you need is not online, take steps to rent the necessary Soundex and census schedules.

6. Consult a map to find your focus ancestor's known county/counties of residence. Make note of, or a map of, the location(s) in relation to surrounding counties. Consult one of the reference books on pages 95–96 to determine when your research county and its neighbors were formed and from what parent county/counties.

ELEVEN

Beyond the Family: County and State Sources

F amily sources and federal census records often give genealogists much of the information they seek. However, these sources often suggest rather than confirm genealogical facts. Remember that records of individuals exist at each level of government or geographical unit. County and state records are key to many genealogical proofs. Thus, genealogists may find an advantage in using these first, or next after federal census records.

COUNTY COURTHOUSES

Counties organize their materials in different ways, but you can generally start at the office of the county clerk or the equivalent. Clerks and staff are usually glad to direct you to the records you want to study but cannot search for you. If you cannot visit the courthouse in person, try to get microfilm records from the state archives or historical society, or your nearest Family History Center.

Some courthouses, especially in the South, have lost records due to fires, floods, and storms over the years. Whether partial or complete losses, they are unfortunate for genealogists. Researchers, therefore, have even more reason to examine records in local, state, and federal jurisdictions.

Warning

Indexes

Before reading county records, familiarize yourself with the indexes. You may find

1. separate indexes for deeds, marriages, divorces, naturalizations, and other records
2. multiple indexes, each covering several volumes (of like records), years, or decades (Look at all that cover your ancestral time period.)
3. record books with indexes at the beginning of each volume
4. computerized indexes
5. records such as court minutes and tax rolls not indexed at all

Inside the index, you may find

- Surnames grouped under their initial letter in chronological order, as the documents came in for filing. Sometimes, they were filed years after the original events took place.
- Names in alphabetical groups: all names beginning with *Pa* indexed on one page, *Pe* on another, then *Ph*, *Pi*, and so forth. This index style usually helps you find entries with alternate spellings.
- Variant spellings. If you seek records of William Thomas Walter and find W.T. or William Watters in the index at the right time, look up the references. They may be for the right ancestor indexed under a misspelled name.

For Your Information

1. Some county courthouse offices answer queries by mail, and some do not. If you try to get information by mail, make your request short, easy to read, concise, and to the point, and enclose a self-addressed, stamped envelope. The clerks may use your envelope or theirs. Sometimes they answer on your letter and return the original to you. Limit your request to something that can be handled quickly: "In working on family history, I am looking for a marriage record from about 1797 to 1803 for Samuel Black and Keturah Shaw. Do you have such a record? If so, what is the cost of obtaining a copy?"

If you know of a specific document in a courthouse office, such as a will in volume D, page 347, you can often get a copy by mail. Call the appropriate clerk's office to verify that they have the volume and can make a copy and find out the cost.

2. Louisiana is organized into parishes rather than counties. Due to its Spanish and French roots, it uses civil law rather than the English common law tradition of the other states. One unique aspect of the civil law system is the office of notary in each parish. Since the early eighteenth century, notaries have drawn up, witnessed, and preserved a multitude of documents that form important resources for genealogists. These documents, or the notarial record books, may contain legal and personal business, including wills, marriage contracts, business agreements, estate inventories, partitions and sales of estates and businesses, mortgages, slave sales and emancipations, and records of family meetings. In Louisiana, family meetings are held on behalf of minor heirs before a sale of estate property or to protect the interests of the minors before the remarriage of the surviving parent. The notes of family meetings are often found in the probate (succession) files of the deceased parents and can be genealogical gold mines.

3. Once you begin to read the record books, document each book with volume and page number, as in "Presidio County, Texas, Deed Book A:24" (page 24). As part of taking notes, record whether the parties could sign their own names or signed with their marks. Remember, the handwriting in these books is rarely that of your ancestors but usually that of the clerk, who indicates whether they signed or made marks. Some courthouses, historical societies, and state archives preserve original marriage bonds and licenses,

wills, and related estate papers. These documents normally show the signatures or marks of the parties involved.

MARRIAGE RECORDS

Marriage records help establish ancestral vital statistics and relationships. They can provide valuable clues for further research as you seek to reconstruct the cluster of an ancestor's relatives and friends.

Before the twentieth century, grooms, before marrying, often had to sign a bond acknowledging that they would owe a stated sum of money to the colonial or state government if there was any lawful cause that would prevent the marriage from taking place. A relative or friend usually acted as surety on the bond. Thus, the thorough researcher will note the name of the surety as part of the cluster of the groom's relatives and friends. Bonds were generally replaced by marriage licenses in the nineteenth century.

Each state sets the age at which a couple can legally marry. Anyone marrying before coming of age was supposed to get permission from a parent or guardian. Some couples, rather than getting parental permission and getting the marriage license in their county of residence, got a license in a county where they were not known and married in spite of one being underage. If both were of age or were marrying with parental consent, it was customary to marry in the bride's county of residence.

Using Marriage Records Effectively

Technique

Study the marriage indexes that cover your research time frame and write down the references that seem pertinent to your search. Sometimes, separate indexes exist for brides and for grooms. After the Civil War some counties had separate marriage books for blacks and whites. Most marriage indexes in the county courthouse do not include participants other than the bride and groom.

- Look up all entries pertaining to your known family, not just your ancestors. You could find your ancestor as a witness, surety, parent, guardian, or clergyman.
- Write down all information: bride, groom, ages and other personal data given, date and place of marriage, the official who performed the ceremony, any witnesses or bondsmen, any parental permission given for an underage person, and of course the volume and page or certificate number of the entry.
- Note clergymen who performed several weddings in your ancestral family. They may be clues to the family's religious affiliation.
- Scan the books of the ancestral time period for evidence of your ancestor, male or female, as a witness, surety, guardian, or clergyman for "nonfamily" or friends. They may or may not be related. The record adds to your knowledge of your ancestor and establishes his or her presence in the place at that time.
- Get copies of the documents pertaining to your ancestors, when possible.

Caution!

1. The marriage entry may give four or five different dates: (a) the clerk's issuing of the license or bond, (b) the marriage ceremony, (c) sometimes, the clergyman's signature, (d) the clergyman (or other official who performed the ceremony) returning the license to the clerk, and (e) the clerk recording it in the official record. Record all dates that are given and what may be missing, especially the record of the ceremony and its return to the clerk.

2. If you find no indication of the wedding date, you cannot assume that the ceremony did or did not take place. Many legitimate marriages do not show a return, which contains the date of the ceremony, in the official record. However, some couples got a license and, for whatever reason, never married. If an ancestor's marriage record does not show the return, look in other records, such as the newspaper or family Bible, for evidence of the ceremony.

3. If you do not find a marriage record that you expected to find in a given county, note that fact as well and look in surrounding or nearby counties.

4. Some states registered not only the names of the bride and groom but their ages, occupations, and parents' names. Other marriage records contain nothing more than the names of the couple.

5. Even if relationships were not stated in the record, many witnesses, bondsmen, clergymen, or justices were relatives of the bride or groom.

6. If you find published transcriptions of marriage records, try to get a copy of the original record to confirm the published information. Human error sometimes occurs in transcribing. For a number of states, statewide sets of marriage transcriptions have been published in books or on microform. Some are available on CD-ROM or online. However, **many of these electronic products are selected records, not complete coverage of your state or county.**

Important

Warning

Original Marriage Records

When the clergyman or ceremonial official returned the license to the courthouse to be recorded in the marriage book, the clerk in many courts filed the original. If your ancestral county maintains a file of the original licenses, by all means get photocopies of ancestral ones. Some counties even give those documents to family members because of limited storage space.

Original marriage bonds or licenses may be stored at the county courthouse, local archives or museum, local historical or genealogical society library, state archives, or state historical society. Often you can get a photocopy by mail.

WILLS AND PROBATE RECORDS

A will is a document by which a person (the testator) directs how his or her property shall be distributed after death. It usually names the spouse, children, and/or other relatives, such as grandchildren or nieces and nephews, and is therefore considered verification of kinship. You can learn such things as what property the deceased owned (at least at the writing of the will, if not at death), religious beliefs, and instructions on burial and the division of the estate.

A will's witnesses and executors were often relatives or friends of the deceased. Thus, wills and other records relating to estate settlements often provide important evidence about a focus ancestor or the cluster of friends and relatives.

For Your Information

1. Depending on the state, you can study will books and probate records in the clerk's office of the county, probate, chancery, or superior court or the town hall. In early years, wills and deeds sometimes were recorded in the same books and therefore indexed together. If the wills were recorded separately, they will be indexed separately.

2. In many places in the nineteenth century and before, married women were not allowed to write wills unless they held separate property in their own names, and this seldom happened. Widows or unmarried women with property did sometimes write wills.

3. **Getting photocopies of wills and probate records, when possible, saves time and gives you valuable references for later study.** If you abstract the information from the documents yourself, copy everything:

- all names
- relationships
- residences
- dates (of will, probate, inventory, administrator reports, estate division, filing, etc.)
- locations of property
- conditions affecting distribution of the estate
- witnesses
- the case number or volume and page number(s) of each document

Timesaver

Studying Wills

In characteristic style of the period, Isaac McFadden of South Carolina began his will in 1818:

> I, Isaac McFadden, . . . feeling the firmities of old age and the wastes of disease making progressive advances upon my bodily frame, yet possessing a competent soundness of mind, do conceive it to be dutiful to make the annexed arrangement of my worldly concernments (Chester County, South Carolina, Will Book 2-G:50).

In traditional order, Isaac commended his "soul to God (from whom it was received) resting on the efficacious mediation and merits of our glorious redeemer." He wished his "body to be committed to the dust in a decent and Christian manner, without parade or unnecessary expense in the hope of the resurrection from the dead, the reunion of Soul and body and the final admission of both into the abodes of bliss in the immediate presence and enjoyment of God." After requesting the payment of debts, he divided his property among his wife and fourteen living children.

Because women's property rights, for the most part, were severely limited until the twentieth century, widows often became destitute and dependent on their children or the community for support. In keeping with common law and applicable statutory law, many early wills set conditions on the wife's inheritance of her husband's estate. Some wills were more generous than the minimum "widow's third" or dower that the law usually provided. (See page 118.)

In 1818, one Elliott Coleman incorporated a common limitation into his will, but the bequest of his personal estate to his widow would be considered advantageous for her and the minor children: "To my wife for whose affection and duty I owe every sence [*sic*] of gratitude and acknowledgment of a husband I give the tract of land wherein I now live and also all my personal estate *during widowhood* in order the better to enable her to support educate and advance our children . . . " (Cumberland County, Virginia, Will Book 7:146, italics added).

The provision "during widowhood" also implied "for the rest of her life, if she remained unmarried." Coleman's personal estate included slaves, livestock, farming implements, furniture, and household goods, all of which allowed the widow to keep the farm operating and generating support for herself and her family.

A different provision is found in the will of Richard Phillips in 1793: "I lend to my beloved wife Lucy all my whole estate both real and personal excepted [*sic*] two feather beds and furniture which I shall hereafter dispose of[,] which estate I desire she may possess and enjoy *during her natural life* . . . my will and desire is that all my estate lent to my said wife be equally divided *at her death* amongst my eight children . . ." (Amelia County, Virginia, Will Book 5:36, italics added). Since Phillips was about age sixty and his children seem to have been grown at the time of his will, he may have felt that his wife probably would not remarry and thus he felt no need to specify that the estate was hers during widowhood only.

Probate Files: More Than Wills

Probate records include a number of documents, most of them dealing with estates of the deceased. These records may exist as original files or records in the county will books or other probate record books. In some states, files of the original documents exist in the county courthouse, or some are available on microfilm. In other states, the originals were destroyed once the clerk copied them into the official record books. The records most often found in such files and record books include

- wills
- applications and appointments of administrators or executors
- administrators' and executors' bonds
- estate inventories and appraisals
- records of estate sales
- guardianship records if the heirs included minors
- annual reports of estate income and expenses, receipts of payment to creditors
- in Louisiana, records of family meetings

- final settlements and divisions of property
- court proceedings generated by disputes among heirs
- any other documents related to the case

The court with probate jurisdiction usually handles other matters such as cases of illegitimacy, adoption, lunacy, orphans, and apprentices. Ancestors sometimes were involved in these matters as well.

Using Probate Records

You will seldom find a death date in old probate records. However, the information given in the will and probate papers may narrow the death date possibilities. See pages 175–176 for additional examples of evaluating probate records.

Even though you may not find in the probate file or record book much information on the death itself, you may learn about the widow's remarriage, the marriage of children, proof of siblings of the deceased, and proof of other relationships. For example, cases exist in which a young, unmarried man died, leaving a will that named his mother, brothers and sisters, and even the children of his siblings.

The 1850 probate file of one married man named his wife and four children. When the wife died three years later, the administrator named her *five* children, including one born apparently after the husband's death. The probate file does not address the issue of paternity for that youngest child, but does state she was a child of this mother. So far, this is the only evidence of this child's existence.

Other records showed appointments of guardians to monitor the affairs of minor children. These documents can help (1) pinpoint a death date for the deceased or an heir or (2) identify relationships.

After one's death, the estate was often inventoried, valued, and recorded—each knife and fork, kettle and candlestick, sheep and horse, bed and chair, hoe and ax. If the estate was sold, a report listed who bought each item and for how much.

Reports of executors or administrators often detailed the income and expenses of the estate year by year and the division of money, land, slaves, and personal property among the heirs. One example is a partial distribution from the estate of Peter T. Phillips in 1833 (Cumberland County, Virginia, Will Book 9:129–131). Eight male and female heirs with the surname Phillips received property valued at five hundred dollars each. Because of this distribution in equal amounts, we know that they were sons and unmarried daughters of the deceased, who seems to have died intestate (without a will). No one else would have had a claim to an equal share unless specified in a will.

Others had "received advancement during the life time" of the said Peter T. Phillips: Benjamin Phillips; Ferdinand G. Coleman and wife, Eliza; and Newton Hazelgrove and Lucy Ann, his wife. Even without other supporting documents, you can infer that Eliza and Lucy Ann were married daughters of Peter T. Phillips, as their husbands are named with them. **If Coleman and Hazelgrove had been heirs in their own right, the wives would not have been listed.** (In this case, the conclusion is supported by their marriage records, deeds, and, later,

Important

their widowed mother's will.) With the settlement record alone, you still would know that if they received their portion in advance, they were more than likely children, not grandchildren. In such a distribution, grandchildren would not be entitled to a share in the estate except to divide the portion due their deceased parent. In that case, their relationship may be spelled out.

For those tracing former slave ancestors, wills and probate records can be vital. They revealed changes in ownership of slaves and often named slave mothers and their children. If they did not state relationships, the researcher can sometimes suggest family units by the way the slaves were grouped in inventories or estate divisions. By tracing a slaveholder's family through several generations in probate records, genealogists can learn of slaves who died, babies who were born, slaves who were hired out to work in a particular craft or trade, ages of slaves at the time of a particular inventory, and residences of some of the owner's heirs, which can suggest new places in which to research. Any of this kind of information can be important in piecing together the ancestral puzzle.

Probate records are valuable sources of information that can give a picture of family relationships, activities, lifestyle, financial status, debts, and even quarrels. Such disputes often generate documents that help solve genealogical problems many years later.

DEEDS AND PROPERTY RECORDS

Deeds transfer ownership of land, buildings, or other property, including slaves before 1865. Warranty deeds, quitclaim deeds, deeds of gift, and deeds of trust are the basic types genealogists use.

1. Warranty deeds, also called simply deeds, transfer property with the assurance of a good title.

2. Quitclaim deeds transfer one person's interest in the property without such a guarantee.

3. Parents sometimes distributed property among their children through deeds of gift, with the key words "for and in consideration of the Natural Love and Affection he hath and bears unto his son." Some used this form of estate division instead of or in addition to a will, often reserving a life estate in the property—the right to use it during their lifetimes. Some deeds of gift do not express a relationship between the giver and receiver; we cannot assume one where none is stated.

4. Deeds of trust were made by one paying off a mortgage or one in debt who was trying to pay creditors. Elliott Coleman in Tennessee executed a deed of trust to his brother and another man in 1867. He listed all his property of value, which was to be sold at auction if he could not pay his debts within one year, including "all interest I have in [the] real and personal estate of my late father Ferdinand G. Coleman, dec'd, late of Cumberland County, Virginia" (Hardeman County, Tennessee, Deed Book U:56). An experience that turned into a nightmare for Elliott and his family became a researcher's dream come true—the identification of his father and a new place to begin research. **This**

Research Tip

For More Info

Chapter ten of *The Sleuth Book for Genealogists* is a case study illustrating the value of such probate records to an African-American genealogy.

Technique

kind of discovery reaffirms these rules of genealogical research: (a) work from the known to the unknown, (b) do not try to skip back in time too soon, and (c) gather clues from one generation's records before trying to move to the previous one.

Deed books in a county courthouse or town hall may include a number of legal instruments other than deeds, including bills of sale (especially for slave sales), prenuptial agreements, powers of attorney, contracts, affidavits, wills and inventories, and even voter and jury lists. Except for these lists, the documents usually were created because of the involvement of property between individuals.

Why Research Deed Records?

Many ancestors owned land and/or slaves, and the records may help establish the names, dates, places, and relationships that make up the family tree. Deed records may

1. show that an ancestor was in a given place at a given time
2. tell where the grantor and grantee were living
3. state relationships, as in the Coleman deed of trust (in number four on page 115) or in a family of slaves
4. suggest relationships
5. help distinguish people with the same name
6. indicate whether or not a person was living at the time
7. reveal occupations and socioeconomic data, such as growing crops and livestock
8. name business associates, friends, fellow church members, or neighbors
9. give history of the ownership of the land
10. help locate or map the land

Deed Indexes

Deed books generally have two indexes: grantor (seller) index and grantee (buyer) index, sometimes called direct and indirect (or reverse) indexes. Use both, and look up your primary surname in that county, as well as other names known or thought to be related. **Consider these research tips:**

Research Tip

- Realize that indexes can contain errors and omissions; sometimes we need to read page by page through record volumes.
- Watch for index entries with *et al.* (Latin for "and others") after a name; it may signal a group of heirs selling land they inherited.
- Watch for index entries with *et ux.* (Latin for "and wife").
- Look in the indexes before and after the time you believe your ancestor to have been in the county; some deeds were recorded years after the transaction.
- Be alert to spelling variations of surnames.
- Understand that if you don't find your ancestor's name in the index, it means only that it was not in the index; the name may still be in the records.

- Recognize that only the buyer and seller are indexed, not witnesses, neighbors, and others.
- Know that if the ancestor's land was sold at auction to satisfy a debt or court order, the record often listed the sheriff as the seller, indexed alphabetically under *S* for *sheriff*.

Survey Systems for Land

The United States uses two categories of land distribution systems: state land and federal land (or public domain). **State land states owned and distributed their land,** often before the federal government began. They are

1. the original thirteen states: Connecticut, Delaware, Georgia, Maryland, Massachusetts, New Hampshire, New Jersey, New York, North Carolina, Pennsylvania, Rhode Island, South Carolina, and Virginia
2. the five states that came out of their land claims or territory: Kentucky, Maine, Tennessee, Vermont, and West Virginia
3. Hawaii and Texas, which entered the Union having been independent republics

Notes

State land states are not uniform in their approach to survey and legal descriptions. However, a number of them use a system of metes and bounds. This practice describes land boundaries with distances and directions to specific markers, either natural (creek or tree) or artificial (a stake in the prairie or a rock pile). Legal descriptions often contain this kind of language: "beginning at a post oak on Mrs. Ward's southeast corner, thence north 30 degrees east 150 poles along her line to a stake in the prairie, thence south 60 degrees east 200 poles. . . ."

The other states are **federal land states created from the public domain, land the United States bought or acquired** and created into territories as the population spread out. Land in these states was generally surveyed according to the rectangular survey system. A map of such land appears as a grid of squares, called townships, containing about thirty-six square miles. Each township contains typically thirty-six sections, each one mile square or 640 acres. One could buy the entire section or portions of it: the northwest quarter, the northern half, half of a quarter, etc. The legal descriptions read very differently from most state land descriptions and are easier to plot on maps: "the northwest quarter of section one, township nine north, range seven east."

Federal records contain the initial transfer of public domain land to individuals. County deed records reflect subsequent sales when individuals sold and bought the same land among themselves. County deed records contain the legal descriptions of the land, which indicate the survey system in use. The legal description is important in locating the property or in identifying neighbors.

Notes

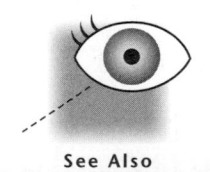

See Also

See chapter thirteen, pages 154–160 for more on federal land and records.

Using Deed Records in Genealogy

Marriage and probate records may provide maiden names, event dates, names of children or parents, clues to relationships, and clues on age or death from which researchers can suggest birth or death dates. Land records may or may not be so specific in the information they provide, but they are extremely valuable resources and often reveal important clues.

Deeds sometimes spell out relationships and events, as in a deed written 18 October 1810, through which Kentucky residents Phoeby Garner, Frances Garner, Nathan Brelsford and Elizabeth Brelsford, his wife, sold their interest in 244 acres in Hampshire County, Virginia, to William Lockhart of that county (Christian County, Kentucky, Deed Book C:133). The text stated that Phoeby, Frances, and Elizabeth were daughters of Henry Garner, deceased, and each was selling her undivided seventh part of the property. From this statement, we learn that there were seven heirs and that Phoeby and Frances were probably not married, for no husband joined in the deed with either. In this case, a researcher would want to

- investigate the possibility that Lockhart was the husband of another sister, for heirs often sold their portions to another heir
- consider that other heirs may have sold their interest to Lockhart (or others) and look for such deeds in the records of the Virginia county to help complete the list of heirs

According to state law in these and other states, Elizabeth, as a married woman, could not own, buy, or sell property on her own, nor could her husband sell her inheritance without her permission. The county court of the Virginia county, thus, asked the court of Christian County, Kentucky, to get from Elizabeth an acknowledgment, obtained by examining her "privily and apart from her said husband whether she willingly signed and sealed the said indenture without the persuasion or threat of her said husband." The records contained no such reference to Phoeby and Frances; this omission also implies that they were not married at the time.

Dower Rights

Most colonies and states, until the mid- or late-nineteenth century, adopted some form of old English common law that, for support, a widow had the right to one-third of any land that her husband had owned during their marriage. In most cases, when a husband sold land, the buyer wanted assurance that the wife would not try to claim her third in the future. Thus, she had to relinquish this "dower right" as part of the transaction. Such documents, which may be the only evidence of a wife's name, tell us that she was alive at that date. They do not suggest she was the first and only wife or the mother of all the children.

When Abraham and Robert Whitesides of Chester County, South Carolina, sold land to Isaac McFadden in November 1804, two ladies relinquished dower rights: Margaret Whitesides, mother of Abraham, and Jane Whitesides, wife of Abraham (Chester County, South Carolina, Deed Book K:266). The facts suggest that Abraham may have inherited the land from his father since his mother was asked to relinquish her dower right to it. The mother would not have had a claim to it if it had not belonged to her husband during their marriage. The

For More Info

For more on researching women, see *A Genealogist's Guide to Discovering Your Female Ancestors,* by Sharon DeBartolo Carmack, and *The Hidden Half of the Family,* by Christina Kassabian Schaefer.

deed suggests that Robert was not Abraham's father since Margaret was identified as Abraham's mother, not as Robert's wife. Was Robert Abraham's brother? Was he not married since no wife was mentioned? Again, the deed gives some specific genealogical information and prompts questions for further study.

Studying Neighbors

Deeds also contain potentially important information that may or may not lead to genealogical discoveries. For example, property descriptions in metes and bounds often mention adjoining landowners: "at Henry Clark's southwest corner," or "bounded on the south by Thomas Ferrel." Genealogists working with federal land states plot ancestral land and neighbors on a grid of townships. In any location, neighbors may have been relatives or in-laws. The genealogist should study the question; this is a good way to pursue cluster genealogy.

Abstracting a Deed Record

As you examine deed records, write down (or get a copy of) all information given:

- date of the deed and of its filing
- type of deed
- buyer(s), seller(s), and their residences
- price and other considerations of the transaction
- size, location, and description of the property
- witnesses
- signatures or marks
- any relationships stated or other names mentioned, such as neighbors
- date the seller's wife relinquished her dower rights and/or date a wife was examined on her willingness to sell
- volume and page numbers for each document

Notes

The following is a rather typical warranty deed. Underlining is added to show what a researcher needs to abstract when taking notes. The transcription keeps the original spelling and punctuation.

(Christian County, Kentucky, Deed Book C:191)

This Indenture made the 13th day of May 1811 between Nathan Brelsford and Elizabeth Brelsford his wife of the one part and Garvener Stuart of the other part all of the county of Christian and State of Kentucky witnesseth that the aforesaid Nathan Brelsford and Elizabeth his wife, for and in consideration of the sum of three hundred dollars to them in hand paid the receipt whereof is hereby acknowledged have granted bargained sold aliened and confirmed unto the aforesaid Garvener Stuart a certain tract or parcel of land containing one hundred and twenty five acres be the same more or less situated lying and being in the county and state aforesaid on the waters of the east fork of little river originally granted by the county court of Christian to Joseph Cravens in February 1802 by survey bearing date the 16th day of March 1803 and patented to the said Brelsford the 15th day of

December 1810 and bounded as follows [legal description follows] to wit beginning at a post oak in Cravens line thence with it south sixty five [degrees] west 112 poles to two post oaks, thence south thirty west 125 poles to a black oak sappling thence south fifty east 150 poles to a black oak on a . . . [?] thence north nine east 250 poles to the beginning to have and to hold the aforesaid tract of land with all and singular the appurtenances thereunto immediately belonging or that may hereafter belong to the only proper use benefit and behoof of him the aforesaid Garvener Stuart his heirs and assigns forever from ourselves our heirs and assigns forever and the aforesaid Nathan Brelsford and Elizabeth his wife for themselves their heirs and assigns doth covenant and agree to and with the aforesaid Garvener Stuart his heirs and assigns that the aforesaid tract of land and bargained premises they will forever warrant and defend unto the said Garvener Stuart his heirs and assigns free from any claim or demand whatever from themselves their heirs and assigns and from all persons and manner of persons whatsoever claiming In witness whereof the said Nathan Brelsford and Elizabeth his wife have hereunto set their hands and seals the day and year first above written in presence of
[left blank—no witnesses given]

Nathan Brelsford [signature] (seal)

Elizabeth Brelsford [signature] (seal)

At Christian County Court, June 18th, 1811
[Wife Elizabeth voluntarily relinquishes her dower right at this time.]

For More Info

These are helpful books for the study of land, property, and inheritance:
- *Inheritance in America: From Colonial Times to the Present.* Carole Shammas, Marylynn Salmon, and Michel Dahlin. New Brunswick, N.J.: Rutgers University Press, 1987.
- *Land & Property Research in the United States.* E. Wade Hone. Salt Lake City: Ancestry, 1997.
- *Women and the Law of Property in Early America.* Marylynn Salmon. Chapel Hill, N.C.: The University of North Carolina Press, 1986.

OTHER COURTHOUSE RECORDS

Courthouses contain additional records that genealogists may find helpful, including birth and death registrations, property tax lists, various court records, divorce records, voter registrations, registrations of livestock marks and brands, military discharge papers of World War I and after, and others. Most of these volumes are not usually indexed, with the exception of birth, death, and divorce records. Sometimes, courthouses also house school records, school censuses, newspapers, manuscript county histories, and other gems.

Vital Records

Each state has its own procedure for birth and death registration. Thus, the county clerk or other courthouse office may or may not have these records, and you may or may not have access to them. Most states have only scattered birth or death records until the late 1800s or early 1900s. Depending on when the state began vital registrations, you may be able to advance your research by collecting birth and death certificates for your ancestors.

Birth certificates may furnish such genealogical information as the child's name, race and sex, birth date and place, parents' names and birthplaces, and the mother's maiden name. Also ask about delayed or probate birth certificates—registrations filed years later by those who were not registered at birth. Supporting documents for delayed certificates are usually returned to the registrant, not kept by the county or state, but may be summarized on the certificate.

Death records may provide the same facts as birth registrations, plus the cause, date, time, and place of death, place and date of the burial, the name of the funeral home and doctor, the name of the informant (often a relative), and the Social Security number for those who died after 1936 and had registered with that administration.

Be aware that the birth information and age at death on an adult's death certificate may or may not (1) be correct or (2) correspond correctly with the death date. For example, a man died on 15 March 1930. His birth date was reported as 1 January 1850. Therefore, his age at death should read "80 years, 2 months, 14 days." The careful researcher will check both the birth date and the age at death against the death date to determine if they agree. If they do not, the researcher (1) cannot assume which one is correct and (2) must seek other sources to help solve the discrepancy.

Important

It is useful to gather copies of siblings' birth or death registrations, because specifics on the parents sometimes differ from one entry to another. For example, four death certificates of six siblings may say that the mother's maiden name was unknown; one may not have a certificate; and the sixth may supply the maiden name. Gathering family death certificates may also help you collect medical history. Birth and death records in some counties and some states may be closed for a period of years for privacy protection. The laws vary, as does their application.

In large cities, the health department or vital statistics office sometimes recorded these events instead of the county. Birth and death certificates and some marriage records may also be obtained from the state vital statistics office in the capital city.

Three references about acquiring vital records in each state are

For More Info

- *International Vital Records Handbook.* Thomas J. Kemp, compiler. Baltimore: Genealogical Publishing Company, latest edition.
- *Where to Write for Vital Records: Births, Deaths, Marriages, and Divorces.* Hyattsville, Md.: U.S. Department of Health and Human Services, Public Health Service, 1998 or later edition. Available from the Superintendent of Documents, U.S. Government Printing Office, Washington, DC 20402, or from a U.S. Government Bookstore. For bookstore locations, see <http://bookstore.gpo.gov/locations/index.html>.
- Web site at <http://www.vitalrec.com/>.

Property Tax Records

Some counties file old property tax records; some keep them only twenty or thirty years. The older records are stored in basements, attics, warehouses, old jails, or at the state archives. Pre-twentieth-century tax records may be available on microfilm.

Use these tax records to learn where in the county the family lived; possibly who their neighbors were; and what taxable property they owned, such as land, horses, cattle, carriages, clocks, or, before 1865, slaves. If you are searching for slave ancestors, tax lists that name slaves and report their ages can be very helpful.

Research Tip

Some tax rolls state or suggest relationships. Some name minor children when the administrator of a parent's estate pays taxes on behalf of the children. A person paying taxes "as agent for" someone else often was a relative or close friend. This information may help you in (1) re-creating and studying the cluster of an ancestor's relatives or associates and (2) identifying the parents. The tax lists can give you clues to when a man became the taxable age, often twenty-one, and appeared on the list because he began owing taxes. Researchers cannot assume, however, that the first appearance on the tax roll is proof of a specific birth year; some men did not enter the tax rolls as soon as they were eligible. Men and widows ceased to appear on the tax rolls when they (1) died, (2) became exempt from paying taxes, or (3) moved out of the county. If, for example, census records suggest the family moved away between 1870 and 1876 and you find them last in the 1875 tax records, you can estimate they moved in 1875 or 1876.

Below are examples of genealogical clues from the Putnam County, Georgia, tax digests between 1817 and 1824:

1. Caty Lamar as guardian for Polley and Dent Lamar (suggests she was their mother or grandmother).
2. Cloy Allen, executor of James Allen, dec'd. (*Executor* means there was a will; look for it.)
3. Peter F. Flournoy as parent to Pamela Brown, Gamantha [*sic*] Slaughter, and Smith W. and Lemuel M. Flournoy (important statement of relationship).
4. John Kennon as guardian for Elizabeth Gorley, for William A. Gorley, and as administrator on the estate of James Gorley, dec'd. (Elizabeth and William may be children of James; *administrator* means there was no will, but there may be a probate file.)
5. Allen Robinson as agent for John A. Robinson (suggests a relationship between the two).
6. William A. Slaughter as guardian for Martin Slaughter's orphans. (Look for probate file of Martin Slaughter.)

Reminder

Figure 11.1, page 124, is a page of an 1820 Georgia tax digest. **Note the marks that appear to the modern eye as ditto marks. In such older records, these marks usually indicate simply a space left blank or "no information" or "not applicable."** In this record, the column headings read

- Names of Person Liable to pay tax
- No. of Poles [*sic*] (number of taxable polls or heads—free males of taxable age and slaves)
- Land of the 1st quality
- Do 2nd (land of the second quality, with *Do* meaning "ditto")
- Do 3rd (land of the third quality)
- Pine (land)
- County (where the land lies)
- Water Course (on which the land lies)
- To Whom granted
- Adjoining To (neighboring landowner)
- Dollars (of tax)
- Cents (of tax)

Court Records

Court records, including dockets, minute books, and case files, give information on civil and criminal cases. Ask courthouse staff which court clerk's office maintains divorce records, as each state has its own system. Court minute books may also contain

- estate divisions
- jury lists and pay records
- evidence of residents hired to do contract work for the county
- naturalization of new citizens
- summaries of divorce, debt, assault, and other court cases
- reports of licensing fees paid by local taverns, ferries, lawyers, and medical professionals
- registration of livestock marks and brands
- grand jury bills charging local citizens with law violations

In some counties, these items of county court business were noted in the minute book, but the records themselves were written in separate volumes marked "Juror Records," "Divorces," "Naturalizations," "Marks and Brands," etc.

Like tax records, court records may be hard to find and time-consuming to use, but they sometimes prove not only interesting but also valuable in solving genealogical problems. On the most basic level, they can place ancestors in a given place at a given time. On another level, they pit neighbor against neighbor, relative against relative in various civil lawsuits. The minute books may give only a bare outline of the case and its resolution. If case files exist, they may give more detail, such as how the parties were related, what the dispute was about, or other relatives involved.

Other Courthouse Records

County clerks' offices and storage shelves sometimes contain miscellaneous volumes and papers of historical interest and potential genealogical value. These may be business ledgers that later became county record books and, thus, contain entries from both uses. They may be papers of an early judge or original

Figure 11.1 Tax Digest, Putnam County, Georgia, 1820

documents salvaged from a courthouse fire. One Kentucky courthouse basement yielded a group of very old, neat little bundles tied with string. They were actual polling lists of which men voted for which candidates in congressional and presidential elections dating back to the 1820s! (Remember, they had no secret ballot as we know it.)

CHECKLIST OF STATE SOURCES

Sources vary by state. Consult books and articles about research in your ancestral states. **References to help you identify sources in your research state include**

- *Ancestry's Red Book: American State, County & Town Sources*. Alice Eichholz, ed.
- *The Genealogist's Companion & Sourcebook*. Emily Anne Croom.
- *Land & Property Research in the United States*. E. Wade Hone.
- *State Census Records*. Ann S. Lainhart.
- *U.S. Military Records: A Guide to Federal & State Sources*. James C. Neagles.

For More Info

Some of the state sources listed below may be available at county courthouses or within the appropriate state agency, but older records may be in a state library, state archives, historical society, or university library. Many records have been microfilmed or published. Check for them at university, public, genealogy, or rental libraries.

Web sites for many of the state libraries, state archives, or state historical societies summarize their special collections and research materials. For online information about these facilities, search for Reference/Libraries or Reference/Archives. At this writing, the Web site at <**http://www.uidaho.edu/special-collections/Other.Repositories.html**> links to university and state archives, public libraries, and museums that have archives collections. The site named "Ready, 'Net, Go! Archival Internet Resources" is at <http://www.tulane.edu/~lmiller/ArchivesResources.html>.

Internet Source

A number of state and university libraries have published guides to their special collections and update them periodically. Such a guide can be an extremely useful tool to own if your research is concentrated in a particular state. Some guides are online on the state library or university Web site. These collections may include public records, family or business papers, early newspapers, maps, church records, and rare historical publications.

Here are some state sources to check as you research. In genealogy, you never know what you may find until you look.

1. Colonial, territorial, or state census records. Many states have had one or more state-prescribed censuses. Many of these name only heads of households and group family members by age or sex. Others give everyone's name, age, birthplace, etc.

2. State land records (primarily in the state land states), including Revolutionary War or other bounty land warrants issued by the states. In these states, land was originally held by the royal, colonial, or other parent government. (Original

See Also

See page 154 for information on public land states.

land records of the public land states are at the Bureau of Land Management, the National Archives, and sometimes at the state's general land office.) In Texas, General Land Office records can also include character certificates for those who immigrated while Texas was a Mexican state.

3. Correspondence of colonial, territorial, or state officials as they interacted with individual citizens and their problems or achievements.

4. State pension records. (Revolutionary War pension applications that were denied may be in the county court minutes.) Some state pensions were granted to Revolutionary War veterans and widows. Confederate veterans and widows could apply for pensions in the former Confederate States (Alabama, Arkansas, Florida, Georgia, Louisiana, Mississippi, North Carolina, South Carolina, Tennessee, Texas, and Virginia) as well as in Kentucky, Missouri, and Oklahoma. For online information on these pensions, see <http://www.archives.gov/research_room/gene alogy/military/confederate_pension_records.html>. It was possible for Confederate veterans to apply for a pension if they lived, after the war, in one of the states listed and met the criteria for eligibility. If they moved to another of these states, they could apply again in their new residence. Of course, not all who were qualified for pensions applied, and not all who applied were accepted.

5. Claims against one of the thirteen original states for losses incurred during the Revolutionary War.

6. Colonial government and Revolutionary War records, many of which were copied by the federal government to replace and reconstruct records destroyed in an 1805 fire in the War Department and in the 1814 British burning of the Capitol and their looting of the War and Treasury Departments, which held the Revolutionary War records.

7. Indian records, especially in Oklahoma, pertaining to the Five Civilized Tribes. Contact the Oklahoma Historical Society or the University of Oklahoma Western History Collection about their holdings, which include copies of National Archives records. See pages 165–167 for more information on Native American records.

8. Tax rolls, from county or state assessments.

9. State militia rolls and records.

10. Cattle brand registers (sometimes in county courthouses).

11. In the South, Confederate records, both civil and military. Many of these records were copied by the federal government in their attempt to identify all those who were guilty of treason against the United States by their participation in and support of the Confederate cause, 1861–65. **The National Archives has microfilmed the *Compiled Service Records of Confederate Soldiers*, the consolidated index to those records, and the *Unfiled Papers of Civil War Soldiers*.**

Microfilm Source

12. Vital statistics registry, primarily birth and death records at the state level. Birth and death certificates are usually available at the Department of Public Health or Bureau of Vital Statistics. (Marriage, birth, and death records are often available in the counties, but the oldest records may be available only at the state archives.) To locate these records, consult the section on vital records earlier in this chapter, on pages 120–121.

13. County records that have been transferred to or copied by the state archives. If these are pre–Civil War records, they may include records of slave emancipations and free blacks.

14. Family and business papers that may be housed at state or university archives. Ask about an index or guide to the manuscript holdings. An index may show your ancestor's name. A guide may show papers or records from his or her hometown, school, church, employer, or an organization to which he or she belonged.

15. Miscellaneous records: memorials and petitions to the state legislature, election records, charters granted by the state, interments in the state cemetery, notary public files, bonds and oaths of office. For the former Confederate States (except Tennessee), amnesty applications and oaths, and the 1867 voter lists.

16. State copies of federal census records and the 1850–1880 agriculture, industry, mortality, and social statistics census schedules (the supplemental schedules).

17. Pay warrants issued by the state.

18. Voter registrations, poll tax records.

19. Records of state law enforcement, public safety, residential or correctional institutions.

20. Vehicle registrations and driver's licenses. States may not keep these vehicle records indefinitely. Some do not keep the license records more than two or three years after the license holder's death. In this case, they may also reassign the driver's license number.

21. Other state agencies, such as state hospitals, departments of education, state courts.

THINGS TO DO NOW

1. Consult one of the vital records information sources on pages 120–121 and list for your ancestral states the dates when vital registration began. Determine which ancestors (or their children or siblings) lived in these states and may have birth and/or death certificates on file.

2. Begin collecting the birth and death certificates for as many ancestors and their siblings as are feasible for your budget and your research.

3. Visit a research facility or Family History Center to learn whether marriage, probate, and land records are available on microfilm for your ancestor's county/counties. Begin to study these three record groups as they pertain to your focus ancestor and pertinent nuclear families.

4. Identify a guide to research on your ancestral state(s); if possible, get a copy.

Idea Generator

TWELVE

Beyond the Family: Local Sources

See Also

See page 143 for more information on rental and lending libraries.

R egardless of when you delve into local sources, you will find that many records are available on microfilm at research libraries and from various rental and lending libraries. Some are online in the form of abstracts, but at this writing, online use of local and county records is limited.

This chapter concentrates on sources created in ancestral localities: cemeteries, newspapers, church and school records, and others. A visit to the local and county research area may give you valuable information available only on location.

CEMETERIES

Tombstones may supply dates, birthplaces, husbands' and wives' names, maiden names, parents' names, and evidence of children who died young, fraternal membership, or military service. Try to locate and photograph the tombstones for as many ancestors as possible. Relatives were often buried in a family plot, so locating one ancestor's tombstone may lead you to others.

To save time, take along a relative who knows where family graves are. Larger cemeteries often have files or maps in their offices to help you find a particular stone or plot. Without such aids, your alternative is to walk up and down the rows reading each stone. You may have to check both sides of the stones, for in older cemeteries, tombstones in the same row may face different directions.

Timesaver

When you find a family stone, copy the information exactly and completely. A photograph provides additional proof of its inscription. If you are not sure of a letter or number, you may need to make a rubbing of it. To do this, put a piece of paper over the stone and rub the paper with a crayon. Then study the rubbing.

Be sure to title your page of notes with the name and location of the cemetery and the date you were there. If the cemetery is large or the stone is difficult to locate, sketch a map of its location for future reference.

Locating Cemeteries

If you do not know where your ancestor is buried, consult older family members, older residents of the area, local funeral home files, death certificates and obituaries of ancestors, books of tombstone transcriptions for the county, and published histories of the area that might contain cemetery listings. If you can pinpoint the ancestor's residence or community, consult a county map for cemeteries nearby. Ask whether the ancestor's church had an adjacent cemetery. If none of these narrows the search, you may have to visit a number of cemeteries in the area.

If you have the name of an ancestral cemetery but do not know its location, what are your options?

1. Ask funeral directors in the county.
2. Get a county map that shows cemeteries. Detailed county maps, such as those from state highway departments, show most of the known cemeteries. If your map does not name them, ask residents or funeral directors in the county for the names. Do they know of others that are not shown on the map?
3. If someone has published a book of tombstone inscriptions for the county, use the descriptions in the book to locate the cemeteries on your county map. Are there cemeteries on or near the county line? Perhaps your ancestral cemetery is just over the line in a neighboring county.
4. If you visit cemeteries in the county, label them on your map as you go.
5. Visit the Web site at <http://mapping.usgs.gov/www/gnis/gnisform.html> or <http://www-nmd.usgs.gov/www/gnis/gnisform.html>. Search using the state, county, and cemetery name. If you get no results, try using *church* instead of *cemetery*, or simply the name alone. Zoom in as far as possible and compare your county or road map with the map on the screen to pinpoint the cemetery location.
6. At a research library, consult the *Omni Gazetteer of the United States of America*, Frank R. Abate, editor, by state and cemetery name, for the county in which the cemetery lies and the longitude and latitude coordinates.

Sources

Internet Source

Caution

In cemetery research, we must remember that

- it is not always possible to find ancestral cemeteries
- not all family members were buried in the same plot or the same cemetery
- not all graves received tombstones
- not all tombstones have survived to the present
- not all tombstone inscriptions remain legible
- tombstones themselves may contain errors, made either by the stonecutter or the family member who furnished the information

Warning

Case Study

CEMETERY RESEARCH: AN EXAMPLE

The search for our great-great-grandfather Harrison's tombstone took my sister and me to many cemeteries and eventually gave us the dates of his life, but the search had two other valuable, unexpected payoffs. The first concerned our Orgain ancestors. Because Harrison had married an Orgain daughter, the Orgain parents should have been in the same area but had not been found in records.

In Williamson County, Texas, where the Harrisons lived, we searched all the cemeteries we could reach, as listed on the county map from the highway department, and did not find Harrison's stone. Did he have one? We tried the Hutto City Cemetery a second time without success. As we stood at the entrance debating what to do next, my brother-in-law squinted ahead, thinking he saw tombstones on a little rise in the distance. I was sure he was seeing a mirage, the kind you see when you close your eyes and see nothing but weeds after you have been weeding the garden all day. Nevertheless, we decided to follow his hunch.

A dirt road led us somehow to the gate of a tiny old and overgrown cemetery. We split up to speed the search. Soon my sister called out, "Hey, have you ever heard of a Reverend Sterling Orgain?" Shrieking with delight, I plunged through the waist to shoulder-high weeds toward her voice. There it was—a double stone for Reverend Sterling Orgain and Mary E. Orgain, his wife, complete with dates! When I calmed down, I had presence of mind enough to (1) copy and photograph the stone and copy other stones around it, which turned out to be those of relatives, and (2) map the little place. Later I took my eighty-year-old great-uncle to see what no one else in the family had known existed, in a place unknown to all of us.

We were still seeking the Harrison tombstone but felt better about visiting so many cemeteries. We returned for a second search at the tiny town where the Harrisons had lived. The feed store was the only business open that Saturday, so we stopped and asked where we might find a local historian who could give us information about other cemeteries in the area.

The feed store man pointed to a house within view and said that the couple who lived there had been in town forever. We knocked on their door and explained our mission. Mrs. Richardson invited us in and began asking questions. Where are you from? Oh, one of you now lives in the county? Has your family ever lived here? Oh, your grandparents once lived in Georgetown? We used to live there too. Who are your grandparents?

When we told them, their faces took on looks of great astonishment. Mr. Richardson grinned, "I used to date your grandmother when your granddaddy was courting her sister." And Mrs. Richardson added, "And I was her maid of honor in their wedding!" What a visit we had!

Before we could get back to the community to search again for the Harrison tombstone, that dear couple went to the city cemetery and found our stone, complete with dates. We had overlooked it because it was facing the opposite direction from all the others around it. The couple copied it and drew us a sketch of where to find it when we did return.

With renewed energy, I looked next for tombstones of Harrison's parents. With their names and the 1850 census entry showing their residence in Victoria, Texas, I visited the cemetery there. In a family plot was the mother's stone, naming her birthplace—Nottoway County, Virginia. That piece of information led to nearly two centuries of Bland ancestors in Virginia. These early experiences made me a firm believer in the value of cemetery research.

Published Cemetery Records

Fortunately for genealogists, many tombstone inscriptions have been copied, published, and placed in libraries, not only in the community where the cemetery is located but around the country. More and more of these transcriptions are available online, especially on Web sites of the counties or in special cemetery databases. If you find a book, periodical, or Web site that includes transcriptions of your ancestors' tombstones, remember that such resources may contain human error. If possible, get photographs of the stones to confirm the information.

Another problem with printed transcriptions is that many are published in alphabetical order. Ancestors were not buried in alphabetical order but in family plots or groups, including relatives with different surnames. When you visit cemeteries, record the cluster of stones in the same plot with or in the vicinity of your ancestor. Especially in small or rural cemeteries, become familiar with names on other tombstones; many were neighbors and friends of your ancestor.

See Also

See page 139 for a discussion of the *Periodical Source Index*, which can help you identify published tombstone inscriptions for your county.

NEWSPAPERS

Some of the most entertaining historical and genealogical information comes from gossip columns, social and personal news, advertisements, and editorials of local newspapers.

The editor of the *Bolivar (Tennessee) Bulletin*, supplied almost everything the family knows about Alfred Coleman. "We notice that A.S. Coleman with a good force has been planting young shade trees in and around the public square this week. . . . We hope Alf will live long to enjoy the fruits of his labor and the thanks of fellow citizens" (13 March 1874).

Other issues told that this bachelor was a busy carpenter, a volunteer firefighter, a cook at all the barbecues, a volunteer on civic committees, an officer in the Odd Fellows Lodge, a member of the Presbyterian church and the Sons of Temperance, and a "sterling" Democrat. Then the editor announced in February 1882 that "Alf Coleman has started for Texas with his celebrated Gate Hinge. Success and safety to him." The 1900 census revealed his presence in

Dallas County, but I haven't learned the fate of his gate hinge.

In addition to news of church, school, lodge, club, political, and civic activities and ancestral participants, newspapers give some local birth, marriage, and death announcements. Even a mention in advertisements, commercial news, hotel guest lists, news of out-of-town visitors, real estate notices, and court case summaries places ancestors in a given place at a given time. **For genealogists, a simple mention of an ancestor can be an important clue.** Sometimes, it gives more specific information, such as a relative's name and relationship, an occupation, or an age.

Tip

The editors also seemed to feel a civic duty to express opinions about local issues. One of my favorites appeared in the *Bolivar Bulletin* on 13 June 1873, where the editor warned boys not to stand and smoke in front of the churches, day or night. If this practice did not stop, he would print names! Don't you wish he had done so!

Using Ancestral Newspapers

Before about 1920, more of our American ancestors lived in rural areas and small communities than in cities. At that time, the small-town weekly newspapers, which often served the entire county, usually contained about four pages. Of course, one page was usually full of advertisements (with genealogical clues); two were often national and state news, with additional ads; and one was local news and editorials. Legal notices, local politics, and news from surrounding communities were spliced in among ads and local news. Sometimes the back page also included serialized fiction and poetry. By examining a few issues of your ancestral newspaper, you can tell where the editor usually placed local items. If you are looking for a specific item, such as a death notice, you may save time by turning directly to the local section. The newspapers are often not indexed, so you need to read or scan each issue.

Citing Sources

When taking notes from these papers, record the name of the paper, the date of the issue, the page number, and where you can find the paper again should the need arise. Most often, we access newspapers on microfilm. If you are fortunate enough to read the originals, handle them with great care, as they become brittle with age.

The parts of ancestral newspapers most likely to be indexed, abstracted, and published are the obituaries and marriage notices. However, some enterprising genealogists have abstracted years of entire issues. This is one kind of book to look for when you go to research libraries. If you find an ancestor's name, try to look at a copy of the actual issue

- to check the abstract for accuracy and completeness
- to see the advertisements or other small notices that often are not abstracted
- to read the rest of the issue and others on the same roll of film for other information about the community, such as the weather, diseases and epidemics, and special events—especially if your ancestor was living there (rather than visiting)

Newspaper Indexes

Microfilm indexes exist for the *Baltimore Sun* and the *Evening Sun* (1819–1951), *The New York Times Tribune* (1875–1906), and the *Washington Star-News* (1894–1973). Also found in large public or university libraries are published indexes for *The New York Times* and the *Times* of London. *The New York Times* published in 1970 and 1980 two volumes of indexes to their obituaries covering the years 1858–1978. Various state archives or state historical societies have indexing projects for their own state newspapers. Contact the individual institution for information.

Two additional publications of value are
- Falk, Byron A., and Valerie R. Falk, comp. *Personal Name Index to "The New York Times Index," 1851–1974*. 22 vols. Succasunna, N.J.: Roxbury Data Interface, 1976.
- Milner, Anita Cheek. *Newspaper Indexes: A Location and Subject Guide for Researchers*. 3 vols. Metuchen, N.J.: Scarecrow Press, 1977–1982.

For More Info

Finding Ancestral Newspapers

Sometimes original or microfilmed newspapers are housed at the newspaper office, the local public library, or the county courthouse. State archives or libraries, historical society libraries, and university libraries often have original and/or microfilm copies for the state or the immediate area. Contact such institutions in your research area for a list or catalog of their holdings. Some provide interlibrary loan of microfilm.

If you have a specific newspaper title and know the years you would like to read, but do not know where the microfilm is housed, ask the interlibrary loan librarian at your local public library to try to get the film for you. The librarian will know how to handle the details.

The newspapers with online text or indexes are usually those from the mid-1980s forward. However, you may find information about ancestral newspapers online. **The United States Newspaper Program site at <http://www.neh.gov/projects/usnp.html> can link you to the Web sites in each state related to the newspaper project.** Some of these sites list their newspaper holdings or inform you of available indexes or abstracts.

Internet Source

If you do not know specific titles and extant issues, you can use union catalogs or United States Newspaper Program Web sites to find this information. Many libraries and state archives (or historical societies) have such union lists for their state. Many libraries have one or more of the following references for identifying and finding newspapers. Listing newspapers by state and town, the first two guides give dates of issues known to exist and where researchers could find them at the time the union list was published.

1. *American Newspapers, 1821–1936: A Union List of Files Available in the United States and Canada*. Winifred Gregory, ed. New York: H.W. Wilson, 1937, reprint by Kraus Reprint Corporation, New York, 1967.
2. *A Check List of American Eighteenth Century Newspapers in the Library of Congress*. John Van Ness Ingram, comp. Washington, D.C.: Government Printing Office, 1912.

3. *Newspapers in Microform.* 2 vols. Washington, D.C.: Library of Congress, 1984.
4. *Union List of Serials in the Libraries of the United States and Canada.* Edna Brown Titus, ed. New York: H.W. Wilson Co., 1965. Lists thousands of periodical publications by state and city. Many of these circulated along with newspapers and are worth checking.
5. *United States Newspaper Program National Union List.* OCLC, 1993 or later edition.

If your ancestral community did not have a newspaper or none survives for the period when your ancestor lived there, you can sometimes get information from a newspaper from a neighboring town, the county seat, or the nearest city. Newspapers that served an entire county occasionally had news from other towns in the county. Newsworthy items could include marriage notices, school graduations, political rallies, or social events reported by a resident correspondent. When two communities vied with each other for status in the county, the correspondent from one sometimes tried to defend or "outclaim" the rival community. Descendants learn about the community from such reports.

City, denomination/religious, ethnic, and organization newspapers, likewise, sometimes printed reports from towns and individuals in the state or region. It may be valuable to investigate these newspapers that your ancestors may have read.

LOCAL SCHOOLS AND COLLEGES

A variety of sources in school and college libraries and archives may help you learn more about an ancestor's alma mater: the yearbook, newspaper, or literary magazine; annual catalogs and bulletins; a school history or scrapbook of clippings; graduation programs; departmental records; and faculty, student, and alumni lists.

The federal privacy law of 1974 has restricted our access to academic transcripts. Usually, only the student (or former student) can request these records. If you are interested in transcripts as a part of the family history and your older relatives agree, consider requesting the copies while these former students are living.

The handling of records of deceased students, especially one's ancestors, is not clear in the law. Some schools will not release records of deceased students without a court order, which is expensive. One college sent my great-grandmother's transcript without questions or delay. Another university refused to send my deceased grandfather's record without his signature! They finally released the transcript when my grandmother, as executor of his estate, although no longer able to sign her own name, made her feeble mark on a request as witnessed by a third relative who had power of attorney over her affairs. Contact the school of interest to learn their policy.

The following are additional sources of education information about ancestors:

Sources

- Local newspaper stories about schools, teachers, sports, graduation, contests, school-sponsored programs and activities.
- Obituaries of the ancestor.
- History of city, county, school, or college.
- Student or alumni lists published in histories or periodicals.
- Family letters, diaries, scrapbooks, mementos.
- Interviews with older relatives and family friends.
- Censuses of 1850 and later asked if children attended school during the year and whether each adult could read and write.
- Censuses of 1890 and later recorded whether each individual could speak English.
- Wills, estate settlements, or guardian accounts sometimes mention tuition and schooling for the children.
- Wills, deeds, and other documents show whether the participants could sign their own names or had to sign with their marks. (Of course, a change over time from a person's signing his name to making his mark could suggest infirmity or disability rather than a lack of schooling.)

LOCAL CHURCHES AND RELIGIOUS ORGANIZATIONS

Local religious organizations sometimes have records that give genealogists dates for births or baptisms, confirmations, marriages, deaths, burials, and transfers in or out; names of parents or children; and minutes of the governing body. The quantity and the genealogical quality of these records vary from organization to organization.

Catholic churches often have remarkable records. Many ancestral Episcopalian/Anglican and Lutheran churches also have fairly comprehensive information. Other Protestant and Jewish congregations in towns and cities have kept their early records or have given them to an archive. The genealogist's greatest problem is the rural churches, many of which are no longer active congregations.

Finding Local Church Records

If you identify an existing church that your ancestral family attended, ask the pastor, secretary, a lay leader, or an officer in the church whether records exist from the ancestral period and where you might find them. Many individual churches simply store or discard records as they choose or as the clergy chooses. Other congregations have an ex officio historian who keeps the old record books. Some store their files in the church office or in a bank vault. Small or rural Methodist, Baptist, and Presbyterian congregations who had circuit rider preachers may have no records beyond the preachers' registers, which the families or descendants may or may not have saved.

Many sources of church records are available, even if you do not know the specific ancestral denomination or congregation. Consider these options:

1. Family tradition or papers, to find a denomination or church name.
2. The ancestral church or a neighboring church of the same denomination. Some hold records of disbanded sister churches.

Sources

3. Local histories, newspapers, historians, or longtime church members in the ancestral community, to find information about local church history and records. Which churches existed when your ancestors were living there?

4. Area families who were once leaders of an ancestral congregation, especially a disbanded one.

5. Local museums, libraries, and archives in the ancestral county.

6. Denominational newspapers, sometimes on microfilm, sometimes at a denominational archive or university library.

7. State or regional denomination offices, such as a diocese office for older Catholic or Episcopalian records or a conference office for Methodist records. Some maintain archives, including records of disbanded congregations.

8. Denominational college libraries and archives near the ancestral community.

9. Public or university libraries in the ancestral area, to find special collections or published church records; consult library catalogs under "[state name]-church records."

10. State historical society collections, state archives, state libraries. Ask in your research area.

11. Genealogical and historical periodicals, to find published church records and tombstone inscriptions from church graveyards.

12. Catalogs of the Family History Library.

13. *National Union Catalog of Manuscript Collections* [NUCMC]. Washington, D.C.: Library of Congress, 1994. See page *xl* under "Religion" for repositories reporting church records in their collections between 1975 and 1993. See the post-1993 updates at university or large public libraries in electronic format, or search NUCMC online at <http://lcweb.loc.gov/coll/nucmc>.

14. *A Survey of American Church Records*. E. Kay Kirkham. 4th ed. Logan, Utah: Everton Publishers, 1978.

15. *The Genealogist's Companion & Sourcebook*, chapter six.

16. Works Progress Administration inventories of church records or other such inventories, found in libraries and archives.

17. *Directory of Archives and Manuscript Repositories in the United States*. 2d ed. Phoenix, Ariz.: Oryx Press, 1988.

18. *A Guide to Archives and Manuscripts in the United States*. Philip M. Hamer, ed. New Haven, Conn.: Yale University Press, 1961.

19. *The Vital Record Compendium*. John D. Stemmons and E. Diane Stemmons, comp. Logan, Utah: Everton Publishers, 1979.

Quakers

Many U.S. genealogists have seventeenth- to nineteenth-century ancestors who were members of the Religious Society of Friends, or Quakers. Since these ancestors did not believe in rituals, they did not have weddings, baptisms, funerals, or tombstones. They did not enter military service or leave personal and financial records. Yet, it is possible to find them in census records and sometimes in tax, land, probate, and court records in county courthouses.

Because local congregations or "meetings" were required to keep detailed records, genealogists have a wealth of records to search for vital statistics and migrations of Quaker ancestors. The best source of such information is the records of the monthly meetings, which list births, marriages, deaths, transfers, committee reports, infractions of the rules, and members "disowned" for (1) marrying a non-Quaker (marrying "out of unity") or (2) being married by a civil servant or minister of another denomination (marrying "contrary to discipline").

Some records of monthly meetings in North Carolina, Pennsylvania, Virginia, and Ohio have been published: *Encyclopedia of American Quaker Genealogy*, by William Wade Hinshaw (Baltimore: Genealogical Publishing Company, 1969–1977). These volumes are available at many genealogy libraries. The Friends Historical Library at Swarthmore College, Swarthmore, Pennsylvania, has the largest collection of Quaker records. For a thorough discussion of searching for Quaker ancestors, see *Our Quaker Ancestors: Finding Them in Quaker Records*, by Ellen T. and David A. Berry (Baltimore: Genealogical Publishing Company, 1987).

The most unusual aspect of Quaker meeting records is their notation of dates. Until 1752, Britain and the American colonies officially used the old Julian calendar, under which each new year began on March 25. Under this Old Style calendar, March was the first month; April, the second, and so forth. The Latin names of the months September, October, November, and December corresponded to their places in the year as the seventh, eighth, ninth, and tenth months, respectively. Because the names of the other months had pagan origins, the Quakers chose to substitute numbers for the names of the months in their records. They usually listed the day, then the month, then the year, as much of the world still does, but in their own style: "12 da 5 mo," or twelfth day of the fifth month, which was July under the Julian calendar but is May under the New Style Gregorian calendar. When only the number of the month is given, you cannot know which name it stands for until you know which calendar was in use.

See Also

See chapter fifteen, pages 190–191, for more on the calendars.

One clerk copied a document into a county will book and recorded the date in Quaker style: ninth day of the eighth month, October, in 1743. His shorthand for October was "8br," as shown here: "Eed & Exd 8br: 9th: p[er] me" meaning "Entered & Examined October 9th by me."

LOCAL HISTORIANS AND ELDERS OF THE COMMUNITY

Cemetery research and travels introduced me to the value of local historians and the elders of any community. Early in my genealogy years, in a small Tennessee town, I spent hours in the private library of a local historian with a sizable collection of letters, diaries, and other papers from local families. He let me read and make notes from these, as they pertained to my family.

One day, in the same town, I walked to the Presbyterian church where my great-grandmother was christened and where her mother was a charter member. As I studied the facade, the door opened, and an elderly lady emerged from the sanctuary where she had been "straightening up." When I introduced myself and told her why I was interested in the church, she invited me in. The most exciting part of the visit was her letting me play the little hundred-year-old pipe organ. She sat at the piano and by ear and from memory played with me any hymn that I started. Not only was it fun to play this antique instrument, but this was the same organ that my great-grandmother, whom I never met, had heard each Sunday. And this was the same sanctuary where she and her parents had worshiped together. Being on ancestral ground was a new and exciting experience.

Experiences like these are not rare. Old-timers are everywhere, happy to share their communities with those of us who are sincere in wanting to know about them. All it takes is asking and listening.

LOCAL LIBRARIES

Fortunately, many public libraries set aside a section or room for a genealogy collection. They may house published histories of counties, area families, schools, and churches. Some maintain vertical files in which local families or their descendants can place copies of their Bible records, family papers, newspaper clippings, and family history charts for other researchers to use.

Of course, some public libraries have extensive genealogy collections that include microfilm, microfiche, books, periodicals, and CD-ROMs. These publications may include reference materials, indexes, microfilmed county records, and National Archives microfilm, as well as compiled abstracts of tombstone inscriptions, newspapers, and various courthouse records. Genealogists certainly appreciate, use, and benefit from the published efforts of other genealogists. However, we still need to see the original records (or microfilm or photocopies) pertaining to our ancestors.

Public and university libraries may have collections of local newspapers, local archives and special collections of manuscripts—diaries, letters, family and business papers, store ledger books, and other items that show ancestors in a cluster of friends and associates. The history sections of university libraries can be especially beneficial to genealogists.

When you visit ancestral hometowns and counties, include a stop at the local public library. You may be pleasantly surprised at what you can accomplish there, and you may be able to contribute to their collection. **To make the most efficient use of your research time, make a list of the sources you want to use, for which ancestors, and for what information.** Anything else you find is a bonus. Call ahead for hours and information on holdings.

Most libraries cannot handle genealogical research by correspondence. In most, the staff simply cannot take the time to answer the multitude of requests they would receive if they offered such a service. Besides, the staff is not always

Timesaver

trained in genealogical research. However, they may agree to send you a copy of a specific item or file that you know they have.

Finding Libraries for Research

1. A good way to learn about libraries near you or in your research locale is to consult the *American Library Directory* in your own public library. The directory describes libraries, state by state, that submitted information, including whether they have a genealogy or local history collection. The directory may also include a genealogical or historical society library in your area. If your ancestral community's library is listed, you can write or telephone the staff with questions about their facility.

2. On the Internet, go to a site for your county or your ancestral county and (a) read about research facilities or (b) post a query about research facilities in the area. A major Web site for such county Web pages is <http://www.usgenweb.org>.

3. Some libraries have Web sites of their own to describe their services, holdings, and special collections. In a search engine such as AltaVista or Yahoo!, from the reference list, choose "libraries." When the different categories of libraries appear on a list, choose "public libraries" and then the state where your research centers. By studying a map of your ancestral state, you can determine the towns or cities nearest your ancestral community. If your community of interest is not listed, find a regional library or public library nearby. Two addresses for such a search are <http://www.altavista.com/> (select "library and resources," "reference") and <http://dir.yahoo.com/reference/libraries>.

Library/Archive Source

Finding Published Materials About Your Research Locale

A library's catalog can tell you what published materials the facility has on your research county. The genealogical materials are often cross-referenced: under (1) the *subject*, e.g., cemeteries, census, deeds, genealogy, history, indexes, inventory of church archives, inventory of county records, archives, manuscripts, immigration, microfilm holdings, militia, tax lists, naturalization, passenger lists, wills, newspapers, etc.; and (2) the *name* of the city, county, state, family, or country to which they pertain.

If you are new to Iowa research and materials, for example, looking at library catalogs online for public libraries in Iowa can tell you about published materials that could be useful in Iowa genealogy—books you did not know about, books you may want to study when you visit the area, books you may be able to borrow on interlibrary loan, or books you may be able to purchase for your personal or local library. In this way, browsing in library catalogs can give you further ideas for your research.

Many libraries do not have their microprint materials, periodicals, or family histories in the computer catalog. However, if you plan to visit the library, ask about these holdings.

Genealogical and historical periodicals have published many county record abstracts, biographical sketches, business records, family Bible entries, tombstone inscriptions, and the like. One of the most comprehensive indexes to these publications is PERSI (*Periodical Source Index*), a product of the Allen County

Public Library in Fort Wayne, Indiana. You can use it in book form in many genealogy libraries or on CD-ROM from Ancestry (also in many libraries). If you are a subscriber to Ancestry.com, you have access to PERSI online. Search by county and state, or surname, to learn about published materials that might help your search. If your local library does not carry the periodical where the article appears, you can get a copy of the article from the Allen County Public Library, 900 Webster St. or P.O. Box 2270, Fort Wayne, IN 46801-2270. Phone: (219) 424-7241.

Finding Library Catalogs

Sources

You can look at many library catalogs online. Even if your ancestral community's library catalog is not online, one in the county or region may be.

1. The Library of Congress has an extensive catalog of family histories and other materials of use to genealogists. You can access it at <http://catalog.loc.gov>. This catalog will help you know what has been published on the subject of your interest.

2. From the Library of Congress Web site, you can search other libraries' catalogs, mostly of state and university libraries, at <http://lcweb.loc.gov/z3 950/>.

3. Through AltaVista or Yahoo!, for example, you can go to library Web sites as described in "Finding Libraries for Research" above. On the Web page of the individual library, check whether its catalog is online.

4. Look at the catalog for the Family History Library in Salt Lake City on the Web site at <http://www.familysearch.org/Search/searchcatalog.asp>. You can conduct a search on a surname or on a place, such as your research county. This catalog contains both books and microprint materials. The books are not available for rent unless they have a microfilm number. The microprint collection is available through local Family History Centers.

OTHER LOCAL SOURCES

Some town and city governments maintain old tax records, vital registrations, minutes of the governing body, and other records that could help place an ancestor in that place at a given time within the context of certain activities. Many local communities have a town or county museum, which sometimes houses artifacts, documents, and early photographs of somebody's ancestors—maybe yours. Local funeral homes may have files dating to the early twentieth century that may yield information on your family members.

Important

Ordinarily, you have to visit the research locale to take advantage of these opportunities. Plan to go during the week, when government offices, businesses, schools, and libraries are open. Call in advance to ask about availability of records and the hours of operation. It is very disconcerting to arrive on Thursday morning for a two-day visit and discover the facility is closing at noon for two days to install new carpet.

CHECKLIST OF LOCAL SOURCES

In searching for your family history, you are the judge of what you want to accomplish and how extensive your search will be. You may decide simply to fill in your charts with basic vital statistics on most lines while you study only one at a time in depth.

Of the many local sources available to genealogists, perhaps only a few will give you information on a particular ancestor. You may find newspapers and tombstones that enlighten you on a dozen ancestors, church records for three or four others, and school records for only two. **It is unrealistic to expect to find information in all these sources for all your ancestors.**

Reminder

Some searchers gather only vital statistics for each ancestor and do not really collect family history. Likewise, by preference or necessity, others do not visit the local hometowns where so much information is often found. Consequently, these people may never try many of the available sources and will therefore miss out on fun, satisfaction, and information, for much of the local data is not available elsewhere.

The checklist presented here does not cover all possible sources but is intended as a summary of the most commonly available local sources in the community or county where ancestors lived.

1. Cemeteries (tombstones).
2. Funeral home files.
3. Newspaper files or microfilm copies in local, state, historical society, or university libraries or archives.
4. Local school records and yearbooks, school censuses, college records and publications.
5. Church registers, vestry books, and other religious archives.
6. Elders in the community: for their stories and memories and for directions to and descriptions of houses, buildings, and cemeteries.
7. Local historians or historical society.
8. Local genealogical library or public library with a genealogy and/or local history collection.
9. Local genealogists or genealogical society.
10. Published county or city history, especially one with biographical sketches. Goodspeed Brothers of Chicago and Nashville published a number of these as state histories with county by county biographies, mostly in the 1880s. Many of the county history and biography sections have been reprinted in recent years or microfilmed.
11. Papers of families or businesses of the ancestor's community on deposit in local, state, historical society, or university libraries or archives.
12. City vital statistics registry at the health department or registrar's office or duplicates at the state level.
13. City archives: tax rolls, law enforcement records, city censuses, etc.
14. County courthouse records. (See chapter eleven.)

RESEARCH TIPS

1. Index to Your Ancestors

As you plan your research, use the Alphabetical Ancestors Chart in Figure 12.2 and Appendix D. The chart becomes an index to your five-generation charts and/or family group sheets. A chart for each state in which you have ancestors, or each county if the ancestors are numerous, is a reference to help you research more efficiently and more thoroughly.

As you research your focus ancestors, you may find other names that ring a bell. Rather than copy a lot of information simply because it pertains to someone of the same surname as one of yours, refer to your chart. If your William Clark died in Missouri before 1840, why copy information about a William Clark born there in 1883 until you have a good reason? Especially for surnames that are common in the state's records, **it is valuable to have at your fingertips the information on your specific ancestors so that you don't spend time unnecessarily barking up the wrong tree.**

For More Info

Three versions of this chart are in *The Unpuzzling Your Past Workbook.*

Timesaver

Alphabetical Ancestors

Locality _____
County and/or State

Surname or Maiden Name	Given Name	Birth Year	Death Year	Residence	Dates of Residence	5-Gen. Chart #

Figure 12.2

2. If the Name's the Same

Numerous early American families had common English, Scottish, or other European surnames. Looking for these somewhere between Maine and Georgia will reveal many same-name families scattered over many counties. Consider these tips for successful research:

1. Focus on the known area where your ancestors lived.
2. Work back one generation at a time from the twentieth century.
3. When the genealogical waters get murky, gather and compare information about other same-name families at the same time and place to narrow the search for your particular family. "Same place" may mean the same county or several neighboring counties.

4. Research in original records to help distinguish your ancestor from others of the same name, using published sources as clues.

When researching a rather unusual surname or one not common in the state where your ancestors lived, you may benefit from collecting information on contemporaries of your ancestor who had the same surname in the same state. They may or may not be related to you, but getting the information when you find it gives you references for later study.

Especially if you find people of the same given name, surname, time period, and place as your ancestor, gather all the data you find. Certainly, not all the early-eighteenth-century Virginia records bearing the name Robert Carter pertain to the same man, but studying all available information can help the genealogist sort them out.

INTERLIBRARY LOAN

You may be able to obtain considerable information by renting or borrowing books and microfilm. Many public libraries offer interlibrary loan service to their local patrons at a nominal postage fee. If you provide accurate title, author, and publication information, including page numbers if applicable, your reference librarian can do the rest. If you do not know what is available from your research area, (1) see "Finding Published Materials About Your Research Locale" on page 139; (2) consult one of the lending libraries listed below; and/or (3) contact the state library, historical society, or university library in your research area for a listing of their interlibrary loan materials. Some state archives, state libraries, or historical societies make microfilm copies of county records, censuses, or newspapers available to researchers in their own state. Some lend microfilm to out-of-state genealogists.

Library/Archive Source

The following are some of the institutions that lend or rent genealogical materials:

1. Family History Library, 35 North West Temple St., Salt Lake City, UT 84150. Rental from this vast collection is handled through numerous Family History Centers. Look in your telephone directory under Church of Jesus Christ of Latter-day Saints for a center in your area, or consult the Web site at <http://www.familysearch.org> for Family History Centers and to search the catalog. The catalog includes National Archives microfilm, censuses, county histories and records, church and cemetery records, family histories, and much more.

2. Genealogical Center Library, P.O. Box 71343, Marietta, GA 30007-1343. <http://homepages.rootsweb.com/~gencenlb/index.html>. E-mail: gencenlib@aol.com. An annual membership fee gives you access to their sizable collection of books, with the largest concentration being from states east of the Mississippi River.

3. National Archives Microfilm Rental Program, P.O. Box 30, Annapolis Junction, MD 20701-0030. Phone: (301) 604-3699. This private company

rents federal population census schedules and selected American Revolutionary War records. For more information, consult the Web site at <http://www.archives.gov/publications/microfilm_catalogs/how_to_rent_microfilm.html>. You can rent from them yourself or, perhaps, through your local public library.

4. National Genealogical Society, 4527 Seventeenth St. North, Arlington, VA 22207-2399. Members may borrow selected books from the society library. Inquire for current catalog price. To see the online library catalog (not all available for loan), visit the Web site at <http://www.ngsgenealogy.org/libprecat.htm>.

5. New England Historic Genealogical Society, 101 Newbury St., Boston, MA 02116. Members may borrow selected materials from the society's large library, which is especially strong in New England materials. View their circulating holdings at <http://www.newenglandancestors.org/researchsection/lendable.asp>. From the home page, select "research resources" for other catalog options.

6. Mid-Continent Public Library, Spring and Highway 24, Independence, MO 64050. Interlibrary loan catalog available. Their full library catalog is online at <http://opac.mcpl.lib.mo.us/>; log in as a guest if you do not have their library card. Their main Web site address is <http://www.mcpl.lib.mo.us>.

THINGS TO DO NOW

Idea Generator

1. Identify from family sources the cemeteries where your family members are buried. For how many ancestors on your five-generation chart can you identify a burial place? Record the name and location of each cemetery.
2. For your focus ancestor's county (or counties) of residence, get a highway department map for cemeteries, communities, roads, watercourses, etc.
3. Look in the Gregory *American Newspapers, 1821–1936: A Union List of Files Available in the United States and Canada* and/or *Newspapers in Microform* or the U.S. Newspaper Program Web site to identify newspapers in your ancestral location(s) and time period(s). Keep this reference list handy. If feasible now, request at least one roll of microfilm on interlibrary loan.
4. Create a list (with addresses and phone numbers) of research facilities near your residence and a list for those near your focus ancestor's residence(s).
5. List any high schools and colleges identified so far that your forebears attended. Write or call at least one institution for their policies and procedures so that you can begin the process of getting a transcript for at least one ancestor.
6. Note on your family group sheets any known religious affiliations for your ancestors. If you know the names of specific congregations, note these as well. Try to locate church or congregational records for at least

one of these bodies for the time period your ancestors were there.

7. Visit the NUCMC Web site and enter your primary research county name or surnames.

8. Start a reference folder or divisions in your focus ancestor's notebook to keep the kinds of materials you gather in numbers 1–7.

THIRTEEN

Beyond the Family: Additional Federal Sources

R esearchers usually benefit from using records at all the jurisdictional levels. At the federal level, the National Archives is the answer to finding most of the federal records genealogists use.

THE NATIONAL ARCHIVES

The National Archives and Records Administration is the home of millions of records of individuals and their dealings with the U.S. government. Fortunately for researchers, thousands of these records are available on microfilm, and many have been indexed. Even more are available for study at the National Archives in Washington, DC.

To learn more about the National Archives, its services and holdings, visit its Web site at <http://www.archives.gov>. To search the microfilm catalogs specifically or to learn about new microfilm, go to <http://www.archives.gov/research_room/genealogy/index.html> and scroll to "new microfilm publications." For the catalogs, click 'Microform catalogs and finding aids." Or click "Genealogical and biographical research," and select the item(s) for new microfilm publications or learn about many other National Archives resources."

Two pamphlets helpful in learning about the National Archives' holdings and services are free upon request from the National Archives, Washington, DC 20408 or from the sales office at (800) 234-8861:

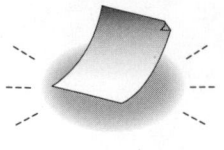

Printed Source

- *Using Records in the National Archives for Genealogical Research.* General Information Leaflet #5.
- *Military Service Records in the National Archives.* General Information Leaflet #7.

Much more comprehensive surveys of the records in the National Archives and its branches are these books, available from the National Archives and genealogy booksellers and in research libraries:

Guide to Federal Records in the National Archives of the United States. 3 vols. Washington, D.C.: National Archives and Records Administration, 1996.

Guide to Genealogical Research in the National Archives. Washington, D.C.: National Archives Trust Fund Board, 1985.

Microfilm Resources for Research: A Comprehensive Catalog. Rev. Washington, D.C.: National Archives and Records Administration, 2000 or later edition.

Scattered throughout the country are branches of the National Archives that hold regional records and microfilm copies of some records stored in Washington.

- Write to or call the one in your research locale to learn what they have that may help you in your search.
- Visit the Web site at <http://www.archives.gov/facilities/index.html>.
- Look at *The Archives: A Guide to the National Archives Field Branches.* Loretto Dennis Szucs and Sandra Hargreaves Luebking. Salt Lake City: Ancestry, 1988.

See Also

See Appendix B for locations.

National Archives records used in genealogy are numerous. In addition to census records, these include military, land, immigration, naturalization, passport, and Native American records; materials of special interest to African Americans; and selected Congressional files. **Microfilmed records are available for use nationwide at research libraries—public, private, society, and university.** You can also rent the microfilm from Family History Centers.

Microfilm Source

MILITARY RECORDS

Servicemen and women, veterans, and the bureaucracy have generated many records pertaining to military and naval service since the Revolutionary War (1775–1783). Of primary interest to genealogists are records in two basic categories: service records and pension records. These military records in the National Archives cover

- regular Army, Navy, and Marine Corps personnel service records
- service records of volunteers
- pension applications and records
- bounty land warrant applications for land offered in return for service

Other service-related records include records of the service academies, National Archives card files on the tombstones of Union army servicemen, histories of many military units, audited accounts on claims of volunteers, and World War I draft registration cards.

To learn about the military records available on microfilm, consult *Military Service Records: A Select Catalog of National Archives Microfilm Publications* (Washington, D.C.: National Archives Trust Fund Board, 1985). To see this catalog online, go to <http://www.archives.gov/publications/microfilm_catal ogs/military/military_service_records.html>.

Did My Ancestor Serve in the Military?

After consulting family papers, relatives, tombstones, and obituaries about an ancestor's possible military service, consult the federal census records.

1. The 1840 census asked for names of those receiving pensions for Revolutionary service or military service after the Revolution. At that time, most of those receiving pensions were disabled (invalid) and/or indigent or widows of servicemen.
2. The special 1890 census of Union (Civil War) veterans and widows exists for (a) the District of Columbia, (b) states alphabetically from Louisiana through Wyoming, and (c) in fragments only, states alphabetically from California to Kentucky. Occasionally, a researcher finds a Confederate veteran mentioned. The microfilm is arranged by state, but the counties are not necessarily in alphabetical order. This census asked for the dates or length of service, rank(s) and unit(s), and information on wounds. Sometimes it included other items reported to the census taker.
3. The 1910 census asked whether a man was a Civil War veteran.
4. The 1930 census asked whether a person was a U.S. military or naval veteran and of which war or expedition.

Library/Archive Source

In books in research libraries, survey large groups of military names for ancestors. Examples of these books fall into these broad categories:

1. Abstracts and Transcriptions of Gravestones of Servicemen; Casualty Lists:

Confederate P.O.W.'s: Soldiers & Sailors Who Died in Federal Prisons & Military Hospitals in the North. Frances Ingmire and Carolyn Ericson. War Department, 1912. Reprint, Nacogdoches, Tex.: the compilers, 1984.

Known Military Dead During Mexican War, 1846–48. Clarence Stewart Peterson, comp. Baltimore: the compiler, 1957.

Soldiers of the American Revolution Buried in Illinois. Illinois State Genealogical Society. Springfield: The Society, 1976.

Soldiers of the War of 1812 Buried in Tennessee. Rev. ed. Mary Hardin McCown, comp. Johnson City, Tenn.: M.H. McCown, 1977.

2. Rosters and Biographical Compilations; Military History; Indexes:

American Militia in the Frontier Wars, 1790–1796. Murtie June Clark. Baltimore: Genealogical Publishing Co., 1990.

DAR Patriot Index. National Society, Daughters of the American Revolution. 3 vols. and supplements. Washington, D.C.: The Society, 1966–86.

An Index-Guide to the Southern Historical Society Papers, 1876–1959. James I. Robertson Jr., editor in chief. 2 vols. Millwood, N.Y.: Kraus International Publications, 1980. Indexes a massive collection of published Confederate archival material.

Summer Soldiers: A Survey & Index of Revolutionary War Courts-Martial. James C. Neagles. Salt Lake City: Ancestry, 1986.

3. County, State, Unit, or Ethnic Compilations, History:

Biographical Rosters of Florida's Confederate and Union Soldiers, 1861–1865. David W. Hartman, comp. 6 vols. Wilmington, N.C.: Broadfoot Publishing Co., 1995.

Connecticut's Black Soldiers, 1775–1783. David O. White. Chester, Conn.: Pequot Press, 1973.

The First Regiment of New York Volunteers. [Mexican War] Francis D. Clark. New York: Geo. S. Evans & Co., printers, 1882.

Tennessee Civil War Veterans Questionnaires. Gustavus W. Dyer and John Trotwood Moore, comp. 5 vols. Easley (now Greenville), S.C.: Southern Historical Press, 1985.

Published bibliographies and online library catalogs can help you identify more such books. A long bibliography appears in James C. Neagles's *U.S. Military Records: A Guide to Federal and State Sources.*

Other ways to find out whether an ancestor served are these:

- Consult the many published indexes to service records or pension applications in libraries nationwide.
- Look at the microfilmed records that are organized alphabetically for ease of searching.
- Consult the Civil War Soldiers and Sailors System in the National Park Service Web site at <http://www.itd.nps.gov/cwss>.

Service Records

Service records in the National Archives pertain to the Revolutionary War, soldiers under the U.S. Command from 1784 to 1811, the War of 1812–15, the Mexican War (1845–48), the Indian wars, the Civil War (1861–65), and the Spanish-American War (1898). Coast Guard records date from 1791 to 1919. Civil War files include many service records and pardon petitions of Confederate soldiers.

The National Personnel Records Center (NPRC), General Services Administration, 9700 Page Ave., St. Louis, MO 63132, houses records relating to more recent service, generally for civilian employees of the Coast Guard's predecessor services (1864–1919) and for those personnel who were discharged ("separated") after

- 1917 (Army officers)
- 1912 (Army enlisted personnel)
- 1947 (Air Force personnel)
- 1902 (Navy officers)
- 1885 (Navy enlisted personnel)
- 1895 (Marine Corps officers)
- 1928 (Coast Guard officers)
- 1914 (Coast Guard enlisted personnel)

Inquiries for information from these records require Standard Form 180, "Request Pertaining to Military Personnel Records." The files are not public;

Step By Step

they are restricted to members of the veteran's immediate family or the veterans themselves. Living veterans must give written consent to release their records. A 1973 fire destroyed many records of World War I service (even separation up to 1959) for army officers and enlisted personnel.

A first step in searching these military records is to examine the indexes to compiled service records. These indexes and large collections of service records are available on microfilm at the National Archives, its regional branches, and many research libraries and from the Family History Library, and the National Archives Microfilm Rental Program. (See pages 143–144.) Arranged alphabetically, they are available for the Revolution, the period 1784–1811, the War of 1812, the Indian wars (1815–1858), the Mexican War, the Civil War (separate indexes for Union and Confederate servicemen), and the Spanish-American War.

Many research libraries hold published indexes and compiled records based on National Archives or state archives records. These are examples:

Index to Volunteer Soldiers, 1784–1811. Virgil D. White, transcriber. Waynesboro, Tenn.: National Historical Publishing Co., 1987.

Index to Volunteer Soldiers in Indian Wars and Disturbances, 1815–1858. Virgil D. White, transcriber. 2 vols. Waynesboro, Tenn.: National Historical Publishing Co., 1994.

Muster Rolls of New York Provincial Troops: 1755–1764. Edward F. DeLancey, ed. 1892. Reprint, Bowie, Md.: Heritage Books, 1990.

Muster Rolls of the Soldiers of the War of 1812: Detached From the Militia of North Carolina in 1812 and 1814. 1851. Reprint, Baltimore: Genealogical Publishing Co., 1976.

Official Army Register of the Volunteer Force of the United States Army for 1861–1865. Washington, D.C.: Adjutant General's Office, 1865. Reprint, Gaithersburg, Md.: Ron R. Van Sickle Military Books, 1987.

Service Records of Confederate Enlisted Marines. Ralph W. Donnelly. Washington, D.C.: the author, 1979. Alphabetical abstracts.

Military service records contain information on when and where the person joined the military, served, and was discharged as well as engagements, capture, rank, promotions, etc. When you find that an ancestor did serve and was discharged at least seventy-five years ago, request a copy of the service records on NATF Form 86, "Order for Copies of Military Service Records" (formerly NATF Form 80). The forms are free on request from the National Archives, Washington, DC 20408 or through the National Archives web site at <http://www.archives.gov/global_pages/inquire_form.html>. Using either address, request the form and the quantity you need, and supply your mailing address.

To process a search and get a copy of these military records, you must provide identifying information, such as the serviceman's name, the war in which he served, the state from which he entered service, and if possible, his unit name and his file numbers or pension application numbers. Additional information

on getting copies of National Archives records is available at <http://www.archi
ves.gov/global_pages/inquire_form.html>.

Colonial military records are records of the original thirteen states, and many
are published. Some of the original states have records of audited accounts—
claims against the state by those who served in the Revolution or lost property
to the military during that war. Many states also have records of state troops
or home guard during the Civil War. The state archives or historical society
may have card or computer indexes to these records.

Military Pensions

Congress and some states authorized pensions to certain veterans of the Revolutionary War:

1. disability or invalid pensions to veterans whose disabilities were a result
   of service,
2. service pensions to those who had served for a specified time, especially
   if they were indigent, and
3. widows' pensions to widows whose husbands were killed in service or
   served for a specified time.

Qualified veterans could also apply for pensions for service in the War of 1812,
the Mexican War, the Indian wars, the Civil War, and the Spanish-American War
and for career service (regular Army or Navy).

Persons applying for military pensions had to prove their service; a widow
had to prove her husband's service. Thus, the records can contain valuable
genealogical information in addition to service history: vital statistics, family
relationships, parents' names, wife's maiden name, marriage information, or
children's names.

Microfilmed pension files, arranged alphabetically, are available for veterans
from the Revolutionary War, Mexican War, Indian wars, and Civil War (Union).
Confederate pension files are in the records of the eleven former Confederate
states and Kentucky, Missouri, and Oklahoma.

**Researchers can rent microfilmed pension applications and related files from
the National Archives Microfilm Rental Program (Revolutionary War only) or
the Family History Library.** The microfilm is also available in many research
libraries. Ledgers of payments made to pensioners between 1818 and 1872 are
on microfilm publication T718.

To determine whether an ancestor was a pensioner, consult such publications
as these:

Genealogical Abstracts of Revolutionary War Pension Files. Virgil D. White,
abstracter. Waynesboro, Tenn.: National Historical Publishing Co., 1990.
By the same abstracter and publisher: *Index to War of 1812 Pension Files*
(1989), *Index to Texas CSA Pension Files* (1989), and *Index to Indian Wars
Pension Files, 1892–1926* (1987).

Index to Confederate Pension Applications [Arkansas]. Desmond Walls Allen.
Conway, Ark.: Arkansas Research, 1991.

Index of Revolutionary War Pension Applications in the National Archives.

See Also

See page 125 for how to
get online information on
the various state archives
or go to <http://www
.cyndislist.com>.

Internet Source

Confederate pension information is online at
<http://www.archives.gov/
research_room/genealogy/
military/confederate_pen
sion_records.html>.

Microfilm Source

Washington, D.C. (now Arlington, Va.): National Genealogical Society, 1976.

List of Pensioners on the Roll January 1, 1883. Senate Executive Document 84 (47th Cong., 2nd Sess.) Serial 2078–2082. This pension roll is part of the United States Serial Set, a standard reference collection in libraries that are federal documents depositories.

Report From the Secretary of War . . . in Relation to the Pension Establishment of the United States. Senate Document 514 (23rd Cong., 1st Sess.) Serial 249–251. 3 vols. Reprint. Baltimore: Genealogical Publishing Company, 1968. Short title: *Pension Roll of 1835.* Also available in its original form at libraries that have the United States Serial Set in their government documents.

Virginia Revolutionary Pension Applications. John Frederick Dorman. 50 vols. with 4-vol. index. Fredericksburg, Va.: the author, 1958–1996. Abstracts of National Archives records.

Published bibliographies and online library catalogs can help you find more works dealing with pension records. Also, an ongoing volunteer project of the USGenWeb organization is the transcription of pension applications and related materials for all wars before 1900. You can get to the Web site in several ways, among them <http://www.usgenweb.org> and <http://www.rootsweb.com/~us genweb/pensions/>.

Once you identify an ancestor with a pension application, even if benefits were denied, get a copy of the file from the National Archives or state archives that holds the original file. For the National Archives, you will need NATF Form 85 "Order for Copies of Federal Pension Records" (formerly NATF Form 80). Use this form also to request copies of service-related bounty land warrant applications. (See the discussion on pages 154–156.)

Other Service-Related Records

Among the microfilmed records in the National Archives are cadet applications to the U.S. Military Academy, records of cadets at the Naval Academy, selected records relating to black servicemen between 1639 and 1886, Confederate casualty lists, records of Civil War prisons and prisoners of war, periodic reports from military post commanders, and compiled histories of Civil War units. National Archives publication M1845 contains records of headstones provided for deceased Union Civil War veterans between about 1879 and about 1903.

The Atlanta (East Point), Georgia, branch of the National Archives houses some 24 million World War I draft registration cards. A search for an individual name can be made for a ten-dollar fee if you supply the person's full name, town and county of residence in 1917, and date of birth. Sometimes it is the birth date we need. If that is your reason for wanting a copy of the ancestor's card, supply an approximate date and tell them it is an estimate.

Genealogists are interested in these cards because they give some physical description, the name of the next of kin, and birth date. We hope the registrant

Figure 13.1 World War I draft registration card, front and back

was telling the truth, as he had to affirm the information with his signature. Figure 13.1, above, is a 1918 registration card.

Contact the East Point branch for the search request form. (See Appendix B, page 241, for the address.) You can request a form via e-mail using center@atlanta.nara.gov. Be sure to provide your mailing address in your request. The records are also available on microfilm at some research libraries such as the Family History Library in Salt Lake City, Utah.

Many public and university libraries have histories and memoirs of Civil War units, especially companies organized in their local area. Although the older books are not usually indexed, they may mention an ancestor in recounting the unit's movements, battles, and daily life. To learn about publications on an ancestral unit, consult

- *Military Bibliography of the Civil War.* Charles E. Dornbusch, comp. 3 vols. New York: New York Public Library, 1971–1972
- the Library of Congress catalog at <http://catalog.loc.gov>
- a public library or state archives in the unit's home territory

By visiting the state archives Web sites or consulting published pamphlets and books about their holdings, you can learn whether the state had homes for indigent, disabled, or elderly Civil War or other soldiers and widows.

Reminder

For More Info

For a comprehensive discussion of research in federal land records, see E. Wade Hone's *Land & Property Research in the United States.*

Microfilm Source

FEDERAL LAND RECORDS

Land records in the National Archives pertain mostly to the thirty public land states created from the public domain—land acquired through purchase or in treaties following wars: (1) all states west of the Mississippi River except Texas and Hawaii, (2) states created from the old Northwest Territory (Illinois, Indiana, Michigan, Ohio, Wisconsin), and (3) the old Spanish, British, French, and Indian lands that became Florida, Alabama, and Mississippi. The land records, mostly 1800–1974, include entries from several types of grants. The ones containing the most genealogical information are usually bounty land warrant applications and homestead applications. However, many others give genealogists good clues.

Bounty land warrant applications in the National Archives are based on a man's wartime military service between 1775 and 1855. To encourage enlistment in the Revolutionary War, some of the thirteen colonies and the Continental Congress promised free land to those who served until the end of the war or to the widows and heirs of soldiers killed. Bounty land grants were also authorized after the Revolutionary War, the War of 1812, the Indian wars, and the Mexican War (1845–48).

Warrants for this bounty land were issued under laws passed between 1796 and 1855. Qualifications varied, and some people made more than one application. In order to apply for the warrant, the veteran or his heirs had to document his service. This documentation process is the source of most of the genealogical information in these files. The *Revolutionary War Pension and Bounty-Land Warrant Applications Files* (National Archives publication M804) are available on microfilm at many research libraries.

Figure 13.2, on page 155, is an excerpt from a widow's application for a Revolutionary War bounty land warrant. Note the genealogical information it provides: her age and maiden name, the county where she and her husband married (although she apparently had forgotten the date), and her husband's death date and place. Notice the added sentence: "She refers for the proof of her husbands services and the proof of her marriage to the declaration on file in the Pension Office for a pension." An application she filed four years earlier for a pension gave the marriage date as "1785 or 6." Her documentation included her register of the births of six of their children. These papers and her husband's pension application are all part of their file in the National Archives.

Some of the thirteen colonies issued warrants for grants on their own unsettled lands and western lands that they claimed. In this way, North Carolina granted land in Tennessee, and Virginia made land grants in Kentucky. Virginia also issued warrants for grants in south central Ohio in an area known as the Virginia Military District. Central Ohio became the location of bounty lands for soldiers (or their assignees) who had served in the Continental Army, under the authority of Congress rather than individual states. Pennsylvania, Massachusetts, New York, and Georgia also issued some bounty land grants. The respective state archives hold records of those grants, and some records have been abstracted and published in books or periodicals.

DECLARATION FOR WIDOW
Who has never received Bounty Land.

STATE OF *South Carolina*
District of *Chesterfield* ss.
COUNTY OF

On this *14th* day of *August* 1855, personally appeared before me, the subscriber, a Justice of the Peace, within and for the County and State aforesaid, (duly authorized by law to administer oaths, *Nancy Blakeney*, aged *90* years, a resident of *Chesterfield* District in the County and State aforesaid, who being duly sworn, according to law, declares that she is the widow of *John Blakeney*, deceased, who was a _____, in the company commanded by Capt. _____, in the Regiment of _____ commanded by Col. _____ In the war with *of the Revolution*

That her said husband entered the service of the United States at _____ on or about the _____ day of _____ 18__ for the term of _____ and continued in actual service in said war for the term of at least fourteen days, and was honorably discharged from said service as will appear by the Muster Rolls of said company, not having any knowledge of the manner of her said husband's discharge. She further states that she was married to the said *John Blakeney*, in the County of *Anson*. State of *North Carolina*, on or about the _____ day of _____ 18__ by *John Jackson* a Justice of the Peace _____ and that her name before her said marriage was *Nancy Heary* _____ that her said husband died at *his residence*, in the district of *Chesterfield* State of *South Carolina* on the *3?* day of *March* 1849, and that she is still a widow. *She refers for the proof of her husbands services and the proof of their marriage to the declaration on file in the Pension office for a pension*

She makes this declaration for the purpose of obtaining the Bounty Land to which she may be entitled under the Act approved March 3, 1855, never having received Bounty Land under this or any other act, nor made any other application for Bounty Land except the present. *Felix Richards of Washington D.C.* is hereby authorized to prosecute this my claim and to receive any warrant that may be issued hereon.

Nancy Blakeney [SEAL]
her mark

AFFIDAVIT OF TWO WITNESSES.

We *Mathias Beavis* and *William L. Funderburk* residents of the District and State aforesaid, upon our oaths declare that the foregoing declaration was signed and acknowledged by the above *Nancy Blakeney* in our presence; and that we believe from the appearance and statements of the applicant, that she is the identical person she represents herself to be. And we further declare that we were well acquainted with the said *John Blakeney* and *Nancy Blakeney* his wife (*now the widow*) during the lifetime of the former and knew them to live together as husband and wife, and to have been so generally reputed. That her said

Figure 13.2 Declaration for Widow, Nancy Blakeney, 1855

Sources

The *American State Papers* contain documents on many subjects, including public lands, military and naval affairs, the post office department, commerce and navigation, and Indian affairs. The thirty-eight volumes are good sources for genealogists and historians.

An important reference is Clifford Neal Smith's *Federal Land Series: A Calendar of Archival Materials on the Land Patents Issued by the United States Government, With Subject, Tract, and Name Indexes*. Volumes I and III index land patents between 1788 and 1814 by subject, tract, and name. Volume II is an index to American Revolution federal bounty land warrants, 1799–1835. Volume IV indexes grants in the Virginia Military District of Ohio.

In studying these resources, remember that veterans or widows who received bounty land warrants did not necessarily move to the new state. Many sold their certificates and stayed put or moved somewhere else.

Individual claims are also found in early land records. Many of the people making these claims had land grants or purchases from foreign sovereigns (mostly French, Spanish, Mexican, and British) and settled the land before the United States acquired it. The United States had to decide who had clear title to each tract. Many records of these claims are published and indexed in the *American State Papers: Public Land Series: Records relating to individual claims presented to federal authorities, 1790–1837.* . . . Federal authorities who handled these claims included district land offices, district courts, the United States Court of Claims, the General Land Office, the Supreme Court, and the Court of Private Claims (for Mexican lands).

Part of the United States Serial Set, the *American State Papers* are often found in public and university libraries, especially federal documents depositories. Although the original public land series volumes are indexed, also consult *Grassroots of America: A Computerized Index to the American State Papers: Land Grants and Claims (1789–1837)*, Philip W. McMullin, ed. Additional documents relating to grants and claims are reproduced, unindexed, in *The New American State Papers* (eight volumes of documents on public lands, 1789–1860).

Donation land claims. In Florida, Oregon, and Washington before the Civil War, the government began giving land to settlers in order to strengthen the U.S. claim to the area when ownership was disputed with another country. Because this land was given or donated to the settlers, the records of the grants are called donation land entries. The files in the National Archives contain records for Florida, 1842–1850, and Oregon and Washington, 1851–1903.

Homestead entry papers are a fourth kind of land record in the National Archives. The Homestead Act of 1862 allowed settlers on public domain lands to obtain a free homestead farm of 160 acres for a small filing fee. In order to obtain title to the land, the homesteader had to live on, cultivate, and improve the property for five years. Other requirements were

- citizenship, or intent to become a citizen
- being a head of household, widow, or single male or female over age twenty-one
- not owning 160 acres or more already
- not having borne arms against the United States (e.g., Confederate servicemen) or given aid and comfort to her enemies (e.g., Confederate supporters)

In requesting this grant, the applicant furnished certain information of genealogical interest: name of the applicant and his wife, size of the family, residence,
age or date of birth, location of the land, and date acquired. His entry papers
would include this application, his certificate of intent to make a claim, the
testimony of two witnesses, the claimant's own testimony, the final certificate
authorizing him to obtain a patent, and, if he was foreign born, his naturalization papers, declaration of intent to become a citizen, or a Union Army discharge certificate. These files can be genealogical gold mines.

Land patents, including the sale of former Indian lands, were the function
of federal land offices. In the early years, these offices were sometimes quite
distant from the lands they sold. The index to the public land series, *Grassroots
of America*, identifies the land offices to 1840. The National Archives has a
four-volume index that lists the land offices responsible for a given region at a
given time.

The government transferred title to public domain land to individual owners
through the patents, recorded in tract books in the land offices. The land offices
east of the Mississippi River eventually transferred their tract books to the
General Land Office, now the Bureau of Land Management (BLM) in the U.S.
Department of the Interior. The Bureau's Eastern States Office (7450 Boston
Blvd., Springfield, VA 22153), holds the tract books for the thirteen eastern
public land states, that is, those east of and those bordering the Mississippi
River: Alabama, Arkansas, Florida, Illinois, Indiana, Iowa, Louisiana, Michigan, Minnesota, Mississippi, Missouri, Ohio, and Wisconsin. The pre-1908
land title records for these states are available

1. on microfilm of the tract books
2. on CD-ROM in libraries, from commercial vendors, and from the Superintendent of Documents (P.O. Box 371954, Pittsburgh, PA 15250-7954)
3. online (except for Iowa, at this writing) at <http://www.glorecords.blm
   .gov> under "Search Land Patents"

The BLM holds some western states tract books in its regional/state offices
in Phoenix, Anchorage, Sacramento, Denver (Lakewood), Boise, Billings, Reno,
Santa Fe, Portland, Salt Lake City, and Cheyenne. Other tract books are in the
National Archives or its regional branches, state and local historical societies,
or state archives or land offices. Many county courthouses have copies of the
tract books pertaining to their land.

Both the National Archives and the BLM have records of land patents from
about 1800 to 1908, although they do not have identical files. The BLM generally has tract books, survey plats, and other land title documents. The National
Archives holds the case files of individual patentees as well as post-1908 entries.

From 1800 to 1820, public lands were sold on credit. The National Archives
contains the credit entry files, 1800–1820, and the credit entry final certificates,
1800–1835. The National Archives also has the cash entry files for 1820–1908
with a master card index for Alabama, Alaska, Arizona, Florida, Louisiana,
Nevada, and Utah. You can get a copy of an ancestor's land entry case file from
the National Archives by mail for a fee, using NATF Form 84. You can request

Internet Source

For locations and tract
book information of these
western BLM offices, visit
the Web site at <http://
www.blm.gov/nhp/
directory/index.htm>.

this form online at <http://www.archives.gov/global_pages/inquire_form.html>.

For a copy of a land entry file, you need to furnish such information as the name of the patentee (person who bought the land), legal description of the property (section, township, and range), land office, and entry or certificate (document) number. If you have the name and legal description, you can find the other data in the appropriate tract book or contact the BLM regional offices or Eastern States Office at the address on page 157.

Why Do You Need Land Entry Files?

1. These files, especially the homestead files, sometimes include important genealogical information.

2. Papers in the file can suggest a former place of residence in which to look for more information on the ancestor.

3. Receipts in the file often predate the final patent certificate and thus tell you when the ancestor actually acquired the land. Sometimes, he sold the land before the final certificate date. If he actually lived on the land, the receipt date may help determine when he moved to the area. (See page 216.)

4. Papers in the file often include an affidavit from someone who knew the applicant well. These affiants were often relatives, in-laws, or close friends—part of an ancestor's cluster. As a genealogist, you may depend heavily on this cluster to find information on your ancestor.

5. With the tract book or the online or CD-ROM versions, you can map an ancestral neighborhood. Although some of the patentees never lived on the land and sold it to others (as shown in county deed records), a number of the landowners around your ancestor were his neighbors and therefore part of his cluster.

Perhaps, some of the neighbors, or your ancestors, bought their land from the original patentees or a subsequent landowner. If so, they will not appear in the tract book records for that land. The tract books list only the original patentees. Thus, **to determine who lived near your ancestor at a given time, combine county records and tract book records.** This process can be an important step in looking for the ancestor's parents, siblings, or in-laws. (See Figure 13.4, page 161.)

Research Tip

Rectangular Survey System

The federal land or public domain states were surveyed into grids that make locating and studying land records relatively straightforward. On paper, the land grid looks like a series of boxes. The boxes, or townships, represent the intersection of vertical rows called ranges and horizontal rows of townships.

For identification, the townships are numbered north or south of a base line. The ranges are east or west of a meridian. Township and range numbers begin at the intersection of base line and meridian: Township 1 South (T1S), Range 1 East (R1E), etc. (See the illustration at the top of page 159.) Township and range numbers can be quite high if the land is a long distance from the base line and meridian. Township and range numbers are important parts of the legal description of any tract of land.

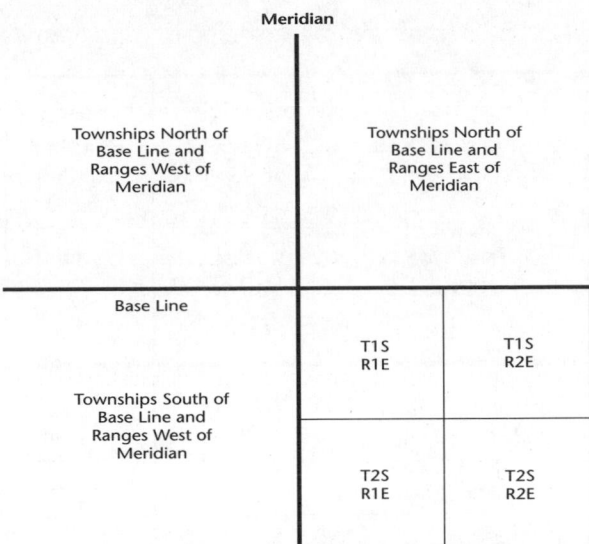

Each township contains up to thirty-six divisions called sections, each a mile square. Sometimes, physical features of the land shape the township in such a way that (1) thirty-six sections are not feasible or (2) some sections are not square. Below is a typical township divided into its thirty-six sections.

Each section within the township contains about 640 acres and can be divided into smaller tracts. Figure 13.3, page 160, shows a typical section and its fractional divisions. The legal descriptions of the tracts use the fractional part of the section, the section number, the township number, and the range number, as in "the northwest quarter, section 1, township 19 north, range 7 east." Abbreviations are common in the records: NE4 or NE1/4 (northeast quarter), S1 (section one), T19N (township 19 north), R7E (range 7 east).

6	5	4	3	2	1
7	8	9	10	11	12
18	17	16	15	14	13
19	20	21	22	23	24
30	29	28	27	26	25
31	32	33	34	35	36

Section 1 (S1)

Northwest Quarter of Section 1 NW4 S1 (NW 1/4 S1) (160 acres)	West Half of Northeast Quarter W2 NE4 S1 or W1/2 NE4 S1	East Half of Northeast Quarter E2 NE4 S1	
North Half of Southwest Quarter N2 SW4 S1 (80 acres)	NW4 SE4 S1 (40 acres)	W2 NE4 SE4 S1	E2 NE4 SE4 S1
South Half of Southwest Quarter S2 SW4 S1	N2 SW4 SE4 S1 S2 SW4 SE4 S1	SE4 SE4 S1	

Figure 13.3 Typical divisions of a section of land, showing legal descriptions of the parts; add the township and range numbers to complete the legal description of any given tract

Mapping an Ancestral Neighborhood

Figure 13.4, page 161, illustrates an 1840s "neighborhood" in Caddo Parish, Louisiana. The research goal was to identify the first husband and/or childhood family of Elizabeth Robertson Croom. When more direct efforts failed to provide an answer, the researcher developed plan C to study the neighborhood where Elizabeth lived with her second husband, Isaac Croom Sr. Were any neighbors related to Elizabeth or perhaps to her unidentified first husband?

Technique

The researcher created the land ownership grid of the surrounding sections from tract book information. **Studying the landowners in census, land, marriage, and probate records helped narrow the search.** Finally, the researcher discovered that one of the neighbors was indeed Elizabeth's brother, James A. Arnold. The grid shows the proximity of his land ("JAA" on the map) to Isaac's. Elizabeth apparently lived with or visited her brother after her first husband died, and she met and married their neighbor, Isaac.

IMMIGRATION AND NATURALIZATION RECORDS

Basically, everyone living in what is now the United States and Canada is a descendant of immigrants—people who came here from somewhere else. Even those who call themselves Native Americans are of immigrant stock, as are the rest of us who are also native to this continent. The genealogical problem is that ancestors came here over hundreds of years from many directions. Except for those who came in about the last 200 years and left government-generated documents to prove it, many of our ancestors came without leaving a trace of previous residence.

Map Showing Isaac Croom's Neighbors

Key:

Map shows land in adjoining ranges: 15 and 16
Map shows land in adjoining townships: 19 and 20

Blank spaces = vacant land
before 1846

Heavy black lines designate sections.
Double lines designate changes in townships and ranges.
Map shows patentees and year of patents in sections surrounding Isaac's

☺ = Turned out to be her
brother's land

☐ Land of Isaac Croom, Elizabeth's second husband
☐ Patents before 1846, when Isaac married his second wife, Elizabeth

Legal descriptions: *Fractional sections & section, **Townships and Ranges***

R16	R16		R16			R15	
	AB-1843 JAA-184? ☺		TMooring 1843	TMooring 1843	*T20 R16*		*T20 R15*
				TMooring 1843		TM '43	
		S34		*S35*		*S36*	*S1*
	RPB 1841		Isaac Croom, 1844 *N2 S2 T19 R16* m Elizabeth, 1846		JH '43 / IC '52	IPW to AN '40 *NE4 S1*	*T19 R15*
			RPB 1841		JH '44 & '48	JH '43 / AN '40	
		S3		*S2*		*S1*	*S6*
SLH 1843	JE 1843		TMooring 1843			IPW 1844 *S12*	
	JE '43 / JT '44		TMooring 1843	TMooring 1843		IPW 1843	
		S10		*S11*		*S12*	*S7*

Figure 13.4

In research, therefore, the immediate problem is not determining the foreign birthplace of our surname but finding the ancestors, one at a time, to identify the immigrants, the ones who were really the first in the line to come here, so that we have a name, place, and time frame in which to research overseas. **Although genealogists have family traditions about the foreign origins of some ancestors, until we confirm the details of each ancestral life and determine the correct immigrant(s), our research needs to focus on this side of the water.**

We often speak of immigration and naturalization records in one breath, as if they are the two halves of a whole, but they are not. The fortunate genealogist will find both kinds of records for an immigrant ancestor and be in a good position to move to foreign research. Sometimes, especially for female ancestors, the immigration record is all we can expect to find. Even for men, naturalization records may exist without the researcher being able to find immigration documents, or vice versa. The ancestor may have participated in both processes, but they were not necessarily connected.

Research Tip

Internet Source

For more on immigration history, visit the Ellis Island Web site at <http://www.ellisisland.org> and its 1892–1924 immigrant database at <http://www.ellisislandrecords.org>. Ellis Island was an entry station from 1892 to 1954.

Sources

Immigration Records

Some records exist for immigrant arrivals before 1820, but no law required ship captains to keep lists or deliver them to governmental authorities. After 1820, captains were to give the customs office in the first port of entry lists of their passengers to show those who had embarked in a foreign port and were disembarking at a U.S. port.

The port where an immigrant ancestor disembarked may be different from the ship's first port of entry; he or she may have continued on the ship from Savannah, for example, to New Orleans or Galveston. As well as first-time immigrants, the passenger lists may show (1) an ancestor making several trips to and from his homeland or (2) U.S. citizens returning home from trips abroad.

Some of these records appear in books and periodicals. Lists of passengers arriving after the 1880s were filed with the Bureau of Immigration. Existing lists are microfilmed for use at the National Archives and its branches, as well as in research libraries.

In the National Archives, in the records of the United States Customs Service, are post-1820 passenger lists and some indexes from vessels arriving at Baltimore, Boston, Detroit, Galveston, New Orleans, New York, Philadelphia, San Francisco, Seattle, and other Gulf and Atlantic ports. Records of the Immigration and Naturalization Service contain passenger and crew lists, with indexes by ports, for the late nineteenth century and the first half of the twentieth century. More indexes appear as more of the records are computerized for publication. To find out which National Archives records and indexes have been microfilmed, consult the online catalog *Immigrant and Passenger Arrivals* at <http://www.nara.gov/publications/microfilm/immigrant/immpass.html>. This catalog is also available in book form at many libraries.

A major resource for immigration research is P. William Filby's *Passenger and Immigration Lists Index: A Guide to Published Arrival Records of About 500,000 Passengers Who Came to the United States and Canada in the Seventeenth, Eighteenth, and Nineteenth Centuries* (called PILI). Annual supplements continue to increase the coverage, and well over two million names have been indexed. This massive work indexes published passenger and naturalization lists and other evidence of immigration. Its companion, *Passenger and Immigration Lists Bibliography, 1538–1900* by the same author, catalogs over 2,500 published lists as a cross-reference. The PILI volumes and many of the books and periodicals that contain the passenger and immigration lists are in larger research libraries. If you find an ancestor's name in the PILI, look next for the published list. Some of the lists contain additional information about the ancestor, and some do not.

Books that list immigrants from particular countries, especially Germany, Ireland, Italy, and Great Britain, are now available. These books are often abstracts of the microfilmed passenger arrival lists at the National Archives, some of which are not indexed other than in these publications. Larger research libraries usually have such books.

Four references in the search for immigrant ancestors are

American Immigration. Maldwyn Allen Jones. 2d ed. Chicago: The University of Chicago Press, 1992. Immigration history.

American Passenger Arrival Records: A Guide to the Records of Immigrants Arriving at American Ports by Sail and Steam. Michael Tepper. Baltimore: Genealogical Publishing Co., 1982.

A Genealogist's Guide to Discovering Your Immigrant & Ethnic Ancestors. Sharon DeBartolo Carmack. Cincinnati: Betterway Books, 2000.

They Came in Ships: A Guide to Finding Your Immigrant Ancestor's Arrival Record. John P. Colletta. 2d ed. Salt Lake City: Ancestry, 1993.

For More Info

Immigration Information in the Census

Federal censuses asked for the following information that can help with immigration research:

1820, 1830	Foreigners not naturalized.
1850–1870	The birthplace of each person, the country of birth for the foreign born.
1870	Whether one's parents were foreign born.
1880 on	The birthplace of each person and each person's parents, the country of birth for the foreign born.
1890	Country of birth for each foreign-born person or parent and how many years each foreign-born male over age twenty-one had been in the United States. Persons ten and older were to report whether they spoke English and, if not, what language they spoke.
1900	Country of birth for foreign-born residents and parents and the year of immigration and number of years in the United States for all males and females of foreign birth, regardless of age. Persons age ten and older were to report whether they spoke English, but not to name their mother tongue.
1910, 1920	(1) Country of birth and the mother tongue (language) for foreign-born residents and anyone's foreign-born parents, (2) for persons ten and older, the language they spoke, especially if not English, (3) for males and females of foreign birth, regardless of age, the year of immigration.
1920	The city or province of foreign birth.
1930	The country of birth, mother tongue, and year of immigration of all foreign-born residents and the country of birth of each foreign-born parent.

Naturalization Papers

Naturalization is the process by which a foreign-born person becomes a citizen. Ancestors arriving in this country before the American Revolution generally did not go through a naturalization process. Of course, many were already British citizens who were simply changing their residence within the British empire. Before the first naturalization law in 1790, the states (or colonies) handled the process on their own.

In order to find naturalization papers for your ancestors, you need to know approximately when they arrived in this country. Passenger lists, census records, land records, family papers, and county tax lists are some of the sources that can help you establish the arrival date.

The first step toward becoming a naturalized citizen was to file a Declaration of Intention. Before 1906, an immigrant could file these "first papers" at any federal, state, or local court. Many did this in their port of entry soon after their arrival in this country. After 1906, the declaration was filed usually in a federal court, sometimes in a state or county court.

The second step was to file "final papers," which included a Petition for Citizenship, an Oath of Allegiance, and papers proving residency for the required number of years. The residency requirement varied from time to time but generally was five years. The final papers did not have to be filed in the same court as the Declaration of Intention. The process was complete when the court issued the Certificate of Naturalization.

Important

Naturalization records sometimes contain valuable genealogical data, such as the subject's birth date and place, spouse's name and origin, children's names and birth information, former and current residence, and immigration data. Other information may include occupation and physical description. Records from the late nineteenth century and the twentieth century generally contain much more detail than earlier records.

Records of naturalizations before 1906 are scattered among state and federal archives, historical societies, libraries, and courthouses (in separate naturalization record books or in the court minutes of various courts). Indexes and guides to each collection may help you locate the records you need.

Papers filed after 1906 are usually kept with the records of the court that handled them. If you do not know which court your ancestor used, inquire at an office of the Immigration and Naturalization Service for the proper form and procedure for having a search made.

Some naturalization records are available from the National Archives and its branches. Taken from federal court files and available on microfilm are indexes and/or records of naturalizations from Alaska, northern California, Colorado, Maryland, Montana, New England, Oregon, Pennsylvania, South Carolina, and Washington. For specific availability, consult the National Archives publication *National Archives Microfilm Resources for Research: A Comprehensive Catalog*, also online at <http://www.archives.gov/publications/genealogy_microfilm_catalogs.html#resource>.

Research Tip

Naturalized citizens who received land under the Homestead Act sometimes filed their citizenship papers with their homestead applications. Therefore, **the land entry case files in the National Archives are also sources to consult when you are looking for naturalization papers.** Two sources to consult when researching in naturalization records are

American Naturalization Processes and Procedures, 1790–1985. John J. Newman. Reprint, Bountiful, Utah: Heritage Quest, 1998.

They Became Americans: Finding Naturalization Records and Ethnic Origins.
    Loretto Dennis Szucs. Salt Lake City: Ancestry, 1998.

Naturalization Information in the Census

Federal census records may help you in naturalization research, if the ancestors supplied correct answers to these questions:

1820, 1830	Foreigners not naturalized.
1890–1910	Whether a person was naturalized or whether naturalization papers "have been taken out" (or first papers had been filed). This applied only to foreign-born males over age twenty-one. In 1900 and 1910, "Na" in the blank indicated a naturalized citizen; "Pa," that first papers had been taken out; "Al," an alien who had taken no steps toward naturalization; "NR," not reported. For those born in the United States, the columns were to be left blank.
1920	Same as 1910 plus the year of naturalization.
1930	Whether any foreign-born person (male or female) was naturalized ("Na"), alien ("Al"), or had begun the process of naturalization ("Pa").

See Also

See the Census Soundex cards showing foreign birthplaces and citizenship status in Figure 10.1, page 101.

NATIVE AMERICAN RECORDS

Native American ancestors basically fall into two research categories: those who remained identified with a tribe or band—many of whom became residents on reservations—and those who blended into non-Indian society. Regardless of which group an ancestor belongs to, tracing the Indian line is a real challenge due to a scarcity of written records prior to about the mid-nineteenth century. Certainly, explorers, scholars, military record keepers, and observers have written about Indians since the first European contact, but these writers, for the most part, did not record genealogical data.

Nontribal Indians are sometimes identified in federal census records, court records, and public land tract books but are less frequently found in deed, marriage, and probate records in the counties. Indian naming and name-changing customs also can complicate one's search in the existing records. In many cases, family records or tradition may be the only indication of an Indian ancestral line. Proving the relationship and the specific identities is the difficulty.

Records of tribal Indians exist in basically two categories: the Five Civilized Tribes of the southeastern United States, most of whom resettled in Oklahoma, and the tribes who were made wards of the government, living on reservations. Documents relating to the Five Civilized Tribes (Cherokee, Choctaw, Chickasaw, Creek, and Seminole) can be found at the National Archives; its branch in Fort Worth, Texas; the Oklahoma Historical Society; the Western History Collection at the University of Oklahoma; and, to a smaller degree, the Atlanta (East Point), Georgia, branch of the National Archives. These include tribal census rolls; enrollment cards; allotment and payroll records; some trading house papers; tribal citizenship applications; service records of those who served in the military, especially for the Confederacy during the Civil War; and miscellaneous records.

A number of the National Archives regional branches and state historical societies or archives have collections relating to reservation Indians. These files include the important tribal census rolls (1884–1940), records of the federal Indian agencies and superintendencies, and correspondence of the Office of Indian Affairs. In addition, there are registers of military service of Indian scouts and Civil War Indian home guards (both on microfilm), some marriage cards and registers, heirship records, Eastern Cherokee claim files (1902–1910), and Indian school records.

Some Native Americans served with the regular army during the Revolutionary War. Their service records and resulting bounty land warrant applications are also on file, as is a special 1880 census of Indians in Washington, Oregon, California, and Dakota Territory. The regional National Archives branches in the western states have field office reports from the Bureau of Indian Affairs.

For More Info

For more detailed information on Indian records in the National Archives, consult such sources as these:

American Indians: A Select Catalog of National Archives Microfilm Publications. Washington, D.C.: National Archives Trust Fund Board, 1972, rev. 1984.

American Indian Records in the National Archives. Edward E. Hill. Salt Lake City: The Genealogical Society of the Church of Jesus Christ of Latter-day Saints, Inc., 1969.

Guide to Records in the National Archives of the United States Relating to American Indians. Edward E. Hill, comp. Washington, D.C.: National Archives and Records Administration, 1984.

Records of the Bureau of Indian Affairs. Edward E. Hill. Preliminary Inventory No. 163. 2 vols. 1965. Reprint, Washington, D.C.: National Archives and Records Administration, 1982.

For More Info

Other reference books that might help in the search for Native American ancestors include these:

Black Indian Genealogy Research. Angela Y. Walton-Raji. Bowie, Md.: Heritage Books, 1993. African-American ancestors among the Five Civilized Tribes.

Dictionary Catalog of the Edward E. Ayer Collection of Americana and American Indians in the Newberry Library. The Newberry Library. 16 vols. Boston: G.K. Hall, 1961.

Ethnic Genealogy: A Research Guide. Jessie Carney Smith, ed. Westport, Conn.: Greenwood Press, 1983. Chapter seven, "American Indian Records and Research," by Jimmy B. Parker, deals mostly with reservation Indians.

Guide to American Indian Documents in the Congressional Serial Set, 1817–1899. Steven L. Johnson. New York: Clearwater Publishing Co., 1977.

Introductory Guide to Indian-Related Records, to 1876, in the North Carolina State Archives. Donna Spindel. Raleigh: North Carolina Division of Archives and History, 1977.

Native American Periodicals and Newspapers, 1828–1982. James P. Danky, ed. Westport, Conn.: Greenwood Press, 1984.

Our Native Americans and Their Records of Genealogical Value. E. Kay Kirkham. 2 vols. Logan, Utah: Everton Publishers, 1980.

"Tracking Native American Family History." Curt B. Witcher and George J. Nixon. In *The Source: A Guidebook of American Genealogy*. Rev. ed. Loretto Dennis Szucs and Sandra Hargreaves Luebking, eds. Salt Lake City: Ancestry, 1997.

Libraries hold books about individual Indian tribes, their history and records. Consult library catalogs for materials on specific tribes or Indians of specific geographic regions.

Although censuses before 1870 show Indians living among the white and black population, the 1870 federal census was the first to include *Indian* as a designation of color (race). Indians living in mostly white settlements were to be enumerated with the general population. In 1900 and 1910, the census also included special enumerations of Indians on and off reservations.

AFRICAN-AMERICAN RESEARCH

Basic genealogical sources, such as family papers, courthouse records, state and federal censuses, state archives, and newspapers, are useful for any genealogist, regardless of ethnic interest, especially after 1870. The challenge for African-American genealogists is finding pre-Civil War slave ancestors. Family tradition and county records are often the key to identification. Since slaves had little or no opportunity to create records, the answers often lie in studying the records created by their owners. Case studies in books and historical journals, such as the *Journal of Negro History*, can acquaint you with source material and the process that others have used successfully.

The National Archives has extensive records pertaining to African-American genealogy. One important group of sources is military records. In addition to service and pension records and their indexes, the National Archives has registers of payments to Colored Troops during and after the Civil War, *Records of the Fifty-Fourth Massachusetts Infantry Regiment (Colored), 1863–1865*, records of Colored Troops in the Adjutant General's Office, and *The Negro in the Military Service of the United States, 1639–1886*. These collections are available on microfilm and can be found at research libraries. The following are two helpful military references:

Data Relating to Negro Military Personnel in the Nineteenth Century. Aloha South. Reference Information Paper 63. Washington, D.C.: National Archives and Records Service, 1973.

List of Black Servicemen Compiled From the War Department Collection of Revolutionary War Records. Debra L. Newman, comp. Washington, D.C.: National Archives and Records Service, 1974.

A comprehensive reference to civilian materials at the National Archives is *Black History: A Guide to Civilian Records in the National Archives*, Debra L. Newman, comp. (Washington, D.C.: National Archives Trust Fund Board, 1984). Among

For More Info

See "Finding Slave Ancestors: The Search for the Family of Archie Davis Sr.," chapter ten in *The Sleuth Book for Genealogists*.

CD Source

Abstracts of records from the Freedman's Savings and Trust Company are available on CD-ROM (Freedman's Bank Records) from the Family History Library and at many libraries and Family History Centers.

For More Info

these are *Records of the United States District Court for the District of Columbia Relating to Slaves, 1851–1863*, including slave manumission papers, 1857–1863, and *Records of the Board of Commissioners for the Emancipation of Slaves in the District of Columbia, 1862–1863*.

Some records, also available on microfilm, come from two post–Civil War agencies: the Freedman's Savings and Trust Company, 1865–1874, and the Bureau of Refugees, Freedmen, and Abandoned Lands, 1865–1872, commonly called the Freedmen's Bureau. The most genealogical of these records are the registers of signatures of depositors in the branches of the Freedman's Savings and Trust Company, which operated in a number of major southern cities, as well as Philadelphia; New York; St. Louis; Baltimore; and Washington, DC. These registers often include personal history and vital statistics, family members, maiden names, and former residences. Freedmen's Bureau records include some marriage records—mostly for Arkansas, Kentucky, Louisiana, and Mississippi—and apprenticeship records. The microfilm is available in some research libraries.

Additional resources for African-American genealogy, in and out of the National Archives, include the following:

African-American Genealogy: A Bibliography and Guide to Sources. Curt Bryan Witcher. Ft. Wayne, Ind.: Round Tower Books, 2000.

African-Americans in the 1870 U.S. Federal Census. Generations Archives. CD-ROM. ACD-0101. North Salt Lake, Utah: Heritage Quest, 2001.

Black Genealogy. Charles L. Blockson, with Ron Fry. Englewood Cliffs, N.J.: Prentice-Hall, 1977.

Black Roots: A Beginner's Guide to Tracing the African-American Family Tree. Tony Burroughs. New York: Simon & Schuster, 2001. Deals only with genealogy from 1870 forward.

Finding a Place Called Home. Dee Parmer Woodtor. New York: Random House, 1999.

The Genealogist's Companion & Sourcebook. Emily Anne Croom. See chapter nine, "Focus on African-American Genealogy."

How to Trace Your African-American Roots: Discovering Your Unique History. Barbara Thompson Howell. Secaucus, N.J.: Citadel Press, 1999.

Slave Genealogy: A Research Guide With Case Studies. David H. Streets. Bowie, Md.: Heritage Books, 1986.

OTHER FEDERAL SOURCES

The National Archives houses records from all three branches of the federal government—legislative, executive, and judicial. Records from each branch aid in genealogical research. For example, most of the military, land, immigration, and census records, as well as most of the Native American and African-American sources discussed earlier in this chapter, are from the files of departments, bureaus, and agencies in the executive branch. Most records dealing with naturalization are from the executive or judicial branch. Genealogical information appears in many government documents.

Legislative archives form a large portion of the holdings of the National Archives. The National Archives maintains records of the Continental Congress and Confederation Congress from the years prior to the writing of the present Constitution, as well as the papers from the Constitutional Convention. These could be helpful to some genealogists, and a number are on microfilm, available at research libraries.

The *Territorial Papers of the United States*

This compilation of records comes mostly from the files of Congress and various executive departments. Several collections are on microfilm. Though unindexed and images of handwritten documents, the microfilm collections cover all the states that were once territories.

One set of transcribed records is available in twenty-eight indexed volumes. These publications represent a small percentage of the entire collection, but they contain information on thousands of ancestors. They are documents created in the course of governing the territories, as individual citizens interacted with Congress or executive departments. The books are arranged by territory and include petitions, letters, jury or militia lists, names of officers appointed to militia or civilian positions, and lists of landowners. Many help place ancestors in a given place at a given time between the federal censuses. Thus, they help genealogists narrow down when the ancestors moved to the territory or died. The documents help researchers learn about governmental, political, economic, military, and geographic issues of the time, their effect on residents, and citizens' reactions to events and issues.

If you had ancestors in these states during the territorial years, prior to statehood, you need to look at these books:

Research Tip

Alabama	Illinois	Louisiana	Missouri	Wisconsin
Arkansas	Indiana	Michigan	Ohio	
Florida	Iowa	Mississippi	Tennessee	

Civil Service Records

Records of civil service employees are somewhat restricted, but inquiries about service that ended after 1909 may be made to the National Personnel Records Center (CPR), 111 Winebago St., St. Louis, MO 63118. The few existing records pertaining to employees before 1909 can be found in the National Archives. Inquiries should contain the employee's full name, the name and address of the federal agency where he or she worked, and the approximate dates of that employment. For very early federal employees, check the lists in the *American State Papers: Miscellaneous* volumes in a research library.

Passports

Passport applications filed between 1791 and 1926 are at the National Archives. Limited searches can be made for age and citizenship information in the records that are at least seventy-five years old. Such searches require the applicant's name and the place and approximate date of the application. Inquiries for information from passport applications less than seventy-five

Microfilm Source

years old should be made to the Passport Office, Department of State, Washington, DC 20520.

The following microfilm publications are available at this writing:

- M1371, *Registers and Indexes for Passport Applications, 1810–1906*
- M1848, *Index to Passport Applications, 1850–52, 1860–80, 1881, 1906–23*
- M1372, *Passport Applications, 1795–1905*
- M1490, *Passport Applications, 2 January 1906–31 March 1925*

Taxes

From the records of the Internal Revenue Service, you can read on microfilm the assessment lists for 1862–1866 by state for thirty-nine states and territories, including former Confederate states. Also on microfilm are the Civil War direct tax assessment rolls for Tennessee (publication T227) and the 1798 direct tax lists for Pennsylvania (publication M372).

Social Security

Social Security applications filed between 1936 and 1978 were microfilmed, and the originals were destroyed. You can get a copy of an original application from the Social Security Administration, Freedom of Information Workgroup, 300 N. Greene St., P.O. Box 33022, Baltimore, MD 21290. Enclose the ancestor's name, Social Security number, and death date or death certificate and the twenty-seven-dollar search fee. These records can often give researchers birth information, parents' names, and residential address and employer at the time of application.

If the ancestor's name appears on the Social Security Death Index online at <http://www.ancestry.com>, the site can generate a letter for you to use in requesting a copy of the application. Mail it along with your search fee.

The Library of Congress

The Library of Congress in Washington, DC, houses an extensive collection of manuscript, published, and microform works of value to genealogists. These include some early state records, newspapers, maps, family papers, and family and county histories. Many bibliographies and finding aids describe the holdings and their use. An excellent reference, especially for those planning to visit the library, is James C. Neagles's *The Library of Congress: A Guide to Genealogical and Historical Research*. Also consult their Web site at <http://lcweb.loc.gov>.

THINGS TO DO NOW

Idea Generator

1. Identify a research facility near you that has National Archives microfilm: public library, university library, Family History Center.
2. Write or call for the free pamphlets from the National Archives mentioned on page 146.
3. If pertinent to your search, inquire about a research facility near you that has the *Territorial Papers* in book form and make plans to use them.
4. On a form such as the military records checklist in *The Unpuzzling Your*

Past Workbook, begin determining whether you had ancestors in the military or eligible for military service, which ones, and which wars or years.

5. If your immigrant ancestors arrived in the United States after the Civil War, begin the process of identifying the country or region of origin or learning when they arrived, especially from census records and family papers.

6. As you identify ancestors with federal homesteads or federal land patents, contact the National Archives to get a copy of at least one file.

7. On a list of research ideas for your focus ancestor, note federal records that you think may help in the search. Add to it as you learn more about the ancestor.

FOURTEEN

Where Do I Look for That?

As you fill in your puzzle for each generation and each ancestor, you will find some pieces more quickly than others. The harder-to-find pieces will require more concentrated effort, but many of them can be found. Sometimes, it is simply a matter of learning about new ways to look for them.

Especially if you gather names and vital statistics from electronic databases or published family or county histories, you owe it to yourself, your family, and your ancestors to take those clues and check them out. This does not mean trying to confirm that what you found is accurate. **It means keeping an open mind, gathering information from a number of sources, and evaluating all that you find—evidence that agrees with or conflicts with the published report.** Then objectively consider whether your research points to a conclusion.

Reminder

BIRTH, DEATH, AND AGE INFORMATION

Sometimes, genealogists find a record with specific birth or death date and/or place information for an ancestor. Because these records may or may not be correct, we should seek confirmation or corroborating evidence in other sources, both family and public.

When we do not find specific birth information, we have to estimate it from age information given in sources such as newspaper clippings. The birth-data suggestions in the next two sections can apply to ancestors of U.S. or foreign birth.

Family Sources

1. Bible records, especially ones made at the time of the event; some Bible records are published in books and periodicals.
2. Interviews with relatives and family friends; family tradition (used cautiously).

3. Family letters, diaries, clippings, obituaries, autobiographical sketches, scrapbooks.
4. Birth announcements, baptism certificates, baby books.
5. Family papers including school transcripts, military discharge papers, passports, driver's licenses, voter registrations, naturalization papers; for immigrants, such papers may indicate whether the ancestor had a name change after arrival in the United States.

Ask distant cousins about sources in their part of the family. Some libraries and archives have collections of donated family papers. Inquire at institutions in your ancestral state, or consult the *National Union Catalog of Manuscript Collections* (NUCMC, pronounced "nuck-muck") and its corresponding *Index to Personal Names in the National Union Catalog of Manuscript Collections, 1959–1984*. Ask a reference librarian how to use these books, or consult *The Genealogist's Companion & Sourcebook* for instructions. Updates of NUCMC since 1993 are electronic publications, available in university and large public libraries. Visit NUCMC online at <http://www.loc.gov/coll/nucmc>.

Public Sources

1. Church registers of births, baptisms, confirmations, marriages (published, on microfilm, or in a church or archives). Baptism or christening facts may help you estimate birth information.
2. Marriage records may show birthplace or age, indicate the parties were of legal age to marry, or show that one or both were underage.
3. Other records require a person to be of age before acting in certain capacities, such as guardian to minor children, juror, officeholder, or seller of land. Appearance in tax records suggests a person was at least of taxable age.
4. Birth certificates (contemporary or delayed), hospital birth records, and newspaper birth notices of the ancestor or a child of the ancestor may show both date and place. Collecting such documents for siblings reveals birth order, family residences, and parents' names.
5. School or college records, publications.
6. Military service or pension files, World War I draft registrations, military discharge papers. A widow's military pension application usually mentions her husband's service and his death.
7. Social Security applications (beginning 1936); Social Security Death Index, on CD-ROM, at many research libraries and Family History Centers, and online at <http://www.ancestry.com>.
8. Organization or lodge membership applications, records, publications.
9. Homestead applications.
10. Declaration of intention to become a citizen, naturalization papers, ships' passenger arrival lists (sometimes give ages of passengers).
11. State or federal censuses that show age on a given date. The 1930 census asked for age at first marriage; this information could be a valuable clue.
12. For people who died in the census year, federal (1850–1880) or state

mortality schedules usually give age at death and month of death within the census year.

13. Tombstones, death certificates, obituaries, funeral cards/programs, funeral home records. Cemetery records may indicate date of burial rather than death date. Birth information in such sources may be inaccurate; verify it with other sources whenever possible.

14. Local business records, such as insurance company files, employment records, and professional organization records.

15. City directories sometimes identify widows. Even telephone directories may indicate a husband's death if the widow was listed by her own name. However, some widows continued the family listing under the husband's name even after his death.

16. Omission of a person from census or tax records may imply death or moving.

17. County or town records, such as jury lists and tax rolls, may give clues to a person's last interaction with public authorities and help narrow down a death date.

18. Published family and county histories; compiled biographical sketches. Use cautiously and try to verify data.

19. Consult *Age Search Information*, by the United States Department of Commerce, Bureau of the Census.

Technique

Estimating Birth Dates From Age Information

When actual birth records are not available, you can sometimes gather evidence of birth information from public records such as newspapers, wills, tax rolls, and marriage records.

Example 1: If an undated clipping in a scrapbook mentions that a female ancestor was part of the first graduating class from a particular local academy, use local history sources to find out when the first class graduated, say 1876. Based on the time and place, were female graduates about sixteen to eighteen years old at graduation? If so, estimate the ancestor's birth year about 1858–1860 (1876 − 16 = 1860; 1876 − 18 = 1858). If that is your first indication of this ancestor's birth, you may want to look next at federal census records for 1880, 1870, and 1860 to get age information from them.

Example 2: On 19 November 1763, Daniel Coleman of Cumberland County, Virginia, gave his consent for his daughter Elizabeth Coleman to marry Phillip Allen. His consent is an indication that Elizabeth was not yet twenty-one. Virginia law at that time required a person under twenty-one to have the permission of father or guardian in order to marry.

Example 3: County tax rolls may suggest age. Depending on legal taxable age at that time, often indicated in the column headings of the record itself, a man's presence on the roll as a poll (a head to be taxed) would indicate that he was at least of taxable age—probably sixteen, eighteen, or twenty-one, depending on the time and place.

Usually, the only women found on tax rolls were widows or unmarried women with taxable property. Thus, no age information can be assumed or estimated from these records alone.

Example 4: Robert Hester of Louisa County, Virginia, wrote his will in November 1769, providing useful information on his children and clues for further research (Will Book 2:71–72).

Case Study

1. To his son Abraham, he gave the 300 acres where Abraham was then living and named him executor of the estate in the event that Robert's widow remarried. These provisions suggest that Abraham was the eldest son, if not the eldest of the thirteen children, and more than likely was well over twenty-one years of age.

2. Daughter Sarah was already married to a Smith and had three children: Robert, Barbara, and Sarah Smith. There is no indication of how old these grandchildren were, but we know they were born by November 1769, the date of the will. Their mother, married with children, was probably no less than twenty years of age and perhaps no more than thirty. These estimates would suggest that she was born between 1739 and 1749.

3. Hester also named his daughter Agness Walton and her two children, Barbara and Anne Hester Walton, information that would place Agness in approximately the same birth range as her sister, about 1739 to 1749.

4. Another daughter, Barbara Walton, was married, but no children were mentioned in the will. It is possible, though not certain from this document alone, that she was the youngest of these three daughters.

5. The other Hester daughters—Anne (Ann in a different entry), Susan, Mary, and Elizabeth—were to receive their inheritance upon reaching the age of eighteen. We know, then, that they were all born after 1751.

6. Hester gave sons James and Nathan land and named them in a provision with Abraham and their married sisters, Sarah, Agness, and Barbara. The father stated that if any child died without heirs, that share of the remaining estate was to be divided equally between the then surviving children *except* these six. This provision suggests that these were the six eldest children and had been given their inheritance to the limit desired by their father.

7. Rounding out the list of children were three younger sons. Francis and Samuel were to receive a sum of money when they reached twenty-one. This information tells us that they were born after 1748 and by 1769.

8. The remaining son, Charles, was to receive the 431 acres where the parents then lived, with the provision that the widow, Barbara, was to have "free and Indisputable authority upon the same during her widowhood." The implication here may be that Charles was still living at home, may have been the youngest son, but without experience running a sizable farm. Thus, the father wanted his wife, not the son, to be in charge.

9. If the father followed a practice that many others have, over the years, of naming his children in his will in birth order, then his sons, in order, were Abraham, James, Nathan, Francis, Samuel, and Charles; his daughters, Sarah, Agness, Barbara, Anne (Ann), Susan, Mary, and Elizabeth.

Other sources—marriage bonds, deeds, other family wills, estate settlement records, census records from 1790 forward, Bible records, or tombstones—may give more birth information on these children and grandchildren. The will alone provides good clues.

Important

Estimating Death Data From County Records

County records often contain clues for death data.

Example 1: The county probate file on Elliott Coleman contained items which placed his death date within a two-week period (Hays County, Texas, probate file #354, County Clerk's office, Courthouse, San Marcos):

- accounting of money paid on behalf of Mr. Coleman, deceased, including cost of medical service, coffin, digging the grave, and clothes for burial, dated 17 February 1892
- bill from doctor dated 18 February 1892 for visits to Mr. Coleman between 16 December 1891 and 3 February 1892

These two items narrow down his death date to some time between February 3 and 17. Since the burial apparently took place by February 17, Coleman died probably between February 3 and 16.

Example 2: Consider the case of Thomas Ballard Smith of Louisa County, Virginia (Will Book 2:309–313). He wrote his will on 13 August 1776 and added a codicil (supplement) to it on 6 October 1777. The will was probated in court on 12 January 1778. Virginia law from 1785 forward provided that no will could be probated until two weeks after the death. If the law simply codified what was already customary, Smith probably died in October, November, or December 1777.

Research Tip

Example 3: Wills, deeds, and estate settlements may give information about family members besides the subject of the record. When Richard Phillips wrote his will in March 1793, he named two grandchildren, John and Lucy Holt, "allowing them to be equal to one of my said children" in the division of his estate, to receive their "deceased mother's" portion (Amelia County, Virginia, Will Book 5:36). We learn here of a daughter, unfortunately not named, who had married, had at least two children, and died before March 1793. This kind of discovery can help in establishing not only the death date of the person who wrote the will, but also birth, death, and marriage information for his family members, married names for daughters, and maiden names, in this case, for John and Lucy Holt's mother.

Example 4: William Harrison's wife Lucy freely acknowledged her husband's sale of land on 11 February 1786 at her home, because she was "about to leave this State and cannot conveniently attend court" (Petersburg, Virginia, Deed Book 1:257). Then on 26 March 1789, William signed a marriage agreement with and deed of gift to Nancy Vaughan, a young neighbor. We cannot tell what had happened to Lucy, his former wife, in just these two sources, but we can realize that divorce was rare, especially for a clergyman, as William was. Besides, William and Nancy named their second daughter Lucy a few years later, and Nancy had no sister named Lucy to honor with such a namesake. It seems more likely that Lucy, the first wife, died during the three years between these documents.

MARRIAGE DATE AND/OR PLACE

The most obvious source for marriage information is the marriage records of the county or town where the marriage took place. Original marriage licenses may also be on file in the county courthouse, town hall, or local archives. Usually the couple married in their, or the bride's, county of residence. If you do not find a marriage record in the supposed home county, check in surrounding counties. Circumstances sometimes led to marriage in a different county, especially in cases of elopement or parental opposition to the marriage.

Other common sources of marriage information are these:
1. Bible records, published or in the family.
2. Letters, diaries, memoirs, scrapbooks, clippings kept within the family.
3. Contemporary newspaper announcements of the event.
4. Church registers.
5. Interviews with relatives and family friends.
6. Obituary, tombstone, pension application, or naturalization papers.
7. Organization publications with news about members.
8. Published family and county histories with biographical sketches. Use cautiously and verify data whenever possible.

Estimating Marriage Date With Census Records

If no other records give a wedding date, you can sometimes approximate a marriage year from census records, but do not assume its accuracy. Federal censuses asked these questions:

Technique

- 1850, 1860: whether the couple married within the census year. Some census takers asked all couples for their marriage year.
- 1870, 1880: whether the couple married within the census year. For 1870, for example, this would mean a wedding between 1 June 1869 and 1 June 1870.
- 1900: the number of years married as of June 1.
- 1910: the number of years in the present marriage as of April 15.
- 1930: age at first marriage.

Using Clues From Census Records

Consider the following example for a pair of great-great-grandparents. Perhaps you first found them listed in the 1880 census, ages thirty-two and thirty, with children ages eight years, six years, five years, three years, and two months.

Case Study

An easy way to narrow the marriage date possibilities is to find the couple in other censuses, especially if you cannot find their marriage record. If they married after June 1870, you may even find them in the 1870 census in their childhood homes with their parents. If they were listed in the 1870 census as a couple with no children, it is possible that they had been married less than two years or had lost a child. Consider these clues:

1880	Great-great-grandmother, age thirty, born about 1849 to 1850. She could have married as early as 1866 (age sixteen). Oldest child, a daughter, age eight, was born about 1871 to 1872. Thus, marriage was likely between 1866 and 1871.
1870	Great-great-grandparents shown as a couple, ages consistent with the 1880 census, with a baby boy born in April of that year and no other children. The child apparently died before 1880, but his presence in 1870 suggests the couple married in 1869 or before. This narrows down the possible marriage date to 1866 to 1869.
1900	Both great-great-grandparents living, ages consistent with the 1880 census, married for thirty-two years. Subtract 32 from 1900; marriage year is about 1868, or 1 June 1867–1 June 1868, based on June 1 census day.
1910	Both great-great-grandparents living, ages consistent with the 1880 census, with forty-one years in present marriage. Subtract 41 from 1910; this suggests marriage 15 April 1868–15 April 1869, based on April 15 census day. We cannot tell whether they followed the census instructions to the letter, but if they did, it is possible the couple married between April 15 and June 1 of 1868. They had not yet reached their forty-second anniversary by census time in 1910, although they had passed the anniversary by census day in 1900.

Finding the Marriage Place

Technique

In looking for the marriage place, consider, for example, where the couple in the above example was living in 1870, where each spouse was born, and where the first child was born. Although many possibilities exist, here are common scenarios that consider typical migration patterns:

1. If the parents were reportedly born in the same state, chances are good that the marriage took place in that state, possibly in the county where they lived in 1870 or a neighboring county. If marriage books for those counties do not provide a record, look for a statewide marriage index or records in other counties in the state.

2. If the parents were born in one state and the first child was born in another, the marriage could have taken place in either or somewhere between the two. More research on the parents is necessary to determine whether they grew up in their birth states.

3. If one spouse and the first child were born in the same state, it is likely the marriage took place in that state and the other spouse moved there at some time prior to their meeting and marrying.

4. If the parents were born in different states and the first child in a third state, they may have married in the state where the first child was born, but there are others to consider. For example, if the first child was born in Alabama, the mother in Georgia, and the father in North Carolina, the marriage likely took place in Alabama or Georgia. Try to determine where the parents grew up. If the father grew up in Alabama, it is possible that the mother moved there

with her family and met and married the father there. You may not be able to answer the question of where they grew up until you identify and study parents and siblings.

Estimating Marriage Date From County Records

Case Study

Other records such as deeds, wills, and estate settlements may help you narrow down a marriage date.

Example 1: William Harrison sold a lot in Petersburg, Virginia, in November 1784, and his wife Lucy was "privately examined as the law directs" and freely acknowledged the sale (Petersburg, Virginia, Deed Book 1:30). We know, then, that William and Lucy were married before this date. Several documents may be necessary to approximate the marriage date itself, but each additional record will help you make a more educated guess.

Example 2: Occasionally, the county records contain a marriage agreement, such as the one William Harrison and Nancy Vaughan signed on 26 March 1789, acknowledging their "promise to marry each other." This document suggests that the couple married in 1789. Because William was giving his new wife the house called Porter Hill "where Harrison now resides," and the couple continued to make their home there, we may guess that they probably married in Petersburg where Nancy's family and Harrison both lived (Petersburg, Virginia, Deed Book 1:492).

Example 3: In Amelia County, Virginia, Richard Phillips wrote his will on 14 March 1793, naming among his family and heirs his daughters, Elizabeth Tolbert Allen and Tabitha Phillips (Will Book 5:36). This document tells us that Tabitha was probably not married when the will was written but that her sister, Elizabeth Tolbert Phillips, had married a man named Allen before this date.

NAMES OF FAMILY MEMBERS

Both family and public sources help identify names of children, siblings, or parents of an ancestor:

1. Letters, diaries, memoirs, photographs, Bible records, interviews with other relatives and family friends, newspaper clippings, obituaries, and wedding stories.
2. Birth and death certificates, birth announcements, church registers of birth or baptism. Death certificates that give parents' names should be corroborated with evidence from other sources since they often contain incorrect or incomplete information. Getting birth and death certificates for several children of the same family can be helpful in identifying parents.
3. Federal and state census records may suggest or state relationships.
4. Tombstones, funeral home files, funeral notices and programs, military pension and bounty land warrant applications sometimes name children, siblings, or parents and can help identify children who died young.
5. County records that sometimes state parent-child or sibling relationships include deeds, court records, parental permission for an underage child in

marriage records, some marriage records that asked for parents' names, wills and probate files, and guardianship records.

6. Passenger arrival records, homestead applications, and naturalization papers often identify family groups.

7. Family and county histories can provide names of siblings, children, or parents. Use cautiously and try to verify data, as these sources vary in reliability and accuracy.

Clues in the Cluster

Children's names and naming patterns within the family may suggest namesakes. Isaac McFadden Patton, Thomas Patton Coleman, and Pitser Blalock Croom were all named for their maternal grandfathers—Isaac McFadden, Thomas Patton, and Pitser Blalock. Of course, other records are necessary to verify these relationships, but genealogists need to be alert to the possibilities.

Cluster genealogy is often the key to discovering names of children or parents. One Texas family lost three infant children and buried them in three different cemeteries in the same county. Had the researcher not been working on the cluster of brothers and sisters of the husband and thus visiting multiple cemeteries in the county, she probably would have missed those three tombstones. After all, how can one know to look for tombstones for people whose existence was unknown? When applicable to your search, the 1900 and 1910 censuses may help by telling you how many children a mother had borne and how many were still living.

Working on the cluster can pay off in another way. For example, a bachelor brother died and named in his will his widowed mother and his brothers and sisters, including married names. If probate records for the parents do not exist or do not name their children, this may be the only evidence of these relationships. **If you do not read the document because he is not your ancestor, you will miss the information.**

Research Tip

Clues in Censuses

The 1880 to 1930 federal censuses provide each person's relationship to the head of the household, as do many state censuses from the same period. Federal censuses of prior years, 1850 to 1870, do not specify relationships but suggest a list of children for each couple: those listed in descending age order immediately after the parents. Usually, the nuclear family was enumerated before children by a previous marriage with a different surname, in-laws, or others living in the house.

If you neglect census records of ancestors' brothers or sisters, you may miss elderly parents or other relatives living with one of the siblings. If you ignore families living around yours in the census, you may miss the parents, a married sister, a married daughter, or relatives of the wife living only a few houses away. The census will not tell you these relationships, but the clues of age, birthplace, parents' birthplaces, naming patterns, or occupation can wave a red flag for you to investigate the similarities for possible connections.

Lest we jump to conclusions about the mother's identity, **we must remember that the wife shown in the census, especially 1850 to 1870 when relationships were not given, was not always the only wife and thus was not automatically the mother of all the children listed.** Especially if children by a different surname appear after the nuclear family, the researcher needs to identify these.

- Were they the mother's children by a previous marriage?
- Were they nieces, nephews, or grandchildren?
- Were they foster children or no relation at all?

If there is a gap of more than three or four years between children in the family, the researcher must ask whether (1) a child (or more) had died, (2) the older group were children of the father by a previous wife, (3) the youngest ones were grandchildren by the same surname, or (4) any of the children were actually the wife's by a previous marriage but were listed under the new husband's surname. Reading all available census records for a family can help answer these questions.

By the same token, a young woman listed just below an older man in a pre-1880 census could be a new wife, an unmarried daughter or granddaughter, a widowed daughter-in-law, or a younger sister or niece. Further study into other records is necessary to sort out such relationships.

MOTHER'S MAIDEN NAME

Sometimes, finding a mother's maiden name is as easy as finding a Bible record, marriage record, newspaper article on her wedding, obituary, or tombstone that states the maiden name. A tombstone reading "Lottie Haynes, wife of H.G. Barnett" indicates Haynes as her maiden name. Sometimes tombstones use the French *nee*, meaning "born," to indicate a wife's maiden name: "Denisha Jane Brelsford nee Turley" (born a Turley). However, the stone that reads "Elizabeth Austin nee Huston" actually reports her name by her first husband, not her maiden name.

Birth or death certificates of the woman's children or her own death certificate may give her maiden name, but these often contain mistakes. (On death certificates, one of the most common maiden names is "don't know," or "d.k.") Of these three certificates, probably the most reliable is the birth certificates of her children. If these are not available, we use whatever clues we can find and investigate them as possibilities.

You may discover maiden names in

- interviews with older relatives and family friends
- family letters and diaries
- a will or probate record of a parent naming a married daughter and her husband
- a deed of gift from a parent to a married daughter and her husband
- a deed whereby a daughter and her husband sold property she inherited
- a prenuptial agreement

You may get a clue from the names of children or grandchildren: Peter *Talbot* Phillips, William *Darby* Orgain, Sarah *Warren* Orgain, Catherine *Ewing* Mc-Fadden, and William Lucius *Heath* Harrison. In these cases, the names are still clues, for no answers have yet surfaced to explain the presence of these surnames as middle names. One Virginian, *Archer Allen* Coleman, seems to bear the maiden names of his maternal grandmother and great-grandmother.

A census record sometimes suggests a wife's maiden name by the presence of a person with a different surname living next door to or with the family. Johnson Godwin, living with George and Effie Keahey in 1870, turned out to be Effie's father. Elizabeth Brelsford, living with Young and Gracey Colvin in 1860, was Gracey's mother. People listed after the immediate family in a census may be younger brothers or sisters or other relatives of the wife. Similarly, tombstones with different surnames within a family group are sometimes for members of the same family. A tombstone of an earlier generation may be that of the wife's mother or father.

ANCESTORS ON THE MOVE

In genealogy, we often have to look for people who moved. Frequently, this scenario occurs as we work backward in time, for few families stayed in one place for several hundred years. For example, a Texas family in the 1880 census reported the parents born in Tennessee and their parents born in North Carolina and South Carolina. An elderly grandparent in the household was born in North Carolina, with parents born in Virginia. Researchers suddenly have four states in which to search as they reach back to those generations.

At other times, we want to study the siblings of an ancestor to complete the cluster and try to learn more about the parents. We discover that several brothers and/or sisters moved away from the family's home county. In these cases, we must work forward from where we last found evidence of these relatives.

In this case, the Internet can be a great tool. Through RootsWeb, USGenWeb, and other sites, you can visit a county, town, or surname site and leave a query for descendants of the lost sibling. This tactic may get you the parents' names with documentation (your ultimate goal). It may introduce you to distant cousins or other researchers who know about the siblings who moved away.

Sources of Information on Former Residence

Many of the same sources that help with birth, death, and age information can suggest ancestral residences. Depending on the time period of the people you are seeking, a variety of additional sources may help you identify places of residence at a given time, including the place to which or from which ancestors moved:

1. Church registers may show transfers in or out.
2. County deed, probate, tax, and other records, especially the indexes that you can read rather quickly.
3. Federal military, land, immigration, naturalization, and other records.

4. Membership applications and records of national organizations and lineage societies.

5. Social Security Death Index (deaths after 1936, but not all deaths).

6. College transcripts and alumni lists may include hometowns.

7. City directories give current, and occasionally former, residences.

8. Statewide Soundex for 1880 to 1930 that allows you to survey the reported birthplaces of many people of the same surname.

9. Family and county histories with biographical sketches; use cautiously and try to verify data.

After identifying the state from which an ancestor came, researchers must identify counties or towns of residence. Survey statewide sources to find ancestors in specific counties, including such published sources as the following. **Be cautious accepting what you find: Your ancestor may be one of several people with the same name.** Seek to verify that you have indeed found the correct ancestor.

Warning

1. Indexes and/or abstracts of census, land grant, or marriage records.

2. Vital records, such as Connecticut's Barbour Collection or a statewide birth/death records index.

3. Compiled biographical sketches, Bible records, obituaries, or tombstone inscriptions, such as Connecticut's Hale Collection.

4. Compilations such as the *Territorial Papers* or books on doctors, legislators, ministers, or specific religious or ethnic groups in a given state.

5. Published countywide tombstone transcriptions, deed and land grant abstracts, will and probate abstracts, tax or jury lists, newspaper abstracts (often regional in coverage).

6. Indexes to statewide and regional genealogical periodicals. Especially for ancestors in Virginia, Kentucky, and West Virginia before the Civil War, become familiar with the *Virginia Historical Index*, commonly called the Swem index, after editor Earl Gregg Swem. It indexes eight major collections and periodicals of Virginia.

7. Published indexes or biographical sketches from a particular state pertaining to groups such as loyalists in the American Revolution, soldiers or pensioners from the Revolutionary War or Civil War, or civilians making claims after these two wars.

Additional Techniques

- Network with other people working on the same family or surname.
- Put queries in regional or national genealogical periodicals.
- Post queries on surname or county sites on the Internet.
- Organize your plan of attack and work on it systematically so that your search is more likely to yield results.

Technique

Research Examples

Several examples illustrate successful use of the sources mentioned above.

1. The National Archives case file from Evan Shelby's purchase of federal

land in Mississippi in 1833 gave his earlier county of residence and a new place to search.

2. A series of newspaper obituaries for one group of Texas siblings showed where the surviving brothers and sisters lived over a period of about forty years in the early twentieth century.

3. Another search presented special, but not unusual, problems in identifying a former residence for Luther White. Genealogists tackling such searches do well to remember this line from Shakespeare's *Henry V*, Act II, Scene 1: "Though Patience be a tired Mare, yet she will plod on." The project is summarized below.

Research Project

Goal: Identify former residence and/or parent(s) for a client's blind ancestor, Luther White.

Information Known: Censuses of 1870 and 1860, in Texas, listed his birthplace as Mississippi. The 1860 census indicated, from the ages of his three children, that the family was probably in Illinois or Mississippi in 1850 and went to Texas after 1855.

Problem: Luther White was not listed as a head of household in the Illinois or Mississippi 1850 index. He may have been living elsewhere or with another family.

Plan: Copy from the 1850 Mississippi index and read in the census all entries for heads of household named White.

Results: Families named White lived in sixty-four Mississippi counties in 1850. Patiently, the researcher read all these families, taking the counties in alphabetical order since they are arranged on the microfilm in approximately that way. Almost at the end, in Pontotoc County, appeared, in this order, James White (age fifty-nine), Luther White (twenty-five and blind), Felix White (fourteen), John White (ten), Luther's apparent wife, Tennessee White (twenty-five, called Frances T. in the later censuses), and children Sarah (five) and William (three, also listed in the later censuses). Persistence paid off. The record suggested that James was Luther's father or uncle, and Felix and John may have been younger brothers, half brothers, or cousins. At last, there was a county in which to search further.

OCCUPATION

A number of sources may help you discover an ancestor's occupation:

1. Family letters, diaries, scrapbooks, obituaries, papers suggesting membership in a union or professional organization, a teacher's certificate, pay stubs, tax returns.

2. Interviews with relatives and family friends.

3. Local newspapers (ads and notices from people in all kinds of occupations), city directories, chamber of commerce membership records.

4. Papers of local lawyers, doctors, or merchants, or other business records from the ancestral community, sometimes at a library or archives and

sometimes showing accounts with their customers, employees, or other businesses.

5. County wills, deeds, tax rolls, records of licensing fees, records of marks and brands.

6. County court minutes may mention craftsmen or others doing work for the county. For example, such minutes revealed that James Shaw owned the ferry across the Cumberland River in early Nashville.

7. County probate records. Estate inventories in the probate records often detail the business property of a deceased individual, such as the stock remaining in a retail business or the growing crop of a farmer. Annual accounts of estates sometimes report the income and expenses of a family business or the receipts for sale of the crops.

8. Published family, county, or company histories; use such sources cautiously and try to verify data with other sources.

Clues in the Census

Census records may supply the following occupation information:

1820, 1850–1880	Manufacturing/industry schedules and agriculture schedules that give more detail about each operation. Many of these schedules exist.
1850 on	Each person's occupation. This is probably the best place to begin looking.
1870	Instructions to the census takers emphasized accurate and precise recording of occupations, including those of children who contributed to the family support with a regular job.
1880	Number of months unemployed during the census year.
1900	Occupation of everyone ten or older; number of months unemployed during the census year; each person's status as employer, employee, or self-employed.
1910	Number of weeks unemployed in 1909; whether one was out of work on census day (15 April 1910); whether one was employer, wage earner, or self-employed.
1920	Whether one was employer, wage earner, or self-employed.
1930	Whether one was at work yesterday.

POLITICAL AFFILIATION

To add interest to your family history, you may want to learn about your ancestors' political affiliations or leanings. Sources for this kind of information include the following:

1. Local newspaper stories and advertisements, especially during campaigns. These often give information about volunteer workers, supporters, and candidates.

2. Interviews with relatives and family friends; letters; diaries; scrapbooks; memorabilia such as campaign buttons or parade photographs; voter registration cards that may show party affiliation.

3. Local or state political party records.
4. Some county records before the Civil War include polling lists that show who voted for whom. (I have found such lists in some Kentucky and Virginia records.)

HOUSING OR LIVING CONDITIONS

To add a social and personal dimension to your family history, you want to learn more about ancestral life, including their homes or living conditions. These are common sources for this information:

1. Family photographs, scrapbooks, memoirs, letters, diaries; interviews with relatives and family friends.
2. Photographs or drawings in local historical societies, archives, or published books on houses of the area.
3. County deed records occasionally describe or illustrate a house on a particular lot or include floor plans for local houses because the contract to build the house was filed for record with the county.
4. County probate records include hundreds of inventories detailing to varying degrees what a person owned at the time of death. These often include lists of furniture, household items, kitchen equipment, linens, and, occasionally, clothing.
5. County tax records sometimes include taxable "luxury" items, such as carriages or clocks.
6. Church records and parish vestry books may describe the minister's house.
7. If a business or new home has been built on the site of a former family home, that company, the builders of the new building, or the new owners may have photographs of the site before construction.
8. City directories, telephone directories, and census records may supply a street address. If the home is still standing, the current residents may talk with you, allow picture taking, or even let you visit inside.
9. Whether or not the home is still standing, older residents of the community or local historians may have drawings or photographs, may be able to describe the home and/or the floor plan, or may tell you what changes were made over the years.
10. The federal censuses of 1850, 1860, and 1870 recorded the value of one's real estate. The 1860 and 1870 returns also asked the value of one's personal estate. Beginning in 1890, the census asked whether homes and farms were rented, owned, or owned free of mortgage.
11. Architectural and social histories for the area may describe the typical house of a given period. This information would allow you to imagine the kind of house your ancestors may have lived in.
12. The Sanborn Company's fire insurance maps, available in larger public and university libraries and state historical societies or archives, provide information such as size and shape of buildings in many towns and cities on specific dates, mostly since 1867.

13. The New Orleans Notarial Archives (421 Loyola Avenue) holds several hundred nineteenth-century watercolor drawings of buildings, mostly in the city and suburban parishes, produced when the buildings were placed on the market. The drawings are of both commercial buildings and residences, and some include floor plans.

14. Some newspaper advertisements of buildings for rent or for sale describe the buildings and name the owners or tenants.

COUNTRY OF ORIGIN

The more recent the immigration, generally the easier it is to find the country of origin. For some immigrant ancestors, we may never know. As I often say, I can't get most of my ancestors down to the beach, much less on the boat. However, a line that stops at the beach or in the hills beyond the beach is not the end of your genealogical world. Most of us still have plenty of ancestors to research and plenty to learn about the immigrants once they got here.

Basic sources to use in identifying a country of origin are the same as those for identifying birth information earlier in this chapter and those discussed in chapter thirteen. Additional suggestions include these:

1. Study everything you can find on your immigrant ancestor in this country, including the closest associates and neighbors. Their origins may have been the same.

2. In naturalization papers the new citizen had to renounce allegiance to the former country and its sovereign; some give specific birthplace information. Sometimes the early naturalization papers show only the most recent residence where the immigrant was a citizen. That may or may not have been the birthplace. (See chapters eleven and thirteen.)

3. Passenger arrival lists sometimes give birthplace or last residence. Many books present abstracts or indexes from these lists of passengers arriving from particular countries and/or in specific ports. Good research libraries will have many of these. (See chapter thirteen.)

4. Studying the ethnic backgrounds in the area where your earliest American ancestors lived may suggest groups to which they belonged. Religious groups often traveled in a body, as did members of extended families or neighbors. You may get clues from maps in published histories and geographies that show migration patterns of particular ethnic and religious groups.

5. If you have evidence to suggest a particular origin for your ancestor, study histories of that group in this country at about the time and place the ancestor lived. Are there similarities that might connect your ancestor with the group: religious affiliation, naming patterns, family customs? Do not assume an origin based on surname alone or family tradition.

6. Talk to someone from the suspected place of origin or contact a genealogical group focusing on that country or region. Consult books on research in that area for ideas.

7. Consult some of the electronic databases online or on CD-ROM to learn

For More Info

See also Sharon DeBartolo Carmack's *A Genealogist's Guide to Discovering Your Immigrant & Ethnic Ancestors*.

whether your ancestor is mentioned or whether others of the same surname are identified with a country of origin. Use any information you find as clues for your own research.

THINGS TO DO NOW

Idea Generator

1. Create or update the chronological profile for your focus ancestor and the pertinent family group sheets. Which topics from this chapter address holes in these charts?
2. Reread the topic in this chapter that you would like to address first and list the sources you would like to try. Begin that effort.

FIFTEEN

What's in a Date?

WRITING DATES

Two methods of writing dates are common in the United States. The more familiar one combines month/day/year: 6/6/76 or June 6, 1976. The other system is used in Europe, in military notation, and increasingly in genealogy, as it eliminates commas and helps prevent confusion in reading. It simply notes day/month/year: 6 June 1976 or 6/VI/1976, with the month written in Roman numerals.

If a writer is consistent, you can usually identify the system in use. In *5/31/1915*, it is obvious the month is first since there are not thirty-one months, but *4/5/1914* is not necessarily clear. Is it May 4 or April 5? To prevent confusion, write out or abbreviate the month instead of using numbers.

If you send a genealogy questionnaire to someone, give them blanks to fill out as you want it done:

_____ / _____ / _____   _____ / _____ / _____
day   month   year   month   day   year

READING DATES

In old newspapers or letters, writers sometimes used shortcuts in noting dates. A person writing on February 17 and referring to a letter "of the 8th instant" meant a letter of February 8, or the same month. The same writer referring to a letter "of the 28th ultimo" meant a letter of January 28, or the previous month. An event on "the 28th proximo" meant the twenty-eighth of next month. Sometimes, writers used abbreviations: *inst.*, *ult.*, *ult°*, or *prox.*

"Tuesday last" meant the most recent Tuesday, and "Thursday next" meant the nearest Thursday to come. "September last" was the most recent September in the past.

OLD STYLE AND NEW STYLE DATES

The Julian, or Old Style, calendar was introduced in Rome in the year we call 46 B.C. and into the Christian world in A.D. 325. It gave the year twelve months and 365 days, with a leap year of 366 days every fourth year, similar to our system today. Later, church scholars realized that the calendar and sun time were not synchronized. Man's calendar was gradually getting behind the sun's natural calendar. In other words, each calendar day was a few minutes too long. These few minutes added up to three days over a period of four hundred years or ten days by the year 1582.

This discrepancy meant the first day of spring, the vernal equinox, fell on March 11 instead of March 21, and the church's calculations for the date of Easter, which are governed by that equinox, were not correct. Therefore, in 1582, Pope Gregory XIII revised the calendar to be more in accordance with the sun. He "made up for lost time" by skipping those ten days to catch up with the sun. The day after October 4 was October 15 instead of October 5.

To prevent the loss of three more days in succeeding four hundred years, we now omit three leap year days every four hundred years. To simplify the process, the Pope chose the double-zero years. The rule is that the double-zero years that can be divided evenly by four hundred are leap years, e.g., 1600, 2000. The ones not evenly divisible by four hundred are not leap years, e.g., 1700, 1800, 1900, 2100.

Reminder

The Pope made another change that affects genealogists. **New Year's Day had been March 25,** nine months prior to the Christmas celebration of Jesus' birth. Thus, 24 March 1532 was followed the next day by 25 March 1533. However, after 1582, New Year's Day would be January 1.

The changes confused many people, and some thought the Pope was trying to shorten their lives by ten days! Even more confusing, however, was the fact that only Spain, Portugal, Poland, France, and parts of Italy made the change in 1582. When it was December 12 in Rome that year, it was December 2 in London. The German Catholic states, Belgium, and parts of Holland followed in 1583–84; Hungary, by 1587. However, for over a century, the countries of Europe and their territories in the New World operated under two different calendars.

Various Protestant states of central and northern Europe adopted the Gregorian calendar by 1701, leaving Great Britain clinging to the old Julian calendar for another half century. By then, the difference between the two systems was eleven days instead of ten because the year 1700 had been leap year, with an extra day, in Britain but not in western Europe. Much of eastern Europe and Asia remained under the Julian calendar or their own system until the twentieth century.

Further complicating the situation, some British individuals (and therefore some American colonists) adopted the Gregorian calendar on their own. You may find in early records what seem to be discrepancies or inaccuracies but are explained by the difference in calendars.

For example, a family Bible record shows that Patty Field Allen was born on 25 August 1746. Her sister Obedience was born on 1 March 1747. It becomes obvious that the family was not using the Gregorian calendar, for a baby born in August is not usually followed by another born about six months later. According to the Julian calendar, still the official calendar of Britain and the colonies, the first day of March following Patty's birth was still 1746. March 25 ushered in 1747. Thus, 1 March 1747 was another twelve months away, about eighteen months after Patty's birth. Obedience, therefore, could write her birth date 1 March 1747/48, meaning 1747 under the old calendar and 1748 under the new one.

If a record is dated "the 5th day of the 5th month of 1729," it could be May 5 under the new calendar but July 5 under the old one, with March being counted as the first month in the Julian system. Thus, you cannot always tell which calendar you are reading, but it seldom really matters. When you know, you can add in your notes *O.S.* (Old Style or Julian) or *N.S.* (New Style or Gregorian) after the date.

A date written with a double day—5/16 April 1704—means that under the old calendar the date would be April 5; under the new calendar, it would be April 16. A double year could be written, but only for the months of January, February, or March. These months could fall under either of two years depending on which calendar the recorder used. Technically, George Washington's birth date could be written "11/22 February 1731/1732," which covers both calendars.

An early will in a county will book illustrates contemporary use of the double year: "In witness whereof I have hereunto Set my hand and Seal the twenty third Day of the twelfth month 1736/7." The twelfth month was February of 1736 under the Julian calendar, 1737 under the new one.

Finally, in 1750, Parliament arranged to make the official change to the Gregorian calendar. The day after 2 September 1752 was September 14 instead of September 3, making up for the eleven days' difference in the two systems. Furthermore, the new year would begin on January 1 instead of March 25.

WHAT DAY OF THE WEEK?

The five-day workweek with a weekend for family and social activities is, of course, a relatively recent phenomenon. Today's predominance of Saturday weddings is surely related to this pattern. On what day of the week did weddings occur in your family's past? Why did Grandma and Grandpa choose Wednesday

Internet Source

Perpetual calendars on the Internet: <http://calendar home.com/tyc>, and <http://www.norbyhus .dk/calendar.html>. Disclaimers warn that human error may cause site errors. This formula is a good way to double-check.

for their wedding? One couple chose that day because the groom, who worked six days a week, found someone who would work for him Wednesday and Thursday. His only free day was Sunday, but no one in that community at that time would have considered having a wedding on Sunday.

Another prospective groom was asked when the wedding would be. The young farmer answered, "Sometime between the peas and the wheat." Apparently any day of the week would do so long as it fell within the slack season.

Some almanacs publish a perpetual calendar by which you can find the day of the week for many dates in the past or future. However, you can figure it yourself with easy arithmetic. The formula on page 193 gives a correct day of the week for any date after 14 September 1752, the day on which Britain and the colonies converted to the Gregorian calendar. Actually you could use the formula for dates before this if you then convert them to the old calendar. The chart gives an example, using an ancestral wedding date.

For fun, practice the formula using 14 September 1752, the day of the great calendar switch. Can you imagine the trauma of trying that kind of change in our culture on that day of the week? Even daylight saving time goes into effect in the early hours of Sunday to cause the least possible confusion. Imagine our making the change to daylight saving time on the same day of the week that the whole calendar changed!

USING DATES

Dates are useful tools, and genealogists use them for many purposes other than vital statistics. These cases illustrate the use and misuse of dates.

Case I

This case could apply to published transcriptions as well as researchers' notes. Tombstones of two Campbell siblings were copied as follows:

Infant daughter
4 September 1891–10 September 1891

Talmadge Ward Campbell
12 January 1892–26 November 1894

Do you see the discrepancy? It has nothing to do with the old calendar. A daughter born in September and a son born four months later? Hardly. The first note seemed to be correct: The unnamed baby girl lived only a few days. Was the other copied wrong or was the stone actually in error? The tombstone was studied again (a good reason to photograph the tombstones), and it actually read June instead of January. The copy contained the error. However, the researcher would also want to study the possibility of error on either stone since the stones show that the babies were born only nine months apart.

```
┌─────────────────────────────────────────────────────────────────────┐
│                      What Day of the Week?                            │
│                                                                       │
│  Formula                                          Example             │
│  ──────────────────────────────────────────────  ──────────────────  │
│           Ancestral wedding date                  9 December 1824     │
│                                                                       │
│  Step 1.  Begin with the last 2 digits of the year.    24            │
│  Step 2.  Add ¼ of this number and disregard any remainder.   6       │
│  Step 3.  Add the date in the month.              9                   │
│  Step 4.  Add according to the month:             6                   │
│                   January     1   (for leap year, 0)                  │
│                   February    4   (for leap year, 3)                  │
│                   March       4                                       │
│                   April       0                                       │
│                   May         2                                       │
│                   June        5                                       │
│                   July        0                                       │
│                   August      3                                       │
│                   September   6                                       │
│                   October     1                                       │
│                   November    4                                       │
│                   December    6                                       │
│  Step 5.  Add for the century:                    2                   │
│                   18th century    4                                   │
│                   19th century    2                                   │
│                   20th century    0                                   │
│                   21st century    6               ────────            │
│  Step 6.  Total the numbers from steps 1–5.       47                  │
│                                                                       │
│  Step 7.  Divide by 7. Check the remainder against this               │
│           chart to find the day of the week:      6 with a remainder of 5.│
│                   1 = Sunday                      The wedding took    │
│                   2 = Monday                      place on a Thursday. │
│                   3 = Tuesday                                         │
│                   4 = Wednesday                                       │
│                   5 = Thursday                                        │
│                   6 = Friday                                          │
│                   0 = Saturday                                        │
└─────────────────────────────────────────────────────────────────────┘
```

Case II

Another tombstone clearly reads:

> To the sacred memory of
> Rev. William Harrison
> who departed this life
> 20th November 1814 . . .

However, his will, dated May 1812, was probated in January 1814 (Petersburg, Virginia, Hustings Court, Will Book 2:91). By law and common sense, the will could not be probated before he died. This leaves the researcher with a discrepancy. Did Harrison die in 1813 or 1812? In this case, at least three other records, created independently of each other and not part of the probate record, indicated that he died in 1813: a Masonic lodge list of deaths for 1813 and two city tax rolls, showing his estate paying 1814 taxes. The probate book itself, with records in chronological order, was clearly correct. The tombstone must contain the error.

Case III

Continued research may produce explanations to puzzling dates, as in Case II. In other instances, perhaps we may never know the answer. Here is an example still "under puzzlement."

The original marriage bond in the archives of the Library of Virginia, showing the intent of William Daniel to marry Patty Field Allen, clearly bears the date 28 March 1768, as does the attached consent of the bride's father, Samuel Allen. Under a Virginia law of October 1748, if either the bride or groom was under twenty-one and not formerly married, consent of the father or guardian of "every such infant shall be personally given before the said clerk" of the county, with two witnesses (Hening's Statutes of Virginia, 6:82).

According to the published Bible record of Patty's brother Archer Allen, Patty's birth date was 25 August 1746 (Bible record of Archer Allen, *The William and Mary Quarterly*, Series 1, 22: 95). This date would have made Patty twenty-one years and seven months old when she married, not legally needing the consent of her father to marry.

At that time, Virginia law required a wife to be brought to the courthouse when her husband sold land to which she had a claim. The justice of the peace or another official took her aside, explained the deed of sale to her, and asked if she willingly signed it. Was the signature hers? Did she wish to retract it? By agreeing to the sale, she relinquished her dower rights to that property.

William Daniel sold a tract of land in August 1761, and no dower right or wife was mentioned. Probably, William was not married at the time. Then in 1763, at least by September 27 when the deed was recorded, William sold 200 acres to John Daniel. No dower right or wife was mentioned at that time. However, in the spring of 1765, John Daniel sold this same tract, and William sold 375 acres in another tract. Seven months later, 28 October 1765, John's wife, Elizabeth, and William's wife, Martha, appeared in court and relinquished their dower rights to the 200 acres that John was selling, and Martha consented to the sale of William's 375 acres (Cumberland County, Virginia, Deed Book 3:193, 416; Book 4:60, 67). Why would Martha have any claim to relinquish on John's land unless she was married to William when he sold it to John? That sale was in 1763, and this document suggests that William and Martha were married by that time, and certainly by 1765, when the dower rights were relinquished. Yet the marriage record clearly shows their marriage in 1768.

The dates of these documents clearly present a dilemma, and perhaps they cannot be reconciled. A possible answer is that William was married to another Martha before he married Patty, who in later records continued to be called Martha. If this were so, the first Martha would have died in 1766 or 1767, leaving no children and perhaps no trace. Another possibility, although less likely in light of other county records and family histories, is that another William and Martha were in the county in the 1760s. This is one of the continuing puzzles of genealogy.

THINGS TO DO NOW

Idea Generator

1. Check your charts. Is your style of writing dates consistent and completely clear to anyone who reads your work, especially those who regularly use the "international" style? Try the international or genealogical style of writing dates.

2. Check your charts for logic and common sense in dates. Watch for people marrying or women bearing children at absurd ages and for children born to fathers long deceased.

3. Use the formula for "What Day of the Week?" to determine the day for the birth, marriage, and death of your focus ancestor or another of your choice. On what day of the week were you born? On what day of the week was the great calendar switch?

SIXTEEN

Read It Right: Handwriting of the Past

T he ability to read handwriting from the past is a skill genealogists need. Developing this skill is easier if you are aware of the characteristics of earlier styles for both letters and numbers.

QUIRKS IN STYLE

Many of the capital letters of the nineteenth and late eighteenth centuries were similar to the styles shown here:

*A B C D E F G H I J K L M N O
P Q R S T U V W X Y Z*

*C G H I J K L S T L W
C G H I J K L S T L Z*

At the same time, most lowercase letters were formed about the same way they are today. Individual variations are found, of course, but there was a general pattern for writers to follow.

There were two styles of *r* and *t*, just as there are today:

Western fork of a branch
running a northernly course

at my decease

Sometimes *u* and *n* looked alike as did *w* and *m*. Like writers today, earlier writers did not always dot their *i*s and cross their *t*s. Because of fading ink, yellowing papers, and the unevenness with which quill pens and pen staffs wrote, these and other strokes in the original may be barely distinguishable to us today.

The most unusual characteristic of older handwriting is the double *s*, written as if it were *fs* or a sprawling *p*. Here are some examples from the nineteenth century.

Putnam

Miss[iss]ippi

witnesseth

blessing

Missouri

Jessee

Agness

Miss Polly

Bass

Divission [*sic*]

possessed

assigns

in the presence of Willm Hill

Individuals used their own variations in form. One of these above writers made the *j* of *enjoyment* exactly the same as the first s in *blessing*. There is no confusion, however, because it is clear what word he was using.

in the enjoyment of

Some capital letters can confuse the modern reader. The *S*, *L*, and *T* may need caution and care in reading.

Susannah, Sally &

Sister

Sons

Subject

Legacy

Lea

Levi

Lucy
Lucy

Thos
Thos [Thomas]

Tenth
Tenth

Tobase
Tobacco

State of So Carolina
State of So Carolina

Last Will
Last Will

Samuel Scattergood
Samuel Scattergood

Samuel L. Saunders
Samuel L. Saunders

Lemuel
Lemuel

Lemuel
Lemuel

Loving Wife
Loving Wife

The *I* and *J* were almost identical—in fact, often interchangeable. Perhaps this similarity is a carryover from the Latin and Greek alphabets in which the two letters were interchangeable, or in which there really was no *J*. Words that we spell with *J* often come from Latin or Greek stems beginning with *I*. A prominent example is the pair of Christian symbols *IHS* and *INRI*. The first is the beginning of the Greek spelling of *Jesus*. The second is an acronym from the Latin words for "Jesus of Nazareth, King of the Jews." Each *I* here stands for a word we begin with *J*.

Another example is the variants in the name John: German *Johannes*, French *Jean*, Spanish *Juan*, Scandinavian *Jan*, Russian *Ivan*, and Gaelic *Ian*. Many of the Biblical names used in the eighteenth and nineteenth centuries were of Hebrew or Aramaic origin and were spelled with an *I*. It was not until the seventeenth century that the *J* was clearly a separate letter in function and form. Is it any wonder then that handwriting reflected this double duty? Here are some examples showing the similarity of *I* and *J*.

In   Isham   I do   January   Sessions

John John   James James   Joshua Joshua

Isaac Johnston Isaac Johnston   Isaac Isaac   John John

In presence of John In presence of John   Jesse Jesse   James Ivey James Ivey

Joseph Harrisson Joseph Harrisson   Isaac Isaac   Juliana Juliana

DECIPHERING

Reading old records can be quite enjoyable because clerks often had very polished, clear handwriting. It takes much more skill to duplicate their style than to read it. The care with which many of them wrote may remind us to review the legibility of our own scribbling.

When you find problems in reading the handwriting, consider different combinations of letters until you decide what the original says. Look at other letters of the same handwriting. Try to find the same letter or word written elsewhere in the same handwriting. Can you guess it by comparing its shape with others you already know? If the letters individually create a problem, look at the word as a whole or the phrase where it appears. What is the context? What is the logical word to fit the meaning?

If you cannot decide, try copying the original as closely as possible, put "?" or "[?]" in your notes to indicate an illegible word, or get a photocopy. If you can narrow the possibilities, put the alternatives in your notes. Examples are the names Lemuel and Samuel, David and Daniel, even Jane/Janie and James. If you cannot tell which name the writer intends, put both in your notes and indicate the problem.

Try a sample problem. This word looks frightful by itself, but in the context of its whole phrase, there is only one possible reading:

"Witness the following signatures & seals"

This is the minister's signature on an 1869 marriage license:

We know the initial is *P* and the last name is Mullally. The first name looks like it ends in *is*. It cannot be Morris or Travis. The first letter is not shaped like the *M* in his last name, and there are too many humps for Travis. If you have access to another source, look to see how someone else wrote his name. His name is Francis.

Another signature to study is the one above Carter H. Trent's name on a contract. The initials are clearly *E. W.* There is a dot for an *I* and the last letter seems to be *s*. The beginning letter, as it turns out, is a large *s* as in the old-style double *s*. But it could give a reader an impression of a *J* or maybe a fancy *T*. In this case, it cannot be compared with letters of the same shape on the document because this is a signature added to another man's instrument. But in the rest of the contract, the man's name appears several times, a little different each time:

Tip

By comparing three slightly different ways of writing the same name, we must conclude the man was E.W. Sims. **Working with records of a particular county over a period of time acquaints researchers with residents' names and thus makes reading their names easier.**

TRANSCRIBING

Copying or transcribing older handwriting takes special care to preserve the message of the original. In copying a passage, copy it just as the original reads. If a letter or word has been omitted and you want to put it in, add it in brackets to indicate that you, not the original writer, supplied it. Another method is to write "[*sic*]" after the word. This is Latin for "thus." It indicates that you know something is wrong, but you've copied it exactly as it was.

"This leaves all well—hopeing this may find [you] and all the family in the enjoyment of the same blessing. I must close write soon—"

"give my love to all of the family and except [*sic*] a portion your self no more"

THE OLDER STYLE

Seventeenth- and early-eighteenth-century handwriting looked different from the later styles. It was not always so sleek and flowing. Some letters were formed differently, particularly the lowercase *e*; others were very similar to nineteenth-century style.

Steⁿ Hughes
Robert Hughes

witnesses hereto

Daniel Croom

Willm Allen

Ent[e]red

Brewer

Andrew Reed

*Adm[inistrato]r
of Benj[a][min] Sullivan*

heretofore made or done

thereof in the Testator's Presence

mercy and merrits of my Lord

did Declare

Item

Quakers

NUMBERS

Numbers written in the eighteenth and nineteenth centuries are very similar to numbers we write now. Sometimes the older ones contain more flourishes or different strokes. Be cautious reading "3," "6," and "8." The first example is "8th day of July 1808."

MARKS

In documents, researchers find the distinctive marks of persons who could not sign their names to documents. In original documents, the marks are theirs, but the names were written by someone else. In record books, the clerk wrote the name and copied the mark as the person made it.

IN DOCUMENTS

Below are some of the terms and symbols researchers find in reading documents. Many people placed their seal, often in wax, on a document after signing it as a way of confirming their signature. The clerk, in copying the document into the official court record, indicated the use of the seal, sometimes with the word *seal* and sometimes with *L.S.*, meaning the place where the seal was affixed.

signed Thomas Smith

This indicates Smith signed the original documents but that this is not his signature.

Taxes p[er] rec[ei]pt

P[er] me [the clerk] (done by me)

Per account

[my] Daughters (Viz) (namely, that is to say)

You may find Viz in wills, preceding the naming of heirs.

Teste

B.B. Woodson C[lerk]

The clerk certifies with his signature that the document is a true copy.

From an estate sale, this excerpt shows the use of *do* to mean "ditto." Someone bought a broad ax; someone bought a "pole Do," or a pole ax; a third person bought another "Do," or pole ax.

A List of the property of Wm Richards dec^d Febr^y 8th 1827. This is the date of the estate sale, not the date of his death.

Idea Generator

THINGS TO DO NOW

Practice reading the following passages:

  1. Portion of an estate inventory listing items and their appraised values

2. A wife's acknowledgment of the sale of land

Cumberland County to wit.

I Isaiah C. England a Justice of the peace for the County aforesaid State of Virginia, do hereby certify, that Mildred A. wife of Archer P. Flippin, whose name is signed to the writing above bearing date on the 23d, day of November 1866. after being examined by me privily and apart from her husband, and having the aforesaid writing fully explained to her, she the said Mildred A. Flippin acknowledged the said writing to be her act and deed, and declared that she executed it willingly, and does not wish to retract it. Given under my hand this 4th day of December 1846.

J. C. England J.P.

3. Promissory note from a probate file

On or before the twenty fifth day of December next I promise to pay Jack S Davenport the sum of fifteen Dollars for value rec'd this twentyeth day of March 1805

his ⊕ mark

Arthur Willis
mark

4. A section of an 1824 will

5.ᵗ. I give & bequeath unto my Daughter Penny Benson three negroes namely, Lilly, Bird & Rachel to be kept together by my Executors for the use & support of herself & children during her natural life. & then to be equally divided among her three Children Patsey Betsey & Jamy Benson so as to prevent the said Negroes from being sold from them & the proceeds wasted by Matthias Benson her husband; together with her distributive share of money that She may be intitled to out of the balance of my estate that may be sold and this part of her legacy to be managed in the same way as the negroes by my Executors for her and her childreny use

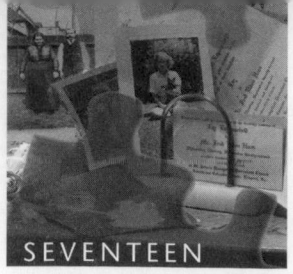

SEVENTEEN

Fitting the Pieces Together: A Case Study

Notes

Endnotes begin on page 221.

Case Study

P utting together a family history involves many strategies, sources, and people. Several interviews with a key person are often necessary. Research into public records may call for several visits to the same courthouse or its microfilmed records as you learn more and ask more questions. Repeated use of all kinds of sources helps make your history as complete and interesting as possible.

Once the links between parents and children are confirmed, with the right ancestors in a given place at a given time, researchers can gather more of the history—social, cultural, and regional—that affected their family. Then weaving the verified genealogical data with historical and cultural information, they can compile a first-rate and meaningful family history.

The case study below details the research for the links—maiden names and parent generations—in one family. The last section illustrates the thinking, planning, and strategies that later focused on trying to identify one ancestor's birth date and place. Endnotes at the end of the chapter detail the sources used to verify two generations of female ancestors and work on the next phase. Please read these along with the case study.

THE FIRST GENERATION: ELLA LEE

Charlotte knew only the names of her grandparents: Bill and Ella Lee White. The lure of the unknown launched a search for her grandmother's family.

Initial Interviews and Preliminary Research

Three elders of this client's family—Aunt Leona, Aunt Zona, and Mama Edna—helped develop the family group sheet for Bill and Ella Lee White, Leona and Zona's parents and Edna's parents-in-law. These two sisters and their sister-in-law named all eighteen children and stepchildren of the parents' combined families, listed as many of the spouses as they could remember, recalled that all the eighteen children were born in Cherokee County, Texas, and confirmed that both parents had lost spouses before marrying each other. In the earliest interview, Edna had recalled that Ella Lee's maiden name was Cummings.[1]

Hidden Treasures

Aunt Zona shared from her mother's Bible the birth information for twelve of the eighteen children. This record revealed that Ella Lee was born on 29 December 1867 in Alto, Texas, as Ella Lee Cummings. In her hometown, she had first married James Alburn Collier on 6 March 1883. He died sixteen years later, on 26 September 1899, three months before the birth of their youngest child.[2] Her husband's death left Ella Lee to support eight children ranging in age from fifteen to newborn.

The same Bible record showed that Ella Lee married her second husband, William J. White, on 12 July 1901 in Alto, Texas.[3] The county marriage record, checked later, gave the marriage date as 14 July 1901.[4] The 1900 census, the most recent one available when the search began and read after this visit, listed both Ella Lee Collier and William J. White in Cherokee County. Ella L. Collier, a thirty-one-year-old widow, lived on her farm with her eight children, including the two young teenage sons who worked on the farm. William J. White, a fifty-one-year-old widower, lived on his farm with his teenage daughter, Lillie White; his mother-in-law, Martha Willis; and a young black farmhand named Sam Alber, who boarded with the family.[5]

Ella Lee's Bible record further revealed that Bill (William J.) White, Leona and Zona's father, had died on 31 October 1910. Since the county death record shows the date as 1 November 1910 at 12 P.M., it is quite possible that he died during the night, the *P.M.* meaning midnight in the eyes of the physician, who seems to have been the informant, or the clerk who made the record.[6] Nevertheless, it is no wonder his two youngest daughters did not remember him; they were ages three and one when he died.

During the visit, Aunt Leona reminisced and told stories; she was really wound up. Each question brought a twenty-minute answer with tales of getting lost in the woods, having seventy-five to a hundred relatives for Christmas, growing up in the tomato patch, a near shotgun wedding, and the old aunt who scolded when the kids fed scraps of biscuit dough to the chickens.

Oral History

On a tour of the Old Palestine Cemetery, where she knew many of the family members were buried, Aunt Leona pointed out names on tombstones and identified each person: "Ida's husband," or "he was killed in a car wreck," or "an adopted son." She also listed the unmarked graves of family members known to be in the cemetery, including her father, Bill White, and his first wife.

Later, Aunt Leona navigated a drive through the county to the old "home place" where she had grown up, although the house was no longer standing; to the school where all the kids "got edgicated"; down the road on which they used to walk to school; and by her Grandma Cummings's house! The very house! This gave the search a new perspective.

A Conversation Full of Clues

Her Grandma Cummings was Ella Lee's mother, the first goal of the search. The presence of the house triggered new questions for Aunt Leona to answer, using her names for the cast of characters—Grandma, Mama, etc.

1. What was Grandma's name? *Grandma.*

2. When did she die? *She lived to be ninety-three; the kids got out of school to go to the funeral.* (**Use this clue.** Leona was born in 1907 and started to school at age six or seven, 1913 or 1914. Her grandma died when she was young but already in school, so after 1913 and maybe around 1920.)

3. Who were Grandma's children? *Mama and a brother, Cumby.*

4. What was his real name? *I don't know.*

5. Was Grandma married more than once? *I don't know.*

6. Did Mama have half brothers and half sisters? *Yes, Mama had a half brother, John Cummings.* (**Use this clue.** Grandpa Cummings had at least one wife before Grandma.)

7. I found a John Cummings in the 1880 census with a wife and a baby girl, Elnora.[7] Is that the same John? *Yes. Nora was the only girl. She had eleven brothers, named for Bible characters, including Matthew, Mark, Luke, and John.*

8. Did Mama have other half brothers or half sisters? *I don't remember.*

9. What was Grandma Cummings's name (again)? *Grandma* (again).

10. Did she live on "the place" a long time? *Yes, forty or fifty years. Grandma needed someone to look after her when she got old, and Mama had too many kids to be Mama and Papa to and [had to] run the farm and feed some of her grandkids, too. She simply could not take care of Grandma. So she deeded her half of the place to her brother, Cumby, if he'd look after Grandma.*

(**Use these clues.** Grandma lived there many years, and Mama "deeded" her half. That means they owned the place. The county clerk's deed index for the appropriate time period listed a number of deed records under the name of Moses Cummings. There had been time to read about six before keeping the appointment with Aunt Leona. Two of the deeds named his wife, Adelia.[8] Were these possibly Ella Lee's parents? The probate records showed that Moses died in 1903, at age seventy-seven, which suggested a birth year of 1826.[9] If he was Ella Lee's father, his approximate age of forty-one at the time of Ella Lee's birth in 1867 would be logical and possible in a father-daughter relationship, especially a father with his second or third wife.)

Now it was time to sort out the facts about the Cummings family.

11. What road is the house on? *Old San Antonio Road.* (**Supporting evidence:** Moses Cummings had purchased at least two pieces of land just outside town on the Old San Antonio Road, as shown in deed records at the courthouse.[10] The 1869 and 1870 dates indicated the purchases were almost forty years before Leona was born, and Grandma could have lived there another ten or more years after Leona's birth. Thus, the deed records supported Leona's statement that Grandma lived on the place forty or fifty years.)

12. Did you ever know Grandpa Cummings? *No.* (**Supporting evidence:** The death record showed that Moses died in 1903, before Leona was born.)

13. What was his name? *Never heard anybody say.*

14. Could it have been Moses? *Don't have any idea.* (At least she was honest.)

15. Could Grandma's name have been Adelia? *Hey, yes! But it was Cordelia.*

Yes, it had to be because sister Delia was named for her. (**Note:** *Adelia* in the deeds makes little difference; clerks sometimes make mistakes.)

16. Moses was her husband, according to deed records of 1869 and 1870. Let's look at the marriages I copied at the courthouse. Here is M.H. Cummings (could be Moses) marrying Mrs. C.E. Everett (C could be Cordelia) in 1865.[11] Your mama was born in 1867, so these could be her parents.

17. Look at these cemetery notes: Nina Cummings, 1872–1945; C.C. Cummings, 1865–1934; Alma Cummings, 1870–1878, daughter of M.H. and C.E. Cummings.[12] Can you identify these? *Well, Cumby's wife was Nina.*[13]

18. Could Cumby be a nickname for Christopher Columbus? *I don't know; I never heard his real name.*

We decided it could be: M.H. and C.E. married in March 1865. Their son Cumby, if the C.C. above, could still have been born in late 1865. Alma, daughter of M.H. and C.E., was born exactly three years to the day after Mama was born, but died young.

19. Do you know any of Cumby's kids or John's kids I could write to for further information? *Yes.* And she gave me a name and address.

Planning

The visit had to end. What was next?

- Study the notes on this family.
- Update the working family group sheets.
- Write down questions that need answers.
- Write the man Leona suggested.
- Reread the 1880 census for Moses and Cordelia Cummings; the first reading probably had missed them.
- Read more census records.
- Plan to revisit the courthouse or rent microfilm for the marriage of a C.E. *Somebody* (Grandma Cummings) to a Mr. Everett (to find her maiden name and marriage) and for vital records.

Notes

Confirmation of Parents

The original goal was to identify Ella Lee's parents. Circumstantial evidence so far suggested they were Moses and Cordelia Cummings. Several additional records solidified the conclusion.

1. The **1870 census**, which did not state relationships, showed Moses and Cordelia with a household full of children: James (20), Martha (16), John A. (14), Mary (12), Columbus (4), Ella (2), Elizabeth Everett (16), and Almanza [*sic*] Everett (14).[14]

2. The **1880 census** confirmed the relationships. Moses and his wife, Cordelia E., had only four children of the combined families in the household: Moses's daughter Mary J. (20), son Columbus (14), daughter Ella (12), and Moses's stepdaughter (Cordelia's daughter), Elizabeth Everett (25).[15] John A. Cummings, James Cummings, and Almanzon Everett were heads of household elsewhere in the county.

3. The **1900 census** listed Columbus C. Cummings (34) and wife Nina (23)

with their family and gave Columbus's birth date as December 1865, which supported the supposition he was born just over nine months after his parents married.[16]

4. The **death certificate** for Chris Columbus Cummings gave his birth information as 23 December 1865 in Alto, Texas; his death information as 8 February 1934 in Cherokee County; and his parents as M.H. Cummings and Cordelia Houston.[17]

5. At first, it appeared that Ella Lee had no death certificate. A review of her Bible record showed that she had married a third time to J.J. Priddy on 13 November 1923 in Alto. This new surname led to her death certificate, which gave her birth information as 29 December 1867 in Texas; her death information as 11 November 1941, burial in Palestine Cemetery, Alto, Texas; and her parents as Moses Cummings and Cordelia Houston.[18] The informant was J(ohn) E(mory) Collier, shown in the Bible record to be her fifth child, born in 1893.

THE SECOND GENERATION: CORDELIA

The new goal was to find the parents of Grandma Cordelia Cummings, wife of Moses Cummings. The death certificates for her children Columbus and Ella Lee had supplied her maiden name as Houston. When she married Moses Cummings, the marriage record had shown her as Mrs. C.E. Everett, but the Cherokee County records did not list the marriage of a Cordelia Houston to an Everett.

The 1870 and 1880 censuses suggested that Cordelia was born between 1832 and 1835.[19] Without a specific family or place in which to look for her in 1860, it was reasonable to skip back to 1850, for which the library had an index. Was she married by 1850? Would she be listed in the census as Houston or Everett?

Potential Parents Emerge

Everett families lived in several area counties. Among these was Cordelia Everett, age seventeen, reportedly born in Pennsylvania, married to William M. Everett, a carriage maker.[20] They lived in the town of San Augustine in San Augustine County, Texas, two counties away from where Cordelia lived after 1865. The same census page listed a Huston family in which Pennsylvania was the reported birthplace of the mother and older son. Was this coincidence, or might they be Cordelia's family? Her age was a clue that could place her between two of the Huston children still living at home.

Marriage records of this new county showed Miss Cordelia E. Huston marrying William M. Everett on Wednesday evening, 27 October 1847.[21] Was this the same Cordelia? If she was born about 1832 to 1835, as three census records suggested, would she have married at twelve to fifteen years of age? Or were the census ages incorrect?

The Huston couple in San Augustine in the 1850 census were Almanzon and Elizabeth.[22] This was promising evidence in light of the same names of the Everett children listed with Cordelia and Moses Cummings in the 1870 and 1880 censuses, cited on page 209. Would Huston probate records in the county

Notes

The records give both name variants, Huston and Houston, for this family; the study reports them as they were in each record.

link Cordelia to this family? They did not. Likewise, Almanzon Huston was a party to many deeds but none with a Cummings or an Everett.

However, two additional census records provided convincing circumstantial evidence.

1. The **1860 census** of San Augustine County enumerated A. and Elizabeth Huston, Cordelia (age twenty-six and listed as Huston), four Huston teenagers, a young woman (who turned out to be a married Huston daughter) and her child, a boarder, and Elizabeth and Almanzon Everett (ages seven and five).[23] Based on the 1870 census listing and the 1880 census statement that Elizabeth Everett was Moses Cummings's stepdaughter, these Everett children were certainly Cordelia's. Were they named for Huston grandparents?

2. An **1835 census** of San Augustine revealed Almanzon and Elizabeth Huston with six children, including Cordelia, age three.[24] This record seemed to push back Cordelia's birth date to about 1832 and suggested her age at the time of her 1847 marriage to be more reasonable and within the norm.

Other Evidence Leads to Confirmation

Moses and "Adelia" Cummings purchased their land on the San Antonio Road in 1869 from Elizabeth Houston and in 1870 from H.H. Houston.[25] Were these Cordelia's mother and brother?

In Alto, where Cordelia lived after 1865, the city cemetery contains one tombstone with a double inscription: Alma, daughter of M.H. and C.E. Cummings, born 29 December 1870, died 31 July 1878, and Elizabeth Austin nee Huston, born 29 March 1805, died 31 July 1878.[26] The significance of this inscription now became apparent.

The surname Austin was the clue leading back to the county courthouse where probate records this time yielded results. Among the heirs (children and grandchildren) of Elizabeth Austin, formerly Huston, were Cordelia Cummings, her two married sisters, her three brothers (including Henry H. Huston of the deed record), and the children of their deceased siblings.[27] In addition, the heirs of A. Huston and Elizabeth Austin, formerly Houston [*sic*], sold 760 acres to one brother to pay the debts of their father's estate. The grantors (heirs) included Cordelia E. and M.H. Cummings.[28]

New Questions, Clues, and Answers

The next question was whether Elizabeth was born a Huston ("nee Huston," from the tombstone) as well as married to one. A trip to the Alto public library unexpectedly provided an answer. A folder in the vertical files included a photocopy and transcription of a Huston Bible record. In typical nineteenth-century handwriting, it showed Almanzon Huston, born 22 October 1799, and Elizabeth Newton, born 29 March 1805. It recorded their marriage twice, as 6 and 16 April 1819 in Erie County, Pennsylvania. This explains why one son was named Newton Huston. The record also showed, and the county marriage record later corroborated, the marriage of Elizabeth Huston to Ira F. Austin on 4 July 1876.[29]

The original research questions were now complete. Ella Lee White was the daughter of Cordelia E. and Moses H. Cummings. Cordelia E. (Huston) Everett Cummings was the daughter of Almanzon Huston, an innkeeper, stagecoach owner, and mail contractor of New York birth. Her mother was Elizabeth Newton, born possibly in northern Pennsylvania. Cordelia herself was one of fourteen children born to the couple and was in Texas with the family prior to the Texas Revolution, in which her father served as quartermaster general.[30] Cordelia died 10 June 1922 at Alto.[31] The funeral home record did not name her burial place, and no death certificate or tombstone has been located.

Case Study

CHALLENGE: CORDELIA'S BIRTH DATE AND BIRTHPLACE

Cordelia's parents were now known. The next research focus was her elusive birth date and birthplace. In such cases, the researcher must accumulate and study evidence from many sources until a likely or definitive conclusion emerges.

Any problem-solving or "brick wall" effort requires a strategy suited to the individual ancestor or question. Each ancestor was unique, so each plan is unique. Of course, every family line and every ancestor's life has questions we cannot answer. **However, many answers are waiting to be found if we approach them appropriately.** Certain general steps guide the way.

Step By Step

- Step one: Focus on one specific ancestor or research problem in order to concentrate on details.
- Step two: Organize, write down, document, and study existing evidence, including facts about the ancestor's cluster of friends, relatives, and neighbors.
- Step three: Use what is known to identify additional sources that may add to the evidence.
- Step four: Research; document new evidence.
- Step five: Evaluate each piece of evidence and the big picture. Is there a convincing answer?
- Step six: Repeat these steps if no convincing conclusion surfaces.

Steps One and Two: The Problem and the Evidence

The Huston family Bible presented a dilemma. The fifth child of Almanzon and Elizabeth Huston was shown as Cordelia A. Huston, born 11 February 1830 and died 14 May 1832. The sixth child was Elizabeth C. Huston, born 16 March 1833. Was this child Elizabeth Cordelia? Possibly. In fact, Cordelia Everett Cummings's daughter Mary Elizabeth also appears in records as Mary, Mary E., Elizabeth, Elizabeth M., and Lizzie. Cordelia too may have gone by her middle name.

No other known evidence corroborates or contradicts the February 11 or March 16 birthdays for these two girls. Thus, we cannot evaluate those dates. The question is whether we can determine the birth year and place for Cordelia E. (Huston) Everett Cummings. The case may require studying the questions of birth date and place together.

The chart and discussion below capsule the known evidence. Summarizing and evaluating the evidence with its documentation is an important part of preparing for further research.

Item	Suggested Birth Year	Suggested Birthplace	Sources and Endnotes
1.	1829	—	Her granddaughter Leona said she lived to be 93; she died in 1922. (Notes 1 and 31 on pages 221 and 223)
2.	1830	—	Family Bible record for Cordelia A. Huston. (Note 29)
3.	1832	—	1835 Census of San Augustine: Cordelia, age 3. (Note 24)
4.	1833	—	Family Bible record for Elizabeth C. Huston. (Note 29)
5.	1833	Pa.	1850 Census, San Augustine County: Cordelia, age 17, living with only her husband. (Note 20)
6.	1833	Tex.	1880 Census, Cherokee County: Cordelia, age 47, living with husband and blended family of children. (Note 15)
7.	1833	—	Funeral record: Cordelia, age 89. Burial place or tombstone not found. (Note 31)
8.	1834	Mich.	1860 Census, San Augustine County: Cordelia, age 26, living with her parents, siblings, and children. (Note 23)
9.	1835	Tex.	1870 Census, Cherokee County: Cordelia, age 35, living with husband and blended family of children. (Note 14)
10.	—	Tex.	Her children's census records: Columbus Cummings in 1880, 1900, 1920;[37] Ella Collier White in 1880, 1900–1920.[33] In 1910, Columbus's household reported his mother's birthplace as Tennessee. The 1910 and 1920 censuses were read after they became available.
11.	—	—	Research has uncovered no further evidence of age or birth year, no death certificate, no pension application, and not even Cordelia herself listed in the 1900–1920 censuses.

Considering the Birth Year Evidence Item By Item

1. (1829) Aunt Leona may have been correct, but she was fifteen when her grandmother died. She said in the first interview that her childhood family was so busy trying to put food on the table they didn't have time to talk, especially about family history. Did she really know her grandmother's age? The date makes sense in light of Cordelia's 1847 marriage date but conflicts with the Bible-reported birth of her brother Thomas Melvin/Malvin in August 1828, only a few months earlier. In his two known census records, Malvin's ages suggest his birth in 1830 and 1828; he has not been found in the 1860 census, and he died in 1864.[34]

2. (1830) This Bible record entry makes sense in light of Cordelia E.'s 1847 marriage. The photocopy of the Bible record is the closest we can get to the original. We do not know if this was the parents' Bible, but the handwriting is

nineteenth-century style. We cannot determine how contemporary the entries were to the events they report.

Problem 1: The Bible also shows the 1832 death of the Cordelia A. born in 1830.

Problem 2: The 1830 census shows only one girl under five years of age in the family. The older sister, Malvina, would have been four on census day; the infant Cordelia would have been about three months old. The family's enumeration included an unidentified girl, age fifteen to twenty, and the apparent Huston wife, age twenty to thirty, along with Almanzon and two young boys, who seem to be the sons Emory S. and Thomas Malvin. Three unidentified males, age twenty to thirty were also in the household.[35] Was a preschooler omitted? Was the Bible record in error?

3. (1832) This is possible in light of Cordelia's 1847 marriage. She was a preschooler living with her parents at this census, and this is the public document closest to the event of her birth. Thus, whoever furnished the information was closer to her birth in time than we are or than later records were. Was it therefore the most accurate?

4. (1833) Cordelia most frequently appeared in the records as Cordelia E. The family Bible records Elizabeth C. Huston, born 16 March 1833. Could these two be the same person? Families sometimes gave children the names of siblings who had died.

5–7. (1833) Three other records indicate this year as Cordelia's birth date, but repeated reporting does not automatically mean the date is accurate.

Problem: This date would mean she was only fourteen when she married in 1847. No parental consent appears with the marriage record; sometimes such a document accompanied the marriage license of a very young bride or groom and stated the age.

8. (1834) Cordelia was living with her parents, siblings, and children in this census. We cannot know who of the large household gave the information. Some of the data provided was accurate, but this date is less likely in light of her 1847 marriage.

9. (1835) Cordelia was living with her husband, children, and stepchildren, and we cannot know who furnished the information. The date is unlikely in light of her 1847 marriage.

No definitive conclusion emerges from the accumulated evidence, but a narrowed range of reasonable dates would be 1830 to 1833.

Considering the Birthplace Evidence

After the censuses of 1910 and 1920 were opened for public study, they added evidence on the birthplace question. The obvious first place to look was Cordelia's census records for 1900–1920. Unfortunately, neither she nor her husband, Moses Cummings, appears in the 1900 Soundex, and she does not appear in the 1910 and 1920 Soundexes under the code for Cummings. Nor is she enumerated in the households or immediate neighborhoods of her children Cumby or Ella Lee in any of those censuses. (What about Aunt Leona's comment that Ella Lee deeded her share of the property to Cumby if he would look after Mama? Does such a deed exist?) Another option is to read the entire county for these years.

The lack of more or less firsthand information means the researcher must look elsewhere. The following evidence emerged.

Pennsylvania. The census of 1850 suggested Cordelia's birth in Pennsylvania. The Huston Bible record and census records support the family's presence in Pennsylvania. The Bible reports the parents' marriage in Erie County in 1819.

Census records during the life of the eldest son, Emory S. Huston, consistently reported Pennsylvania as his birthplace (1821). However, shortly after his death, Michigan appeared as his birthplace in the 1880 census.[36] A family member may have known of the Hustons' Michigan residence and reported it as his birthplace. In light of a different birthplace given in the 1880 census report, Emory may well have been the source of the 1850 to 1870 information.

In addition, the 1850 census reported the fourth Huston child, Emory's brother Malvin, born in Pennsylvania (1828).[37] The Bible record indicates that the second Huston child died in infancy (1824).

Emory's brother Newton Houston's censuses of 1900 and 1910 and their sister Priscilla Palmer's 1910 census reported their parents' birthplaces as New York and Pennsylvania.[38] The 1850 census also reported the Huston parents' birthplaces as New York and Pennsylvania.[39]

If Elizabeth (Newton) Huston's parents were in Pennsylvania at the time of Cordelia's birth, it is at least possible that Elizabeth was with her parents for that event. This possibility is an option for study if necessary. So far, it appears that Almanzon lived in Pennsylvania no later than 1829. As contrary evidence, the only census record found for the third Huston child, Malvina C. (Huston) McShan, gives her birthplace as Ohio (1826).[40]

Michigan. The initial reference to Michigan as Cordelia's birthplace was from the 1860 census, at which time she and her Everett children lived with her parents and five siblings. Whoever gave the information may have had the siblings' birthplaces correct and the parents' birthplaces incorrect—Pennsylvania and Ohio instead of New York and Pennsylvania—if other censuses and Texas records are correct.

The following records document the family's and father's presence in Michigan:

1. Almanson [*sic*] Huston signed a "Petition of residents of St. Joseph County, Michigan" in October 1829. In December 1829 and November 1831, an A. Huston signed additional petitions from the residents.[41]

2. The Almanzon Huston household appears in the 1830 census in Berrien County, Michigan, as previously described.[42]

3. The first deed recorded in Berrien County, Michigan, was Almanzon Huston's 23 November 1831 purchase of town lot fifty-three in the part of the village of Niles laid out and sold by William Justice. The day before, an A. Huston witnessed a deed by which Almanzon's reported parents, Thomas and Mary Huston, sold lot ten and its "small frame dwelling" in the same village. On December 22, Almanzon witnessed another deed. Then on 30 December 1831, he and his wife, Elizabeth, sold eighty acres of federal land in township seven south, range

seventeen west. In the presence of the justice of the peace, Elizabeth acknowledged that she willingly signed the deed and agreed to the sale.[43]

4. Berrien County deed records show the purchase of land by another A. Huston—Angelina—on 23 November 1831, but would she, as a woman, have been the A. Huston who signed the two petitions in December 1829 and November 1831 or witnessed the 22 November 1831 deed mentioned above?[44]

5. Almanzon Huston patented two adjoining tracts of federal land, both final certificates bearing the date of 4 June 1833. Only the file for certificate 403 contains a receipt for payment, and it shows a purchase date of 21 June 1831 (Figure 17.1). The Hustons sold the smaller tract (file 134) in December 1831, above.[45] Nevertheless, the 1831 receipt is one more piece of evidence placing the Hustons in Michigan between 1829 and the end of 1831.

Texas. The earliest record found so far in Texas for Almanzon Huston was his purchase of a town lot in San Augustine on 22 September 1834.[46] Almanzon's character certificate, necessary for a foreigner settling in Mexican Texas, was dated 23 September 1834. It states he was a native of New York and headed a family of six persons.[47] It did not give his year of arrival in Texas, as many such certificates did. The numerous land records and character certificates dated in the fall of 1834 in east Texas reflect the large backlog of settlers waiting for

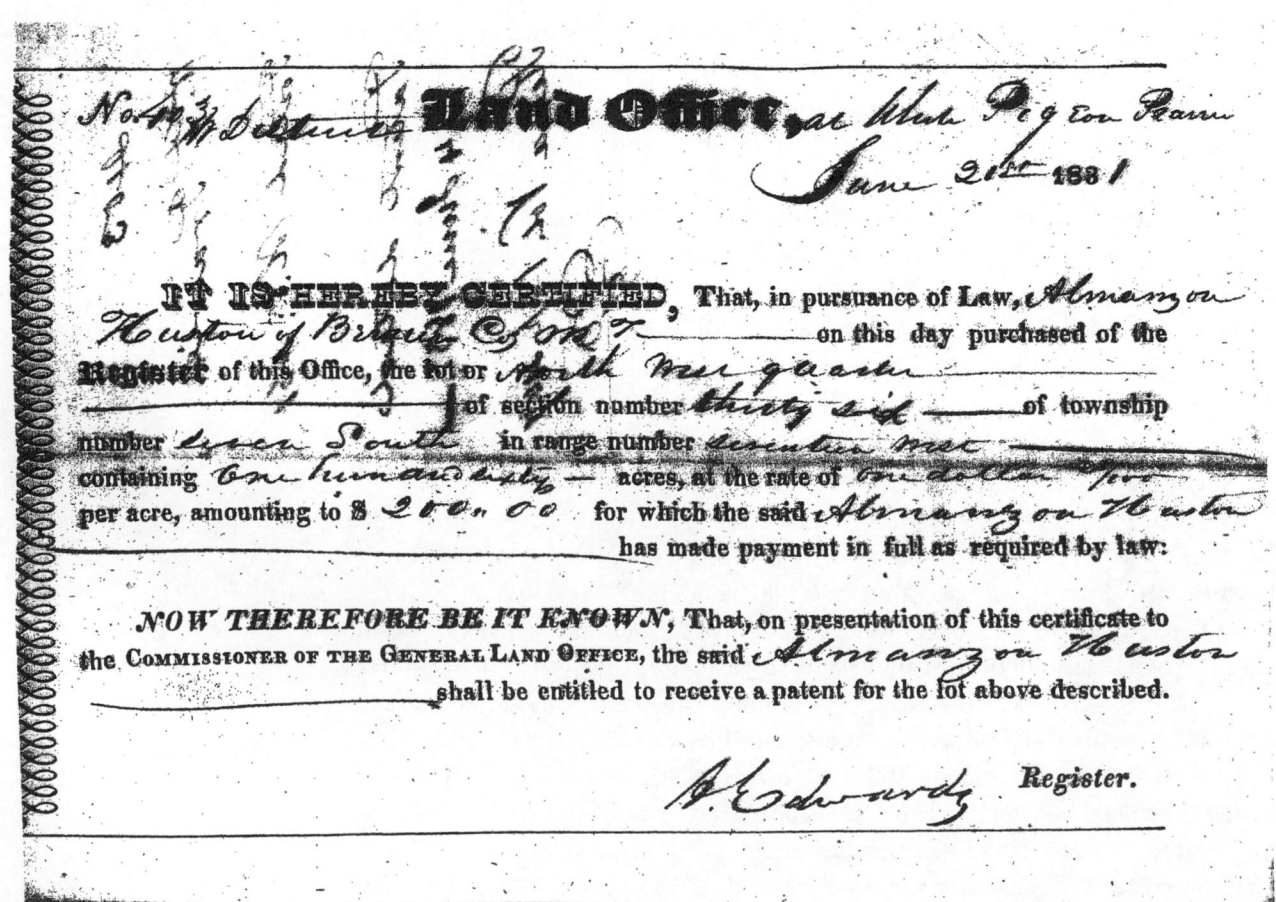

Figure 17.1 Almanzon Huston's receipt for land purchase in Michigan

titles and not simply an influx of new residents. Almanzon's records, therefore, suggest only that he was in the state with his family by September 1834. The makeup of the family reported in the certificate—six persons—corroborates the family Bible record: Almanzon, Elizabeth, son Emory, daughter Malvina, son Thomas Malvin, and daughter Cordelia/Elizabeth.

Twentieth-century historical accounts place Almanzon at various battles and events in Texas prior to 1834. They need to be studied.

Answers? Sherlock Holmes cautioned detectives, which include genealogists, not to create a theory and try to fit the facts to it, but to let the facts lead to a theory and an answer. In the case of Cordelia's birthplace, the facts so far indicate no clear answer. If she was the child born in 1830, she was born probably in Michigan. More research is needed to determine where the family was from 1832 to 1834.

Step Three: Identifying Sources and Research Questions

Many questions arise from thinking about a genealogical problem. Write them down and choose one at a time to address. In this case, the first question below seemed a good place to begin.

1. What happened to Cordelia's Everett children? Will their records help identify her birthplace?
2. Identifying Cordelia's birthplace may hinge on where her father resided from 1832 to 1834.
   a. Study other Michigan records to estimate his length of residence there.
   b. Study San Augustine County, Texas, deed records again, from their begining in 1833. Is there evidence of Almanzon prior to 22 September 1834? The Mexican municipality of San Augustine was organized in March 1834 from the municipality of Nacogdoches.[48] Do records for Almanzon exist in the parent municipality?
   c. Get the files of Almanzon's Texas land grants. Do they suggest when he arrived in Texas and whether his family was with him, or are they based solely on military service?
   d. What pre–Texas Revolution (pre-1836) documents and contemporary accounts place him in Texas prior to 1834?
   e. Investigate federal military records to check out reports of Almanzon's pre–Texas participation in Indian wars.
3. Narrowing Cordelia's birth date may hinge on (a) determining the birthplace first and (b) studying her siblings in more depth.
4. Elizabeth Huston's parents are tentatively identified. Work on proving that relationship. Where were they from 1830 to 1833? If they were in Pennsylvania, would Elizabeth have stayed or gone "home" for Cordelia's birth? Were they in Michigan?
5. Almanzon's parents are identified in family papers and tradition. Work on proving that relationship. Where were they 1830–1833? Early evidence places them in Michigan.
6. Although a public marriage record probably does not exist for Almanzon and Elizabeth in Pennsylvania, could a church record be found?[49]

Step Four: New Research and Documentation of New Evidence

The first question for study was Cordelia's Everett children. The following is a summary of the new evidence.

1. **Probate records** of San Augustine County indicate that W.M. Everett's will, written 8 February 1864, was probated four days later and left his property to his children: Mary Elizabeth and Almanzon H. Everett. The will also named Everett's parents as Zackariah and Mary Everett, both deceased, of Clay County, Missouri. This document leads to the conclusion that the daughter, Mary Elizabeth, carried the names of both her grandmothers. The children's appointed guardian was their mother, Cordelia E. Everett.[50]

Figures 17.2 and 17.3, below and on page 219, show the end of this will and Cordelia's petition for guardianship, both dated 1864.

Figure 17.2 End of Wm. M. Everett's will, showing signature and date

2. A **typescript of a "committee of safety" trial** in San Augustine, held in February 1864, indicated that William M. Everett and his wife, a sister of Malvin Houston, were divorced. The trial was held "on the morning of the day fixed for the execution of Malvin Houston and William M. Everett, who had been sentenced to be hung for the murder and robbery of Col. [Richard] Waterhouse." Everett testified that his wife had said "if he could get money enough to maintain her, and relieve her from so much hard work, she would consent to live with him again." He said he gave his "wife" $1,250 of the $1,500 that was his part of the robbery and burned the remainder out of remorse. Malvin Houston testified that he gave all his share of the money ($1,500) to his mother.[51] The record does not indicate whether anyone made an attempt to retrieve the money or what the form of the money was—coin, paper, Confederate, etc.

Malvin Houston at first was "unwilling to tell on [H.M.] Kinsey," who originated the plan of the crime, because "he had promised to marry his sister, Mrs. Everett, and take care of her."[52] Kinsey apparently was not tried and, after the deaths of Everett and Huston, moved to nearby Nacogdoches, Texas. Waterhouse's son instigated H.M. Kinsey's death in Nacogdoches shortly after the close of the Civil War (1865).[53]

Figure 17.3 Cordelia's petititon for guardianship, showing signature and date

3. **Deed records** suggest that in or after February 1864, Mrs. Everett and her mother, Mrs. Huston, moved to Alto. On February 5, Elizabeth Houston, "widow of A. Houston" and still "of San Augustine County," paid $1,000 in gold coin for 562 acres in Cherokee County along the San Antonio Road and

Lawson's Creek.[54] This transaction perhaps raises more questions than it answers. Then, Mrs. Everett married M.H. Cummings at Alto in March 1865.

4. The **1870 census** of Cherokee County lists Elizabeth Huston, age sixty-six, with her youngest daughter and several apparent grandchildren in the household, next to the families of her sons Newton Houston and Henry H. Houston.[55]

5. **Almanzon H. Everett**, Cordelia's second child, married Mary Forshee in Cherokee County, on 5 September 1877.[56] The 1900 census reported that Houston Everett and his wife, Mollie, had been married twenty-three years and that Mollie had borne ten children, five of whom were living and four of whom were listed with the family, including a one-year-old daughter. This census gave his birth date as February 1855, consistent with his age of five in the 1860 census, cited earlier. He and his son Newton both worked in a sawmill. By 1910, only four of eleven children were living, the youngest being a seven-year-old daughter, the only child at home.[57] The entries call him Almanzon, Houston, and A.H. Everett and thus tell us he was indeed named for his grandfather. His death certificate gives his birth date as 9 February 1852 (too early), his death date as 8 August 1931, his father's name as W.M. Everitt, and his mother as Miss D. [Delia?] Houston.[58]

What about his mother's birthplace? In his 1880 census entry, "birthplace of mother" is blank. The 1900–1920 censuses report his mother's birthplace as Texas.[59] The death certificate lists it as "don't know."

6. **Mary Elizabeth Everett**, Cordelia's eldest child, lived with her mother at the time of the 1860, 1870, and 1880 censuses. Lizzie Everett married E.M. Atterberry on 6 June 1883.[60] His occupation was housepainter, and they owned a home in the town of Rusk in Cherokee County. They had no children of their own but adopted a daughter, Addie. Census records of 1900–1920 report the husband's name as Mitchell, Elam M., and E.M. Atterberry; her death certificate names him Mitchell.[61] Likely he was Elam Mitchell Atterberry. The 1900 census gives her birth date as October 1853, consistent with her age in the 1870, 1900, and 1910 censuses. Her death certificate gives her birth date as 14 February 1853 (consistent with the 1860 census), her death information as 3 May 1934 at Alto, and her parents as John [sic] Everett and Cordelia E. Cummings.

What about her mother's birthplace? Her household's 1920 census reports it as Missouri; the 1880 census shows it as Texas. The 1900 and 1910 censuses and her death certificate list it as Michigan. The death certificate informant, Mrs. Nancy Cummings, though not yet positively identified, at least places the birthplace information within the family tradition.

Step Five: Evaluate New Evidence and the Big Picture

Further research has found no new evidence on Cordelia's birth date. What does Cordelia's birthplace question look like now? Overall, two records admitted the informant's lack of knowledge on the subject. One census each suggested Cordelia was born in Pennsylvania, Tennessee, and Missouri; we can eliminate this data for the time being due to lack of further evidence to support it. If strong new evidence points to one of these, we can always reopen its case.

Evidence from ten households in census records overwhelmingly suggests that Cordelia was born in Texas. Four records ask us to consider Michigan, and we must. Ten "votes" to four? These numbers alone do not decide a genealogy case. (1) We do not know who furnished the information for the censuses. (2) As the eldest child, who lived with the grandparents and several aunts and uncles, would Mary have been in a better position than her younger siblings or her stepfather to hear about her mother's birthplace? (3) Evidence does not yet show conclusively where the family was in 1832 and 1833.

Step Six: Repeat the Steps If No Convincing Conclusion Surfaces

No strongly convincing conclusion is apparent. Thus, the research will proceed to item two on the research list on page 212: Study Almanzon's whereabouts between 1832 and 1834.

Because Texas was a Mexican state, not keeping the kinds of records the counties kept after independence, records there may be scarce. We may not find a clear and convincing answer, but we may uncover new evidence. Hope springs eternal.

ENDNOTES

Notes

Note: Family History Library is cited as FHL.

1 Visits by the author, with her client, to Leona Holsomback and Zona Bailey of and in Cherokee County, Texas, beginning 25 July 1975, and with Edna (Holmes) White of and in Houston, Texas, beginning June 1975, notes in author's possession.

2 Family Bible of Ella Lee White, in possession of Zona Bailey, Wells, Texas (publication information not available), copied by author, July 1975; Collier's full name furnished and marriage and death date corroborated in a Collier family Bible, in possession of Leo Maddux, Conroe, Texas, when author saw it in July 1980; Collier's death date and Ella Lee's dates in the Bible are the same as on their tombstone, Old Palestine Cemetery, Alto, Texas, visited by author, 25 July 1975; the Collier-Cummings marriage date is corroborated in the Cherokee County, Texas, Marriage Book I:232, County Clerk's office, Courthouse, Rusk; all Cherokee County records cited are from this office in the courthouse unless otherwise cited.

3 Family Bible of Ella Lee White.

4 Cherokee County, Texas, Marriage Book M:361, marriage of W.J. White and Mrs. E.L. Collier, 14 July 1901 (license date, 13 July 1901), FHL microfilm 0988079; the county record may be the most contemporary with the event.

5 U.S. Census of 1900, Cherokee County, Texas, roll 619, e.d. 20, sheet 12, family 214, widow Ella L. Collier household; e.d. 19, sheet 19, family 323, widower William J. White household.

6 Family Bible of Ella Lee White; Cherokee County, Texas, Death Records, Book 1:183, #1558, entry of W.J. White (age 61, died in Alto).

7 U.S. Census of 1880, Cherokee County, Texas, roll 1295, e.d. 13, sheet 39,

family 325, John A. Cummings household, with Mary and Elnora (age $^{5}/_{12}$, born in December 1879).

8 Cherokee County, Texas, Deed Book U:28, 333.

9 Cherokee County, Texas, Death Records, Book 1:24, #327, entry of M.H. Cummings (age 77, died 16 October 1903, in Alto of "endorcortitis exhaustion," perhaps a corruption of endocarditis).

10 Cherokee County, Texas, Deed Records U:28 (1869), 333 (1870).

11 Cherokee County, Texas, Marriage Book D2:313, license and ceremony on 13 March 1865.

12 Helen Wooddell Crawford, *Cemeteries of Mid Cherokee County, Texas* (n.p.: the compiler, 1973), 80-Alto City Cemetery; cemetery visited and Cummings family tombstones copied by author, June 1980.

13 Cherokee County, Texas, Marriage Book K:161 shows the marriage of C.C. Cummings and Nina Derrett on 1 November 1891; Book J:380 shows the marriage of a C.C. Cummings to Hallie McKnight on 12 February 1888, possibly an earlier marriage of the same man.

14 U.S. Census of 1870, Cherokee County, Texas, roll 1578, page 166, Moses Cummings household.

15 U.S. Census of 1880, Cherokee County, Texas, e.d. 13, sheet 19, family 162, Moses Cummings household; also in the county were John A. Cummings, e.d. 13, sheet 39, family 325; next household enumerated, Almanzon Everett, e.d. 13, sheet 39, family 326; James Cummings, e.d. 13, sheet 35, family 291.

16 U.S. Census of 1900, Cherokee County, Texas, e.d. 19, sheet 11, family 191, Columbus C. Cummings household.

17 Death certificate for Chris Columbus Cummings (1934, Cherokee County), #6212, Texas Bureau of Vital Statistics, Austin.

18 Family Bible of Ella Lee White; death certificate for Mrs. Ella White Priddy (1941, Alto, Cherokee County), #49286, Texas Bureau of Vital Statistics, Austin.

19 U.S. Census of 1870, Cherokee County, Texas, p. 166, Moses Cummings household; U.S. Census of 1880, Cherokee County, Texas, e.d. 13, sheet 19, Moses Cummings household.

20 U.S. Census of 1850, San Augustine County, Texas, roll 914, p. 339, family 115, William M. Everett household.

21 Frances T. Ingmire, *San Augustine County, Texas, Marriage Records 1837–1880* (St. Louis: n.p., 1980), 6; San Augustine County, Texas, Marriage Book 1:95, FHL microfilm 1003680.

22 U.S. Census of 1850, San Augustine County, Texas, p. 339, family 120, Almanzon Huston household.

23 U.S. Census of 1860, San Augustine County, Texas, roll 1304, p. 6, A. Huston household.

24 Marion Day Mullins, comp., *The First Census of Texas, 1829–1836* (Washington, D.C. [now Arlington, Va.]: National Genealogical Society, 1959), 2, which shows only a date of 1834–1836; "Census of San Augustine, latter part of 1835," in Robert Bruce Blake Research Collection (Austin: R.B.

Blake, compiler, 1958–1959), XIX:346, shows the same family information, with a few transcription differences, but a more specific date.

25 Cherokee County, Texas, Deed Book U:28, 333.

26 Alto City Cemetery, Cummings family tombstones.

27 Cherokee County, Texas, Probate Minutes Book A:288, Book B:89, estate of Elizabeth Austin, will dated 26 July 1878, probated 5 August 1878.

28 Cherokee County, Texas, Deed Book I-2:339–341, dated 3 August 1878.

29 Huston family Bible record, Houston file, vertical files, Stella Hill Memorial Library, Alto, Texas, copied by author about 1980, photocopy made in 2000 in author's possession; the file does not say who owned the Bible or made the early entries; several other entries show different handwriting; Cherokee County, Texas, Marriage Book H:208, marriage of I[ra] F. Austin to Mrs. Elizabeth Huston, 4 July 1876, FHL microfilm 0988077.

30 Arrant-Haralson file, Stella Hill Memorial Library, Alto, Texas; R.B. Blake, "Almanzon Huston," in Walter Prescott Webb, ed., *The Handbook of Texas* (Austin: Texas State Historical Association, 1952), I:869; Carolyn Ericson, "Almanzon Huston," in *Nacogdoches County Families* (Nacogdoches, Tex.: Nacogdoches County Genealogical Society, 1985), 371.

31 M.J. Hogan's register of funerals in Alto, Texas, 1922, showing Cordelia E. Cummings, as reported by C.C. Cummings, in *Miscellaneous Genealogical Records of Cherokee County, Texas* (Jacksonville, Tex.: Major Thaddeus Beall Chapter, National Society, Daughters of the American Revolution, 1979), 21.

32 U.S. Census of 1880, Cherokee County, Texas, e.d. 13, sheet 19, family 162, Moses Cummings household; U.S. Census of 1900, Cherokee County, Texas, e.d. 19, sheet 11, family 191, Columbus C. Cummings household; U.S. Census of 1910, Cherokee County, Texas, roll 1538, e.d. 14, sheet 5, Cumby Cummings household, giving mother's birthplace as Tennessee; U.S. Census of 1920, Cherokee County, Texas, roll 1786, e.d. 21, sheet 10A, Columbus Cummings household.

33 U.S. Census of 1880, Cherokee County, Texas, e.d. 13, sheet 19, family 162, Moses Cummings household; U.S. Census of 1900, Cherokee County, Texas, e.d. 20, sheet 12, Ella L. Collier household; U.S. Census of 1910, Cherokee County, Texas, e.d. 14, sheet 8, William J. White household; U.S. Census of 1920, Cherokee County, Texas, e.d. 21, sheet 11B–12A, Ella White household.

34 U.S. Census of 1850, San Augustine County, Texas, p. 339, Almanzon Huston household; Mullins, *The First Census of Texas*, 2; R.B. Blake Research Collection, XIX:346.

35 U.S. Census of 1830, Berrien County, Michigan, roll 69, p. 184, Almanzon Huston household; census day was June 1 and the infant Cordelia was reportedly born in February, so she should have been reported if 1830 was her birth year.

36 U.S. Census of 1850, San Augustine County, Texas, p. 355, Emery [*sic*] S. Huston household; U.S. Census of 1860, Nacogdoches County, Texas, roll 1301, p. 117, E.S. Huston household; U.S. Census of 1870, Nacogdoches

County, Texas, roll 1599, p. 425, Emory F. [*sic*] Houston household; U.S. Census of 1880, Nacogdoches County, Texas, roll 1320, e.d. 47, sheet 3, Rose Huston (widow) household, reporting birthplace of children's father as Michigan rather than Pennsylvania; U.S. Census of 1880, Mortality Schedule, microfilm, Nacogdoches County, Texas, p. 1, reporting November 1879 death of Emory S. Huston and giving his birthplace as Michigan.

37 U.S. Census of 1850, San Augustine County, Texas, p. 339, Almanzon Huston household.

38 U.S. Census of 1900, Cherokee County, Texas, e.d. 20, sheet 10, family 174, Newton Houston household; U.S. Census of 1910, Cherokee County, Texas, e.d. 14, sheet 5, family 83, Percilla Palmer household, with Nute Houston and wife as boarders.

39 U.S. Census of 1850, San Augustine County, Texas, p. 339, Almanzon Huston household.

40 U.S. Census of 1850, San Augustine County, Texas, p. 353, family 322, William B. McShan household, with Malvina C., reportedly born in Ohio; this family has not yet been found in the 1860 or later censuses.

41 "Petition of residents of the St. Joseph Country, Michigan" in October, 1829, *Territorial Papers of the United States* (Washington, D.C.: Government Printing Office, 1934–1975), Michigan Territory, 1829–1837, XII:86; "Petition to Congress by Inhabitants of the St. Joseph Country," December 1829, XII:106, showing signer A. Huston; "Memorial to Congress by Citizens of the Territory," signed 8 November 1831, XII:369, showing signers A. and T. Huston; Vol. XI, Michigan Territory 1820–1829, shows no Huston or variant spelling in the index.

42 U.S. Census of 1830, Berrien County, Michigan, p. 184.

43 Berrien County, Michigan, Deed Book A:1 (Almanzon Huston, grantee), 4 (Thomas and Mary Huston, grantors), 6 (A. Huston, witness, 23 November 1831; record does not say which A. Huston it was), 36–37 (Almanzon Huston, witness, 22 December 1831), 38–39 (Almanzon and Elizabeth Huston, grantors), FHL microfilm 1029444.

44 Ibid., A:6, 12 (Elijah and Edith Lacey to Angelina Huston, 23 November 1831).

45 Land entry case files no. 134 (W1/2 SW1/4 S25 T7S R17W) and 403 (NW 1/4 S36 T7S R17W), for Almanzon Huston, both patented 4 June 1833, White Pigeon Prairie land office, Michigan, Records of the Bureau of Land Management, Record Group 49, National Archives, Washington, D.C., copies in author's possession.

46 San Augustine County, Texas, Deed Book C:140, County Clerk's office, Courthouse, San Augustine.

47 Gifford White, *Character Certificates in the General Land Office of Texas* (St. Louis: Ingmire Publications, 1985), vii, certificates 1012 (Almanzon Huston), 1474 (mentioning his survey, 22 September 1834), and 1828 (mentioning his survey, 17 November 1834); certificates are in numerical order.

48 Imogene Kinard Kennedy and J. Leon Kennedy, *Genealogical Records in*

Texas (Baltimore: Genealogical Publishing Co., 1987), 141, 153.

49 Alice Eichholz, ed., *Ancestry's Red Book: American State, County & Town Sources*, rev. ed. (Salt Lake City: Ancestry, 1992), 620, saying that "nineteenth-century civil vital records in Pennsylvania are practically nonexistent."

50 Probate packet of William M. Everett, with original will, dated 8 February 1864, probated 12 February 1864, naming his children, and Cordelia Everett's petition for guardianship of her children after their father's death, San Augustine County, Texas, County Clerk's office, Courthouse, San Augustine, copy in author's possession; typescript from May term 1864, San Augustine County Court, showing Cordelia's appointment as guardian of her children, County Clerk's office, copy in author's possession.

51 "The Murder of Colonel R. Waterhouse of San Augustine, Decr. 30th 1863," a description of the Committee of Safety "trial" of Everett and Huston, William Everett testimony, George Lewis Crocket papers, Box 31, File 130, East Texas Research Center, Stephen F. Austin State University Library, Nacogdoches, Texas, photocopy in author's possession; according to Crocket, he copied this document from a handwritten account by Judge William W. Wallace, with original committee signatures affixed, found among the papers of William Garrett, one of the committee members, and at the time (date not given) in the possession of Garrett's grandson, Wm. G. Sharp; Crocket's typescript gives the dates of the trial as 13–15 February 1865, clearly in conflict with the entire probate packet, all of whose documents indicate that 1864 was the correct year and that the men died between February 8 and 12; Huston family Bible record (note 29) indicates that Malvin Huston died 10 February 1864.

52 Committee of Safety trial account, Malvin Houston testimony, Crocket papers.

53 "Killing of H.M. Kinsey," handwritten copy of an eyewitness account of David Lee, undated, George Lewis Crocket papers, Box 18, File 40, p. 43, East Texas Research Center, Stephen F. Austin State University Library, photocopy in author's possession; telephone conversation, 21 August 2000, with Harry Noble of San Augustine, Texas, who told author that his research found that Waterhouse's son was a Confederate officer stationed in Louisiana and he and friends took revenge on Kinsey very soon after the close of the war (1865) and that two court cases pending in San Augustine County in the spring of 1864 were dismissed because a party to each case (one, Everett; the other, Huston) was deceased.

54 Cherokee County, Texas, Deed Book R:87, Jennings and wife to Elizabeth Houston, County Clerk's office, Courthouse, Rusk.

55 U.S. Census of 1870, Cherokee County, Texas, p. 173, family 138, Elizabeth Houston household; family 139, Newton Houston household; family 140, Henry H. Houston household.

56 Cherokee County, Texas, Marriage Book H:278, A.H. Everett to Mary Forshee, FHL microfilm 0988077.

57 U.S. Census of 1900, Cherokee County, Texas, e.d. 30, sheet 11, Houston

Everett household; U.S. Census of 1910, Polk County, Texas, roll 1578, e.d. 88, sheet 7, Almanson [*sic*] Everett household.

58 Death certificate for A.H. Everitt (1931), Angelina County, Texas, County Clerk's office, Courthouse, Lufkin, copy in author's possession.

59 Ibid.; U.S. Census of 1900 and 1910, just cited for Almanson/Houston Everett; U.S. Census of 1880, Cherokee County, Texas, e.d. 13, sheet 39, Almanzon Everett household; U.S. Census of 1920, Angelina County, Texas, roll 1773, e.d. 9, sheet 18, A.H. Everett household.

60 Cherokee County, Texas, Marriage Book I:257, Miss Lizzie Everett to E.M. Atterberry, 6 June 1883, FHL microfilm 0988077.

61 U.S. Census of 1900, Cherokee County, Texas, Rusk, e.d. 16, sheet 4, family 70, Mitchell Atterberry household, with wife Mary; U.S. Census of 1910, Cherokee County, Texas, Rusk, e.d. 10, sheet 5, family 83, Elam M. Atterbury household, with wife Mary; U.S. Census of 1920, Cherokee County, Texas, Rusk, e.d. 19, sheet 14, family 175, E.M. Atterberry household, with wife Mary E.; death certificate for Mary Elizabeth Atterberry (1934), Cherokee County, Texas, County Clerk's office, Courthouse, Rusk, copy in author's possession.

THINGS TO DO NOW

Idea Generator

1. Check your documentation on your family group sheets, other charts, or notes. Are there holes in any of the citation information, such as a missing publisher's name, publication date, author or compiler's full name, roll or page number(s) for the information you are using? Take steps to complete those citations.

2. In other books or genealogical journals, read other case studies, including all the endnotes or footnotes. If possible, discuss with another researcher at least one case study, including the nature of the problem, the techniques used to answer the question, and the sources cited. Did the author present the case in a convincing manner? What kinds of sources did the researcher use? Do you think the author sufficiently answered the research question?

3. Write a report for at least one of your research questions, however simple or complex it was to answer. Present your question and the process by which you arrived at an answer. In footnotes or endnotes, document each piece of evidence you used. Cite several different sources, such as interviews, specific family papers, census records, vital records, or others.

EIGHTEEN

Sharing Your Family History

O nce you have gathered information on your focus ancestor(s), you may want to share the results with the family at large. Notebooks and clippings may fascinate those who gathered them, but they do not entertain those who have not shared in the search. What then?

WRITING A FAMILY HISTORY

One approach is to write a narrative of the information on one surname lineage, from its earliest confirmed ancestor to the present generations. Each chapter becomes a biography of an ancestor or ancestral couple, from birth to death, including your documentation for the facts you report.

Chapters are more interesting if they describe the society and culture in which the ancestors lived and the history they experienced. You can find some of this material in county, state, and regional histories. Social histories and reprints of contemporary diaries and letters can tell you about the customs, clothing, and everyday life in the ancestral era and place. You can set the stage for your ancestor's birth by describing the family into which he or she was born: the number and ages of the older children, something about the parents and other adults in the household, the residence, the family's living conditions, work, neighbors, and so forth.

At the close of each biographical chapter, it is helpful to include a family group sheet or descendancy chart listing the subject, children, and grandchildren. Other sheets can update each branch of the family.

Some genealogists prefer to let their genealogy software prepare their book and its charts. Depending on the software in use, notes on any individual can be as lengthy as necessary to present biographical information with documentation.

If family history is to mean anything, it must be more than just lists of names and dates. A narrative, in addition to descendancy charts and family group sheets, can be a good way to share stories, letters, and documents, or to set the family in the society in which it lived.

We often think of people in the past living in one large generation at the same time, or we tend to consider those who became famous as always being famous. We forget that they began life more or less as the rest of us did. It is fun to identify some of those famous individuals who were contemporaries of your ancestor. Mentioning them adds some perspective and interest to your stage setting. Which ones were children when your ancestor was a child? Who was well known during your ancestor's adulthood? Information of this kind can be found in such books as the *Dictionary of American Biography*, Dumas Malone, et al., eds. (New York: Charles Scribner's Sons, 1928–1974) and the *Encyclopedia of American History*, Richard B. Morris and Jeffrey B. Morris, eds. (New York: HarperCollins, 1996).

These and other standard reference books also give you information about events that took place in the community or nation during your ancestor's life. For example, if the ancestor lived in Vicksburg, Mississippi, during the Civil War, find out about life there during the siege of Vicksburg. The family probably had a rough time. Many sources share experiences of city residents at that time. You may not find your family mentioned in these sources, but you can relate in your account what their fellow citizens experienced and suggest that your family may have had similar experiences. Word your account carefully so that you do not claim as fact something that is only an educated guess.

Other resources are available to help you with this kind of family history book. Some are included in the bibliography.

FAMILY HISTORY COLLECTION

Perhaps you do not consider yourself a writer, but you still want to share the history you have found. Here are ideas that have worked for other genealogists.

Compile your charts and copies of the actual documents that have taught you about your ancestors, put them in a logical and probably chronological order, and add a little explanation here and there. Such a collection makes special Christmas, birthday, or anniversary gifts for family members and may stimulate interest in your larger project. Grandparents can prepare it for children and grandchildren; aunts, for nieces and nephews; brothers or sisters, for parents, siblings, and cousins.

Letters or diaries are the foundation of many family histories. The compiler adds editorial comments, explanations, and photographs to tie the material together. In this way, the researcher preserves the text and flavor of the original but interprets it for the present and future generations.

Even while you are working on a more complete family history, you can collect, preserve, and organize valuable and interesting family history, as discussed in chapters six through nine. This kind of project is an exciting, even entertaining way to share the more recent family history of three to five generations.

For More Info

For more on placing your ancestors into appropriate societal and historical context, see *Bringing Your Family History to Life Through Social History*, by Katherine Scott Sturdevant.

- If you are a grandparent and knew your grandparents, you have firsthand, personal, and valuable knowledge of five generations.
- If your grandparents are living and they knew their grandparents, you have access to five generations of interesting family stories and memories.

Your collection can contain whatever you want to include and in any order. Once the pages are arranged, you can photocopy them and bind each set into booklets or binders for family members. You can also use archival sheet protectors for any original documents, photographs, or keepsakes you include.

When you put together such a collection and want it to last for future generations, why not spend a little more and use materials that are made to last, such as acid-free, chemically stable, archival-quality paper, binders, sheet protectors, and storage containers. Two sources of such preservation materials are

- Heritage Quest, P.O. Box 329, Bountiful, UT 84011-0329. Phone: (800) 760-2455.
- Light Impressions, P.O. Box 22708, Rochester, NY 14692-2708. Phone: (800) 828-6216.

Possible Contents of a Family History Collection

1. **Title page:** title, your name as compiler, date, perhaps your address, any dedication statement.
2. **Table of contents:** items grouped by topic, generation, surname, decade, or any way you think best, given the content.
3. **Foreword:** a letter to your family, possibly in your handwriting or signed, explaining what the collection is, why you want to share it, and what you hope it will mean to the family in years to come—whatever you want to say.
4. **Five-generation charts** that represent facts you have verified.
5. **Family group sheets** with their documentation: each nuclear family in the collection.
6. **Names and addresses** of relatives on the family group sheets, especially any who have worked on family history or have information on the family's past.
7. **Biographical sketches or chronological profiles,** one person or couple to a sketch. Somehow, include your documentation. (See chapter three, page 31.)
8. **Interesting tidbits and "spice,"** by generation or topic.
   - Religious history: who belonged to which denominations or congregations.
   - Occupational history: working men and women in the family history, their occupations, and what you have learned about them.
   - Medical and genetic history: causes of death, diseases or physical problems that have repeated themselves, longevity, occurrence of twins or triplets (one family identified fourteen sets of twins!), physical characteristics that run in the family.

- Educational history: who went where, college attendance and degrees.
- Military history: who served when and where, any family members who are members of the Daughters of the American Revolution or other lineage groups whose membership is based on military service.
- Talents or outstanding characteristics of family members: musicians, authors, artists, terrific cooks, seamstresses; sense of humor, gentleness, meanness; beauties, those who excel or excelled in sports, etc.
- Special traditions and customs: holiday and birthday traditions, vacations the family took, everyday customs in different generations (What was a typical day like?).
- Hobbies and pastimes of family members, especially of previous generations; pets.
- Favorites, especially of previous generations: foods, sports, books, movies, authors, teams, music, performers, places to visit, cars, pets, colors, hymns, scripture, friends, etc.
- Interesting habits of family members, especially previous generations. Sayings or expressions that family members use(d).

9. **Keepsakes and collectibles** (probably copies): documents, photographs of people and houses, letters, recipes, handwriting samples, samples of creativity from family members (poetry, music, drawings, short stories, etc.).
10. **Memories:** recollections or story handed down, memories of your grandparents.
11. **Map** showing residences of the family in certain years or movement of one family over the years. (See page 83.)
12. **Index**

Regardless of how you share your family history, it can have meaning for the family only when it is shared. Whether done formally or informally, published or photocopied from a typed original, it holds insight and fascination for the whole family for years to come. Even if no one seems interested today, someone in the future will applaud you for preserving your (and their) heritage.

THINGS TO DO NOW

Idea Generator

1. Choose one ancestor and write an introduction for a biographical sketch, making the effort to set that ancestor's life into appropriate social, historical, and regional context.
2. Choose one ancestral family and plot their known residences on a map.
3. Choose one couple or family as the subject of a possible family history project such as the one outlined in this chapter. Make an outline or list of the items you could include in a project about that couple or family.
4. Choose an ancestor you knew and write your memories of time you spent together, describing events, personality, appearance, etc.

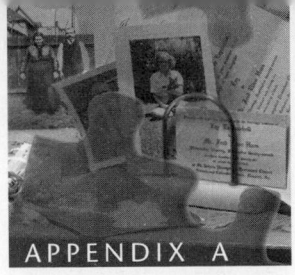

Glossary and Relationship Chart

Additional References:

Black, Henry Campbell. *Black's Law Dictionary*. 6th ed. St. Paul, Minn.: West Publishing Co., 1990.

Drake, Paul. *What Did They Mean by That?: A Dictionary of Historical Terms for Genealogists*. 2 vols. Bowie, Md.: Heritage Books, Inc., 1994, 1998.

Evans, Barbara Jean. *A to Zax: A Comprehensive Dictionary for Genealogists and Historians*. 3d ed. Alexandria, Va.: Hearthside Press, 1995.

Harris, Maurine, and Glen Harris. *Ancestry's Concise Genealogical Dictionary*. Salt Lake City: Ancestry, 1989.

Lederer, Richard M., Jr. *Colonial American English*. Essex, Conn.: Verbatim, 1985.

McCutcheon, Marc. *Everyday Life in the 1800s*. Cincinnati: Writer's Digest Books, 2001.

Taylor, Dale. *The Writer's Guide to Everyday Life in Colonial America: From 1607–1783*. Cincinnati: Writer's Digest Books, 1997.

Varhola, Michael. *Everyday Life During the Civil War*. Cincinnati: Writer's Digest Books, 1999.

Abstract—summary of important points of a text or document.

Administrator—person appointed to manage or divide the estate of a deceased person, especially one who died without a will. *feminine*: administratrix.

Alien—*noun*: a foreigner, citizen of another country; *verb*: to transfer property to another.

Ancestor—person from whom you are descended; a forefather; a forebear.

Ancestry—all forebears of a person, from parents backward in time.

Archives—records of a government, organization, institution; the place where such records are stored.

Attest—to affirm; to certify by signature or oath.

Banns—public announcement of an intended marriage.

Bequeath—to give personal property to a person in a will. *noun*: bequest.

Bond—a binding agreement to perform certain actions or duties or be required to pay a specified sum of money as a penalty; at different times required of estate administrators or executors, grooms, certain elected officials. A bondsman, often a relative, acted as surety.

Bounty land—land promised as reward or inducement for enlisting in military service.

Christian name—the name given at christening or baptism, the *given* name.

Codicil—addition to a will.

Collateral relatives—people with common ancestors, but descended from different brother or sister lines.

Common ancestor—one shared by any two or more people.

Confederacy—Confederate States of America, the southern states that seceded from the United States in 1860–61. *adjective*: confederate.

Consort—wife or husband whose spouse is living.

Conveyances—deeds, transfers of title to property.

Cousin—child of one's aunt or uncle in any generation; once used informally for any close relative or friend.

Deceased—dead.

Declaration of Intention—first paper, sworn to and filed in court, by an alien stating the desire to become a citizen.

Deed—transfer of ownership of and title to property.

Descendancy chart—chart of a person's offspring: children, grandchildren, and succeeding generations.

Descendant—an offspring of a person: child, grandchild, great-grandchild, etc.

Devise—to give property, usually land, in a will.

Devisee—one to whom property is given in a will.

Devisor—one who gives property in a will.

Dissenter—one who did not belong to the established church, especially the Church of England.

Dower—legal right or share that a wife acquired by marriage in the real estate of her husband, allotted to her after his death for her lifetime.

Emigrant—one leaving a country and moving to another.

Enfeoff—to grant property in fee simple. In deeds, the sellers "do grant, bargain, sell, alien, enfeoff, release, and confirm unto" the buyer certain property.

Entail—*law.* to restrict the inheritance of real property to one's lineal descendants or one line of descendants.

Enumeration—a listing or counting, such as a census.

Estate—all property and debts belonging to a person.

Executor—one appointed in a will to carry out its provisions. *feminine*: executrix.

Fee simple—absolute ownership of a piece of land, to sell or devise as the owner chooses.

Fieri facias—*Latin, law.* cause it to be done; an order to a sheriff to sell enough of a person's property to satisfy a court judgment of debt against that person.

Friend—member of the Religious Society of Friends; a Quaker.

Given name—name given to a person at birth or baptism; one's first and middle names.

Grantee—one who buys property or receives a grant.

Grantor—one who sells property or makes a grant.

Great-aunt—sister of one's grandparent.

Great-uncle—brother of one's grandparent.

Guardian—person appointed to care for and manage property of a minor (underage), orphan, or adult incompetent of managing his own affairs.

Half brother or sister—child by another marriage of one's mother or father; the relationship of two people who have only one parent in common.

Heir—one entitled by law or by terms of a will to inherit property from another.

Illegitimate—born to a mother who was not married to the child's father.

Immigrant—one moving into a country from another.

Indentured servant—one bound into the service of another person for a specified number of years, often in return for transportation to this country; a redemptioner.

Infant—*law.* one who is under legal age.

In primis—*Latin.* in the first place.

Instant—*archaic.* of the current month; of this month.

Intestate—*noun*: one who dies without a will; *adjective*: dying without a will.

Issue—offspring; children; descendants; progeny.

Late—recently deceased; now deceased.

Legacy—property or money left to someone in a will.

Legatee—one who inherits money or property through a will.

Lineage—ancestry; descent from a specific ancestor. *adjective*: lineal.

Loyalist—Tory; an American colonist who supported the British side in the American Revolution.

Maiden name—a girl's surname before marriage.

Majority—legal age; age to have adult status and privileges; "coming of age." The age and benefits attached to it vary with time and place.

Maternal—related through one's mother. Maternal grandmother is the mother's mother.

Microform—reproduction of images, reduced in size, in one of several ways: microcard, microfiche, or microfilm.

Militia—citizens of a state who are not part of the national military forces but who can be called into military service in an emergency; a citizen army, apart from the regular military forces.

Minor—one who is under legal age; not yet a legal adult; an infant.

Mortality—death; death rate.

Namesake—person named after another person.

Necrology—listing or record of persons who have died recently.

Nee—*French*. born. Used to identify a woman's maiden name: Mrs. Susan Mood nee Logan.

Orphan—person who has lost one or both parents by death.

Patent—grant of land from a government to an individual.

Paternal—related through one's father. Paternal grandmother is the father's mother.

Pedigree—family tree; ancestry; lineage.

Pension—money paid regularly to an individual, especially by a government for military service during wartime, or upon retirement from government or company service.

Pensioner—one who receives a pension.

Pole—in land surveys, a measurement of 16½ feet (5.035 meters) in length; a rod or perch.

Poll—list or record of persons, especially for taxing or voting; one "head" or taxable person.

Prenuptial agreement (antenuptial agreement)—legal document made by a couple before marriage, usually involving property.

Primogeniture—*law*. the right of the eldest child, usually the eldest son, to inherit the entire estate of the parents.

Probate—legal process of (1) determining that a will is valid before authorizing distribution of the estate, (2) appointing someone to administer an intestate estate, or (3) overseeing the settlement of estates. See *succession*. Probate court jurisdiction may also include cases of lunacy, adoption, bastardy, and the like.

Progenitor—ancestor.

Proximo—*Latin, archaic.* in the following month, the month after the present one.

Public domain—land owned by the government.

Quitclaim deed—transfer of claim or title (usually to land) without guarantee of valid title.

Relict—*archaic.* widow.

Rod—See *pole.*

Section—640 acres; one of thirty-six divisions of a township in the rectangular survey system.

Sibling—person having one or both parents in common with another; brother or sister.

Sic—*Latin.* thus; copied exactly as the original reads. Often suggests a mistake or surprise in the original.

Statute—law.

Stepbrother, stepsister—child of one's stepmother or stepfather by a previous marriage.

Stepchild—child of one's husband or wife by a previous marriage.

Stepfather—husband of one's mother by a later marriage.

Stepmother—wife of one's father by a later marriage.

Succession—especially in Louisiana, the process of determining a will's validity, identifying heirs, ordering inventory of the estate, ordering family meetings to determine the best interest of minor heirs, putting heirs in possession of the estate. *Probate* is the same process; term used in most states. *Succession* as a legal term in other states is the transfer of property to legal heirs of an intestate estate. The right to inherit and to what degree is determined by the state's laws of descent and distribution.

Surname—family name; last name.

Territory—area of land owned by the United States, not a state, but having its own legislature and governor.

Testator—person who makes a valid will before death.

Teste—*law.* to bear witness, to certify with one's signature that a record is a true copy or a document is genuine.

Tithable—taxable. *noun*: a person who owes tax to a specified jurisdiction.

Tithe—formerly, money due as a tax for support of the clergy or church.

Tory—Loyalist; one who supported the British side in the American Revolution.

Township—division of U.S. public land that usually contains thirty-six sections, or thirty-six square miles. Also a subdivision of the county in some states.

Tutor—*Louisiana, civil law*. guardian of minor children. *feminine*: tutrix.

Ultimo—*Latin, archaic*. in the month before this one; last month.

Union—the United States; also the North during the Civil War, the states that did not secede.

Vital records—records of birth, death, marriage, divorce.

Vital statistics—data dealing with birth, death, marriage, divorce.

Warranty deed—deed in which the seller of the property guarantees a clear title to the buyer.

Will—document declaring how a person wants his or her property divided after death.

Abbreviations

(commonly used in genealogy or documents)

b—born.

B—black; Negro.

c, ca—about, approximately; from Latin *circa*.

co—county, or company.

col—colored; black; Negro.

Col—colonel.

CSA—Confederate States of America, the association of southern states that seceded from the United States 1860–1861.

d—died.

dau—daughter.

dea—deacon.

decd or dec'd—deceased.

Do—ditto; what we use as ditto marks often simply indicated a blank column or "no information."

et al—Latin *et alii*, meaning "and others."

etc—Latin *et cetera*, meaning "and other things."

et ux—Latin *et uxor*, meaning "and wife."

F—female.

fi fa—Latin *fieri facias*; see glossary.

fmc—free man of color.

fwc—free woman of color.

govt—government.

ibid—Latin *ibidem*, meaning "in the same place." Used in footnotes to mean the same work as just cited.

IOOF—Independent Order of Odd Fellows, fraternal organization.

IS—Interim Supply, meaning that a minister is appointed as full-time minister to the congregation but on an interim or temporary basis.

JP—justice of the peace.

LDS—The Church of Jesus Christ of Latter-day Saints, the Mormons.

LE—Local Elder.

LS—Latin *locus sigilli*; on documents, the place where a person's seal is placed.

M—male.

m—married.

m1—married first.

m2—married second.

ME South, ME North—Methodist Episcopal Church South, North.

MG—Minister of the Gospel.

Mu—Mulatto, person of mixed Caucasian and Negro ancestry.

nd—no date given.

n m—never married.

np—no page, or no publisher, given.

NS—New Style, referring to the Gregorian calendar.

OM—Ordained Minister.

OS—Occasional Supply, referring to a minister appointed to serve when needed, not on a regular basis.

OS—Old Style, referring to the Julian calendar.

pp—pages.

Sen, Sr—senior.

SS—Stated Supply, referring to a minister appointed as the regular minister of a congregation.

unm—unmarried.

VDM—Latin *Verbi Domini Ministerium*, minister of the Word of God.

viz—Latin *videlicet*, meaning "to wit," "that is to say," or "namely."

W—white; Caucasian.

(w) or wit—witness.

Relationship Chart

Instructions for using the chart on page 239 to identify the relationship between any two people.

1. Identify the common ancestor of the two people. Locate the box in the upper left corner for the common ancestor.
2. Across the top row of the chart, find the relationship of one of the two people to their common ancestor.
3. Down the left edge of the chart, find the relationship of the second person to their common ancestor.
4. Read down the column of the first person and across the chart on the row of the second person. Where the two rows intersect is the box that identifies the relationship.

Example:

1. The common ancestor is Margaret Catharine (Patton) Coleman.
2. H.T. is the grandson of Margaret Catharine (Patton) Coleman, two generations away from her. Read across row 2.
3. Judith is the great-great-granddaughter of Margaret Catharine, four generations away from her. Read down column 4.
4. Row 2 and column 4 intersect at the box that reads "1 cou 2 R," or first cousin two generations removed. Judith and H.T. are first cousins twice removed.

	1	2	3	4	5	6	7	8	9
	COMMON ANCESTOR	SON / DAU.	GRAND-SON	GREAT GRAND-SON	G-G GRAND-SON	G-G-G GRAND-SON	4G GRAND-SON	5G GRAND-SON	6G GRAND-SON	7G GRAND-SON
1	SON / DAU.	BRO / SIS.	NEPHEW / NIECE	GRAND NEPHEW	GREAT GRAND-NEPHEW	G-G GRAND-NEPHEW	G-G-G GRAND-NEPHEW	4G GRAND-NEPHEW	5G GRAND-NEPHEW	6G GRAND-NEPHEW
2	GRAND-SON	NEPHEW / NIECE	1ST COUSIN	1 COU 1 R	1 COU 2 R	1 COU 3 R	1 COU 4 R	1 COU 5 R	1 COU 6 R	1 COU 7 R
3	GREAT GRAND-SON	GRAND NEPHEW	1 COU 1 R	2ND COUSIN	2 COU 1 R	2 COU 2 R	2 COU 3 R	2 COU 4 R	2 COU 5 R	2 COU 6 R
4	G-G GRAND-SON	GREAT GRAND-NEPHEW	1 COU 2 R	2 COU 1 R	3RD COUSIN	3 COU 1 R	3 COU 2 R	3 COU 3 R	3 COU 4 R	3 COU 5 R
5	G-G-G GRAND-SON	G-G GRAND-NEPHEW	1 COU 3 R	2 COU 2 R	3 COU 1 R	4TH COUSIN	4 COU 1 R	4 COU 2 R	4 COU 3 R	4 COU 4 R
6	4G GRAND-SON	3G GRAND-NEPHEW	1 COU 4 R	2 COU 3 R	3 COU 2 R	4 COU 1 R	5TH COUSIN	5 COU 1 R	5 COU 2 R	5 COU 3 R
7	5G GRAND-SON	4G GRAND-NEPHEW	1 COU 5 R	2 COU 4 R	3 COU 3 R	4 COU 2 R	5 COU 1 R	6TH COUSIN	6 COU 1 R	6 COU 2 R
8	6G GRAND-SON	5G GRAND-NEPHEW	1 COU 6 R	2 COU 5 R	3 COU 4 R	4 COU 3 R	5 COU 2 R	6 COU 1 R	7TH COUSIN	7 COU 1 R
9	7G GRAND-SON	6G GRAND-NEPHEW	1 COU 7 R	2 COU 6 R	3 COU 5 R	4 COU 4 R	5 COU 3 R	6 COU 2 R	7 COU 1 R	8TH COUSIN

RELATIONSHIP CHART ABBREVIATIONS

BRO = brother
SIS = sister
DAU = daughter
COU = cousin
R = removed (generations removed)

G-G = great-great
GRANDSON = grandson or granddaughter
SON = son or daughter
NEPHEW = nephew or niece

The chart may be extended in either direction for identifying more distant relationships.

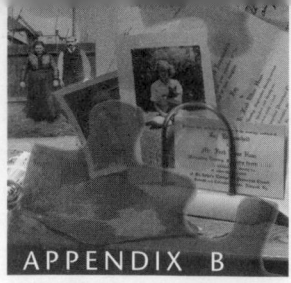

National Archives and Regional Branches

National Archives and Records Administration
700 Pennsylvania Ave. NW
Washington, DC 20408
Phone: (800) 234-8861 or (301) 713-6800
E-mail: inquire@nara.gov

National Archives II
8601 Adelphi Rd.
College Park, MD 20740-6001
Phone: (800) 234-8861
E-mail: inquire@arch2.nara.gov

National Archives home page: http://www.archives.gov

National Archives—information on nationwide facilities, including regional
branches and presidential libraries, holdings, research at each facility, hours,
and directions to each location: http://www.archives.gov/facilities/index.html

REGIONAL BRANCHES OF THE NATIONAL ARCHIVES

Alaska

National Archives, Pacific Alaska Region (Anchorage)
654 W. Third Ave., Anchorage, AK 99501-2145
Phone: (907) 271-2441
Serving Alaska.

California

National Archives, Pacific Region
24000 Avila Rd., Laguna Niguel, CA 92677-3497 or
P.O. Box 6719, Laguna Niguel, CA 92607-6719
Phone: (949) 360-2641
Serving Arizona; southern California; Clark County, Nevada.

National Archives, Pacific Sierra Region
1000 Commodore Dr., San Bruno, CA 94066-2350
Phone: (650) 876-9001
Serving northern California, Hawaii, Nevada except for Clark County,
American Samoa, Pacific Trust Territories.

Colorado

National Archives, Rocky Mountain Region
Bldg. 48, Denver Federal Center
P.O. Box 25307, Denver, CO 80225-0307

Phone: (303) 236-0804

Serving Colorado, Montana, New Mexico, North Dakota, South Dakota, Utah, Wyoming.

District of Columbia

Washington National Records Center

4205 Suitland Rd., Suitland, MD 20746.

For information, visit the Web site:

http://www.nara.gov/records/wnrcpub.html

Georgia

National Archives, Southeast Region

1557 St. Joseph Ave., East Point, GA 30344-2593

Phone: (404) 763-7474

Serving Alabama, Florida, Georgia, Kentucky, Mississippi, North Carolina, South Carolina, Tennessee.

Illinois

National Archives, Great Lakes Region (Chicago)

7358 S. Pulaski Rd., Chicago, IL 60629-5898

Phone: (773) 581-7816

Serving Illinois, Indiana, Michigan, Minnesota, Ohio, Wisconsin.

Massachusetts

National Archives, Northeast Region (Boston)

Murphy Federal Center, 380 Trapelo Rd., Waltham, MA 02452-6399.

Phone: (781) 647-8104

Serving Connecticut, Maine, Massachusetts, New Hampshire, Rhode Island, Vermont.

National Archives, Northeast Region (Pittsfield)

10 Conte Dr., Pittsfield, MA 01201-8230

Phone: (413) 445-6885

A microfilm reading room, serving primarily the Northeast but with census, military, and other records with national coverage.

Missouri

National Archives, Central Plains Region (Kansas City)

2312 E. Bannister Rd., Kansas City, MO 64131

Phone: (816) 926-6920

Serving Iowa, Kansas, Missouri, Nebraska.

National Archives, Central Plains Region (Lee's Summit)

200 Space Center Dr., Lee's Summit, MO 64064-1182

Phone: (816) 478-7089

Serving Department of Veterans Affairs; agencies and courts in New Jersey, New York, Puerto Rico, U.S. Virgin Islands.

New York

National Archives, Northeast Region (New York City)
201 Varick St., New York, NY 10014-4811
Phone: (212) 337-1300
Serving New Jersey, New York, Puerto Rico, U.S. Virgin Islands.

Ohio

National Archives, Great Lakes Region (Dayton)
3150 Springboro Rd., Dayton, OH 45439-1883
Phone: (937) 225-2852
Serving Indiana, Michigan, Ohio.

Pennsylvania

National Archives, Mid Atlantic Region (Center City Philadelphia)
900 Market St., Philadelphia, PA 19107-4292
Phone: (215) 597-3000
Serving Delaware, Maryland, Pennsylvania, Virginia, West Virginia.
Genealogical records are at this facility.

National Archives, Mid Atlantic Region (Northeast Philadelphia)
14700 Townsend Rd., Philadelphia, PA 19154-1096
Phone: (215) 671-9027.
Serving Delaware, Maryland, Pennsylvania, Virginia, West Virginia.

Texas

National Archives, Southwest Region
501 W. Felix St., Bldg. 1, P.O. Box 6216, Fort Worth, TX 76115-0216
Phone: (817) 334-5515
Serving Arkansas, Louisiana, Oklahoma, Texas.

Washington

National Archives, Pacific Alaska Region (Seattle)
6125 Sand Point Way NE, Seattle, WA 98115-7999
Phone: (206) 526-6501
Serving Idaho, Oregon, Washington.

Federal Census, 1790–1930

WHICH CENSUS REPORTS . . . ?

age, sex, race of each individual in free household	1850 forward
agricultural schedules	1850–1880
attendance in school	1850 forward
months attending school	1900
birth date (month/year) of each person	1900
month of birth if born within the year	1870, 1880
birthplace of each person	1850 forward
citizenship, see *male . . . ; naturalized citizen . . .*	
convict	1850, 1860, 1890
crippled, maimed, deformed	1890
deaf, dumb, or blind	1850–1890, 1910
defective, dependent, delinquent schedules (DDD)	1880
disabled: crippled, maimed, bedridden, or other disability	1880
employer, self-employed, or wage earner	1910–1930
months unemployed	1880–1900
whether person worked yesterday	1930
home or farm as residence	1890–1910, 1930
home owned or rented	1890–1930
home owned free of mortgage	1890–1920
farm owned or rented	1890
farm owned free of mortgage	1890
value of home or monthly rent	1930
homeless child	1890
illness, current, or temporary disability	1880
chronic or acute illness, length of time afflicted	1890
immigration year	1900–1930
number of years in United States	1890, 1900
industry/manufacturing schedules	1820, 1850–1880
insane, idiot	1850–1880
defective in mind	1890
language, native	1890, 1910–1930
native language of parents	1920
speaks English	1890–1930
male, eligible/not eligible to vote	1870

marital status	1880 forward
age at first marriage	1930
married within the census year	1850–1890
month of marriage, within census year	1870
number of years of present marriage	1900, 1910
mortality schedules	1850–1880
mother of how many children, number living	1890–1910
name of each individual in free household	1850 forward
name of head of household only	1790–1840
naturalized citizen "Na" or first papers "Pa"	1890–1930
year of naturalization	1920
occupation	1850 forward
parents, whether foreign born	1870
birthplace of parents	1880 forward
pauper	1850, 1860, 1890
prisoner	1890
radio set in home	1930
reading and writing, whether able to read or write	1890–1930
persons unable to read and/or write	1850–1880
relationship to head of household	1880 forward
slaves by age and sex	1820–1860
number of slaves in household	1790–1860
social statistics schedules	1850–1880
Soundex (see chapter ten)	beginning 1880
street address of family	1880 forward
value of real estate owned	1850–1870
value of home or monthly rent	1930
value of personal estate	1860–1870
veterans: pensioners	1840
Union veterans and widows, special schedule	1890
Civil War veteran or widow, Union or Confederate	1890
Civil War veteran, Union or Confederate	1910
veteran of U.S. military or naval forces, which war	1930

FIRST FEDERAL CENSUS AVAILABLE FOR EACH STATE*

Alabama	1830	Florida	1830
Alaska	1900	Georgia	1820+
Arizona	1850	Hawaii	1900
Arkansas	1830	Idaho	1870
California	1850	Illinois	1810
Colorado	1860	Indiana	1820
Connecticut	1790	Iowa	1840
Delaware	1800+	Kansas	1860
District of Columbia	1800	Kentucky	1810+

Louisiana 1810
Maine 1790
Maryland 1790
Massachusetts 1790
Michigan 1820
Minnesota 1850
Mississippi 1820
Missouri 1830
Montana 1860
Nebraska 1860
Nevada 1870
New Hampshire 1790
New Jersey . . . . .1830+
New Mexico 1850
New York 1790
North Carolina 1790
North Dakota 1860
Ohio 1820

Oklahoma 1860**, 1900
                      forward
Oregon 1850
Pennsylvania 1790
Rhode Island 1790
South Carolina 1790
South Dakota 1860
Tennessee 1820 (1810
                      partial)
Texas 1850
Utah 1850
Vermont 1790
Virginia . . . . .1810+
Washington 1860
West Virginia . . . . .1870+
  (part of Virginia until 1863)
Wisconsin 1820
Wyoming 1870

+Published substitutes exist for the 1790 census, created from other records. For other states or counties missing from the 1790 schedules, see published, microform, town or county courthouse records of the period.

*Censuses may be missing for several reasons:
1. State or territory not yet organized, or enumerated with parent territory.
2. Census was taken but schedule misplaced, not turned in, ruined, lost, destroyed.

**Free, non-Indian residents of Oklahoma area are enumerated at the end of roll 52 (Arkansas) under Indian Lands.

APPENDIX D

Blank Forms

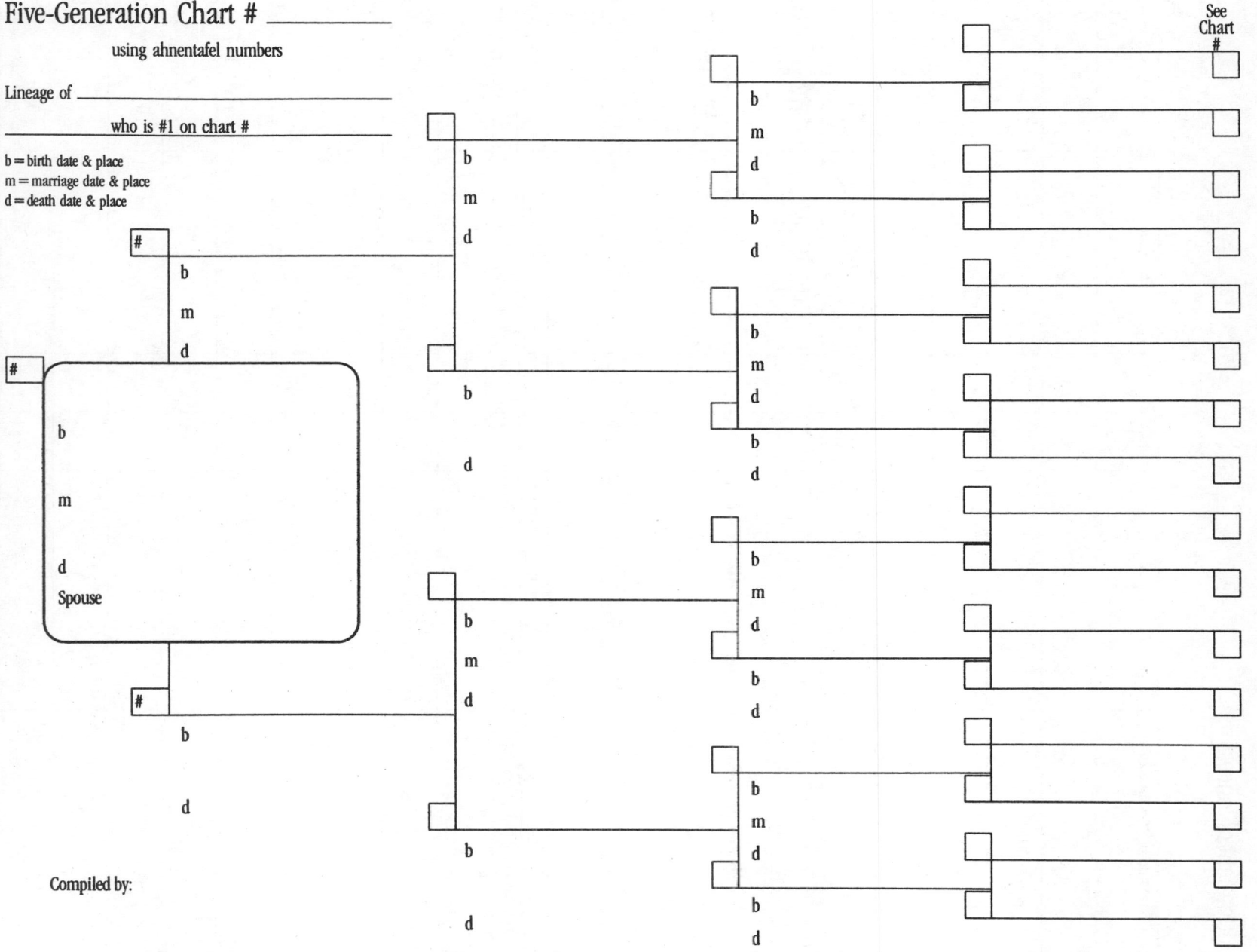

Reprinted from Unpuzzling Your Past Workbook

Five-Generation Chart # _____

using ahnentafel numbers

Lineage of _____

_____ who is #1 on chart # _____

b = birth date & place
m = marriage date & place
d = death date & place

#

b

m

d

#

b

m

d

Spouse

#

b

d

b

m

d

b

d

b

m

d

b

d

b

m

d

b

d

b

m

d

b

d

b

m

d

b

d

b

m

d

b

d

See Chart #

Compiled by:

Alphabetical Ancestors

Locality _____
County and/or State

Surname or Maiden Name	Given Name	Birth Year	Death Year	Residence	Dates of Residence	5-Gen. Chart #

Reprinted from Unpuzzling Your Past Workbook

Family Group Sheet of the _____ Family

Full name of husband	Birth date
His father	Birth place
	Death date
	Death place
His mother with maiden name	Burial place

Full maiden name of wife	Birth date
Her father	Birth place
	Death date
	Death place
Her mother with maiden name	Burial place

| Other Spouses | Marriage date, place, etc. |
| Source #s | Source #s |

Children of this marriage	Birth date & place	Death date, place, & burial place	Marriage date, place & spouse
Source #s			
Source #s			
Source #s			
Source #s			
Source #s			
Source #s			

Reprinted from Unpuzzling Your Past Workbook

Source #   Sources (Documentation)
_____

Reprinted from Unpuzzling Your Past Workbook

Family Group Sheet of the _____ Family, continued

Father _____ Mother _____

Children of this marriage	Birth date & place	Death date, place, & burial place	Marriage date, place & spouse
Source #s			
Source #s			
Source #s			
Source #s			
Source #s			
Source #s			
Source #s			
Source #s			

Notes

Reprinted from Unpuzzling Your Past Workbook

Source #	Sources (Documentation)

Reprinted from Unpuzzling Your Past Workbook

Census Check on _____
<small>Name</small>

Birthdate/place _____ First Census _____

Father's Name _____ Mother's Name _____

Marriage date/place _____ Spouse _____

Death date/place _____ Burial place _____

Census Year	Age	State/Counties Searched	County Where Found & Notes	Film #, Roll #, E.D., Pg, etc.

Reprinted from Unpuzzling Your Past Workbook

Gaylord Stickle Company, Houston Texas

Reprinted from Unpuzzling Your Past Workbook

1790 Census

Reprinted from Unpuzzling Your Past Workbook

Township or Local Community _____ County _____ State _____

Enumerator _____ Date Census Taken _____ Enumerator District # _____

[Official census day—first Monday in August, 2 August 1790]

Page	Name of Head of Family	Free White Males 16 years & upwards including heads of families	Free White Males under 16 years	Free White Females including heads of families	All Other Free Persons	Slaves	Dwellings/ Other information

Reprinted from Unpuzzling Your Past Workbook

1800 or 1810 Census

Local Community _____ County _____ State _____

Enumerator _____ Date Census Taken _____ Enumerator District # _____

[Official census day—first Monday in August: 4 August 1800 & 6 August 1810]   Supervisor District # _____

Written Page No.	Printed Page No.	Name of Head of Family	Free White Males					Free White Females					All other free persons except Indians not taxed	Slaves
			under 10	of 10 & under 16	of 16 & under 26 including heads of families	of 26 & under 45	of 45 & up	under 10	of 10 & under 16	of 16 & under 26 including heads of families	of 26 & under 45	of 45 & up		

Reprinted from Unpuzzling Your Past Workbook

1820 Census

Local Community _____

Enumerator _____

County _____

Date Census Taken _____

[Official census day—7 August 1820, first Monday]

State _____

Enumerator District # _____

Supervisor District # _____

Written Page No.	Printed Page No.	Name of Head of Family	Free White Males including heads of families						Free White Females including heads of families					Foreigners Not Naturalized	Persons engaged in Agriculture	Persons engaged in Commerce	Persons engaged in Manufacture	Free Colored Persons Males				Free Colored Persons Females				All other persons	Slaves
			to 10	10 to 16	*16 to 18	16 to 26	26 to 45	45 & up	to 10	10 to 16	16 to 26	26 to 45	45 & up					to 14	14 to 26	26 to 45	45 & up	to 14	14 to 26	26 to 45	45 & up		

*Those males between 16 & 18 will all be repeated in the column of those between 16 and 26.

258

Reprinted from Unpuzzling Your Past Workbook

1830 or 1840 Census—Part 1

Local Community _____ County _____ State _____

Enumerator _____ Date Census Taken _____ Enumerator District # _____

[Official census day—1 June 1830-1840] Supervisor District # _____

Written Page No.	Printed Page No.	Name of Head of Family	Free White Persons (including heads of families)																								
			Males													Females											
			under 5	5-10	10-15	15-20	20-30	30-40	40-50	50-60	60-70	70-80	80-90	90-100	100 & over	under 5	5-10	10-15	15-20	20-30	30-40	40-50	50-60	60-70	70-80	80-90	90-100	100 & over

Reprinted *from* Unpuzzling Your Past Workbook

1830 Census—Part 2

Local Community _____ County _____ State _____

Enumerator _____ Date Census Taken _____ Enumerator District # _____

[Official census day—1 June 1830] Supervisor District # _____

Written Page No.	Printed Page No.	Name of Head of Family (from previous page)	Slaves — Males						Slaves — Females						Free Colored Persons — Males						Free Colored Persons — Females						TOTAL	White Persons included in the foregoing who are					Slaves & Colored Persons included in the foregoing who are			
			under 10	10 - 24	24 - 36	36 - 55	55 - 100	100 & up	under 10	10 - 24	24 - 36	36 - 55	55 - 100	100 & up	under 10	10 - 24	24 - 36	36 - 55	55 - 100	100 & up	under 10	10 - 24	24 - 36	36 - 55	55 - 100	100 & up		deaf & dumb under 14	deaf & dumb 14 - 25	deaf & dumb 25 & up	blind	foreigners not naturalized	deaf & dumb under 14	deaf & dumb 14 - 25	deaf & dumb 25 & up	blind

1840 Census—Part 2

Local Community _____

Enumerator _____

County _____

State _____

Date Census Taken _____

Enumerator District # _____

Supervisor District # _____

[Official census day—1 June 1840]

Written Page No.	Printed Page No.	Name of Head of Family (Previous Page)	Slaves — Males						Slaves — Females						Free Colored Persons — Males						Free Colored Persons — Females						TOTAL	Number of Persons employed in each family in							Revolutionary or Military Service Pensioners in the foregoing	
			under 10	10 - 24	24 - 36	36 - 55	55 - 100	100 & up	under 10	10 - 24	24 - 36	36 - 55	55 - 100	100 & up	under 10	10 - 24	24 - 36	36 - 55	55 - 100	100 & up	under 10	10 - 24	24 - 36	36 - 55	55 - 100	100 & up		Mining	Agriculture	Commerce	Manufacturing & Trades	Ocean Navigation	Canal, Lake, River Navigat'n	Learned Prof'ns & Engineers	Name	Age

Reprinted from Unpuzzling Your Past Workbook

1850 Census

Reprinted from Unpuzzling Your Past Workbook

Post Office or Local Community _____ County _____ State _____

Enumerator _____ Date Census Taken _____ Enumerator District # _____

[Official census day—1 June 1850] Supervisor District # _____

Written Page No.	Printed Page No.	Dwelling in order of visitation	Family Number in order of visitation	Name of every person whose usual place of abode on 1 June 1850 was with this family	Description			Profession, Occupation, or Trade of each Male over 15	Value of of Real Estate Owned	Place of Birth naming state, territory, or country	Married within the year	In school within the year	Persons over 20 unable to read & write	If deaf & dumb, blind, insane, idiot, pauper or convict
					Age	Sex	Color							
		1	2	3	4	5	6	7	8	9	10	11	12	13

Reprinted from Unpuzzling Your Past Workbook

1860 Census

Post Office or Local Community _____ County _____ State _____

Enumerator _____ Date Census Taken _____ Enumerator District # _____

[Official census day—1 June 1860] Supervisor District # _____

Written Page No.	Printed Page No.	Dwelling Number	Family Number	Name of every person whose usual place of abode on 1 June 1860 was with this family	Description			Profession, Occupation, or Trade of each person over 15	Value of Real Estate Owned	Value of Personal Estate Owned	Place of Birth naming state, territory or country	Married within the year	In school within the year	Persons over 20 unable to read & write	Deaf & dumb, blind, insane, idiotic, pauper or convict
					Age	Sex	Color								
		1	2	3	4	5	6	7	8	9	10	11	12	13	14

1850 or 1860 Census   Schedule 2—Slaves

Reprinted from Unpuzzling Your Past Workbook

Local Community _____ County _____ State _____

Enumerator _____ Date Census Taken _____ [Official census day—1 June]

Written Page No.	Printed Page No.	Names of Slave Owners	Number of Slaves	Description			Fugitives from the State	Number Manumitted	Deaf & dumb, blind, insane or idiotic	Number of Slave Houses	Names of Slave Owners	Number of Slaves	Description			Fugitives from the State	Number Manumitted	Deaf & dumb, blind, insane or idiotic	Number of Slave Houses
				Age	Sex	Color							Age	Sex	Color				
		1	2	3	4	5	6	7	8	9	1	2	3	4	5	6	7	8	9
		1									1								
		2									2								
		3									3								
		4									4								
		5									5								
		6									6								
		7									7								
		8									8								
		9									9								
		10									10								
		11									11								
		12									12								
		13									13								
		14									14								

Reprinted from Unpuzzling Your Past Workbook

1870 Census

Local Community _____ County _____ State _____

Enumerator _____ Date Census Taken _____ Enumerator District # _____

[Official census day—1 June 1870]   Supervisor District # _____

Written Page No.	Printed Page No.	Dwelling No.	Family No.	Name of every person whose place of abode on 1 June 1870 was in this family	Description			Profession, Occupation, or Trade	Value of		Place of Birth	Parents		Month born within the year	Month married within the year	In school within the year	Cannot read	Cannot write	Deaf & dumb, blind, insane or idiotic	Males eligible to vote	Males not eligible to vote
					Age	Sex	Color		Real Estate Owned	Personal Estate Owned		Father Foreign-born	Mother Foreign-born								
		1	2	3	4	5	6	7	8	9	10	11	12	13	14	15	16	17	18	19	20

Reprinted from Unpuzzling Your Past Workbook

1880 Census

Local Community _____ County _____ State _____

Enumerator _____ Date Census Taken _____ Supervisor District # _____

[Official census day—1 June 1880] Enumerator District # _____

Written Page No.	Printed Page No.	Street Name	House Number	Dwelling Number	Family Number	Name of every person whose place of abode on 1 June 1880 was in this family	Description			Month born if during census year	Relationship to head of this household	Single	Married	Widowed / Divorced	Married during year	Profession, Occupation or Trade	Months unemployed this year	Health						School this year	Cannot read	Cannot write	Birthplace	Birthplace of Father	Birthplace of Mother
							Color	Sex	Age									Currently ill? If so, specify.	Blind	Deaf & dumb	Idiotic	Insane	Disabled						
			1	2		3	4	5	6	7	8	9	10	11	12	13	14	15	16	17	18	19	20	21	22	23	24	25	26

1900 Census

Reprinted from Unpuzzling Your Past Workbook

Local Community _____

Ward _____

Enumerator _____

County _____

[Official census day—1 June 1900]

Date Census Taken _____

State _____

Supervisor District # _____

Enumeration District # _____

Written Page No.	Printed Page No.	Street	House Number	Dwelling Number (1)	Family Number (2)	Name of every person whose place of abode on 1 June 1900 was in this family (3)	Relationship to head of family (4)	Color (5)	Sex (6)	Birth Date — Month / Year (7)	Age (8)	Marital status (9)	# Years married (10)	Mother of how many children? (11)	# of these children living (12)	Birthplace of — This Person (13)	Birthplace of — This Person's Father (14)	Birthplace of — This Person's Mother (15)	Year of Immigration (16)	# Years in U.S. (17)	Naturalized Citizen (18)	Occupation of every person 10 & older (19)	# months not employed (20)	Education — # months in school (21)	Education — Can read (22)	Education — Can write (23)	Education — Speaks English (24)	Owned or rented (25)	Owned free of mortgage (26)	Farm or house (27)	No. of farm schedule (28)

Reprinted from Unpuzzling Your Past Workbook

1910 Census

Local Community ——————
Ward ——————
Enumerator ——————

County ——————
[Official census day—15 April 1910]
Date Census Taken ——————

State ——————
Supervisor's District # ——————
Enumeration District # ——————

		Page No.											
		Street											
		House No.											
	1	Dwelling No.											
	2	Family No.											
	3	Name of each person whose place of abode on 15 April 1910 was in this family											
	4	Relationship											
	5	Sex											
	6	Color											
	7	Age											
	8	Marital status											
	9	# Years— Present Marriage											
	10	Mother of how many children?											
	11	# living children											
Birthplace of	12	This Person											
	13	Father											
	14	Mother											
	15	Year of Immigration											
	16	Naturalized or alien?											
	17	Speaks English? If not, give name of language.											
	18 / 19	Profession or Occupation & nature of business											
	20	Employer or Wage Earner or Working on Own Account											
	21	Out of work 15 April 1910?											
	22	# weeks out of work in 1909											
	23	Can read											
	24	Can write											
	25	School since 1 September 1909											
	26	Owned/rented											
	27	Owned free or mortgaged											
	28	Farm or house											
	29	No. of farm schedule											
	30	Civil War Veteran											
	31	Blind											
	32	Deaf & dumb											

Reprinted from Unpuzzling Your Past Workbook

1920 Census

Local Community ——————
Ward ——————
Enumerator ——————

County ——————
[Official census day—1 January 1920]
Date Census Taken ——————

State ——————
Supervisor's District # ——————
Enumeration District # ——————

No.	Column
	Page No.
1	Street
2	House No.
3	Dwelling No.
4	Family No.
5	Name of each person whose place of abode on 1 Jan 1920 was in this family
6	Relationship
7	Own or rent home
8	Owned free or mortgaged
9	Sex
10	Color or race
11	Age
12	Marital status
13	Immigration year
14	Naturalized or alien?
15	Naturalization year
16	School since 1 Sept 1919
17	Can read
18	Can write
19	Birthplace of — This person
20	Mother tongue
21	Birthplace of — Father
22	Mother tongue
23	Birthplace of — Mother
24	Mother tongue
25	Speaks English?
26	Profession or Occupation & nature of business
27	
28	Employer, wage earner, or self-employed
29	No. of farm schedule

1930 Census

From *Unpuzzling Your Past*

State _____ Incorporated place _____ Enumeration District No. _____ Sheet No. _____

County _____ Ward of city _____ Block No. _____ Supervisor's District No. _____ Roll or CD-ROM No. _____

Township or other division of county _____ Unincorporated place _____ Institution _____

[Census Day — 1 April 1930] Enumerated by _____ on _____ 1930

Place of Abode				Name of each person whose place of abode on 1 April 1930 was in this family	Relationship to head	Home owned or rented	Value of home if owned, or monthly rent	Radio set	Does family live on farm?	Sex	Color or race	Age at last birthday	Marital condition	Age at first marriage	School since 1 Sept 1929	Can read and write?	Birthplace of			Mother tongue of foreign born	Year immigrated to U.S.	Naturalization, first papers, or alien	Speaks English?	Occupation			Class of worker	Worked yesterday?	Veteran of U.S. military or navy?	What war?
Street	House no.	Dwelling no.	Family no.														This person	Father	Mother					Trade, profession, or kind of work	Industry or business					
1	2	3	4	5	6	7	8	9	10	11	12	13	14	15	16	17	18	19	20	21	22	23	24	25	26	27	28	30	31

Note: Column 29, line on Unemployment Schedule, and Column 32, no. of farm schedule are omitted here since those schedules no longer exist.

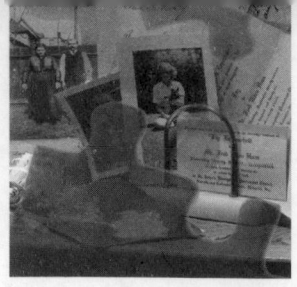

Bibliography

BIBLIOGRAPHIES IN THE TEXT

African-American research and reference, pages 167–168
Church records, sources for locating, page 136
Everyday life references, page 231
Genealogical dictionaries, page 231
General history and biography, page 228
Hereditary societies and rosters, page 80
Immigration references, page 163
Land and property, page 120
Locating church records, page 136
Military pensions, page 151–152
Military personnel and history, pages 148–149
Military service records, page 150
National Archives research, pages 146–147
Native American records and research, pages 166–167
Naturalization records, pages 164–165
Newspaper indexes, page 133
Newspaper union lists, pages 133–134
Photograph dating, page 78
Property and inheritance, page 120
Quaker references, page 137
State sources, page 125
Vital records, page 121

CITED OR SELECTED WORKS FOR FURTHER REFERENCE

Abate, Frank R., ed. *Omni Gazetteer of the United States of America*. Detroit: Omnigraphics, Inc., 1991.

American State Papers: Documents, Legislative and Executive of the Congress of the United States. 38 vols. Washington, D.C.: Gates and Seaton, 1832–1861.

Bentley, Elizabeth P. *Directory of Family Associations*. Baltimore: Genealogical Publishing Co., 1991 or later edition.

Carmack, Sharon DeBartolo. *A Genealogist's Guide to Discovering Your Female Ancestors*. Cincinnati: Betterway Books, 1998.

———. *A Genealogist's Guide to Discovering Your Immigrant & Ethnic Ancestors*. Cincinnati: Betterway Books, 2000.

———. *Organizing Your Family History Search*. Cincinnati: Betterway Books, 1999.

Croom, Emily Anne. *The Genealogist's Companion & Sourcebook*. Cincinnati: Betterway Books, 1994.

———. *The Sleuth Book for Genealogists*. Cincinnati: Betterway Books, 2000.

———. *The Unpuzzling Your Past Workbook*. Cincinnati: Betterway Books, 1996.

Drake, Paul. *You Ought to Write All That Down: A Guide to Organizing and Writing Genealogical Narrative*. Bowie, Md.: Heritage Books, 1998.

Eichholz, Alice, ed. *Ancestry's Red Book: American State, County & Town Sources*. Rev. ed. Salt Lake City: Ancestry, 1992.

Everton, George B., Sr., ed. *The Handy Book for Genealogists*. Logan, Utah: Everton Publishers, latest edition.

Filby, P. William. *Passenger and Immigration Lists Bibliography 1538–1900*. 2d ed. Detroit: Gale Research, 1988.

———. *Passenger and Immigration Lists Index: A Guide to Published Arrival Records of . . . Passengers Who Came to the United States and Canada in the Seventeenth, Eighteenth, and Nineteenth Centuries*. Detroit: Gale Research, 1981–.

Greenwood, Val D. *The Researcher's Guide to American Genealogy*. 3d ed. Baltimore: Genealogical Publishing Co., 2000.

Hatcher, Patricia Law. *Producing a Quality Family History*. Salt Lake City: Ancestry, 1996.

Hinckley, Kathleen W. *Locating Lost Family Members & Friends*. Cincinnati: Betterway Books, 1999.

Hone, E. Wade. *Land & Property Research in the United States*. Salt Lake City: Ancestry, 1997.

Index to Personal Names in the National Union Catalog of Manuscript Collections, 1959–1984. Alexandria, Va.: Chadwyck-Healey, 1988.

Kirkham, E. Kay. *How to Read the Handwriting and Records of Early America*. Salt Lake City: Deseret Book Co., 1961.

Lainhart, Ann S. *State Census Records*. Baltimore: Genealogical Publishing Co., 1992.

McMullin, Philip W., ed. *Grassroots of America: A Computerized Index to the American State Papers: Land Grants and Claims (1789–1837)*. Salt Lake City: Gendex Corp., 1972.

Meyerink, Kory L., ed. *Printed Sources: A Guide to Published Genealogical Records*. Salt Lake City: Ancestry, 1998.

Mills, Elizabeth Shown. *Evidence! Citation & Analysis for the Family Historian*. Baltimore: Genealogical Publishing Co., 1997.

Neagles, James C. *The Library of Congress: A Guide to Genealogical and Historical Research*. Salt Lake City: Ancestry, 1990.

———. *U.S. Military Records: A Guide to Federal and State Sources*. Salt Lake City: Ancestry, 1994.

The New America State Papers. Wilmington, Del.: Scholarly Resources, 1972–1981.

Schaefer, Christina Kassabian. *The Hidden Half of the Family*. Baltimore: Genealogical Publishing Co., 1999.

Smith, Clifford Neal. *Federal Land Series: A Calendar of Archival Materials on the Land Patents Issued by the United States Government, With Subject,*

Tract, and Name Indexes. Chicago: American Library Association, 1972–1986.

Sperry, Kip. *Reading Early American Handwriting.* Baltimore: Genealogical Publishing Co., 1998.

Sturdevant, Katherine Scott. *Bringing Your Family History to Life Through Social History.* Cincinnati: Betterway Books, 2000.

Szucs, Loretto Dennis, and Sandra Hargreaves Luebking, eds. *The Source: A Guidebook of American Genealogy.* Rev. ed. Salt Lake City: Ancestry, 1997.

Thorndale, William, and William Dollarhide. *Map Guide to the U.S. Federal Censuses, 1790–1920.* Baltimore: Genealogical Publishing Co., 1987.

United States Department of Commerce, Bureau of the Census. *Age Search Information.* Washington, D.C.: Government Printing Office, 1990.

Index

THE Unpuzzling Your Past WORKBOOK

TABLE OF CONTENTS

Alphabetical Ancestors by Alphabetical Headings (1)
to index a collection of family group sheets or pedigree charts.

Alphabetical Ancestors by Surname (1)
to index all relatives by the same surname.

Alphabetical Ancestors by Locality (1)
to form a master list of all ancestors from one location (county, state, etc.).

Index to Workshop Notes and Handouts, *with* alphabetical headings given (1)
to index notes and handouts collected from seminars and workshops.

Index to Workshop Notes and Handouts, *without* alphabetical headings provided (1)
to allow searchers to develop their own index or for already large collections.

Notes (3)
to encourage proper documentation of notes and facilitate notetaking.

Deed Abstract (3)
to facilitate abstracting deed records and encourage thoroughness.

Census Forms
to expedite census extraction and encourage thoroughness.
1790 Census (4)
1800–1810 Census (4)
1820 Census (4)
1830–1840 Census—Part 1 (4)
1830 Census—Part 2 (4)
1840 Census—Part 2 (4)
1850 Census (5)
1860 Census (5)
1850–1860 Slave Schedules (5)

1870 Census (5)
1880 Census (5)
1900 Census (5)
1910 Census (5)
1920 Census (5)

Interview Forms
to aid in interviewing relatives for family history in the twentieth century.
Pre-1930 Period (1)
Depression–1930s (1)
World War II and the 1940s (1)
Decade of the 1950s (1)
Decade of the 1960s (1)

Family Group Sheet (10)
to present vital statistics and documentation for each nuclear family.

Ahnentafel Table (2)
to compile known ancestors for any one individual.

Five-Generation Chart (2)
to show one individual and four generations of ancestors, with vital statistics.

Ahnentafel Five-Generation Chart (2)
to show any five generations, using ahnentafel identification numbers.

Biographical Outline (4)
to consolidate all information known about one individual, with documentation.

United States Map (2)
to track migrations and residences of ancestral families.

Timelines
to place ancestors into history as an aid to study and comparison.
1600–1800 (1)
1750–1950 (1)

INTRODUCTION

Genealogy is an intriguing, engrossing, captivating, fascinating, popular hobby and profession. In order to be successful, the genealogist must (1) plan and organize and (2) do careful, accurate, thorough research. The genealogist who plans and organizes without good research has no real success, for the results are meaningless. The one who tries to do the appropriate research using little scraps of paper, without planning or organization, finds that success is elusive, literally lost in the shuffle. But the genealogist who plans *and* organizes *and* researches carefully will experience the excitement and gratification of accomplishment. This is true when one finds a great-grandmother's "long-lost" maiden name, proves the identification of the long-sought father or mother of an ancestor, or determines that a certain elusive ancestor was alive in a given year and place. The smallest detail can make the avid genealogist squeal.

If you are relatively new to genealogy, use this book as a workbook to accompany *Unpuzzling Your Past*, as the two are intended to complement each other and the beyond-the-basics *The Genealogist's Companion & Sourcebook*. Both of these books, by Emily Croom, are published by Betterway Books in Cincinnati, Ohio. *Unpuzzling Your Past* and *The Genealogist's Companion & Sourcebook* are primarily concerned with the research aspect of genealogy. This book deals with planning and organization.

A book of genealogical forms has one basic purpose—to help organize research and its results. When we organize our *research*, we tend to be more efficient and more thorough, and our efforts stay focused on our goals. When we organize the *results*, we are in a better position to study and evaluate. We avoid duplicating our efforts, and we have a better picture of where we are in our search. Best of all, we can find our information readily.

Organizing systems are probably more numerous than genealogists, for who has not begun with one system and switched at least once to what seemed a better one? This book does not promote any particular system; each genealogist must develop or adapt one best suited to personal style and needs. The key is to use consistently the system that works best for you.

Many people use three-ring binders for collecting and organizing data, by surname or locality or both. Some transfer notes to file folders, large index cards or computer word processing documents. Many use genealogy computer programs to link known relatives and store basic information on them. Still others use a combination of these systems.

My own preference is three-ring binders, one (or more) for each surname, divided by locality. When the amount of material for one locality outgrows its space, it becomes a separate binder, such as METCALFE-Texas or COLEMAN-Cumberland County, Virginia. What I want in an organizing system is to gather and file notes in one operation, without having to transcribe, sort and file notes once I get home from the library or courthouse. This means that note taking is limited to one surname in one locality per page. I find it helpful to write at the top of each page of notes, usually in the upper right corner, the surname to which the notes pertain: BLAKENEY-Jasper County or SHELBY-South Carolina. In keeping with this practice, many of the forms in the book begin with a title that includes the surname written at the top of the page.

The forms in this book can be used with practically any organizing system. Some, such as the census check, military records checklist, and biographical outline, are indispensable in seeing at a glance what has been done and planning the next step. Others, such as the interview and census forms, are valuable in both the information-gathering and -storage processes. Still others, including family group sheets, five-generation charts and biographical outlines, consolidate information already gathered, evaluated and accepted to give an overall picture of the ancestor(s).

Blank forms make up the bulk of the book. Some appear only once, as master copies from which readers should make photocopies for their own use. Others are provided in multiple copies for your convenience. You may want to keep at least one blank form of each type as a master.

The examples and suggestions which follow are some of the ways these forms can be used. Be creative and adapt them to suit your own needs as you begin or continue unpuzzling your past!

PART ONE

Forms for Planning and Organizing Research— Checklists

Each checklist in this book is a tool to help genealogists focus on a particular aspect of their research. The forms include a census check, a military records checklist, a research planning worksheet (called a problem search form in *Unpuzzling Your Past*), and a contact log. What makes these forms unique is that you can tailor them to your own research. They will guide you to define your problem, to evaluate your progress, and to decide what to do next.

CENSUS CHECK

The census check lets you consolidate census information on any one person. Use one form for information from the decennial federal censuses on that person and another form for colonial, territorial or state census information. Each form allows you to see at a glance

- Where you hope to find the person in each census during his or her lifetime
- Where you *do* find this person
- What problems you have encountered
- Which records you have searched
- Which records remain to be searched
- Ideas for future research

This form does not take the place of the census forms for each federal census, which appear later in this book. Instead, it summarizes your research and records the reference or bibliographic information on each find.

The reference information at the top of the form keeps pertinent vital statistics handy as your search progresses. Example 1 on page 5 is for an ancestor who married four times and outlived all four husbands. Because her name was different in five successive federal censuses, it was helpful to have the marriage information readily available during the census searches. (Fortunately, my grandmother had alerted me to different surnames, so I began my search in the marriage records of the county where this ancestor had lived. By the time I began the census search, I knew Sarah's surname in each census year.)

The column for age provides another perspective to aid in the search and study. Several people by the same name may show up in a given county or state. When searching for your own ancestor, knowing his or her age as well as potential family members can aid in sorting out the candidates. The age to write in the column is the age you believe the person to be on *census day* of the census year. As the instructions to the federal census takers stated, all information they recorded was to be correct as of census day, regardless of when the enumerator actually visited the household. Some enumerators and/or families followed these instructions and some did not. This is one reason we also record the date of the enumerator's visit. For 1790-1820, census day was the first Monday in August. For 1830-1900, it was June 1. Thereafter, census day was April 15 (1910), January 1 (1920) and April 1 (1930-1940). See chapters 12, 13 and 15 in *Unpuzzling Your Past* and chapter 2 of *The Genealogist's Companion & Sourcebook* for further discussion and case studies of census research.

MILITARY RECORDS CHECKLIST

The military records checklist allows you to record each ancestor or person of interest and search the military records appropriate to that person's life. For example, you would not want to spend time searching Civil War service records for an ancestor born in 1855 or 1760. On the other hand, you would not want to overlook a set of potentially helpful records just because "Nobody ever said he was in that war." Lists of corresponding military records to search can be found in such reference books as these:

1. *The Genealogist's Companion & Sourcebook*, by Emily Croom. Cincinnati: Betterway Books, 1994. Chapter 4 surveys microfilm resources available through the National Archives and at many libraries.
2. *Military Service Records: A Select Catalog of National Archives Microfilm Publications*. Washington, DC: National Archives Trust Fund Board, National Archives and Service Administration, 1985. Catalog of descriptions and film numbers, especially helpful in determining which rolls of film you may need to study.
3. *U.S. Military Records: A Guide to Federal & State Sources, Colonial America to the Present*, by James C. Neagles. Salt Lake City: Ancestry Inc., 1994. An excellent resource for genealogists, detailing the kinds of records generated and kept at both state and federal levels, whether microfilmed or not.

Military records concern all the services (army, navy, marines, militia, national guard, coast guard, merchant marine, and eventually, air force), both volunteers and those in regular service. These records deal with many aspects of military business, such as service records, pensions and bounty land warrants, prisoners, deserters, casualties, burials, soldiers' homes, medical and battle reports, courts-martial, the service academies and correspondence. Some federal and state censuses also report certain information about veterans. Thus, many records exist. Each genealogist must decide the extent to which the records may be pertinent to a particular search.

The form furnished here is a general reminder to begin with the service records available from a particular period for ancestors who might have served at that time. If indeed you find an ancestor in one of the services, you may want to investigate further in other kinds of military records, such as those for Civil War prison camps. We must remember that the more recent records are open only to servicemen or women or next of kin. We must also remember that colonial, some Revolutionary, and some Confederate records are found in state rather than federal archives. Ask in the state archives or historical society of your research area to determine what military records they have, or consult *U.S. Military Records*, listed above.

The checklist can be used in several ways. One option is to limit each form to one surname and search for direct ancestors and their brothers and cousins. Another option is to list all male ancestors from a pedigree chart, regardless of surname, and use the form as a master checklist. (Add females to the checklist as you deem appropriate to your family). To aid in the search, it is helpful to record, with the ancestor's name, his life dates and residences so that you can (1) cross out the wars or service periods for which he was too young, too old or not alive and (2) have a frame of reference for where he may have enlisted, applied for a pension or, for World War I and after, filed his discharge papers at the county courthouse.

In the columns that fall within the subject's life, you could write in his age at the beginning of that conflict or period. Then you can decide whether to spend time searching records for a seventy-five-year-old man or a twelve-year-old child. As the example shows, when the record is found, it can be noted. You can establish your own system, such as using *P* to indicate a pension record, *S* for a service record, *BLW* for bounty land warrant, etc. The example simply uses *pension*, *serv* for service record, and *CSA* for Confederate States of America. Notes in your notebooks and files will detail the search and its results. The checklist is simply a tool to give visual perspective and help make the search more thorough.

As Example 2 shows, a horizontal line through the non-applicable columns is easy to use and does not visually clutter the chart, and a diagonal slash through other columns can indicate a decision not to search due to a person's advanced age, known illness or disability, or absolute certainty that he did not serve. For one man in the example, family *tradition* reports his service in the Revolution, but the searcher has not yet found records to that effect. For another man, a record was found for someone with the same name, but, because the name is common in that family, it has not yet been determined whether it is the same person. However you use the checklist, be creative and let it serve you.

RESEARCH PLANNING WORKSHEET

The research planning worksheet is an aid for planning a search strategy. It is a checklist you create for a specific individual or family, at any point in a search, to help you lay out the beginning steps or deal with the tougher and narrower questions after trying the first sources. Used in conjunction with the contact log explained below, it focuses on a given problem:

- What is the problem to be studied?
- What have you tried (sources, contacts, evaluation) and with what results?
- What questions now need to be asked to find a solution?
- What is your next course of action? (research, sources, contacts, evaluations, crystal ball?)

Of course, the form is not intended to be used as a list of all possible sources for a specific search. Rather, it is a place to list the ones you want to try *next* in your search. Depending on the results, you can continue on a new form to concentrate on a real challenge from new angles or to tackle a different aspect of the same family.

Example 3 reflects an ongoing search for which the first sources—census, tombstone inscriptions, newspapers, marriage records, and successions (probate)—yielded very little information. The most inter-esting discovery from these sources was the revelation that both mother and daughter had married men named Isaac Croom, uncle and nephew to each other.

CONTACT LOG

A contact log is another planning device and serves as a checklist for personal contacts, such as letters, telephone calls and interviews. It is especially helpful to make such a list early in a search as you gather preliminary information from relatives. However, the form can be used at any point in a search. I like to write down ideas for contacts even if I cannot get to them right away.

Example 4 illustrates a search which had already gathered information from the few remaining relatives and census and was confronted with conflicting vital statistics on a late-nineteenth-century grandfather. Fortunately, I was able to make a number of local inquiries and appointments by telephone. Some of the list I generated in advance. Other contacts I added as the search progressed. For example, two church secretaries suggested other churches to contact which had existed in the time period I was searching.

Census Check on SARAH W. ORGAIN HARRISON TISDALE EVANS SMITH

Name "Grandma Smith"

Birthdate/place 3 APRIL 1840 NEAR PARIS, HENRY Co. TN   First Census 1840

Father's Name STERLING ORGAIN   Mother's Name MARY E. JONES

m1. WILLIAM L. HARRISON

Marriage date/place:
m1 JULY 1861, WILLIAMSON Co Tx
m2 MAR 1871 "
m3 Nov 1896 "

Spouse:
m2 · J.E. TISDALE (d 1894)
m3 · WILLIAM T. EVANS (d 1905)

Death date/place 1 MAY 1928   Burial place STAMFORD, JONES Co Tx
m4 ?   m4 · JOHN S. SMITH (d 1915)

Census Year	Age	State/Counties Searched ✓=found there x= not found	County Where Found & Notes	Film #, Roll #, E.D., Pg, etc.
1840	2/12	WITH STERLING ORGAIN Madison Co TN X Henry Co TN ✓	All males in family are accounted for in entry. Extra female 5-10—Who? Daughter?	M704 roll 522 p425
1850	9	WITH STERLING ORGAIN Williamson Co Tx X Madison Co TN ✓ Henry Co TN X	Age 9 dau listed as Jane. Sister Jane also listed. family 542	M432 roll 889 M 327B wp 654 dist 12
1860	19	WITH STERLING ORGAIN Williamson Co Tx ✓	In Round Rock. Kids at home: John, Sterling, Sarah, Benj. D.	M653 roll 1308 p47 family 304 dwell 295
1870	29	SARAH W. HARRISON widow Williamson Co Tx X	not found in county or in Texas index. Haven't found parents either.	M593
1880	39	SARAH W. TISDALE Williamson Co Tx ✓	Precinct 8. printed p 583. J.E. + Sarah*, his-hers-ours kids + brother Sterling Orgain Jr. *(Sallie)	T9 roll 1333 e.d. 162 sheet 53 family 459
1900	59	SARAH W. EVANS Williamson Co Tx ✓	Precinct 8. Her b-date wrong (May 1837). With them are brother Sterling Jr + son Dick Tisdale. (Sallie)	T623 roll 1680 e.d. 140 sheet 3A family 53
1910	69	SARAH W. SMITH Bastrop Co Tx ✓	In Elgin, m 2 years. Mother of 5, 4 living. With them, brother Sterling + grandson Joseph Metcalfe! (Sarah)	T624 roll 1529 e.d. 9 sheet 2B dwelling 36
1920	79	SARAH W. SMITH widow Bexar Co 4 Metcalfe X Jones Co 4 Harrison ✓	At 514 E. Reynolds, Stamford 4 son Edward B. Harrison + wife + brother Sterling Jr (84) (Sallie)	T625 roll 1824 e.d. 128 sheet 6B-7A
/		d 1928	THESE NOTES ARE ONLY HIGHLIGHTS. THEY DO NOT TAKE THE PLACE OF CENSUS FORMS.	

Military Records Checklist for Ancestors of Robert T. Shelby

Ancestor Name & Life Dates	Colonial Wars (state records)	American Revolution 1775–1783 (check state & federal records)	1784-1811	War of 1812 (1812–1815)	Indian Wars 1815–1858	Patriot War 1838	Mexican War 1846–1848	Civil War 1861–1865 (for Confederates, check state & federal records)	Service 1866 forward	Spanish-American War 1898–1899	Philippine Insurrection 1899–1902	World War I 1917–1918	World War II 1941–1945
Evan Shelby NC 1775–1850s MS		No record found	One Evan 3 Reg SC State Troops 37	41+	63	71	/	/					
John P. Shelby SC 1818–1900 TX						20	28	CSA Pension + Serv. 43+	48+	80	/	/	
George M. Shelby MS 1845–after 1912 Tx brother of Travis								CSA Pen. App. serv. 16+		ill 53	ill 54	d? 72	/
Irving R. Shelby GA 1849–1912 TX brother of Travis								not found 16 at end	17+	49	50		
Travis O. Shelby MS 1864–1943 TX									Family knowledge did not serve	34	35	that he 53	77
John Blakeney c1732–1832	check NC, SC			80	84+	/	/	/	/	/			
John Blakeney II NC 1758–1848 SC		Pension	No record found 54	No record found 58+	No record found 80	88	/	/	/	/			
John Blakeney III SC 1791–1876 SC			No record found 21	No record found 25+	No record found 47	55	70	/	/				
Stephen J. Ford MS 1839–1885 LA								CSA Serv. POW 22	27	/			
Samuel David Williamson AL 1827–1911 LA								CSA Service 34	39	71	72	/	
John Wesley Williamson LA 1879–1956 LA										20		draft regis. 38	/ 62

Annotations:
- "Age at the time"
- "Horizontal lines indicate period not applicable to this person."
- "Slash means we won't look for records in these cases."
- "Have found service record + prisoner record – Confederate"

Example 2
UNPUZZLING YOUR PAST WORKBOOK
6

Research Planning Worksheet

Maiden name in parentheses

Date ___summer 1992___

Statement of the Problem __to find father of Ann (Robertson) Croom & first husband__

of Elizabeth Robertson Croom. Ann b GA c1836

(m2 LA, 1846)   bro Thos.J. b GA c 1841-42

Questions Related to the Problem:

1. How did Isaac Croom Sr get the land he sold & gave away? Was any of it Elizabeth's? **NO**

2. Can I find any evidence of Elizabeth before or after her 1846 m to Isaac Sr other than 1850 census?

3. What can I find on the Robertson kids or half sister Louisiana (Croom) Harris? Locate any descendants?

4. Do records of neighboring parishes help? Maybe Eliz. came to Caddo Parish <u>after</u> Robertson died.

5. If Robertson died in GA, why would Eliz. come to LA & with whom?

6. Might study witnesses and surety on the 2 marriage records (Eliz. & Ann).

[already searched US census, parish tombstone inscriptions, newspaper, marriages, successions]

↳ *No Isaac or Eliz. in 1860 or 1870. We know Isaac was alive in both years.*

Try next: deeds, tract books, tax records, New Orleans Notarial Archives   *Not found in LA or TX.*

Sources to Try	Results
1. Caddo Parish deeds 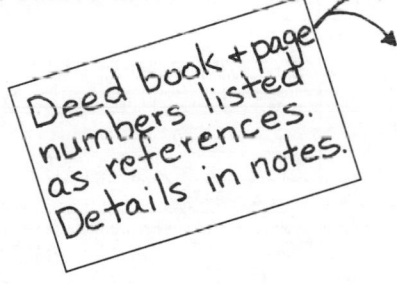 Deed book + page numbers listed as references. Details in notes.	*Nothing found in deeds (so far) pointing to a Robertson husband/father. Did find* (1) S:855 – Thomas J. Robertson in Lafayette Co AR in Dec 1871. (2) S:855,721 – Elizabeth's middle initial – C. (3) L:194 – Elizabeth alive in Nov 1857. (4) S:721 – Elizabeth d by Oct 1871. (5) P:975 – Indication that Elizabeth d by April 1868. (6) S:721 – Isaac moved to Panola Co Tx by Oct 1871.
2. Panola Co Tx Marriages	Isaac remarried there, Nov 1868.
3. Caddo Parish tract books (1995)	Bureau of Land Mgt. CD-ROM – Automated Land Records. Isaac's land accounted for here & in deeds. Apparently none of it had been Elizabeth's. No Robertson patents in right time period (pre-1846).
4. New Orleans Notarial Archives	• must go there – records not microfilmed. • need names of notaries from Caddo Parish 1840s – c1870 • any marriage agreement or family meeting before Elizabeth m Isaac Sr? or anything at all …

Example 3

Contact Log # 2   Surname or Search GRANDPA KING   d 1941
ALFRED THOMAS KING

Contact plan	Subject	Contact made, date	Results & notes
Call County Clerk	old voter registration records	6 Feb 94	says they don't keep them
Call E. Point GA nat'l archives branch	form for WWI draft	7 Feb 94	sent form
Call Noni	John's new phone #	7 Feb 94	✓
Write Tx DPS	Did Grandpa have driver's license?	8 Feb 94	no records before 1976
Call Trinity Epis. Church - Baytown	any record of him	8 Feb 94	none 1920-1941
Write SS Admin.	his SS5 (application)	10 Feb 94	answer 10 April 94 ★ BINGO! birthdate + place
Write Texas Grand Lodge - Waco	his Masonic record	9 Feb 94	answer Feb 16 ★ BINGO! birthdate + place 1879-1912
Call Trinity Lutheran	Appointment to see records - looking for Grandpa baptism + ma. Tom + Emilia deaths	11 Feb 94	no record found
Call 1° Evangelical Lutheran		11 Feb 94	no record of them
Call Houston Endowment	Employee records - Grandpa	11 Feb 94	Archivist has never found any employee records.
Call Missouri Synod office in Austin	Identify old Lutheran ch. in Austin	X - found at Clayton Lib.	history of Synod in Tx. No Luth. Ch. in Austin then.
Write E. Point GA archives	Grandpa WWI draft registration	20 Feb 94	no record found
Call Forest Park - Lawndale	directions to cemetery	27 Mar 94	went out there Apr 2
Call Fred	Obits for Tom + Emilia	22 Feb 94	He sent microprints 23 Feb
Call SP Railroad Personnel off. Calif.	H+TC and SP personnel records	22 Feb 94	has records only after 1980
Call Fred	Obits < Grandpa < Preuss in-laws	20 Mar	found Grandpa only - sent 31 Mar
Call Annunciation Catholic Ch.	Alf + Annie 1907 m rec.	11 Apr 94	no record found
Call St. Joseph Catholic Ch.	—— " ——	"	—— " ——
Call Catholic Cathedral	—— " ——	"	records in Latin, stored in boxes, weeks to search
Call Christ Church (Epis) Cathedral	—— " ——	"	no record of them
Call Joe Wells	—— " ——	wait til after tax season...	
Call John			

Example 4   UNPUZZLING YOUR PAST WORKBOOK
8

Forms for Organizing Research and Files—Indexes

Two kinds of indexes are provided here. First, the public records indexes facilitate the use of deed and marriage indexes and the Soundex and serve as checklists for your work. The second group indexes ancestors and various notes and handouts in your own files.

DEED INDEX FORM

The deed index form (1) provides space to record the basic information often found in town or county deed indexes and (2) saves time in transcribing it. Armed with the indexes, you are ready to read the original record books, even on microfilm. For filing in appropriate binders or folders, use a separate form for each surname in each locality.

The form matches the grantor (direct) and grantee (indirect or reverse) organization of most courthouse indexes. For example, when you search for all deeds under the surname Williamson, you may find Williamsons selling (grantors) as well as buying (grantees). Thus, on the form that shows "Grantor" in the first column, you will record all Williamson sellers in that locale during your chosen time period. The back of the form provides space to list all Williamson buyers (grantees) from the reverse index. Example 5 illustrates the use of this form.

You will want to study not only your immediate ancestors in the deed records but also the cluster formed by their relatives, friends and neighbors. Studying the *cluster* helps you learn about your direct lineage. Relatives and neighbors often bought from and sold to each other and witnessed each other's transactions. Even if your ancestor owned no land, he could have been a witness for a neighbor who may turn out to be his brother-in-law, father-in-law or stepfather. In addition, finding an ancestor as a witness also shows he was alive on that day and may help narrow down a death date or moving date.

Refer to chapter 11 of *Unpuzzling Your Past* for explanation of various indexing systems used for courthouse records. Consult chapter 11 in *Unpuzzling Your Past* or chapter 5 in *The Genealogist's Companion & Sourcebook* for discussion of deed records and their genealogical value.

MARRIAGE INDEX FORM

The marriage index form is organized in a similar manner. Grooms of your target surname can be listed on the front of the form; brides, on the back. The form provides space to document your notes—where you used the index and how you could find the same information again. This index information helps you locate vital statistics on direct ancestors and study the cluster of relatives in a given county or state. Example 6 illustrates the use of this form.

STATEWIDE MARRIAGE INDEX FORM

The statewide marriage index form is useful for searches in those states which have centralized marriage indexes in print, in microform, or in files in the state archives, historical society or other depository. These indexes can help you identify brides and grooms of your research surname, the town or county of record, a date (of license, marriage or filing), and sometimes a reference or other information. With this index data, you can contact the appropriate agency or institution for copies of the ones you need or perhaps rent the microfilmed records to see them for yourself and abstract any additional information they may contain.

Example 7 shows two ways that this form can be used. One option, shown at the bottom of the example, simply lists the information straight off the index. It just happens that all but one of the brides are from the same county. The groom index at the top of the example is an alternative way of organizing the information from a statewide index. Listed first are all the Cato/Cater grooms who were marrying in Monroe

County, the county being studied. Next are those from neighboring counties. Grooms from one county sometimes married in a next-door county if that was the bride's residence. Also, people by the same surname living in neighboring counties were often relatives. Grooms from the parent county (the county from which Monroe originated) were grouped next. With a less common name such as Cato/Cater, grooms living in the same area of the state need to be studied as possible relatives.

Chapter 11 of *Unpuzzling Your Past* and chapter 5 of *The Genealogist's Companion & Sourcebook* discuss marriage records and their genealogical use.

SOUNDEX SEARCH FORM

The soundex search form provides space to record the basic information from the microfilmed Soundex (or Miracode) cards. The form can be adapted to at least two kinds of searches. First is the search for all households of a given surname in a given locale, whether town, county or state, such as all Crooms in Texas in 1900. The second is a search for a particular person, whether or not a head of household. The shaded row on the form can be used to list information on that person that will help in the identification on the Soundex: name, race, age, birth place, residence, and other persons you expect to find in the same household. This shaded area keeps that information handy as you search and record households with likely candidates.

Example 8 shows two searches for specific individuals in the 1900 Soundex. The search for the first girl, Minnie, was complicated by the fact that nothing concrete was known about her as the search began, except an approximate birth date. Four possible candidates were found, but the four birth dates given in the census were all different from the date the family had been given. Thus, the search had to continue into other censuses and other documents to compile and sort out enough data to make an informed decision on which Minnie was the correct one. The second search, for Bettie May, had an exact birth date, known to be correct, and the name of a brother. Only one Bettie M. turned up on the Soundex, and she had a brother by the right name. The searcher then used other sources to verify that this was indeed the correct family, in spite of the fact that the birth date given in the census was wrong. However, it is not unusual for birth dates in the 1900 census to be off by even two or three years. (The 1900 census is the only one before 1960 that asked for month and year of birth).

The earliest Soundexed census is the 1880 census. The 1880 census covers only families listed with children ten and under, and the 1910 Soundex is not available for all states. Refer to chapter 12 and Appendix E in *Unpuzzling Your Past*, third edition, and chapter 2 in *The Genealogist's Companion & Sourcebook* for discussion of the Soundex and for 1910 Soundex availability. For your convenience, the appendix on pages 43 and 44 provides two references: a list of information reported in the federal censuses, showing which information appears in which censuses, and a review of the Soundex coding system.

ALPHABETICAL ANCESTORS CHART

The alphabetical ancestors chart can be used in a number of ways. Adapt it to your own needs. I use it in the following ways, and a blank form is provided for each:

1. As a master list for *one surname*, placed at the beginning of a notebook or file, to identify and sort out the people in that family.
2. As a finding and identifying aid for *one locality* (city, county, state or country) of ancestors from that place. This is especially handy when you visit that locale and don't want to spend valuable research time looking for someone in the wrong place or time period. Example 9 is a master list of this kind: ancestors from the state of Kentucky.
3. As a master list, *one or two alphabet letters to a page*, of all known ancestors, placed first in a notebook of family group sheets and/or pedigree charts. For example, all surnames beginning with *A* and *B* may fit on one page; all beginning with *C* may need their own page.

INDEX TO WORKSHOP NOTES AND HANDOUTS

The index to workshop notes and handouts is the only way I have found to keep up with all the pages of notes and handouts from seminars, in such a way that I can refer to them and benefit from them long after the event itself. Some people file these notes and handouts in file folders or half-inch binders, one for each occasion. Others put them in that "someday stack" of "papers I don't know what to do with right now but will get around to later." After trying the latter method unsuccessfully for some years, I sorted them all into large three-ring binders and then needed a way to find specific information easily. This index has worked well for me.

All-day seminars usually deal with several topics, each of which needs to be listed in the index. I find that I need to look up information by topic more often than by the lecturer's name, so I file all items from one seminar or speaker together in the notebook and index alphabetically by topic. The index refers me to the speaker who presented that topic. (See Example 10.) When one binder is full, I add another. I use a notebook divider for each lecturer and arrange it alphabetically in the binder.

Regardless of how you organize, you can get the most out of a seminar only when you *do* organize. Speakers often put much time and effort into preparing useful topics and handouts, and audiences seldom go away empty-handed. All this effort is fruitless if we never look at the notes and handouts again. This index can fix the problem!

An alternative form for indexing workshop notes and handouts is provided for those who already have or hope to have many such entries and prefer to designate their own alphabetical headings on the columns of the form. With this form, you can use one letter of the alphabet for each column and use multiple pages, or create any other division that fits your need.

Deed Index—Grantors

Deed Index for __Caddo Parish__ (County) __LA__ (State) Surname __CROOM__

Source: Courthouse or Library __Caddo Parish Courthouse, Shreveport__ Call #, Film # ____

Grantor Surname: CROOM	Grantee	Book, Page	Date	# Acres	Type Transaction or Legal Description
Isaac "	T. Mooring	H-488	1853	land	S2 T19 R16
Isaac "	Calvin S. Croom	donation A-14	1853	240 A	S2 T19 R16
C. S. "	James Christian	H-540		land	S2 T19 R16
Isaac "	" "	L-194	1857		S1 T19 R16
Isaac "	Jno D. Bickham	L-656	1858		slaves-sale
C. S. "	" " "	M-422	1859	67½ A	S19 T20 R15
" " "	Saml Gerald	N 598	1860	land	S19+20 T30 R15
John "	Benj. B. Bonham	P 15	1866	land	S30 T20 R15
Isaac "	Louisa C. Harris	P 975	1868	donation	S29+30 T20 R15
Calvin S. "	Methodist Ch. S.	V 442	1875	¼ A	S25 +36 T20 R15

Deed Index—Grantees

Deed Index for __Caddo Parish__ (County) __LA__ (State) Surname __CROOM__

Source: Courthouse or Library __Caddo Parish Courthouse, Shreveport__ Call #, Film # ____

Grantee Surname: CROOM	Grantor	Book, Page	Date	# Acres	Type Transaction or Legal Description
Isaac "	Jos. Allen	C 225	1844		NW¼ S2 T19 R16
" "	Jos. R. Belton	C 227	1844		NE¼ S2 T19 R16
" "	Timothy Mooring	H 478	1853		W½ NW¼ S1 T19 R16
" "	Thos. Philyan et ux.	L 248	1857		
C. S. "	T. Mooring	T 45	1873		power of attorney
" " "	Jno + Lou Harris	X 459	1879		
Calvin S. "	Timothy Mooring Sr.	N 267	1860		
" " "	" " Tutor	N 279	1860		
Wm H. B. "	Heirs of CS + MA Croom	18 - 700	1897		various

Example 5

UNPUZZLING YOUR PAST WORKBOOK

12

Marriage Index—Grooms

Marriage Index for **CADDO PARISH** County **LA** State Surname **CROOM**

Source: Courthouse or Library **parish courthouse, Shreveport** — Call #, Film # —

Groom	Bride	Date	Book, Page	#
Calvin S. Croom	Margaret A. Mooring	12 Jan 1851	1 - 262	
Isaac Croom	Mrs. Elizabeth Robinson (sic)	22 June 1846	1 - 143	bond
F. H. B. Croom	Bennie Lindsay	22 Nov 1905	30 - 541	
Isaac Croom Jr	Ann Maria Robertson	16 May 1856	1 - 484	license
Isaac Croom	Maria Ann Robertson	15 Sept 1856	2 - 10	solemnized

Marriage Index—Brides

Marriage Index for **CADDO PARISH** County **LA** State Surname **CROOM**

Source: Courthouse or Library **parish courthouse, Shreveport** — Call #, Film # —

Bride	Groom	Date	Book, Page	#
Isabella Croom	Jno. Bland	18 Aug 1846	1 - 111 / 1 - 102	
Lucille M. "	Andrew J. Brewer	14 Jan 1909	34 - 507	
F. C. "	Thos. Cooper	20 Aug 1884	15 - 181	
Roberta "	R. M. Hales	1 Nov 1883	14 - 694	
Elvira "	R. Kelly	11 Jan 1847	1 - 138	
Elvira "	Roderick Kelly	15 Jan 1848	1 - 147	
Piety "	Robt. D. Packer	30 July 1850	1 - 213	bond
Eliza "	D. H. Powell	3 Oct 1877	10 - 191	
Irene Margaret "	Jas. Taylor Hood	2 Oct 1889	18 - 121	
Nina E "	S. O. Williams	23 Nov 1910	36 - 245	

Example 6

Statewide Marriage Index for _____AL_____ Surname _Cato/Cater_

State Soundex Code

Source of this information: _Early Alabama Marriages 1813-1850_ (Call #) Film # _Gen. 976.1 E12 ALA_
(San Antonio: Family Adventures, 1991) Vol. 3C Clayton Library

Groom		Bride	Date	County	Reference
A. J.	Cato	Sarah J. McPherson	20 Dec 1865	Monroe	none given
Alex J.	"	Elizabeth East	8 Feb 1865	Monroe	"
Elbert W.	"	Sabrina Ann Booker	10 July 1840	Monroe	"
Lamenthurn W.	"	Catherine Rawls	6 May 1834	Monroe	"
William	Cater	Margaret A. Sigler	5 Aug 1858	Monroe	"
neighboring counties					
William	Cato	Emeline Maness	31 Oct 1831	Wilcox	"
William D.	Cater	Marinda Powell	11 July 1839	Wilcox	"
parent county					
B. P.	Cato	Lottie Moore	22 July 1828	Washington	"

Statewide Marriage Index for _____N C_____ Surname _Shelby_

State Soundex Code

Source of this information: _1977 microfiche, NC State Archives_ Call #, Film # _card 35_
(also gives bondsmen & witness-see notes) at Clayton-C52D5 bond #

Bride		Groom	Date	County	Reference
Betsy	Shelby	Jacob Clonts	16 Feb 1815	016-01-043 Cabarrus	7457
Dorcas	"	Wm. Alexander Kerr	9 Feb 1807	065-01-130 Mecklenberg	82032
Harriett	"	Alanson Alexander	17 Dec 1823	065-01-002	79985
		bondsman Milton Shelby			
Isabella	"	Stephen Alexander	22 Nov 1797	065-01-007	80080
Marg't J.	"	Wm. Marshal	m. 16 June 1864	065-01-160	82537
Susan Cornelia	"	John T. Harry	m. 25 Mar 1858	065-01-098	81524
Sarah	"	John Alexander	15 Aug 1798	065-01-005	80050
Susanah	"	Dan Alexander	11 June 1800	065-01-003	80004
(At Clayton, finding aids notebook has list of county codes)					
065 = Mecklenberg Co.					

Example 7 UNPUZZLING YOUR PAST WORKBOOK
14

Soundex Search for __BLALOCK__   B 442   Year __1900__   State __TN__

Surname — Code

Given Name or Head of Household	Color & Age	Birth-place & Citizen.	County	City, Street Address	Vol, E.D., Sheet, Line	Other Family Members or Enumerated With
Search for: _Minnie Blalock_	WF c16 "b May 1884 I think"	TN	nothing more known at time of search — (Minnie is sometimes a nickname for Mary.)			*Knowing siblings' names could be a great help —*
	Date from an old aunt who knew her	*1900 census gave month + year of birth, but not always correctly.*				
James T. Blalock	W Sept 1860	TN	Lincoln		ed 62 sheet 28 line 18	wife Mary + Geo 1880, Clara 1882, Minnie Feb 1884, Clayton 1886 all b TN
John Blalock	W Mar 1861	TN	Putnam	*Not enough data here to determine who is correct girl. Gather more info on these + subject.*	ed 68 sheet 5 line 13	wife Louisa Ann Charlie 1885 Minnie 1887 Maggie 1890 Bertha 1895 Emery 1897
Pitser M. Blalock	W June 1845	TN	Hardeman		ed 145 sheet 8 line 35	wife Catheran Loe 1877 Minnie Mar, 1885 Jesse 1889 all b TN
Giles Blalock	W May 1858	TN	White	*Census ages and birthdates often are wrong.*	ed 155 sheet 8 line 46	wife Rosie Mary Oct 1885 andy 1888 David 1896 allice 1898

〜〜〜〜〜〜〜〜〜〜〜〜〜〜〜〜〜〜〜〜〜〜〜〜〜〜〜〜〜〜〜〜〜〜〜〜〜

Soundex Search for __BLALOCK__   B 442   Year __1900__   State __TN__

Surname — Code

Given Name or Head of Household	Color & Age	Birth-place & Citizen.	County	City, Street Address	Vol, E.D., Sheet, Line	Other Family Members or Enumerated With
Search for: _Bettie May Blalock_	Known b 11 July 1885 age 14-15	TN	(Bettie is sometimes a nickname for Elizabeth.)			had brother Jesse Dee
Edward Blalock	W M Feb 1869	TN	White		ed 154 sheet 2 line 62	wife Nancy Ellzie Oct 1890 addison Lavena Earnest + Isaac *B-date too late*
Fannie Blalock widow	W F May 1858	TN	Hardeman	New Castle	ed 145 sheet 7 line 66	son Trimble Apr 1877 ★son Dee Jan 1881 ★dau Bettie M May 1886 *Right girl but wrong date*

〜〜〜〜〜〜〜〜〜〜〜〜〜〜〜〜〜〜〜〜〜〜〜〜〜〜〜〜〜〜〜〜〜〜〜〜〜

Alphabetical Ancestors

Locality __KENTUCKY__
County and/or State

Surname or Maiden Name	Given Name	Birth Year	Death Year	Residence	Dates of Residence	5-Gen. Chart #
ALLISON	ROBERT	by 1765	1816	SHELBY Co.	by 1800 –1816	5
ALLISON	JOSEPH	c1790 –1794	1831	SHELBY Co.	by 1800– 1831	5
ALLISON (m Metcalfe)	MARY BELL	1820	1868	SHELBY Co. DAVIESS Co.	all life	1, 5
JAGGERS	DANIEL		1808	HARDIN Co.	after 1800 –1808	8
LITTLER (m Metcalfe)	REBECCA	1770 –1776	after 1840	SHELBY Co.	c1802 –death	5
METCALFE	JOSEPH SR.	1765 –1770	1840	SHELBY Co.	c1802 –1840	5
METCALFE	JOSEPH JR.	1814	TX 1887	SHELBY Co. DAVIESS Co.	1814— c1877-79	5,1
METCALFE	THOMAS MOODY	1852	Tx 1930	DAVIESS Co.	1852— c1871-76	1

Index to Workshop Notes and Handouts

Topics M–N	Lecturer	Topics O–P–Q–R	Lecturer
Military Records	Bockstruck	Ohio Research	Witcher
Migration & Settlement	Hooverson	Okla Historical Society	See Okla 1988 Boyle
" see also	Bockstruck	Old Southwest	Bockstruck
Mississippi Research	"	Organizing	Dollarhide
		"	G. Carter
New England sources	Schoeffler		
New Orleans Notarial archives	Reeves	Passenger Lists	Hansen

Examples 9,10

UNPUZZLING YOUR PAST WORKBOOK
16

PART THREE

Forms for Gathering Information

Once your search is planned and organized and you get to the library, courthouse or interview session, you can work faster and more efficiently in certain searches with prepared forms. The ones provided here include a form for note taking from books, articles or documents; a form for abstracting deeds; census extraction forms; and forms to stimulate interviewing for family history.

NOTE-TAKING FORM

You may not need a prepared form for writing down notes from cemetery transcriptions or tax records or a county history. However, a form is provided for your convenience and to help in remembering the documenting process. That process is the primary caution in note taking. Ask yourself, "How can I (or someone else) find the same information again? How can I give proper credit to the source if I use this information in an article, book or family history? What evidence backs up my conclusions and data? What am I taking directly (quoting) from this source and what am I paraphrasing?" Perhaps this form will offer a not-so-subtle reminder and help establish good research habits. The form can be used for almost any book, public record or family papers. Examples 11 and 12 illustrate three of these applications.

Genealogists need to record *all* sources they consult. Usually, we don't know whether a source contains something useful until we look through it. Thus, writing down the bibliographic information *first* creates a record. We can always put in our notes: "No Shelbys in index. No mention found in chapter on King's Mountain." However, if the book or article discusses a place or event which was pertinent to the family, even if it did not refer to them by name, the text may contain useful background or details which add to your understanding of the family's experience and surroundings. Notes taken now from such a work could prove helpful later in your search.

DEED ABSTRACT FORM

Especially when genealogists begin their search, they may not have had much experience with courthouse records. Deeds are one kind of valuable public document found in courthouses (and on microfilm) and often can be abstracted more quickly with the help of a form set up much like the document itself. This form is organized to handle the most common situations found in deed records. Example 13 is an abstract of a warranty deed, often called simply a *deed*, which has considerable genealogical value.

Remember that the grantor is the seller and the grantee, the buyer. Refer to chapter 11 in *Unpuzzling Your Past* and chapter 5 in *The Genealogist's Companion & Sourcebook* for discussion of deeds and their genealogical use. The example on the research planning worksheet, page 7, illustrates genealogical gleanings from several deeds as applied to one search.

CENSUS FORMS

Many people begin their genealogical efforts with census records once they have done preparatory work in family sources. It seems there is always census work to do. Thus, one of the most widely used forms in genealogy is the census extraction form. The census forms in this book, 1790 through 1920, plus the slave schedule forms, follow the original government forms, column by column, so that note taking is easy. Remember that before 1850, only heads of household were named and members of the household were listed by sex and age groups. Beginning in 1850, every free person was listed by name. Thus, two examples are provided here, one before and one after 1850. Example 14, from 1830, demonstrates the ease of making multiple entries of the same surname since a number of families will fit on one form. The 1830 example also illustrates the value of finding every census for a given individual. If the searcher skipped the 1830 census for Abiel Fellows, what a gem he or she would miss!

Example 15, from 1880, however, holds only one family because everyone in the household is listed individually. This family is an example of a his-hers-and-ours blended family, something to keep in mind in studying censuses.

Here are a few reminders about census research:

1. Be sure to copy *everything* given in the original, as it appears in the original, including people with diffcrent surnames. Such persons may be relatives. Copy information at the top of the page, including enumeration date, and every column where something is marked. (See page 2 for a brief explanation of *census day*. See also page 64 of *Unpuzzling Your Past*, third edition, and chapter 2 in *The Genealogist's Companion & Sourcebook* for further discussion of *census day*.)

2. Read ten to twenty families on either side of yours, or the entire enumeration district or county, looking for relatives. Because the census was usually recorded in the order of visitation down a street or road, relatives living near each other often appear near each other in the census. Remember that ancestors lived, worked and worshiped within a cluster of relatives, friends and neighbors. Studying this cluster often provides clues or information on the ancestor(s) we are seeking.

3. Look for every ancestor in all available censuses taken during that lifetime.

4. Reading the Soundex or index never takes the place of reading the original. If you do not find your family-of-interest in the Soundex or index, read the entire county or enumeration district where you expect them to be at that time. If they lived in a city, use other sources such as city directories, maps and newspapers to narrow down the area in which to search.

5. Remember that people were missed in every census, and some censuses for some locations have been lost. In the case of the burned 1890 census, see *The Genealogist's Companion & Sourcebook*, page 18, for a detailed survey of the surviving fragments.

6. Chapter 2 of *The Genealogist's Companion &*

Sourcebook is an entire chapter devoted to federal census records, finding aids and supplemental schedules. See *Unpuzzling Your Past*, third edition, pages 63-66 and 75-78 for discussion of census research.

INTERVIEW FORMS

Forms for interviewing family members can help elicit information on personal and family *history*. You can gather vital statistics and basic genealogical information on family group sheets, but many of us need reminders and memory-joggers to ask pertinent questions about history as the family experienced it. The interview forms in this book are therefore organized by decade or era. The questions provided are by no means all the questions to ask. They are intended as a springboard to memories. Expand into whatever areas your interviewee takes you. Ask additional questions about how history affected the family, how and why people did the things they did, when and where events took place within the family, who had interesting experiences, what daily life was like, and the ways life is different now. Refer to chapters 7, 8 and 9 in *Unpuzzling Your Past* for more questions and suggestions for successful interviewing.

Some of the questions, such as those asking about membership in organizations and religious groups, could produce valuable answers which lead you to other sources for research. If a male interviewee says he is a Mason, for example, ask whether his father, uncles or grandfathers were also Masons. Masonic records, depending on place and time, can be helpful in locating birth, death, and residence information on men who were members. Discovering a family's religious affiliation in the early twentieth century may lead you to congregational records or cemeteries where more vital data may be found, even on previous generations.

The questions on the forms, by necessity, are general. Make them specific to your own family. Expand into other sheets of paper as needed when you get stories or lengthy answers. Encourage your interviewee to give you details and specifics. Example 16 shows a slight change in the dates covered, at the request of the interviewee, to discuss his life before his marriage.

Notes

Surname _Black (Rev. Sam)_

Title of ⟨book,⟩ article, or document _The Tinkling Spring: Headwater of Freedom_ # vols. in set _____

For articles, title of journal _____
  volume # _____ , issue # and date _____ , page #s _____

⟨Author,⟩ compiler, and/or editor _Howard McKnight Wilson_

City of publication _Fishersville, VA_ Publisher and date of publication _Tinkling Spring & Hermitage Presbyterian Churches 1954_

Where I used it and when _Clayton Library_ date _July 1978_

Call # or Film # _975.5 W748 Va_

Get all index references first + check off as you use them.

Vol # (when applicable), _Index:_
Page # Notes _Rev. Samuel Black 80-82, 151, 154, 156-7, 159, 167, 170, 176, 430-31_

Page #	Notes
80	North & South Mountain congregation asking for supply preacher. located on head of "Shenandoe." Joined in the call when Donegal Presbytery 1745 voted unanimously to transport Rev. Sam Black after his acceptance & installed him as regular pastor. At first he refused to move to VA. For this disobedience, he was publicly reproved by the presbytery.
81	*quoted from the book* "After Mr. Black's unfortunate experience over the transfer to N & S Mt in 1745, he was reinstated in his old pastorate at Conewago, but was soon in trouble 'y them again.'" It

Notes

Article title in quotes

Surname _Harrison (William)_

Title of book, ⟨article⟩ or document _"The Right Reverand William Harrison of Revolutionary Virginia, First 'Lord Archbishop of America'"_ # vols. in set _____

For articles, title of journal _Historical Magazine of the Protestant Episcopal Church_
  volume # _53_ , issue # and date _1 (March 1984)_ , page #s _25-43_

Author, compiler, and/or editor _Otto Lorenz, Kearney State College, Kearney NE_

City of publication _____ Publisher and date of publication _____

Where I used it and when _Rice Univ Library (UH too)_ date _Feb 1993_

Call # or Film # _BX 5800. H5_

Vol # (when applicable),
Page # Notes

Page #	Notes
25	Harrison had been chaplain to Lord Cornwallis at Gloucester, British garrison across York R from Yorktown. Harrison was rector, Bristol Parish, Dinwiddie & Prince

Notes   Surname _SHAW_

Title of book, article, or (document) _Davidson County TN Court Minutes_ # vols. in set ____

For articles, title of journal _____

     volume # _____ , issue # and date _____ , page #s _____

Author, compiler, and/or editor _____

City of publication _Nashville_   Publisher and date of publication _Tenn. State Archives_

Where I used it and when _microfilm, rented_   date _Aug 1978_

Call # or Film # _____

Vol # (when applicable), _Vol. A (6 Oct 1783 – 15 July 1791)_

Page #	Notes
7	7 Jan 1784 – James Shaw recorded his stock mark as half crop in left ear & under kiel in right ear & brand: ƗƆ
21	July 1784 – grand jury included James Shaw.
26	July 1784 – James Shaw established ferry cross the Cumberland R at Nashville. Shaw requested "that he keep a Ferry at the place afforesaid [sic] with good & sufficient boats & well attended for the purpose of passage of such as are desirous of crossing the said river" at the following fees: 1 shilling – man & horse 1 shilling – every pack horse & pack 8 pence – lead horse without pack 6 pence – every footman 6 pence – every head of horned cattle 4 pence – every head of sheep & hogs
146	7 July 1785 – deed from Thomas Molloy to James Shaw acknowledged.
253	2 July 1787 – James Shaw is security for David Fry (?), sheriff.
282	8 Apr 1788 – James Shaw on jury. Case: State vs. Samuel Martin, accused of stealing bull from James Bosley. Defendant pleaded not guilty. Jury found him not guilty.

Example 12

Deed Abstract

Surname __BRELSFORD__

Source (Courthouse, microfilm & #, other) __Courthouse__

County or town where filed __Christian__ State __KY__ Deed Book # __C__ Inclusive pages __137__

Quitclaim deed _____ Warranty deed ✓ Bill of sale _____ Deed of trust _____ Deed of gift _____

This indenture made this day __11 Oct__ in the year __1810__

between (grantor) __Phoeby + Frances Garner, Nathan Brelsford + wife Elizabeth, 3 of the__ of _____ __KY__
name(s) __heirs of Henry Garner, dec'd.__ county (or town), state

This shows that Elizabeth's maiden name was Garner.

and (grantee) __Peter Dick__ of __Frederick Co VA__
name(s) county (or town), state

The said grantor(s) for and in consideration of the sum of __$950__ [Is it dollars or other currency?] paid by grantee(s)

and/or notes in the amount of _____ at _____ percent interest, due on date(s) _____,

or other considerations [describe] _____

have sold (or given, if deed of gift) to the grantee(s) the following property: __384__ acres, situated in __Frederick__

county, state of __VA__, described as follows: [Copy waterway, boundaries, neighbors, whatever it says] _beginning at double white oak on West point of a hill of the Pine Cabin Ridge, then N20E 200 poles to 2 white oaks + a locust sapplin[g] on S side near _____ of a ridge, then S60 E 320 poles to 2 pines on the top of a ridge, then S30 W 214 poles to a white oak + black oak on E side of a ridge, then N57 W 278 poles to the beginning ... being land conveyed to said Henry Garner by deed of bargain + Sale by Henry Garner + wife Jane, dated 6 Sept 1776 + recorded in Frederick Co. Henry Garner d intestate + these heirs are selling their portions of the estate._

The deed should encourage the searcher to study both Henrys further.

and/or other property described as: _____

In witness whereof the grantors have set their hands and seals. [Note who signed and who made a mark instead.]
Nathan, Frances, + "Pheba" signed.
Elizabeth made her X.

Witnesses: _none listed_

This request shows that the Brelsfords + probably the sisters were living in Christian County.

Does the seller's wife relinquish her dower right? _____ When? _____

Does the seller's wife willingly sign and seal the indenture? _The Frederick Co. court asked the Christian Co. court to get answer + send to them since Elizabeth could not conveniently come to Frederick Co. to be examined._

Date the deed is acknowledged in court _____ Date recorded _____

[See Frederick Co records for Elizabeth's answer + recording date.]

Example 14

1830 or 1840 Census—Part 1

Local Community TOWNSHIP OF BRADY   County ST. JOSEPH   State MICHIGAN

Enumerator ELIAS TAYLOR   Date Census Taken 12 NOV 1830   Enumerator District # —

[Official census day—1 June 1830-1840]   Supervisor District # —

Written Page No.	Printed Page No.	Name of Head of Family	Males under 5	5-10	10-15	15-20	20-30	30-40	40-50	50-60	60-70	70-80	80-90	90-100	100 & over	Females under 5	5-10	10-15	15-20	20-30	30-40	40-50	50-60	60-70	70-80	80-90	90-100	100 & over
	180	Abiel Fellows	0	2	0	3	0	0	0	0	1					1	1	3	0	0	0	1						
	181	James Fellows	0	0	0	0	1									0	0	0	1									
	20	Festus A. Fellows	0	0	0	0	1									1	0	0	0	1								
	20	Rise L. Fellows	1	0	0	0	0	1								1	0	0	0	1								
	22	James Fellows	0	0	0	0	0	0	0	1						0	0	0	2	0	0	0	1					
	22	Albert G. Fellows	2	0	0	0	2	1								0	0	0	0	1								

Free White Persons (including heads of families)

Census taker added this note: "This man is sixty five [years] of age has nineteen living children ten of which is under his care was a soldier in the Revolution is a man of Sober Habits of unusual enterprise and great strenght [sic] of mind has never received any thing from our government for his Early and Youthful strugle [sic] for Independence is it to [sic] late to hope??"

19 children minus 10 at home leaves 9 to find. This James may well be one of them.

Other Fellows in Michigan — all in Wayne County, outside of Detroit.

Gathering the others in the state, especially when there are only a few, will help in studying a family. These 4 Fellows are likely to be related to each other + may be related to Abiel.

1880 Census

Local Community _Precinct 8_ County _Williamson_ State _TX_ roll #1333
(county is split on 2 rolls)
Enumerator _H. A. Highsmith_ Date Census Taken _23+24 June 1880_ Supervisor District # _5_

[Official census day—1 June 1880] Enumerator District # _162_

Written Page No.	Printed Page No.	Street Name	House Number	Dwelling Number	Family Number	Name of every person whose place of abode on 1 June 1880 was in this family	Color	Sex	Age	Month born if during census year	Relationship to head of this household	Single	Married	Widowed / Divorced	Married during year	Profession, Occupation or Trade	Months unemployed this year	Currently ill? If so, specify.	Blind	Deaf & dumb	Idiotic	Insane	Disabled	School this year	Cannot read	Cannot write	Birthplace	Birthplace of Father	Birthplace of Mother
		1	2			3	4	5	6	7	8	9	10	11	12	13	14	15	16	17	18	19	20	21	22	23	24	25	26
53	583	1	1	459	459	JE Tisdale	W	M	51				1			farmer											AL	AL	AL
						Sallie H "	W	F	40		wife		1			keeps house											TN	VA	NC
						Bland Harris [sic]	W	M	18		son- step	1				works on farm											Tx	VA	TN
						Mattie E Harrison	W	F	16		step- dau	1				at home											"	"	"
						Wm. L. Harrison	W	M	14		step- son	1				"								1			"	"	"
						Sigar [sic] Tisdale	W	F	13		dau	1				"								1			"	AL	"
						Sterling O. Tisdale	W	M	6		son	1				"								1			"	AL	"
						Benjamin D. Tisdale	W	M	4		son	1				"								1			"	blank	
						Sterling Organ	W	M	44		bro- law	1				works on farm											TN	VA	TN

Sallie's kids by first husband! Bland was also a Harrison.

These 3 are JE's kids, but only the 2 boys are also Sallie's. Other sources show that JE + Sallie had been married 9 years in 1880.

This is the first census to ask for relationships.

Sterling + Sallie were siblings. This should be NC, not TN, based on all other evidence.

Example 15

Pre-1930 Period

Interview with ___Ray Loden___

Interviewer, date, place ___EAC, 13 Jan 1996, his home, Houston Tx___
He asked to keep interview pre-1925. He and Ruby married in 1925 + just celebrated 70th anniversary!

Your age in ~~1930~~ 1925 ___ or circle as appropriate: child teenager (young adult) adult

Size of your family in the 1920s: ___9___. Names of persons in the household & relationship to you:
Father + mother, 4 brothers + 2 sisters. Details on attached page.

Residence(s) before ~~1930~~ 1925, with dates, street, town, state ___farm near Wills Point Tx, Route 1___
made calls through operator. Were on rural party line. Their ring was 3 longs and a short.

When did the family get any of these "modern conveniences"? Telephone ___1918___ Car ___1915___ Electricity ___none___
Indoor plumbing ___none___ Running water in the house ___none___ Vacuum cleaner ___none___ Electric fans ___none___
Washing machine ___none___ Other?

What kind of cooking stove did you or your mother use before 1930? What kind of refrigeration for food? Wood-burning stove. Ice box for refrigeration. Had no well, but had brick-lined + concrete cistern. Lowered syrup buckets full of buttermilk into cistern to keep milk cool.

How was your house heated in the winter? ___fireplaces + wood heater. First had Kerosene lamps for light, then Coleman lights (gasoline).___

Did your family own its home? ___yes___ Rent? _____ How much was rent? _____

What can you tell me about your house(s) before 1930? Rooms? 6 Size? (One) two or more stories? (Wood) brick, etc.? House had dogtrot through middle: Living room (doubled as bedroom), 1 bedroom, dining room, kitchen on 1 side; 2 bedrooms on other side. Fireplace in 2 rooms. Smokehouse.

Did your family ever experience a house fire? ___no___ flood? ___no___ other natural disaster? ___no___ Elaborate.
Had storm cellar but few occasions to use it.

Were you a student before ~~1930~~ 1925? ___yes___ How far in school did you go? ___through college___
How far from home was your school? ___1¼ mi from rural school - grades 1-10.___ 10 miles from high school - last year year (11th grade) he boarded in town. School went only to 11th grade then.
Did you have to buy your books or did the school provide them? ___bought books___
What can you tell me about your elementary or high school experiences?
drama, debate, athletics - basketball + tennis

What jobs did family members hold in the 1920s or before? (Did any of the women work outside the home?) No.
farming.

Did you work in the 1920s? Doing what? On farm. (had cattle tanks + ponds for water)

How did you decide "what you wanted to be when you grew up"? (Methodist minister) Was conscious of a spiritual call. Had encouragement from Christian parents + a loyal pastor.

What did you do for entertainment in the 1920s or before? hunting, fishing, basketball made their own crystal set. Could get 1 Dallas station. Loved to hear Hawaiian music.
When did you or your family get a radio for the first time? ___1922___ a phonograph? ___none___

Did anyone in the family play a musical instrument? Who? What? Brother George + sister Mildred played piano.

How often did you go to movies? Favorites? Maybe once a year.
Westerns were his favorites.

Example 16　　UNPUZZLING YOUR PAST WORKBOOK

24

Did the family have pets? Explain. a dog to work cattle, cats to control rodent population

What part did sports or games play in your life in this period? entertainment - basketball, tennis, marbles + keeps, sometimes mumblety peg.

During childhood, what is your earliest memory of home and family? How old were you? 4 years old. Father was seriously injured working on railroad. Had to be hospitalized — which was rare. Births + illnesses usually treated at home. This experience made him realize there were hospitals + what they were.

What is your earliest memory of events outside the family? How old were you? same

During childhood, what were your favorite toys and games? Did you make any of your own toys? made stick horses, go-carts, + play wagons.

To what extent were family gatherings part of your life before 1930? Explain.

To what extent were religious activities a part in your life before 1925/1930? Explain. Religious activities were as essential as good conduct + honesty in the home.

What, if any, rules governed Sunday or the Sabbath in your home before 1925/1930? (1) No manual labor except feeding the livestock. (2) No cooking — baking was done on Saturday. (3) No athletic games or picture shows, except croquet — because his father loved to play croquet.

Was dancing allowed in your family? no Card playing? no Dating without a chaperone? no
Were family members restricted in what they could read for pleasure? yes. Mother or dad would read it first to approve or disapprove.
What other rules or customs governed behavior?

How did your family celebrate or observe birthdays? Christmas or other religious holidays? July 4?
Special days were celebrated with friends, family + loved ones.

What wedding or funeral customs do you remember in your family or community in this period? Weddings were conducted in the home or at church. Brides wore what they had or got a dress they could use again — not usually white.

Do you remember when you or your family got a camera for the first time? 1921

What kind of transportation did you use most? wagon, buggy, car after 1915

How did you get to school or work? walked to rural school for 10 grades. Boarded in town for last year of high school.

What did the family do at lunch time? Come home or eat elsewhere? What do you remember about school lunches? All meals were eaten at home. School lunches were carried in lunch pail or syrup bucket. Took syrup in quinine bottle — held enough syrup for 2 biscuits.

Was the main meal at noon or in the evening? What did you call that meal? main meal at noon, called it dinner.

If you lived on a farm, what crops did the family raise? What food? Crop - cotton. Food - wheat (exchanged for barrel of flour), corn (went to grist mill on Saturdays), oats, fruit orchard, vegetables, hogs, beef, + chickens.

Did any family members serve in the military in World War I? Who? Where? Brother George Dee was in student army officers group, could continue school + get training. Was still training at end of war.

How did the family celebrate the end of World War I? They celebrated in every way they could make noise. /

Was this a good period in your life? yes How did your experiences before 1930 affect your life thereafter?

Example 16 Cont'd.

PART FOUR

Forms for Reference and Study

This group of forms provides an organized way of recording and storing information already known to be true or accepted as a result of careful evaluation of data. The forms capsule a search so that you can see how much you know about a given person or family and where there are holes in your information. They give you "the big picture" and help you view your progress in ways that will surprise you. Using these forms can be an extremely valuable exercise.

FAMILY GROUP SHEET

The family group sheet is one of the most universally used and valuable forms for genealogists. It contains vital information on one nuclear family, i.e., parents and their children. As I study a family in depth, I create a group sheet for every ancestral couple and separate forms for each of their children and each of their brothers and sisters. For example, if great-grandpa was one of six siblings, I make a separate sheet for each of his brothers and sisters. If great-grandpa and great-grandma had four children, I make a separate form for each of the four, including the one who was my own grandparent. Why? Because ancestors did not live in a vacuum, but in a cluster of friends, neighbors and relatives. By studying the cluster in which these ancestors lived, worked and worshiped, we not only get a better picture of their lives and times but may learn more about them than we could by studying only the ancestral couple itself. Group sheets of the extended family show us important parts of the cluster, generation by generation, and identify many of the names we find in the same documents with our own ancestors.

Many versions of family group sheets are available. I prefer one that reads vertically like most other papers in a notebook and one that has writing space big enough that I don't have to use a magnifying glass to read what is there. This particular group sheet format has served me well. It can display vital information as well as the sources which provided the details. With each person on the chart, list the source number(s) applicable to that person, and list the references on the back. Please refer to chapter 3 of *Unpuzzling Your Past* for further discussion of these charts.

Example 17 is one of my own families. The group sheet has gone through a number of versions over the years as I have added data about my family. It is to a point now where I can add new sources as I find them without having to retype the whole form. This format was especially useful in making me answer very basic questions: How do I know Thomas was the son of William and probably the son of Elizabeth? How do I know Catey was the daughter of Isaac? How do I know Elizabeth Steele was Isaac's wife (actually, his first wife) and Catey's mother? (Some researchers list only his second wife as if she were the only one). How do I know Steele was her maiden name? How do I know all of these children were really children of Thomas and Catey? And on and on. Although the census records before 1850 do not name the children living at home, they at least account for the children who were supposed to be in the family in each of those years. Thus, I listed those census reports in the sources, and they support the other data. They also place the family in a given location in those years.

AHNENTAFEL TABLE

The ahnentafel table is a concise way of listing the ancestry of any one person and assigning a standard identification number to each ancestor. (*Ahnentafel* is a German word meaning *ancestor table* or *family tree*.) Many pedigree charts, such as the five-generation chart on page 33, employ these numbers for the most recent four or five generations (numbers 1-31). Then, when you begin a new chart to add more generations of ancestors, you begin with the same numbers 1-31 again. However, many genealogists find it logical and helpful to continue the ahnentafel numbering beyond the first chart (most recent 31 people) to the more remote generations. The ahnentafel chart in this book is a reference for seven generations. The reader is invited to extend the list as necessary beyond that point.

Calculating the ahnentafel number for any person

is very easy. Double any person's number to identify the father. Double the number and add one to identify the mother. For example, if you want to prepare your own pedigree on the table, begin with yourself as number one. Doubling *one* to *two* gives your father's number; doubling that to *four* gives his father. Doubling your own number and adding one gives $2 + 1 = 3$, which is your mother's number. Thus, the parents of ancestor number twelve would be twenty-four and twenty-five. You can carry the system as far back as you find ancestors.

Using this chart helps you see readily where the holes are and may spur you on to tackle the search for the more elusive ancestors. Because these numbers can get a little unwieldy in long lists, I prefer to divide them into paternal and maternal halves. Besides, we usually think of ancestors by the "side" to which they belong. Dividing them into the two halves may help us keep them straight. Example 18 shows one page of the ahnentafel table.

FIVE-GENERATION CHART

The five-generation chart, also called a pedigree chart, illustrates one person with four generations of ancestors: parents, grandparents, great-grandparents and great-great-grandparents. Each vertical column represents one generation. This chart gives you a different viewpoint from the family group sheets, which (1) detail two generations, (2) include siblings, and (3) can go forward as well as back in time. In contrast, the five-generation chart allows you to evaluate the generations, especially for proper dates and places, by viewing several generations at once. If you use this form for information that you have already proved or accepted as true based on evidence, you may not need to list documentation on the back since you would have the sources documented elsewhere on your family group sheets and in your notes and files. However, if you feel you need a reminder of where you found each piece of data, you can list sources for each person on the back of the chart. If you have not used this kind of form before, see chapter 3 of *Unpuzzling Your Past* for instructions.

Example 19 represents an in-progress search which has hit some "brick walls," one due to adoption. Nevertheless, the search goes on, gathering evidence which is yielding data for family group sheets and biographical outlines even where vital statistics for the five-generation chart are still wanting.

FIVE-GENERATION AHNENTAFEL CHART

The five-generation ahnentafel chart is for those searchers who want to extend their ahnentafel numbers to the five-generation charts so that each ancestor has one consistent identification number. On this form, you supply your own numbers from your ahnentafel table. Example 20 illustrates the process.

BIOGRAPHICAL OUTLINE

The biographical outline can be a working record of your progress in studying a particular ancestor, or it can be used for a more-or-less finished presentation. By listing specific events in the life of the ancestor as you find them in records and documents, you can study the person with greater perception than by having the events scattered in isolated documents throughout a file or notebook. Listing the events chronologically allows you to evaluate your findings: to relate events to each other, to see cause and effect, to discover patterns, to identify migrations, to review dates for conflicts or inconsistencies, to find holes in your research, to identify new places and sources to search, and perhaps even to enjoy the fruits of your search! Recording the documentation for each piece of information encourages you (1) to research carefully and thoroughly, (2) to use more primary sources than secondary ones, and (3) to question yourself: How do I *know* this date is correct? How do I *know* the list of children is accurate? How do I know the event took place *here*? How do I *know* the maiden name?

If we rely heavily on published (or unpublished) family and county histories for our information, we probably will accumulate little real evidence to back up our conclusions. Why? Few family and county histories, for many reasons, are thorough in their documentation of details. The most reliable evidence that we genealogists find usually comes from such sources as contemporary family Bibles, deeds and land records, wills and probate files, public marriage records, church records, tax rolls, military records, some census records and some newspapers. Dozens of sources exist in public records as well as in family papers. Mistakes can be found in nearly any kind of source, but the sources that are closer in time to the original event and those involving eyewitnesses or firsthand accounts are usually more reliable.

The outline can include whatever you choose and be as detailed as you want to make it. It is more interesting and more useful with a thorough coverage of whatever you find on the subject: birth, marriage, death, birth of children, military service, land transactions, court appearances, professional or occupational events, religious milestones, participation in community affairs, etc. In mentioning these events on the outline, some searchers list only a brief "headline" entry, knowing the details are in notebooks or files. Other genealogists want more explanation, comment or clarification in the outline. The example provided here leans on the side of more comment.

Example 21 is from a search that has accumulated more than will fit into two pages. Only the first two of its pages are used here. Additional records and information are still being sought to answer questions which arise from studying the data collected so far: What is the earliest evidence of Sterling in Tennessee? Is there any evidence of Sterling himself in Virginia? What evidence may narrow down the dates of his moves from county to county in Tennessee and his move to Texas?

UNITED STATES MAP

Studying maps in relation to genealogy can help us see the effects of geography on the life and decisions of a family. They may lead us to study migration routes and patterns and can aid in our understanding of how history affected the family. Maps are visual reminders of where the family was during the lives of its members and during wars, natural disasters and events of national importance. Sometimes, we even discover that ancestors in different parts of the family were at one time neighbors. In other words, maps are very useful tools for genealogists. In fact, every genealogist needs a good atlas and a good historical atlas of the United States, and any other country from which you study ancestors.

As you determine the migrations within each ancestral family, you can plot the various migrations and residences on a map such as the one provided in this book. One map may show migrations of several lines before they became joined by marriage in one county or town. Or you may choose to show only the male members of one surname on each map. Use it as it fits your needs and to illustrate what you want to show.

Example 22 depicts two Southern families who followed very different migration routes over several generations until certain members ended up together along the Texas gulf coast in the late nineteenth century. Because of space limitations on the map itself, a key is provided to detail each stop along their way.

TIMELINE

As you study ancestors and try to fit them into appropriate surroundings, circumstances and events, a timeline may prove useful as well as interesting. Such a device also allows comparison of one ancestor's life with the lives of other relatives. Where do they overlap? Who was alive during "the war"? Who lived longest? Who lived through both the American Revolution and the Civil War? What may have prompted the family to move over the mountains or down the valley when they did? What events in the "old country" may have caused the family's immigration to America?

The purpose of the chart is to remind us that our ancestors lived not in a vacuum but in a time and place surrounded by other people. They lived through the history we once studied in school and may have forgotten. We sometimes need to be reminded of that history. For example, we need not spend time trying to find Pennsylvania records from the 1650s because that colony was not settled until 1682. Sometimes a visual representation is the best way to keep such things in perspective.

Although timelines such as those provided here cannot list all pertinent events, they can include certain key events to trigger further investigation into ancestors' lives and times. The two timelines included in this book cover the periods 1600 to 1800 and 1750 to 1950, overlapping a little so that fewer ancestors have to be split between charts. The solid lines divide the charts into segments of twenty-five years each. Place the ancestors with their life dates on the chart any way you choose. It may be helpful to include the ahnentafel numbers of the ancestors charted.

As with the military records checklist, you can limit each form to one surname or use it as a master chart for all ancestors who lived in the same period. (Example 23 is a master chart with ancestors from both the paternal and maternal lines.) Be creative and use it as it suits you.

Family Group Sheet of the ___Thomas Patton___ Family

	Source #			Source #
Thomas Patton Full name of husband	1	Birth date	4 Feb 1794	3
		Birth place	SC, possibly York Co.	4
William Patton His father	4	Death date	24 April 1852	3,2
		Death place	Fayette Co, TN	32
Elizabeth His mother with maiden name	4	Burial place	Rehobeth Cemetery, Fayette Co (Presbyterian church gone)	31
Catherine Ewing McFadden Full maiden name of wife	1,3, 24	Birth date	22 Jan 1798	3
		Birth place	SC, probably Chester Co.	1
Isaac McFadden Her father	1	Death date	30 Mar 1873	3
		Death place	probably Hardeman Co, TN	9,10
Elizabeth Steele Her mother with maiden name	22	Burial place		

Other Spouses none	Marriage date, place, etc. 4 July 1816, in SC, probably Chester or York Co.
Source #s	Source #s 3

Listed in birth order, using full names.

Children of this marriage	Birth date & place	Death date, place, & burial place	Marriage date, place & spouse
1. William Ewing Patton Source #s 3, 5, 6, 7, 11, 13	22 Nov 1817 SC possibly York Co.	14 Jan 1897 Senatobia, Tate Co, MS	28 Jan 1840 Fayette Co, TN Agnes Abigail Kerr/Karr
2. Sarah Jane Patton Source #s 3, 5, 6, 7, 9, 10, 12	18 Sept 1819 SC possibly York Co.	Apr 1885	 John L. Day
3. James McFadden Patton Source #s 3, 6, 7, 13, 14, 16, 29	1 Aug 1824 SC probably York Co.	3 May 1870 Fayette Co, TN Mt Pleasant Cem, Hickory Withe	19 Jan 1848 Fayette Co, TN Emily Narcissa Kerr/Karr
4. Elizabeth Olevia Patton Source #s 3, 6, 7, 17	18 Dec 1825 SC probably York Co.	Feb 1887	before 1850 Allen P. Gilliam
5. Isaac Steele Patton Source #s 3, 6, 7, 18, 19	11 Dec 1827 (1826?) SC probably York Co.		13 Sept 1848 Fayette Co, TN Mary A. Dickson
6. Margaret Catherine Patton Source #s 3, 6, 7, 9, 10, 20, 21, 23, 33	25 Feb 1829 (Bible record) Tombstone—1828. SC prob. York Co.	19 June 1901 Brown Co, TX Zephyr Cem.	12 Oct 1847 Fayette Co, TN Elliott Glen Coleman

Discrepancy in b-date for #6 creates possible question on b-date for #5. Must study both.

Example 17

Source #   Sources (Documentation)

1   Probate records, Chester Co, SC, Bk K, Folios 123-126, SC Archives.
    Isaac McFadden estate records show Thomas Patton as heir (in right of wife). Return of debts
    and accounts of estate of Isaac McFadden, 19 Mar 1829, showing 4 payments to Thomas Patton
    "on legacy." Isaac and family lived in Chester Co. as shown in many deeds and church records:

1b <u>Early Records of Fishing Creek Presbyterian Church, Chester County, South Carolina, 1799-
    1859</u>, Brent H. Holcomb and Elmer O. Parker, compilers, Bowie, MD: Heritage Books, 1991,
    facsimile reprint of original records.

2   Letter from "Catherin M. Coleman" (dau of Thomas Patton) to brother-in-law Aurrelious F.
    Coleman, 18 May 1852, giving her father's death date. Copy in possession of Emily Croom.
    Original in possession of Thyrza McCollum, Greenville MS, until her death, June 1995.

3   Turner Coleman Bible, copied 5 May 1971, by his son Word Coleman. Bible then in possession
    of Word's sister Norma Irene McGary of Mullin, TX.

4   Will of William Patton, blacksmith, 30 May 1795, York Co, SC Wills, Bk 1, p 173 and case #61,
    file #2806, Will Bk A-12, p 139, guardianship proceedings. A few other SC Patton families
    had sons named Thomas, but various factors help rule out those as ours. Wife Elizabeth named
    in will.

5   US Census of 1820, York Co, SC, p 158A (Thomas Patton family)
6   US Census of 1830, York Co, SC, p 338   ''   ''   ''
7   US Census of 1840, Fayette Co, TN, Dist 15, p 164 ''   ''
8   US Census of 1850, Fayette Co, TN, Dist 13, p 749 ''   ''
9   US Census of 1860, Hardeman Co, TN, p 73 (Catey Patton, Day, Coleman)
10 US Census of 1870, Hardeman Co, TN, Dist 3, p 139 (Catey Patton, Coleman)

11 Fayette Co, TN, Marriage Bk A, p 32 (William E Patton)
12 US Census of 1850, Fayette Co, TN, p 242 (Wr p 482) (John & Sarah Day)
13 Letters from Rachel & Leslie Karr Patton, grandson of Wm E Patton, to Emily Croom, 2 Jan
    1981, 4 June 1971, with Wm E Patton info and 30 Mar 1974 with dates of James McF Patton from
    cemetery.

> pr p = printed page #
> wr p = written page #

14 US Census of 1860, Fayette Co, TN, Dist 7, p 101-102 (James McF Patton)
15 Fayette Co, TN, Marriage Bk A, p 152 (James M. Patton)
16 Letters and chart from Lily McElroy Harrison, g-granddau of James & Emily Patton, to Emily
    Croom, about 1978 (not dated).

17 US Census of 1850, Fayette Co, TN, Dist 4, wr pg 528, pr pg 264B, family #445. Gilliam. No
    indication whether any of the children are Elizabeth's.

18 Fayette Co, TN, Marriage Bk A, p 161 (Isaac S. Patton)
19 US Census of 1850, Fayette Co, TN, wr pg 499, pr pg 250. Isaac S Patton. Have not found this
    family after this.

20 Fayette Co, TN, Marriage Bk A, p 143 (Patton-Coleman)
21 US Census of 1850, Hardeman Co, TN, family #222, pr p 84, wr p 167 (Coleman)
22a Jones Co, NC, Deeds, Bk G, p 154-155, names Elizabeth <u>Steele</u> as wife of Isaac McFadden, 1790.
    Chester Co, SC, Deeds, Bk B, p 85, dated 10 June 1789, names Elizabeth as his wife, without
    maiden name.

22b Elizabeth d 26 June 1802, age 39. <u>Tombstone Records of Chester County, SC</u>, Louise Kelly
    Crowder, comp. Chester, SC, 1970, Vol 1, p 45.

23 US Census of 1880, Ganzales Co, TX, e.d. 72, pr p 376 (Coleman)
24 Fayette Co, TN, Marriage Bk A, p 238 (Patton-Day)
25 US Census of 1860, Fayette Co, TN, Dist 2, p 37 (Day)
26 US Census of 1870, Fayette Co, TN, Dist 1, p 25 (Day)
27 Fayette Co, TN, County Court Minute Book E, p 23, guardianship of 3 youngest children and
    support for widow.

Example 17 Cont'd.

Family Group Sheet of the ___Thomas Patton___ Family, continued

Father ___Thomas Patton___   Mother ___Catherine Ewing McFadden___

Children of this marriage	Birth date & place	Death date, place, & burial place	Marriage date, place & spouse
7. Mary Susan Patton "deaf and dumb" Source #s 3, 7, 8, 9, 10, 27, 28	2 Mar 1834 TN probably Fayette Co	30 Mar 1873 Hardeman Co TN	never married
8. Frances Stephanie Patton Source #s 3, 7, 8, 24, 25, 26, 27, 30	8 Aug 1835 TN probably Fayette Co	2 May 1857 Fayette Co TN Somerville Cemetery	7 Dec 1853 Fayette Co TN Wiley G. Day
9. Margaritta Clementine Steadman (Steadovan) Patton Source #s 3, 8, 9, 10, 27, 28, 29	31 Oct 1840 TN probably Fayette Co	20 Oct 1869 Hardeman Co TN	Trowill
   Source #s			

Source #   Sources (Documentation)

28   Bolivar, TN, Presbyterian Church Register from copy made by Louise J. McAnulty, 1969, and copied by Emily Croom, 1972. Gives membership dates of Mary and Margaritta L (sic) Patton. Beside Margaritta's name is the note "dead" without date. No indication that she had any name but Patton.

29   US Census of 1870, Mortality Schedule, TN, is missing, according to reference librarian at TN State Library and Archives, who said it apparently left the National Archives to go to Duke University (NC) but never arrived there. The other 3 mortality schedules are available.

30   Somerville Cemetery, Somerville, Fayette Co, TN, tombstones. Visited and copied by Emily Croom, July, 1973.

31   Letter from Mrs. W.L. Cargill to Emily Croom, 18 May 1993, giving burial place of Thomas Patton. Also confirmed that he left no will.

32   Fayette Co, TN, Inventory Bk H, p 66, Thomas Patton estate, 1854. My copy from TN State Archives.

33   Tombstone of Catherine Patton Coleman, Zephyr Cemetery, Brown Co, TX, visited, copied, rubbing made, by Emily Croom, Easter, 1971.

Example 17 Cont'd.

Ahnentafel Table for No. 1 EMILY CROOM

Double a person's number to find the father. Double the number and add 1 to find the mother.

Paternal Line	Maternal Line
Parents	
2 Pitser Blalock Croom	3 Fletcher Metcalfe
Grandparents	
4 Albert Sidney J. Croom	6 Hunter Orgain Metcalfe
5 Emily Louise Blalock	7 Fletcher Elizabeth McKennon
Great-Grandparents	
8 Isaac Croom "Jr"	12 Thomas Moody Metcalfe
9 Ann Maria Robertson	13 Martha Emma Harrison
10 Pitser Miller Blalock	14 John Fletcher McKennon
11 Mary Catherine Coleman	15 Margaret Richardson Mood
Great-Great-Grandparents	
16 Charles Croom Jr.	24 Joseph Metcalfe
17 Sivil / Sybil ?	25 Mary Bell Allison
18 Robertson	26 William Lucius Harrison
19 Elizabeth C.	27 Sarah H. Orgain
20 Jesse Blalock	28 Rev. William Richard McKennon
21 Rosanna Lea	29 Martha Elizabeth McBride
22 Elliott Glen Coleman	30 Rev. Francis Asbury Mood
23 Margaret Catherine Patton	31 Susan William Ann Richardson Logan
Great-Great-Great-Grandparents	
32 Charles Croom Sr.	48 Joseph Metcalfe
33 Temperance	49 Rebecca Littler
34	50 Joseph Allison
35	51 Mary (Polly)
36 Robertson	52 George Washington Harrison
37	53 Margaret Emma Bland
38	54 Rev. Sterling Orgain
39	55 Mary Elizabeth Jones
40 William Blalock	56 George Garner McKennon
41 Mary Cash	57 Nancy Liles
42	58 John McBride
43	59 Mary "Polly" Jaggers
44 Ferdinand Glen Coleman	60 Rev. John Mood
45 Elizabeth A. Phillips	61 Catherine McFarlane
46 Thomas Patton	62 Thomas Muldrup Logan MD.
47 Catherine Ewing McFadden	63 Susan William Ann Richardson

Example 18

Five-Generation Chart # 2

#1 on this chart is the same as

3 ___ on chart # 1 ___.

b = birth date & place
m = marriage date & place
d = death date & place

2 John Wesley Williamson
b 29 Mar 1879
Natchitoches (Vernon) Par. LA
m 19 Dec 1900, Rapides
Par. LA
d 4 May 1956, Hineston
LA

1 Elsie Mae Williamson
b 4 May 1914, Hineston,
Rapides Par. LA
m 5 Apr 1934, Harris Co Tx
d 10 Mar 1984, Houston,
Harris Co Tx
Spouse Robert Orten Shelby

4 James Cater Williamson
b 24 Oct 1856
Monroe Co AL
m c 1876
d 2 May 1936, Hineston,
Rapides Par. LA. Buried-
Smith Cem, Leander LA

5 Matilda Ann Bennett
b 17 Jan 1859
Natchitoches Par. LA
d 31 Jan 1933
Buried-Smith Cem,
Leander LA.

8 Samuel David Williamson
b 4 Oct 1827
Monroe Co AL
m 17 Jan 1850 Monroe Co AL
d 17 Oct 1911, Simpson,
Vernon Par. LA

9 Ann Cater
b 1827-29 AL
d 1865-66 LA

10 Caleb P. Bennett
b 1812-1815 GA
m 18 Aug 1843
Talbot Co GA
d Sept 1864 LA

11 Harriett Ellender Hudson
b 12 July 1829 SC
d 26 Sept 1890 LA.
Buried-Pine Island Cem,
Simpson, Vernon Par LA

16 Samuel D. Williamson
bc 1780-90   d 1835 AL

17 Esther/Easter

18 James M.   Cater
bc 1803 SC

19 probably
Sarah
bc 1806 SC

20 Edmund Bennett
bc 1786 GA   d 1850s LA

21 Mary
bc 1797-98 GA

22 Hudson
b NC

23 b NC

24 Fry

3 Hettie Margie Fry
b 10 Oct 1882 LA
Adopted by James M + Melissa
Smith, about age 2.
d 27 May 1965, Leesville,
Vernon Par. LA. Buried
with husband at
Fellowship Cem, Hineston LA.

6 b
m
d

7 Annie J.   Herndon
bc 1859 MS
m2 Edwin Rainwater
d c 1890 LA

12 b
m
d

13 b
d

14 b
m
d
m2 ____ House?

15 b
d

25

26

27

28

29

30

31

UNPUZZLING YOUR PAST WORKBOOK

Example 19

Compiled by:
EAC + RTS

Example 20

Five-Generation Chart # 3

using ahnentafel numbers

Lineage of EMILY CROOM

who is #1 on chart # 1

b = birth date & place
m = marriage date & place
d = death date & place

Compiled by: EAC

#7 Fletcher Elizabeth McKennon
b 21 Sept 1893
Georgetown, Tx

m 2 Sept 1914
Georgetown, Tx

d 27 Dec 1976, Houston, Tx
bur. Marfa Tx with husband
Spouse Hunter Orgain
Metcalfe 1887-1968

#14 John Fletcher McKennon
b 1863 TN near Henryville
m 19 Sept 1888, Waco,
McLennan Co Tx
d 22 Jan 1894
Philadelphia PA

#15 Margaret Richardson Mood
b 26 Apr 1867
Charleston SC

d 2 Jan 1948
Beverly Hills CA

28 William Richard McKennon
b 25 Aug 1831
TN prob. Maury Co.
m
d 10 July 1898
Maury Co, TN
bur. Rose Hill Cem.

29 Martha Elizabeth McBride
b 16 Sept 1834
TN, prob. Maury Co.
d 1 Feb 1910
Maury Co, TN
bur. Rose Hill Cem.

30 Rev. Francis Asbury Mood
b 23 June 1830
Charleston SC
m 28 Dec 1858
Columbia SC
d 12 Nov 1884
Waco Tx

31 Susan William Anne Richardson Logan
b 5 Aug 1843
Sumter SC
d 13 Nov 1916
Georgetown Tx

56 George Garner McKennon
bc 1808
SC
m 20 Nov 1828
Maury Co TN
d 1860s prob. Maury Co.

57 Nancy Liles/Lisles
b VA
d TN by 1850
prob. Maury Co.

58 John McBride
b 24 July 1791
NC
m 12 Mar 1818,
Maury Co TN
d 18 Dec 1857

59 Mary "Polly" Jaggers
b 9 Dec 1800 SC or TN
d 14 Apr 1836
Maury Co TN

60 Rev. John Mood
b 11 Jan 1792
Charleston SC
m 23 May 1815 "
d 1 Mar 1864 "

61 Catherine McFarlane
b 23 July 1798
Charleston SC
d 31 Jan 1857
Charleston SC

62 Thomas Muldrup Logan MD
b 31 Jan 1808
Charleston SC
m 9 Mar 1828
Charleston SC
d 13 Feb 1876 Sacramento

63 Susan William Richardson
b 1811 Charleston SC
d 27 Aug 1864
Charleston SC

#	Name	See Chart #
112	William McKennon — bc 1775 SC	
113		
114	Liles	
115		
116	McBride	
117		
118	Daniel Jaggers	
119	Hester	
120	Peter Mood — 1766-1821	4
121	Mary Dorothy Sigwald — 1766-1819	4
122	Alexander McFarlane	5
123	Catherine Reader — c1773-1839	5
124	George Logan — 1778-1861	6
125	Margaret White Polk — 1780-1826	6
126	Hon. John Smythe Richardson — 1777-1850	7
127	Elizabeth Lucretia Buford	7

Biographical Outline of the Life of ___STERLING ORGAIN Sr.___

(Name of person)

With information on education, military service, marriage(s), children, illnesses, religious milestones, migrations,
residences, jobs, family events, land purchases, court appearances, death & burial, etc.

Date	Age	Event and Place	Documentation
Birth 31 Jan 1787		Place VA, probably Brunswick Co. Son of Wm Darby O. & possibly wife	Tombstone gives date (Shiloh Cem, Hutto, TX). Father in county records.
1782 & 1785		Elizabeth, named in his will. Father in Brunswick Co tax list	The First Census of the U.S., GPO, Wash., DC, 1908. Tax list used as substitute for 1790 census. No other Orgains in county tax lists.
15 Mar 1787	2/12	Father taxed in Brunswick for self & 6 slaves, 4 horses, 17 cattle.	The Personal Property Tax Lists for the Year 1787 for Brunswick Co, VA. Netti Schreiner-Yantis & Florene Love. Springfield, VA: Gen Bks in Print, 1987.
1799 & 1801	12, 14	Father on St Andrews Par, Bruns. Co. tax list (no 1800 census)	Personal property tax lists, Brunswick Co, St Andrews Parish, VA, microfilm from VA State Lib, at Clayton Lib, Houston.
1808	21	Would appear first time on poll tax	No taxes collected that year. . .
1809	22	Pers. property tax list, father's entry shows 2 white polls. Is the 2nd one Sterling?	Same as 1801.
26 June 1810	23	Father wrote will, naming kids, including Sterling	Brunswick Co VA Wills Bk 9:361-362
Aug 1810	23	Sterling not accounted for in father's household, tax list or census.	Tax list, same as 1801. US Census, 1810, Brunswick Co, VA, p 725.
1818	31	marries Mary Elizabeth Jones, dau Edmund Jones, Murfreesboro TN	Sterling named in Jones' will, Madison Co TN Will Bk 2:274-278. Letter from James Robert Orgain Jr, Alberta VA, 6-6-91, gives her full name & place.
17 Sept 1818	31	Sterling & Alfred Moore (bro-in-law), merchants/partners bought an a/c against US govt for $120 for blacksmith labor for 120 pr horseshoes for TN Mtd Volunteers in Seminole War, from Morris Lindsay.	List of Private Claims Brought Before the Senate, Vol 2:734-735. S.misc. doc.67(30-2)534.
c 1819	32	Son William E, born TN	All children living in 1852 named in Madison Co TN Deed Bk 18:464-465. Date suggested in 1850 census, Madison Co TN, Family #527.
1820	33	Not shown as head of family in census. Appears to be with in-laws (Edmund Jones) w/Mary & son Wm.	US Census, 1820, Rutherford Co TN, p 37
c 1820-21	33	dau Martha E born TN	suggested by 1830 census, her early 1840 marriage & birthdates of siblings.
Dec 1821- Feb 1822	35	Moore & Orgain petitioned Congress to be paid the $120 (see 1818). Petition referred to claims com. & tabled. 8 Feb, referred to claims committee, rejected by Treas. Dept. on grounds that volunteer gunmen got 40¢/day for use of horses & should pay own expenses for horseshoes.	S.doc.37(17-1)59
8 Feb 1822			S.doc.34(18-1)90, document B, and S.misc.doc.67(30-2)534, Vol 2:734-735.

[handwritten annotation, boxed, pointing to 1782 & 1785 row:] Used to show William's residence in the county before + after Sterling's birth

Example 21

Date	Age	Event and Place	Documentation
1822–1823	c35	Son Edmund Jones O, born TN	US Census, 1850, Madison Co TN, p 654 suggests date & gives state.
12 Feb 1824	37	Moore/Orgain petition referred to mil. affairs committee, approved, reported out as bill #47, passed in May. Said they couldn't imagine that the Act of Jan 1795, under which volunteers were called out & pd, intended soldiers to pay for shoeing own horses during service to country. $120 had been approved by unit & regiment colonels.	S.doc. 34(18-1)90 *See The Genealogist's Companion & Sourcebook for explanation and discussion of the U.S. Serial Set.*
May 1824			
24 May 1824	37	Father's will probated, Brunswick Co VA	Brunswick Co VA Will Bk 9:361-362.
c 1824-25	c37	Son James born TN	Date suggested in US Census, 1850, Madison Co TN, p 654.
1825	38	Taxed for 1 poll, wife Mary taxed for 3 slaves	Madison Co TN tax roll, 1825.
1825-1826	38-39	As minister of Methodist Episcopal Church South performed weddings	Madison Co TN marriage records, various dates.
10 Nov 1825	38	Assigned power of attorney to Alfred Moore	Madison Co TN Court Minute Bk II, p 11.
Feb, May 1826	39	Hands assigned to road work	Madison Co TN Court Minute Bk II, 31, 85.
1826	39	Taxed for 1 poll, 3 slaves	Madison Co TN tax rolls, 1826.
1828	41	Taxed for 1 poll, 4 slaves	Madison Co TN tax rolls, 1828.
Nov, 1829	42	Son John Henry b near Paris, Henry Co TN	Reminiscences of the Boys in Gray. Mamie Yeary, comp. Dayton OH: Morningside, 1986 reprint of 1912 original.
1830	43	Census: 4 boys, 2 girls, 12 slaves	US Census, 1830, Henry Co TN, p 42.
1831-32	44	Dau Jane born TN	Dates for these 2 suggested in 1850 census, Madison Co TN, p 654.
1833-34	46	Dau Emily born TN	
1834	47	Local preacher elected to deacon's orders at annual conference	History of Methodism in Tennessee. John B. M'Ferrin. Nashville, 1886, III: 441.
1834-1842	47-55	Served as Trustee, Henry Co TN	The Goodspeed History of Tennessee, Carroll, Henry, Benton cos. Southern Historical Press, 1978 reprint, p 820.
1835-36	48-49	Son Sterling Jr born TN	Date suggested consistently in 1850-60-80-1920 censuses. 1900 census gives Apr 1830, but no other evidence to support that.
c 1837	50	Father-in-law Edmund Jones dies	Will probated Feb, 1838. Madison Co TN Will Bk 2:274-278.
c 1838	51	A dau born ?, name not known, indicated in 1840 census but not shown in 1850 census.	See 1840, 1850.
11 Feb 1840	53	Dau Martha m Thos P. Hall in Henry Co TN	Henry Co TN Marriages, I (1838-1852). W.O. Inman, comp. Paris, TN, 1974.
2 Apr 1840	53	Dau Sarah W. born TN, Henry Co	Her funeral notice (1928) gives date.

Death 4 Jan 1878	90	Place Probably Williamson Co TX Wife Mary d 19 days later, 23 Jan 1878	Tombstone gives dates for him & wife Mary.
Burial		Place Shiloh Cem, near Hutto, Williamson Co TX	
Probate ?		Place No probate record found in Williamson Co.	

Example 21 Cont'd.

Thomas Glascock, 1642

William Frierson, 1732

by 1761

by 1794

1820s

1808

by 1837

by 1843

by 1873

1870

1898

Glas(s)cock
1642 Old Rappahannock Co VA
(Richmond Co)
by 1761 Fauquier Co VA
by 1794 Rowan Co NC
1820s Rutherford Co TN
by 1837 Jackson Co AL, island in river near
Bridgeport
1870 Lamar & Fannin counties TX
1898 Angleton, Brazoria Co TX.

Frierson • • • • • •
1732 Williamsburg SC
1808 Maury Co TN
by 1843 College Hill, Lafayette Co MS
by 1873 Sumner, Tallahatchie Co MS
1898 Angleton, Brazoria Co TX. William
Livingston Walter, son of Sarah Dixie
Frierson & William Thomas Walter,
m Mary Cordelia Glascock in 1907.

Gaylord Stickle Company, Houston Texas

Example 22

Example 23

Family or Surname *Various, with ahnentafel numbers*

Timeline 1600-1800

Timeline events:
- 1607 Jamestown VA founded
- 1620 Pilgrims land at Plymouth MA
- 1630 Massachusetts Bay Colony
- 1634 First settlers to Maryland
- 1642-1649 English Civil War
- 1649 Charles I beheaded. Cromwell & Parliament rule England.
- 1660 Restoration of established church & monarchy. Charles II crowned.
- 1670 First permanent English settlement in South Carolina
- 1682 Pennsylvania colony begins.
- 1709-1710 First large German immigration (Palatine)
- 1717 Large Scotch-Irish immigration begins, first wave.
- 1733 First settlers to Georgia
- 1754-1763 French & Indian War
- 1763 Treaty of Paris — Britain gets Canada & most land east of Mississippi River
- 1775-1783 American Revolution
- 1788 US Constitution adopted
- 1790 First US federal census

Timeline scale: 1600 — 1625 — 1650 — 1675 — 1700 — 1725 — 1750 — 1775 — 1800

Individuals and ahnentafel numbers:

- #1696 — Theodorick Bland, 1629–1671
- #1697 — Anne (Bennett) Bland, 1639–1687
- #1698 — William Randolph, 1651–1711
- #849 — Elizabeth (Randolph) Bland, 1680s–1720 (wife)
- #848 — Richard Bland I, 1665–1720 (husband, father)
- #424 — Richard Bland II, 1710–1776 (son, father)
- #425 — Anne (Poythress) Bland, 1712–1758 (wife, mother)
- #506 — Gabriel Guignard, 1708–1757 (husband)
- #240 — Johann Peter Muth (Mood), 1730–1778 (husband)
- #128 — Daniel Croom, 1680–1734–1735 (father)
- #64 — Jesse Croom, c.1713–1812 (son)

PART FIVE

Letter Writing

Genealogists occasionally need to write letters to agencies, institutions or individuals to request information or copies of documents. Sometimes, however, a telephone call will suffice. For example, instead of writing to the National Archives branch in East Point, Georgia, to request the form necessary for obtaining a copy of a certain World War I draft registration card, you can spend a few cents and call them at (404) 763-7477, ask that the form be mailed to you, and give them your name and address. (They have all the cards for the entire nation, not just the southeastern region. Microfilm copies are becoming available at other National Archives branches and research libraries as well.)

Likewise, if you plan to visit ancestral counties, a few telephone calls in advance can get you valuable information: the days and hours when the courthouse or library will be open, whom to contact for records of a certain church, whether the court clerks have the older records in their offices, whether some records are in storage, and whether these are accessible. This advance calling can be helpful, too, in locating certain records—finding out, for example, whether they are at the state historical society or archives, the local courthouse, or a university or public library. By telephone, you may be able to set up appointments to see certain church or funeral home records or to visit a private library that is open by appointment only. By telephone, you can learn whether a publisher or bookseller has a certain book in stock and place an order.

Instead of writing a long interview letter to a relative or friend, a telephone call or two may be easier, even if more expensive. A phone call assures you of getting an answer, and getting it quickly, and allows you to cover more thoroughly the information you want. The major concerns with such calls are whether you are able to write fast enough to take good notes as the conversation progresses and how well your interviewee hears over the telephone.

Occasionally, when your questions are specific to your research, such as pulling a given volume from library or courthouse shelves and copying the two pages you need, you may be able to arrange the transaction by telephone. Much depends on the practice of the particular library or courthouse, how busy they are at the moment, and whether they want payment in advance.

When you do need to write letters for your research, you may have better luck if you remember the tips listed below.

LETTER WRITING TIPS FOR GENEALOGISTS

- Make the letter concise and to the point.
- Include in the letter the date, your address, and your name printed legibly. Put your return address on the envelope as well.
- Offer to pay for the service you are requesting. Most agencies which require payment will send you instructions on how they handle the fee. Many require it in advance.
- If asking for information, especially from a library, institution or government agency, generally limit yourself to one or two questions relating to one ancestor.
- When asking correspondents for information they may have on a particular ancestor, especially if the surname is common, include the ancestor's life dates and place(s) of residence for your correspondent's reference.
- Thank your correspondent in advance for the help you are requesting.
- You may want to include your phone number and suggest your correspondents call you. However, many people do not want to make long-distance calls so you may want to ask for their phone number and permission to call them.
- If writing to an individual or non-government agency or institution and expecting a reply, enclose a self-addressed *stamped* envelope (SASE). Please remember the stamp, and use the correct postage.
- Type or print your letter if at all possible. If using a computer printer or typewriter, be sure

the print is dark, sharply imprinted and easy to read. I, for one, will not answer letters that I cannot read readily.

- Proofread your letter for correct spelling and grammar, and make sure the information you give in your letter is as accurate as possible.

- You may want to keep copies of your outgoing letters so that you can have a reference when you get a response. In my early days of writing genealogy letters, I received an answer to a letter of which I had no copy. Enough time had passed that I had forgotten what I had asked. It went something like this:

Dear Emily,
In answer to your questions:

1. Yes.
2. I think she did.
3. I have no record of it.
4. The fourth child was indeed Mary Louise. I remember her well. Red-headed and plump. She was just older than my mother.
5. I can't remember, but you might contact your Aunt Sue. She knows much of this family.
6. No, I don't know who she married. I think she had 2 sons and 1 daughter.

It's good to hear from you! Good luck with your project.

When writing to relatives for information, I like to suggest that they answer *on* the letter I send them and return it to me so that I have my questions and their answers together. I leave space for answers when I type the letter. Example 24 on page 42 is this kind of letter. Sometimes public officials answer on your original letter because it is a quick way to handle correspondence. The following is one example I received years ago. Some county clerks will answer letters of this kind, and some will not. Much depends on the volume of genealogy letters they receive and the load of day-to-day business they have.

[to county clerk of Livingston County, Smithland, KY, 9 August 1978]

Dear Sir,
In working on family history, I am researching James Shaw, an early resident of Livingston County. He died there in May 1803. Do your records include a will or inventory or estate set-

tlement for him? If so, please tell me the cost of obtaining a copy.
Thank you very much for your help.
Sincerely,

In searching our records, I did not find a will, inventory or settlement for a James Shaw.
[signed] James Jones, Liv. Co. Clerk

SAMPLE LETTERS

The following are a few examples of genealogy letters. Adapt the form to your own style and needs. A query letter to a journal or newspaper column needs to be concise and to the point. If the journal has a prescribed form for queries, use that. Otherwise, keep your information pertinent to your request but with enough information to let readers know whether it may be someone on whom they have information.

Query Letters

Dear Query Editor,
Seek descendants of Alexander Armstrong (c1808 MS-1872 LA) and 2nd wife Sarah Ford (c1831/33 MS-1917 LA), m 1850 in Franklin Parish LA. Issue: William A, Aaron B, Elizabeth R (m Glasscock), Margaret J (m Davidson), John, Sallie (m Lindsey), Eliza, & Robert E. Lee Armstrong, all born in LA between 1851 and 1869, probably Franklin Parish. Seek parents & siblings of wife Sarah.
Thank you for printing my query.
Sincerely,

Another kind of query letter may be sent to several families of one surname, especially in a county or town from which ancestors came, asking for information or seeking descendants. In this kind of letter, it is wise to spell out words that we genealogists often abbreviate—*born, married, died, about.*

Dear Mr. Oldham,
We are working on the genealogy of several Robertson County, TX, families and are trying to find descendants of John Charles Lafayette Oldham (born about 1856) and wife Annie (Shelby) Oldham (born about 1861, died before 1912). They married in Robertson County in 1878 and continued to live there. Their known children (born between 1879 and 1898) were Vida, John Preston, Roachal, Lycurgus (died

1973), Lula (married a Pringle), Hetty (married an Ingram), and Elam Jennings. Some of these moved to Limestone, Navarro, McLennan, and Tarrant counties. Lafayette was son of James N. and Mary W. Oldham of Robertson County. We believe Annie to be the daughter of John P. and Matilda Shelby. Lafayette had a sister Arabella Jelks, a sister M.A. McDaniel, a sister V.A. Hightower, and a brother B.F. Oldham. One grandson of Lafayette and Annie was Alvin Preston Oldham, living in Waco about 1969.

If you have information about or knew any of these Oldhams, we would appreciate hearing from you. A stamped envelope is enclosed for your convenience. Many thanks for any help you can offer.

Sincerely,

Letter Requesting Copies

One of the most common situations when genealogists need to write letters is to request a copy of a document from the institution or agency which holds it. If you know they charge a set fee for such copies, or can find out by telephone, enclosing a check for that amount may speed up an answer. Some archives, however, bill you according to the document's length. Other archives add fees for research, handling and out-of-state residents. Many will not accept partial payment in advance but want the whole fee paid before they send you the material. Therefore, you must send in a request, often on their special form (call to request one), wait for an order form to be returned to you, mail your check and wait again for your copy.

The following is an example of a letter requesting a copy of an ancestor's Social Security application, called an *SS-5*. This document often contains valuable information, such as birth date and place, parents' names, and residence and employment at the time of application.

Social Security Administration
Freedom of Information Office
4-H-8 Annex
6401 Security Blvd.
Baltimore, MD 21235

To Whom It May Concern,
In working on family history, I need to obtain

a copy of the SS-5 for this ancestor: Alfred Thomas King, SS# 467-00-0001, born about 1885–1886, possibly in Houston, Texas, and died 27 April 1941. Enclosed is a check for $7, which I understand will offset the cost of the copy. Please send it to me at the address shown above. Thank you very much.

Sincerely,

Interview Letters

Interview letters are my way of writing questions to an individual and getting the answers back on the same page. The only problem is anticipating how much space to leave for an answer. I could never judge correctly for my Great-aunt Emily, for she had much to share, and I am very grateful that she was thorough in her responses. After all, she had grown up among many of the people about whom I needed information. Sometimes, she and other correspondents have left questions blank. Expect that to happen. And remember to enclose a self-addressed stamped envelope with your request.

Example 24 is part of an interview letter dealing not with genealogical data but with historical detail that is interesting and pertinent in genealogy.

IN CLOSING

The forms provided in this book offer many options for the genealogist who wants time-saving conveniences, wants to be thorough, tries to be accurate, and makes lists or progress reports to determine how far the search has come and where it needs to go. The forms are for you to use as you wish, to adapt to your own style and needs. You may not want to use them all for every family in your search, but perhaps you will find many of them useful and will glean new ideas for planning, organizing, searching, record keeping and letter writing. Some of the forms have been adapted from those originally published in *Unpuzzling Your Past*, and others are new. All make an effort to be user-friendly.

Over the years, as I have used these, or earlier versions, I have found that they really do make a difference in how thoroughly I research, study and evaluate. I trust we all will be better genealogists as a result of this kind of effort. That is ultimately what this book is all about.

Happy Unpuzzling!

Interview Letter

Emily Croom to Emily Blalock, 4 Dec 1970

Dear Aunt Emily,
Here are some of the questions I need help with. Please answer on this page and return it to me in the enclosed envelope. Thank you so much!
1. When my granddad Albert moved to Hardeman County, did he work for the Blalocks?
    No. If my memory serves me right, he bought the farm when he married Laura Keller. Albert and Lou moved from that farm to Texas.

2. About the log house which Albert and Lou lived in. . . . Did you and Lowe move into it when Albert and Lou moved to Texas?
    Lowe bought the farm from Mr. Croom and Lou when they moved to Texas and he rented it out until we married. After our marriage in Dec. 1903, we moved into the house in January of 1904.

3. How many rooms did it have and which ones? In the picture I have, there is a window upstairs. Was that a bedroom?
    Yes. It had a big room, a kitchen, a combination bedroom and dining room, a big room upstairs over the large room downstairs, a back porch and a room over the back porch which led to the large upstairs room. The house was made of sawed logs and "chinked" as you would call it. It had a tun-and-grooved [*sic*] floor (wooden). It had been built only a few years. It had a barn, smokehouse, chicken house, as all farm houses had. There was a garden fenced with chicken-proof wire fencing to protect the vegetables. Albert and Lou were comfortably situated in every way.

4. The picture shows a lean-to addition in the back. What was it?
    A back porch with a room upstairs over the porch.

5. Did the kitchen have a fireplace or a wood stove?
    It had a very adequate large wood stove.

6. Do you remember what furniture they had in the house?
    The house was well-furnished but they had an auction sale and sold all of the furniture and took only their clothes and personal belongings with them to Texas. They went to Texas by train.

7. Were the walls on the inside covered over with wood, plaster, paper, or anything?
    The logs were sawed and chinked. Walls were as smooth as panelling is now.

8. Was the house warm in winter? cool in summer?
    Yes

9. I'd appreciate anything else you can tell me about Albert.
    I always thought of him as being a good man, and I liked him very much. He was a good neighbor. Lou and I prepared his first wife, Laura, for burial. She was sick a long time which made it very hard on Mr. Croom.

Federal Census, 1790-1930

WHICH CENSUS REPORTS . . . ?

age, sex, race of each individual in household	1850 forward
agricultural schedules	1850-1880
attendance in school	1850 forward
months attending school	1900
birthdate (month/year) of each person	1900
month of birth if born within the year	1870-1880
birthplace of each person	1850 forward
deaf, dumb, or blind	1830, 1850-1890, 1910
defective, dependent, delinquent schedules (DDD)	1880
pauper or convict	1850-1860
prisoner, convict, homeless child, pauper	1890
disabled: crippled, maimed, bedridden, or other disability	1880
crippled, maimed, deformed	1890
employer, self-employed, or wage earner	1910-1930
months unemployed	1880-1900
whether person worked yesterday or number on unemployment schedule	1930
home or farm as residence	1890-1910, 1930
home owned or rented	1890-1930
home owned free of mortgage	1890-1920
value of home or monthly rent	1930
farm owned or rented	1890
farm owned free of mortgage	1890
illness, current, or temporary disability	1880
chronic or acute illness, length of time afflicted	1890
immigration year	1900-1930
number of years in U.S.	1890-1900
industry/manufacturing schedules	1820, 1850-1880
insane, idiot	1850-1880
defective in mind	1890
language, native	1890, 1910-1930
native language of parents	1920
speaks English	1890-1930

male, eligible/not eligible to vote	1870
marital status	1880 forward
age at first marriage	1930
married within the [census] year	1850-1890
month of marriage, within the [census] year	1870
number of years of present marriage	1900-1910
mortality schedules	1850-1880
mother of how many children, number living	1890-1910
name of each individual in household	1850 forward
name of head of household only	1790-1840
naturalized citizen or first papers	1890-1930
year of naturalization	1920
occupation	1850 forward
parents, whether foreign-born	1870
birthplace of parents	1880 forward
radio set in home	1930
reading and writing, whether able to read or write	1890-1930
persons unable to read and/or write	1850-1880
relationship to head of household	1880 forward
slaves by age, sex	1830-1860
number of slaves	1790-1860
social statistics schedules	1850-1880
Soundex	1880 forward, mostly
street address of family	1880 forward
value of real estate owned	1850-1870
value of personal estate	1860-1870
veterans: pensioners	1840
Union vets and widows, special schedule	1890
Civil War veteran, Union or Confederate, or widow	1890
Civil War veteran, Union or Confederate	1910
veteran of U.S. military or naval forces, which war	1930

Soundex Codes

1	b, p, f, v
2	c, s, k, g, j, q, x, z
3	d, t
4	l
5	m, n
6	r

Strike out vowels and _y, w, h_. Use remaining letters for form three-digit code.
(Use initial letter of name to begin code.)
Wilhite = W430   Northway = N630

Double letters count only once.   Hill = H400   Patterson = P362

Consecutive letters in one code count once: Adcock = A322   Sumner = S560
Schmidt = S530   but Hughes = H220 (g and s are not consecutive)

Run out of letters before you get a three-digit code? Add zero.
Lee = L000   Mays = M200   Willis = W420

Get three code numbers before you finish the name? Disregard the remainder of the name.
Robertson = R163 (disregard s and n)

Census Check on _____
_{Name}

Birthdate/place_____ First Census _____

Father's Name _____ Mother's Name _____

Marriage date/place _____ Spouse _____

Death date/place _____ Burial place _____

Census Year	Age	State/Counties Searched	County Where Found & Notes	Film #, Roll #, E.D., Pg, etc.

Census Check on _____
<small>Name</small>

Birthdate/place _____ First Census _____

Father's Name _____ Mother's Name _____

Marriage date/place _____ Spouse _____

Death date/place _____ Burial place _____

Census Year	Age	State/Counties Searched	County Where Found & Notes	Film #, Roll #, E.D., Pg, etc.

Census Check on _____
Name

Birthdate/place _____ First Census _____

Father's Name _____ Mother's Name _____

Marriage date/place _____ Spouse _____

Death date/place _____ Burial place _____

Census Year	Age	State/Counties Searched	County Where Found & Notes	Film #, Roll #, E.D., Pg, etc.

Census Check on _____
Name

Birthdate/place _____ First Census _____

Father's Name _____ Mother's Name _____

Marriage date/place _____ Spouse _____

Death date/place _____ Burial place _____

Census Year	Age	State/Counties Searched	County Where Found & Notes	Film #, Roll #, E.D., Pg, etc.

Census Check on _____
Name

Birthdate/place _____ First Census _____

Father's Name _____ Mother's Name _____

Marriage date/place _____ Spouse _____

Death date/place _____ Burial place _____

Census Year	Age	State/Counties Searched	County Where Found & Notes	Film #, Roll #, E.D., Pg, etc.

Military Records Checklist for _____

Ancestor Name & Life Dates	Colonial Wars (state records)	American Revolution 1775–1783 (check state & federal records)	1784-1811	War of 1812 (1812–1815)	Indian Wars 1815–1858	Patriot War 1838	Mexican War 1846–1848	Civil War 1861–1865 (for Confederates, check state & federal records)	Service 1866 forward	Spanish-American War 1898–1899	Philippine Insurrection 1899–1902	World War I 1917–1918	World War II 1941–1945

Military Records Checklist for _____

Ancestor Name & Life Dates	Colonial Wars (state records)	American Revolution 1775–1783 (check state & federal records)	1784-1811	War of 1812 (1812–1815)	Indian Wars 1815–1858	Patriot War 1838	Mexican War 1846–1848	Civil War 1861–1865 (for Confederates, check state & federal records)	Service 1866 forward	Spanish-American War 1898–1899	Philippine Insurrection 1899–1902	World War I 1917–1918	World War II 1941–1945

Research Planning Worksheet

Date _____

Statement of the Problem _____

Questions Related to the Problem:

Sources to Try	Results

Research Planning Worksheet

Date _____

Statement of the Problem _____

Questions Related to the Problem:

Sources to Try	Results

Research Planning Worksheet

Date _____

Statement of the Problem _____

Questions Related to the Problem:

Sources to Try	Results

Research Planning Worksheet

Date _____

Statement of the Problem _____

Questions Related to the Problem:

Sources to Try	Results

Contact Log # _____ Surname or Search _____

Contact plan	Subject	Contact made, date	Results & notes

Contact Log # _____ Surname or Search _____

Contact plan	Subject	Contact made, date	Results & notes

Deed Index—-Grantors

Deed Index for _____ Surname _____
County   State

Source: Courthouse or Library _____ Call #, Film # _____

Grantor Surname:	Grantee	Book, Page	Date	# Acres	Type Transaction or Legal Description

Deed Index—Grantees

Deed Index for _____ Surname _____
County   State

Source: Courthouse or Library _____ Call #, Film # _____

Grantee Surname:	Grantor	Book, Page	Date	# Acres	Type Transaction or Legal Description

Deed Index—Grantors

Deed Index for _____   Surname _____
                    County   State

Source: Courthouse or Library _____ Call #, Film # _____

Grantor Surname:	Grantee	Book, Page	Date	# Acres	Type Transaction or Legal Description

Deed Index—Grantees

Deed Index for _____ _____ Surname _____
              County   State

Source: Courthouse or Library _____ Call #, Film # _____

Grantee Surname:	Grantor	Book, Page	Date	# Acres	Type Transaction or Legal Description

Marriage Index—Grooms

Marriage Index for _____ Surname _____
County   State

Source: Courthouse or Library _____ Call #, Film # _____

Groom	Bride	Date	Book, Page	#

Marriage Index—Brides

Marriage Index for _____ Surname _____
County   State

Source: Courthouse or Library _____ Call #, Film # _____

Bride	Groom	Date	Book, Page	#

Marriage Index—Grooms

Marriage Index for _____ Surname _____
County   State

Source: Courthouse or Library _____ Call #, Film # _____

Groom	Bride	Date	Book, Page	#

Marriage Index—Brides

Marriage Index for _____ _____ Surname _____
County　　　　　　　　　　　　　　State

Source: Courthouse or Library _____ Call #, Film # _____

Bride	Groom	Date	Book, Page	#

Statewide Marriage Index for _____ Surname _____

State   Soundex Code

Source of this information: _____ Call #, Film # _____

Groom	Bride	Date	County	Reference

Statewide Marriage Index for _____ Surname _____

State   Soundex Code

Source of this information: _____ Call #, Film # _____

Bride	Groom	Date	County	Reference

Statewide Marriage Index for _____ Surname _____

State

Soundex Code

Source of this information: _____ Call #, Film # _____

Groom	Bride	Date	County	Reference

Statewide Marriage Index for _____ Surname _____
State   Soundex Code

Source of this information: _____ Call #, Film # _____

Bride	Groom	Date	County	Reference

Soundex Search for _____ Year _____ State _____

Surname   Code

Given Name or Head of Household	Color & Age	Birth-place & Citizen.	County	City, Street Address	Vol, E.D., Sheet, Line	Other Family Members or Enumerated With
Search for:						

Soundex Search for _____ continued. Year _____ State _____

Surname Code

Given Name or Head of Household	Color & Age	Birth-place & Citizen.	County	City, Street Address	Vol, E.D., Sheet, Line	Other Family Members or Enumerated With

Soundex Search for _____ Year _____ State _____

Surname   Code

Given Name or Head of Household	Color & Age	Birth-place & Citizen.	County	City, Street Address	Vol, E.D., Sheet, Line	Other Family Members or Enumerated With
Search for:						

Soundex Search for _____ continued. Year _____ State _____

Surname   Code

Given Name or Head of Household	Color & Age	Birth-place & Citizen.	County	City, Street Address	Vol, E.D., Sheet, Line	Other Family Members or Enumerated With

Alphabetical Ancestors

Alphabetical Group _____
such as A-B, C-D, etc.

Surname or Maiden Name	Given Name	Birth Year	Death Year	Residence	Dates of Residence	5-Gen. Chart #

Alphabetical Ancestors

Alphabetical Group _____

Surname or Maiden Name	Given Name	Birth Year	Death Year	Residence	Dates of Residence	5-Gen. Chart #

Alphabetical Ancestors   Surname or Family Group _____

Surname or Maiden Name	Given Name	Birth Year	Death Year	Residence (Town, County, State)	Dates of Residence	5-Gen. Chart #

Alphabetical Ancestors, continued for Surname or Family Group _____

Surname or Maiden Name	Given Name	Birth Year	Death Year	Residence (Town, County, State)	Dates of Residence	5-Gen. Chart #

Alphabetical Ancestors

Locality _____
County and/or State

Surname or Maiden Name	Given Name	Birth Year	Death Year	Residence	Dates of Residence	5-Gen. Chart #

Alphabetical Ancestors, continued for Locality _____

County and/or State

Surname or Maiden Name	Given Name	Birth Year	Death Year	Residence	Dates of Residence	5-Gen. Chart #

Index to Workshop Notes and Handouts

Topics A–B–C	Lecturer	Topics D–E–F	Lecturer

Topics G–H–I	Lecturer	Topics J–K–L	Lecturer

Index to Workshop Notes and Handouts

Topics M–N	Lecturer	Topics O–P–Q–R	Lecturer

Topics S–T–U	Lecturer	Topics V–W–X–Y–Z	Lecturer

Index to Workshop Notes and Handouts

Fill in alphabet headings as desired.

Topics:	Lecturer	Topics:	Lecturer

Topics:	Lecturer	Topics:	Lecturer

Notes

Surname _____

Title of book, article, or document _____ # vols. in set _____

For articles, title of journal _____
        volume # _____ , issue # and date _____ , page #s _____

Author, compiler, and/or editor _____

City of publication _____ Publisher and date of publication _____

Where I used it and when _____ date _____

Call # or Film # _____

Vol # (when applicable),
Page #   Notes

Vol. #

Page #   Notes

Notes

Surname _____

Title of book, article, or document _____ # vols. in set _____

For articles, title of journal _____
      volume # _____ , issue # and date _____ , page #s _____

Author, compiler, and/or editor _____

City of publication _____ Publisher and date of publication _____

Where I used it and when _____ date _____

Call # or Film # _____

Vol # (when applicable),
Page #   Notes

Notes

Surname _____

Title of book, article, or document _____ # vols. in set _____

For articles, title of journal _____

      volume # _____ , issue # and date _____ , page #s _____

Author, compiler, and/or editor _____

City of publication _____ Publisher and date of publication _____

Where I used it and when _____ date _____

Call # or Film # _____

Vol # (when applicable),
Page #   Notes _____

Deed Abstract

Surname _____

Source (Courthouse, microfilm & #, other) _____

County or town where filed _____ State _____ Deed Book # _____ Inclusive pages _____

Quitclaim deed _____ Warranty deed _____ Bill of sale _____ Deed of trust _____ Deed of gift _____

This indenture made this day _____ in the year _____

between (grantor) _____ of _____
                 name(s)   county (or town), state

and (grantee) _____ of _____.
                 name(s)   county (or town), state

The said grantor(s) for and in consideration of the sum of _____ [Is it dollars or other currency?] paid by grantee(s)

and/or notes in the amount of _____ at _____ percent interest, due on date(s) _____,

or other considerations [describe] _____

have sold (or given, if deed of gift) to the grantee(s) the following property: _____ acres, situated in _____

county, state of _____, described as follows: [Copy waterway, boundaries, neighbors, whatever it says.]

and/or other property described as:

In witness whereof the grantors have set their hands and seals. [Note who signed and who made a mark instead.]

Witnesses: _____

Does the seller's wife relinquish her dower right? _____ When? _____

Does the seller's wife willingly sign and seal the indenture? _____

Date the deed is acknowledged in court _____ Date recorded _____

Deed Abstract

Surname _____

Source (Courthouse, microfilm & #, other) _____

County or town where filed _____ State _____ Deed Book # _____ Inclusive pages _____

Quitclaim deed _____ Warranty deed _____ Bill of sale _____ Deed of trust _____ Deed of gift _____

This indenture made this day _____ in the year _____

between (grantor) _____ of _____
                name(s)   county (or town), state

and (grantee) _____ of _____.
                name(s)   county (or town), state

The said grantor(s) for and in consideration of the sum of _____ [Is it dollars or other currency?] paid by grantee(s)

and/or notes in the amount of _____ at _____ percent interest, due on date(s) _____,

or other considerations [describe] _____

have sold (or given, if deed of gift) to the grantee(s) the following property: _____ acres, situated in _____

county, state of _____, described as follows: [Copy waterway, boundaries, neighbors, whatever it says.]

and/or other property described as:

In witness whereof the grantors have set their hands and seals. [Note who signed and who made a mark instead.]

Witnesses: _____

Does the seller's wife relinquish her dower right? _____ When? _____

Does the seller's wife willingly sign and seal the indenture? _____

Date the deed is acknowledged in court _____ Date recorded _____

Deed Abstract

Surname _____

Source (Courthouse, microfilm & #, other) _____

County or town where filed _____ State _____ Deed Book # _____ Inclusive pages _____

Quitclaim deed _____ Warranty deed _____ Bill of sale _____ Deed of trust _____ Deed of gift _____

This indenture made this day _____ in the year _____

between (grantor) _____ of _____
                  name(s)   county (or town), state

and (grantee) _____ of _____.
              name(s)   county (or town), state

The said grantor(s) for and in consideration of the sum of _____ [Is it dollars or other currency?] paid by grantee(s)

and/or notes in the amount of _____ at _____ percent interest, due on date(s) _____,

or other considerations [describe] _____

have sold (or given, if deed of gift) to the grantee(s) the following property: _____ acres, situated in _____

county, state of _____, described as follows: [Copy waterway, boundaries, neighbors, whatever it says.]

and/or other property described as:

In witness whereof the grantors have set their hands and seals. [Note who signed and who made a mark instead.]

Witnesses: _____

Does the seller's wife relinquish her dower right? _____ When? _____

Does the seller's wife willingly sign and seal the indenture? _____

Date the deed is acknowledged in court _____ Date recorded _____

1790 Census

Township or Local Community _____ County _____ State _____

Enumerator _____ Date Census Taken _____ Enumerator District # _____

[Official census day—first Monday in August, 2 August 1790]

Page	Name of Head of Family	Free White Males 16 years & upwards including heads of families	Free White Males under 16 years	Free White Females including heads of families	All Other Free Persons	Slaves	Dwellings/ Other information

1790 Census

Township or Local Community _____ County _____ State _____

Enumerator _____ Date Census Taken _____ Enumerator District # _____

[Official census day—first Monday in August, 2 August 1790]

Page	Name of Head of Family	Free White Males 16 years & upwards including heads of families	Free White Males under 16 years	Free White Females including heads of families	All Other Free Persons	Slaves	Dwellings/ Other information

1790 Census

Township or Local Community _____ County _____ State _____

Enumerator _____ Date Census Taken _____ Enumerator District # _____

[Official census day—first Monday in August, 2 August 1790]

UNPUZZLING YOUR PAST WORKBOOK

Page	Name of Head of Family	Free White Males 16 years & upwards including heads of families	Free White Males under 16 years	Free White Females including heads of families	All Other Free Persons	Slaves	Dwellings/ Other information

1790 Census

Township or Local Community _____ County _____ State _____

Enumerator _____ Date Census Taken _____ Enumerator District # _____

[Official census day—first Monday in August, 2 August 1790]

UNPUZZLING YOUR PAST WORKBOOK

Page	Name of Head of Family	Free White Males 16 years & upwards including heads of families	Free White Males under 16 years	Free White Females including heads of families	All Other Free Persons	Slaves	Dwellings/ Other information

1800 or 1810 Census

Local Community _____ County _____ State _____

Enumerator _____ Date Census Taken _____ Enumerator District # _____

[Official census day—first Monday in August: 4 August 1800 & 6 August 1810]   Supervisor District # _____

UNPUZZLING YOUR PAST WORKBOOK

Written Page No.	Printed Page No.	Name of Head of Family	Free White Males					Free White Females					All other free persons except Indians not taxed	Slaves
			under 10	of 10 & under 16	of 16 & under 26	of 26 & under 45	of 45 & up	under 10	of 10 & under 16	of 16 & under 26	of 26 & under 45	of 45 & up		
					including heads of families						including heads of families				

1800 or 1810 Census

Local Community _____ County _____ State _____

Enumerator _____ Date Census Taken _____ Enumerator District # _____

[Official census day—first Monday in August: 4 August 1800 & 6 August 1810]   Supervisor District # _____

Written Page No.	Printed Page No.	Name of Head of Family	Free White Males					Free White Females					All other free persons except Indians not taxed	Slaves
			under 10	of 10 & under 16	of 16 & under 26	of 26 & under 45	of 45 & up	under 10	of 10 & under 16	of 16 & under 26	of 26 & under 45	of 45 & up		
					including heads of families					including heads of families				

UNPUZZLING YOUR PAST WORKBOOK

1800 or 1810 Census

Local Community _____ County _____ State _____

Enumerator _____ Date Census Taken _____ Enumerator District # _____

[Official census day—first Monday in August: 4 August 1800 & 6 August 1810]   Supervisor District # _____

UNPUZZLING YOUR PAST WORKBOOK

Written Page No.	Printed Page No.	Name of Head of Family	Free White Males					Free White Females					All other free persons except Indians not taxed	Slaves
			under 10	of 10 & under 16	of 16 & under 26	of 26 & under 45	of 45 & up	under 10	of 10 & under 16	of 16 & under 26	of 26 & under 45	of 45 & up		
					including heads of families					including heads of families				

1800 or 1810 Census

Local Community _____ County _____ State _____

Enumerator _____ Date Census Taken _____ Enumerator District # _____

[Official census day—first Monday in August: 4 August 1800 & 6 August 1810]   Supervisor District # _____

Written Page No.	Printed Page No.	Name of Head of Family	Free White Males					Free White Females					All other free persons except Indians not taxed	Slaves
			under 10	of 10 & under 16	of 16 & under 26 including heads of families	of 26 & under 45	of 45 & up	under 10	of 10 & under 16	of 16 & under 26 including heads of families	of 26 & under 45	of 45 & up		

UNPUZZLING YOUR PAST WORKBOOK

1820 Census

[Official census day—7 August 1820, first Monday]

Local Community _____ County _____ State _____

Enumerator _____ Date Census Taken _____ Enumerator District # _____

Supervisor District # _____

Written Page No.	Printed Page No.	Name of Head of Family	Free White Males including heads of families						Free White Females including heads of families						Foreigners Not Naturalized	Persons engaged in Agriculture	Persons engaged in Commerce	Persons engaged in Manufacture	Free Colored Persons								All other persons	Slaves
																			Males			Females					
			10 to 10	10 to 16	*16 to 18	16 to 26	26 to 45	45 & up	10 to 10	10 to 16	16 to 26	26 to 45	45 & up						14 to 14	14 to 26	26 to 45	45 & up	14 to 14	14 to 26	26 to 45	45 & up		

*Those males between 16 & 18 will all be repeated in the column of those between 16 and 26.

1820 Census

Local Community ——————

Enumerator ——————

County ——————

Date Census Taken ——————

[Official census day—7 August 1820, first Monday]

State ——————

Enumerator District # ——————

Supervisor District # ——————

Written Page No.	Printed Page No.	Name of Head of Family	Free White Males including heads of families							Free White Females including heads of families							Foreigners Not Naturalized	Persons engaged in Agriculture	Persons engaged in Commerce	Persons engaged in Manufacture	Free Colored Persons												All other persons	Slaves
																					Males				Females							
			10 to 10	10 to 16	*16 to 18	16 to 26	26 to 45	45 & up		10 to 10	10 to 16	16 to 26	26 to 45	45 & up						to 14	14 to 26	26 to 45	45 & up	to 14	14 to 26	26 to 45	45 & up		

*Those males between 16 & 18 will all be repeated in the column of those between 16 and 26.

1820 Census

Local Community _____

Enumerator _____

County _____ State _____

Date Census Taken _____ Enumerator District # _____

[Official census day—7 August 1820, first Monday] Supervisor District # _____

Written Page No.	Printed Page No.	Name of Head of Family	Free White Males						Free White Females						Foreigners Not Naturalized	Persons engaged in Agriculture	Persons engaged in Commerce	Persons engaged in Manufacture	Free Colored Persons								All other persons	Slaves
			to 10	10 to 16	*16 to 18	including heads of families 16 to 26	26 to 45	45 & up	to 10	10 to 16	including heads of families 16 to 26	26 to 45	45 & up					Males to 14	14 to 26	26 to 45	45 & up	Females to 14	14 to 26	26 to 45	45 & up		

*Those males between 16 & 18 will all be repeated in the column of those between 16 and 26.

1820 Census

Local Community _____

Enumerator _____

County _____ State _____

Date Census Taken _____ Enumerator District # _____

[Official census day—7 August 1820, first Monday] Supervisor District # _____

Written Page No.	Printed Page No.	Name of Head of Family	Free White Males						Free White Females					Foreigners Not Naturalized	Persons engaged in Agriculture	Persons engaged in Commerce	Persons engaged in Manufacture	Free Colored Persons								All other persons	Slaves
			to 10	10 to 16	*16 to 18	16 to 26	26 to 45	45 & up	to 10	10 to 16	16 to 26	26 to 45	45 & up					Males to 14	14 to 26	26 to 45	45 & up	Females to 14	14 to 26	26 to 45	45 & up		

*Those males between 16 & 18 will all be repeated in the column of those between 16 and 26.

1830 or 1840 Census—Part 1

Local Community _____ County _____ State _____

Enumerator _____ Date Census Taken _____ Enumerator District # _____

[Official census day—1 June 1830-1840] Supervisor District # _____

Written Page No.	Printed Page No.	Name of Head of Family	Free White Persons (including heads of families)																								
			Males													Females											
			under 5	5-10	10-15	15-20	20-30	30-40	40-50	50-60	60-70	70-80	80-90	90-100	100 & over	under 5	5-10	10-15	15-20	20-30	30-40	40-50	50-60	60-70	70-80	80-90	90-100	100 & over

UNPUZZLING YOUR PAST WORKBOOK

1830 or 1840 Census—Part 1

Local Community _____ County _____ State _____

Enumerator _____ Date Census Taken _____ Enumerator District # _____

[Official census day—1 June 1830-1840] Supervisor District # _____

Written Page No.	Printed Page No.	Name of Head of Family	Free White Persons (including heads of families)																								
			Males													Females											
			under 5	5-10	10-15	15-20	20-30	30-40	40-50	50-60	60-70	70-80	80-90	90-100	100 & over	under 5	5-10	10-15	15-20	20-30	30-40	40-50	50-60	60-70	70-80	80-90	90-100	100 & over

UNPUZZLING YOUR PAST WORKBOOK

1830 or 1840 Census—Part 1

Local Community _____ County _____ State _____

Enumerator _____ Date Census Taken _____ Enumerator District # _____

[Official census day—1 June 1830-1840] Supervisor District # _____

Written Page No.	Printed Page No.	Name of Head of Family	Free White Persons (including heads of families)																									
			Males													Females												
			under 5	5-10	10-15	15-20	20-30	30-40	40-50	50-60	60-70	70-80	80-90	90-100	100 & over	under 5	5-10	10-15	15-20	20-30	30-40	40-50	50-60	60-70	70-80	80-90	90-100	100 & over

UNPUZZLING YOUR PAST WORKBOOK

1830 or 1840 Census—Part 1

Local Community _____ County _____ State _____

Enumerator _____ Date Census Taken _____ Enumerator District # _____

[Official census day—1 June 1830-1840] Supervisor District # _____

UNPUZZLING YOUR PAST WORKBOOK

Written Page No.	Printed Page No.	Name of Head of Family	Free White Persons (including heads of families)																								
			Males														Females										
			under 5	5-10	10-15	15-20	20-30	30-40	40-50	50-60	60-70	70-80	80-90	90-100	100 & over	under 5	5-10	10-15	15-20	20-30	30-40	40-50	50-60	60-70	70-80	80-90	90-100	100 & over

1830 Census—Part 2

Local Community ——————

Enumerator ——————

County ——————

Date Census Taken ——————

[Official census day—1 June 1830]

State ——————

Enumerator District # ——————

Supervisor District # ——————

Written Page No.	Printed Page No.	Name of Head of Family (from previous page)	Slaves — Males						Slaves — Females						Free Colored Persons — Males						Free Colored Persons — Females						TOTAL	White Persons included in the foregoing who are				Slaves & Colored Persons included in the foregoing who are			
			under 10	10 - 24	24 - 36	36 - 55	55 - 100	100 & up	under 10	10 - 24	24 - 36	36 - 55	55 - 100	100 & up	under 10	10 - 24	24 - 36	36 - 55	55 - 100	100 & up	under 10	10 - 24	24 - 36	36 - 55	55 - 100	100 & up		deaf & dumb under 14	deaf & dumb 14 - 25	deaf & dumb 25 & up	blind	foreigners not naturalized	deaf & dumb under 14	deaf & dumb 14 - 25	deaf & dumb 25 & up	blind

1830 Census—Part 2

Local Community _____

Enumerator _____

County _____

Date Census Taken _____

State _____

Enumerator District # _____

Supervisor District # _____

[Official census day—1 June 1830]

Written Page No.	Printed Page No.	Name of Head of Family (from previous page)	Slaves — Males						Slaves — Females						Free Colored Persons — Males						Free Colored Persons — Females						TOTAL	White Persons included in the foregoing who are					Slaves & Colored Persons included in the foregoing who are			
			under 10	10 - 24	24 - 36	36 - 55	55 - 100	100 & up	under 10	10 - 24	24 - 36	36 - 55	55 - 100	100 & up	under 10	10 - 24	24 - 36	36 - 55	55 - 100	100 & up	under 10	10 - 24	24 - 36	36 - 55	55 - 100	100 & up		deaf & dumb under 14	deaf & dumb 14 - 25	deaf & dumb 25 & up	blind	foreigners not naturalized	deaf & dumb under 14	deaf & dumb 14 - 25	deaf & dumb 25 & up	blind

1830 Census—Part 2

Local Community _____

Enumerator _____

County _____

Date Census Taken _____

State _____

Enumerator District # _____

Supervisor District # _____

[Official census day—1 June 1830]

Written Page No.	Printed Page No.	Name of Head of Family (from previous page)	Slaves												Free Colored Persons												TOTAL	White Persons included in the foregoing who are					Slaves & Colored Persons included in the foregoing who are			
			Males						Females						Males						Females							deaf & dumb under 14	deaf & dumb 14-25	deaf & dumb 25 & up	blind	foreigners not naturalized	deaf & dumb under 14	deaf & dumb 14-25	deaf & dumb 25 & up	blind
			under 10	10-24	24-36	36-55	55-100	100 & up	under 10	10-24	24-36	36-55	55-100	100 & up	under 10	10-24	24-36	36-55	55-100	100 & up	under 10	10-24	24-36	36-55	55-100	100 & up										

1830 Census—Part 2

Local Community _____ County _____ State _____

Enumerator _____ Date Census Taken _____ Enumerator District # _____

[Official census day—1 June 1830] Supervisor District # _____

UNPUZZLING YOUR PAST WORKBOOK

Written Page No.	Printed Page No.	Name of Head of Family (from previous page)	Slaves												Free Colored Persons												T O T A L	White Persons included in the foregoing who are					Slaves & Colored Persons included in the foregoing who are			
			Males						Females						Males						Females															
			under 10	10 - 24	24 - 36	36 - 55	55 - 100	100 & up	under 10	10 - 24	24 - 36	36 - 55	55 - 100	100 & up	under 10	10 - 24	24 - 36	36 - 55	55 - 100	100 & up	under 10	10 - 24	24 - 36	36 - 55	55 - 100	100 & up		deaf & dumb under 14	deaf & dumb 14 - 25	deaf & dumb 25 & up	blind	foreigners not naturalized	deaf & dumb under 14	deaf & dumb 14 - 25	deaf & dumb 25 & up	blind

1840 Census—Part 2

Local Community _____ County _____ State _____

Enumerator _____ Date Census Taken _____ Enumerator District # _____

[Official census day—1 June 1840] Supervisor District # _____

UNPUZZLING YOUR PAST WORKBOOK

Written Page No.	Printed Page No.	Name of Head of Family (Previous Page)	Slaves												Free Colored Persons													TOTAL	Number of Persons employed in each family in								Revolutionary or Military Service Pensioners in the foregoing	
			Males						Females						Males						Females								Mining	Agriculture	Commerce	Manufacturing & Trades	Ocean Navigation	Canal, Lake, River Navigat'n	Learned Prof'ns & Engineers		Name	Age
			under 10	10 - 24	24 - 36	36 - 55	55 - 100	100 & up	under 10	10 - 24	24 - 36	36 - 55	55 - 100	100 & up	under 10	10 - 24	24 - 36	36 - 55	55 - 100	100 & up	under 10	10 - 24	24 - 36	36 - 55	55 - 100	100 & up											

1840 Census—Part 2

Local Community _____ County _____ State _____

Enumerator _____ Date Census Taken _____ Enumerator District # _____

[Official census day—1 June 1840] Supervisor District # _____

UNPUZZLING YOUR PAST WORKBOOK

Written Page No.	Printed Page No.	Name of Head of Family (Previous Page)	Slaves												Free Colored Persons												T O T A L	Number of Persons employed in each family in							Revolutionary or Military Service Pensioners in the foregoing	
			Males						Females						Males						Females							Mining	Agriculture	Commerce	Manufacturing & Trades	Ocean Navigation	Canal, Lake, River Navigat'n	Learned Prof'ns & Engineers	Name	Age
			under 10	10 - 24	24 - 36	36 - 55	55 - 100	100 & up	under 10	10 - 24	24 - 36	36 - 55	55 - 100	100 & up	under 10	10 - 24	24 - 36	36 - 55	55 - 100	100 & up	under 10	10 - 24	24 - 36	36 - 55	55 - 100	100 & up										

1840 Census—Part 2

Local Community ——————

Enumerator ——————

State ——————

County ——————

Date Census Taken ——————

Enumerator District # ——————

Supervisor District # ——————

[Official census day—1 June 1840]

Written Page No.	Printed Page No.	Name of Head of Family (Previous Page)	Slaves — Males						Slaves — Females						Free Colored Persons — Males						Free Colored Persons — Females						TOTAL	Number of Persons employed in each family in — Mining	Agriculture	Commerce	Manufacturing & Trades	Ocean Navigation	Canal, Lake, River Navigat'n	Learned Prof'ns & Engineers	Revolutionary or Military Service Pensioners in the foregoing — Name	Age
			under 10	10 - 24	24 - 36	36 - 55	55 - 100	100 & up	under 10	10 - 24	24 - 36	36 - 55	55 - 100	100 & up	under 10	10 - 24	24 - 36	36 - 55	55 - 100	100 & up	under 10	10 - 24	24 - 36	36 55	55 - 100	100 & up										

1840 Census—Part 2

Local Community _____ County _____ State _____

Enumerator _____ Date Census Taken _____ Enumerator District # _____

[Official census day—1 June 1840] Supervisor District # _____

UNPUZZLING YOUR PAST WORKBOOK

Written Page No.	Printed Page No.	Name of Head of Family (Previous Page)	Slaves Males						Slaves Females						Free Colored Persons Males						Free Colored Persons Females						TOTAL	Number of Persons employed in each family in							Revolutionary or Military Service Pensioners in the foregoing	
			under 10	10 - 24	24 - 36	36 - 55	55 - 100	100 & up	under 10	10 - 24	24 - 36	36 - 55	55 - 100	100 & up	under 10	10 - 24	24 - 36	36 - 55	55 - 100	100 & up	under 10	10 - 24	24 - 36	36 - 55	55 - 100	100 & up		Mining	Agriculture	Commerce	Manufacturing & Trades	Ocean Navigation	Canal, Lake, River Navigat'n	Learned Prof'ns & Engineers	Name	Age

1850 Census

UNPUZZLING YOUR PAST WORKBOOK

Post Office or Local Community _____ County _____ State _____

Enumerator _____ Date Census Taken _____ Enumerator District # _____

[Official census day—1 June 1850] Supervisor District # _____

Written Page No.	Printed Page No.	Dwelling in order of visitation	Family Number in order of visitation	Name of every person whose usual place of abode on 1 June 1850 was with this family	Description			Profession, Occupation, or Trade of each Male over 15	Value of of Real Estate Owned	Place of Birth naming state, territory, or country	Married within the year	In school within the year	Persons over 20 unable to read & write	If deaf & dumb, blind, insane, idiot, pauper or convict
					Age	Sex	Color							
		1	2	3	4	5	6	7	8	9	10	11	12	13

1850 Census

Post Office or Local Community _____ County _____ State _____

Enumerator _____ Date Census Taken _____ Enumerator District # _____

[Official census day—1 June 1850] Supervisor District # _____

UNPUZZLING YOUR PAST WORKBOOK

Written Page No.	Printed Page No.	Dwelling in order of visitation	Family Number in order of visitation	Name of every person whose usual place of abode on 1 June 1850 was with this family	Description			Profession, Occupation, or Trade of each Male over 15	Value of of Real Estate Owned	Place of Birth naming state, territory, or country	Married within the year	In school within the year	Persons over 20 unable to read & write	If deaf & dumb, blind, insane, idiot, pauper or convict
					Age	Sex	Color							
		1	2	3	4	5	6	7	8	9	10	11	12	13

1850 Census

UNPUZZLING YOUR PAST WORKBOOK

Post Office or Local Community _____ County _____ State _____

Enumerator _____ Date Census Taken _____ Enumerator District # _____

[Official census day—1 June 1850] Supervisor District # _____

Written Page No.	Printed Page No.	Dwelling in order of visitation	Family Number in order of visitation	Name of every person whose usual place of abode on 1 June 1850 was with this family	Description			Profession, Occupation, or Trade of each Male over 15	Value of of Real Estate Owned	Place of Birth naming state, territory, or country	Married within the year	In school within the year	Persons over 20 unable to read & write	If deaf & dumb, blind, insane, idiot, pauper or convict
					Age	Sex	Color							
		1	2	3	4	5	6	7	8	9	10	11	12	13

1850 Census

Post Office or Local Community —————

Enumerator —————

County —————

Date Census Taken —————

[Official census day—1 June 1850]

State —————

Enumerator District # —————

Supervisor District # —————

Written Page No.	Printed Page No.	Dwelling in order of visitation	Family Number in order of visitation	Name of every person whose usual place of abode on 1 June 1850 was with this family	Description			Profession, Occupation, or Trade of each Male over 15	Value of of Real Estate Owned	Place of Birth naming state, territory, or country	Married within the year	In school within the year	Persons over 20 unable to read & write	If deaf & dumb, blind, insane, idiot, pauper or convict
					Age	Sex	Color							
		1	2	3	4	5	6	7	8	9	10	11	12	13

1850 Census

County ——————

State ——————

Date Census Taken ——————

Enumerator District # ——————

Supervisor District # ——————

[Official census day—1 June 1850]

Written Page No.	Printed Page No.	Dwelling in order of visitation	Family Number in order of visitation	Name of every person whose usual place of abode on 1 June 1850 was with this family	Description			Profession, Occupation, or Trade of each Male over 15	Value of of Real Estate Owned	Place of Birth naming state, territory, or country	Married within the year	In school within the year	Persons over 20 unable to read & write	If deaf & dumb, blind, insane, idiot, pauper or convict
					Age	Sex	Color							
		1	2	3	4	5	6	7	8	9	10	11	12	13

1860 Census

Post Office or Local Community ————————

Enumerator ————————

County ————————

Date Census Taken ————————

[Official census day—1 June 1860]

State ————————

Enumerator District # ————————

Supervisor District # ————————

Written Page No.	Printed Page No.	Dwelling Number	Family Number	Name of every person whose usual place of abode on 1 June 1860 was with this family	Description			Profession, Occupation, or Trade of each person over 15	Value of Real Estate Owned	Value of Personal Estate Owned	Place of Birth naming state, territory or country	Married within the year	In school within the year	Persons over 20 unable to read & write	Deaf & dumb, blind, insane, idiotic, pauper or convict
					Age	Sex	Color								
		1	2	3	4	5	6	7	8	9	10	11	12	13	14

1860 Census

Post Office or Local Community _____ State _____

Enumerator _____ Date Census Taken _____ Enumerator District # _____

County _____ [Official census day—1 June 1860] Supervisor District # _____

Written Page No.	Printed Page No.	Dwelling Number	Family Number	Name of every person whose usual place of abode on 1 June 1860 was with this family	Description			Profession, Occupation, or Trade of each person over 15	Value of Real Estate Owned	Value of Personal Estate Owned	Place of Birth naming state, territory or country	Married within the year	In school within the year	Persons over 20 unable to read & write	Deaf & dumb, blind, insane, idiotic, pauper or convict
					Age	Sex	Color								
		1	2	3	4	5	6	7	8	9	10	11	12	13	14

1860 Census

Post Office or Local Community _____

Enumerator _____

County _____   State _____

Date Census Taken _____   Enumerator District # _____

[Official census day—1 June 1860]   Supervisor District # _____

Written Page No.	Printed Page No.	Dwelling Number (1)	Family Number (2)	Name of every person whose usual place of abode on 1 June 1860 was with this family (3)	Age (4)	Sex (5)	Color (6)	Profession, Occupation, or Trade of each person over 15 (7)	Value of Real Estate Owned (8)	Value of Personal Estate Owned (9)	Place of Birth naming state, territory or country (10)	Married within the year (11)	In school within the year (12)	Persons over 20 unable to read & write (13)	Deaf & dumb, blind, insane, idiotic, pauper or convict (14)

Note: Columns 4, 5, 6 are grouped under "Description".

1860 Census

Post Office or Local Community _____ County _____ State _____

Enumerator _____ Date Census Taken _____ Enumerator District # _____

[Official census day—1 June 1860]

Supervisor District # _____

Written Page No.	Printed Page No.	Dwelling Number	Family Number	Name of every person whose usual place of abode on 1 June 1860 was with this family	Description			Profession, Occupation, or Trade of each person over 15	Value of Real Estate Owned	Value of Personal Estate Owned	Place of Birth naming state, territory or country	Married within the year	In school within the year	Persons over 20 unable to read & write	Deaf & dumb, blind, insane, idiotic, pauper or convict
					Age	Sex	Color								
		1	2	3	4	5	6	7	8	9	10	11	12	13	14

UNPUZZLING YOUR PAST WORKBOOK

1860 Census

Post Office or Local Community _____ County _____ State _____

Enumerator _____ Date Census Taken _____ Enumerator District # _____

[Official census day—1 June 1860] Supervisor District # _____

Written Page No.	Printed Page No.	Dwelling Number	Family Number	Name of every person whose usual place of abode on 1 June 1860 was with this family	Description			Profession, Occupation, or Trade of each person over 15	Value of Real Estate Owned	Value of Personal Estate Owned	Place of Birth naming state, territory or country	Married within the year	In school within the year	Persons over 20 unable to read & write	Deaf & dumb, blind, insane, idiotic, pauper or convict
					Age	Sex	Color								
		1	2	3	4	5	6	7	8	9	10	11	12	13	14

UNPUZZLING YOUR PAST WORKBOOK

1850 or 1860 Census   Schedule 2—Slaves

Local Community ———————

Enumerator ———————

County ———————   Date Census Taken ———————

State ———————   [Official census day—1 June]

Written Page No.	Printed Page No.	Names of Slave Owners 1	Number of Slaves 2	Description			Fugitives from the State 6	Number Manumitted 7	Deaf & dumb, blind, insane or idiotic 8	Number of Slave Houses 9
				Age 3	Sex 4	Color 5				
		1								
		2								
		3								
		4								
		5								
		6								
		7								
		8								
		9								
		10								
		11								
		12								
		13								
		14								

Names of Slave Owners 1	Number of Slaves 2	Description			Fugitives from the State 6	Number Manumitted 7	Deaf & dumb, blind, insane or idiotic 8	Number of Slave Houses 9
		Age 3	Sex 4	Color 5				
1								
2								
3								
4								
5								
6								
7								
8								
9								
10								
11								
12								
13								
14								

1850 or 1860 Census   Schedule 2—Slaves

Local Community _____   County _____   State _____

Enumerator _____   Date Census Taken _____   [Official census day—1 June]

Written Page No.	Printed Page No.	Names of Slave Owners (1)	Number of Slaves (2)	Description						
				Age (3)	Sex (4)	Color (5)	Fugitives from the State (6)	Number Manumitted (7)	Deaf & dumb, blind, insane or idiotic (8)	Number of Slave Houses (9)
		1								
		2								
		3								
		4								
		5								
		6								
		7								
		8								
		9								
		10								
		11								
		12								
		13								
		14								

Written Page No.	Printed Page No.	Names of Slave Owners (1)	Number of Slaves (2)	Description						
				Age (3)	Sex (4)	Color (5)	Fugitives from the State (6)	Number Manumitted (7)	Deaf & dumb, blind, insane or idiotic (8)	Number of Slave Houses (9)
		1								
		2								
		3								
		4								
		5								
		6								
		7								
		8								
		9								
		10								
		11								
		12								
		13								
		14								

1850 or 1860 Census   Schedule 2—Slaves

Local Community _____ County _____ State _____

Enumerator _____ Date Census Taken _____ [Official census day—1 June]

UNPUZZLING YOUR PAST WORKBOOK

Written Page No.	Printed Page No.	Names of Slave Owners	Number of Slaves	Description			Fugitives from the State	Number Manumitted	Deaf & dumb, blind, insane or idiotic	Number of Slave Houses	Names of Slave Owners	Number of Slaves	Description			Fugitives from the State	Number Manumitted	Deaf & dumb, blind, insane or idiotic	Number of Slave Houses
				Age	Sex	Color							Age	Sex	Color				
		1	2	3	4	5	6	7	8	9	1	2	3	4	5	6	7	8	9
		1									1								
		2									2								
		3									3								
		4									4								
		5									5								
		6									6								
		7									7								
		8									8								
		9									9								
		10									10								
		11									11								
		12									12								
		13									13								
		14									14								

1850 or 1860 Census   Schedule 2—Slaves

Local Community _____ County _____ State _____

Enumerator _____ Date Census Taken _____ [Official census day—1 June]

UNPUZZLING YOUR PAST WORKBOOK

Written Page No.	Printed Page No.	Names of Slave Owners	Number of Slaves	Description			Fugitives from the State	Number Manumitted	Deaf & dumb, blind, insane or idiotic	Number of Slave Houses	Names of Slave Owners	Number of Slaves	Description			Fugitives from the State	Number Manumitted	Deaf & dumb, blind, insane or idiotic	Number of Slave Houses
				Age	Sex	Color							Age	Sex	Color				
		1	2	3	4	5	6	7	8	9	1	2	3	4	5	6	7	8	9
		1									1								
		2									2								
		3									3								
		4									4								
		5									5								
		6									6								
		7									7								
		8									8								
		9									9								
		10									10								
		11									11								
		12									12								
		13									13								
		14									14								

1850 or 1860 Census   Schedule 2—Slaves

Local Community _____ County _____ State _____

Enumerator _____ Date Census Taken _____ [Official census day—1 June]

UNPUZZLING YOUR PAST WORKBOOK

Written Page No.	Printed Page No.	Names of Slave Owners	Number of Slaves	Description			Fugitives from the State	Number Manumitted	Deaf & dumb, blind, insane or idiotic	Number of Slave Houses	Names of Slave Owners	Number of Slaves	Description			Fugitives from the State	Number Manumitted	Deaf & dumb, blind, insane or idiotic	Number of Slave Houses
				Age	Sex	Color							Age	Sex	Color				
		1	2	3	4	5	6	7	8	9	1	2	3	4	5	6	7	8	9
		1									1								
		2									2								
		3									3								
		4									4								
		5									5								
		6									6								
		7									7								
		8									8								
		9									9								
		10									10								
		11									11								
		12									12								
		13									13								
		14									14								

1870 Census

Local Community _____ County _____ State _____

Enumerator _____ Date Census Taken _____ Enumerator District # _____

[Official census day—1 June 1870] Supervisor District # _____

Written Page No.	Printed Page No.	Dwelling No.	Family No.	Name of every person whose place of abode on 1 June 1870 was in this family	Description			Profession, Occupation, or Trade	Value of		Place of Birth	Parents		Month born within the year	Month married within the year	In school within the year	Cannot read	Cannot write	Deaf & dumb, blind, insane or idiotic	Males eligible to vote	Males not eligible to vote
					Age	Sex	Color		Real Estate Owned	Personal Estate Owned		Father Foreign-born	Mother Foreign-born								
		1	2	3	4	5	6	7	8	9	10	11	12	13	14	15	16	17	18	19	20

UNPUZZLING YOUR PAST WORKBOOK

1870 Census

Local Community _____

Enumerator _____

County _____

Date Census Taken _____

[Official census day—1 June 1870]

State _____

Enumerator District # _____

Supervisor District # _____

Written Page No.	Printed Page No.	Dwelling No.	Family No.	Name of every person whose place of abode on 1 June 1870 was in this family	Description			Profession, Occupation, or Trade	Value of		Place of Birth	Parents		Month born within the year	Month married within the year	In school within the year	Cannot read	Cannot write	Deaf & dumb, blind, insane or idiotic	Male eligible to vote	Males not eligible to vote
					Age	Sex	Color		Real Estate Owned	Personal Estate Owned		Father Foreign-born	Mother Foreign-born								
		1	2	3	4	5	6	7	8	9	10	11	12	13	14	15	16	17	18	19	20

1870 Census

Local Community _____ County _____ State _____

Enumerator _____ Date Census Taken _____ Enumerator District # _____

[Official census day—1 June 1870] Supervisor District # _____

UNPUZZLING YOUR PAST WORKBOOK

| Written Page No. | Printed Page No. | Dwelling No. | Family No. | Name of every person whose place of abode on 1 June 1870 was in this family | Description | | | Profession, Occupation, or Trade | Value of | | Place of Birth | Parents | | Month born within the year | Month married within the year | In school within the year | Cannot read | Cannot write | Deaf & dumb, blind, insane or idiotic | Males eligible to vote | Males not eligible to vote |
					Age	Sex	Color		Real Estate Owned	Personal Estate Owned		Father Foreign-born	Mother Foreign-born								
		1	2	3	4	5	6	7	8	9	10	11	12	13	14	15	16	17	18	19	20

1870 Census

Local Community ———————

Enumerator ———————

County ———————

Date Census Taken ———————

[Official census day—1 June 1870]

State ———————

Enumerator District # ———————

Supervisor District # ———————

Written Page No.	Printed Page No.	1 Dwelling No.	2 Family No.	3 Name of every person whose place of abode on 1 June 1870 was in this family	Description			Profession, Occupation, or Trade	Value of		Place of Birth	Parents		13 Month born within the year	14 Month married within the year	15 In school within the year	16 Cannot read	17 Cannot write	18 Deaf & dumb, blind, insane or idiotic	19 Males eligible to vote	20 Males not eligible to vote
					4 Age	5 Sex	6 Color	7	8 Real Estate Owned	9 Personal Estate Owned	10	11 Father Foreign-born	12 Mother Foreign-born								

Local Community ———
Enumerator ———

County ———
Date Census Taken ———

[Official census day—1 June 1870]

State ———
Enumerator District # ———
Supervisor District # ———

Written Page No.	Printed Page No.	1 Dwelling No.	2 Family No.	3 Name of every person whose place of abode on 1 June 1870 was in this family	Description			7 Profession, Occupation, or Trade	Value of		10 Place of Birth	Parents		13 Month born within the year	14 Month married within the year	15 In school within the year	16 Cannot read	17 Cannot write	18 Deaf & dumb, blind, insane or idiotic	19 Males eligible to vote	20 Males not eligible to vote
					4 Age	5 Sex	6 Color		8 Real Estate Owned	9 Personal Estate Owned		11 Father Foreign-born	12 Mother Foreign-born								

1880 Census

Local Community ——————
Enumerator ——————

—————— County
Date Census Taken ——————

[Official census day—1 June 1880]

—————— State
—————— Supervisor District #
—————— Enumerator District #

Written Page No.	Printed Page No.	Street Name	House Number	1 Dwelling Number	2 Family Number	3 Name of every person whose place of abode on 1 June 1880 was in this family	4 Color	5 Sex	6 Age	7 Month born if during census year	8 Relationship to head of this household	9 Single	10 Married	11 Widowed / Divorced	12 Married during year	13 Profession, Occupation or Trade	14 Months unemployed this year	15 Currently ill? If so, specify.	16 Blind	17 Deaf & dumb	18 Idiotic	19 Insane	20 Disabled	21 School this year	22 Cannot read	23 Cannot write	24 Birthplace	25 Birthplace of Father	26 Birthplace of Mother

Description: columns 4–6 (Color, Sex, Age). *Health:* columns 16–20 (Blind, Deaf & dumb, Idiotic, Insane, Disabled).

1880 Census

Local Community ————————

Enumerator ————————

County ————————

Date Census Taken ————————

[Official census day—1 June 1880]

State ————————

Supervisor District # ————————

Enumerator District # ————————

Written Page No.	Printed Page No.	Street Name	House Number	Dwelling Number (1)	Family Number (2)	Name of every person whose place of abode on 1 June 1880 was in this family (3)	Description				Relationship to head of this household (8)	Single (9)	Married (10)	Widowed / Divorced (11)	Married during year (12)	Profession, Occupation or Trade (13)	Months unemployed this year (14)	Health						School this year (21)	Cannot read (22)	Cannot write (23)	Birthplace (24)	Birthplace of Father (25)	Birthplace of Mother (26)
							Color (4)	Sex (5)	Age (6)	Month born if during census year (7)								Currently ill? If so, specify. (15)	Blind (16)	Deaf & dumb (17)	Idiotic (18)	Insane (19)	Disabled (20)						

1880 Census

Local Community ——————
Enumerator ——————

County ——————
Date Census Taken ——————
[Official census day—1 June 1880]

State ——————
Supervisor District # ——————
Enumerator District # ——————

Written Page No.	Printed Page No.	Street Name	House Number	Dwelling Number (1)	Family Number (2)	Name of every person whose place of abode on 1 June 1880 was in this family (3)	Color (4)	Sex (5)	Age (6)	Month born if during census year (7)	Relationship to head of this household (8)	Single (9)	Married (10)	Widowed / Divorced (11)	Married during year (12)	Profession, Occupation or Trade (13)	Months unemployed this year (14)	Currently ill? If so, specify. (15)	Blind (16)	Deaf & dumb (17)	Idiotic (18)	Insane (19)	Disabled (20)	School this year (21)	Cannot read (22)	Cannot write (23)	Birthplace (24)	Birthplace of Father (25)	Birthplace of Mother (26)

Description spans columns 4–6 (Color, Sex, Age). *Health* spans columns 16–20 (Blind, Deaf & dumb, Idiotic, Insane, Disabled).

1880 Census

Local Community ―――――――
Enumerator ―――――――
County ―――――――
Date Census Taken ―――――――
State ―――――――
Supervisor District # ―――――――
Enumerator District # ―――――――

[Official census day—1 June 1880]

Col. No.	Heading
	Written Page No.
	Printed Page No.
	Street Name
	House Number
1	Dwelling Number
2	Family Number
3	Name of every person whose place of abode on 1 June 1880 was in this family
	Description
4	Color
5	Sex
6	Age
7	Month born if during census year
8	Relationship to head of this household
9	Single
10	Married
11	Widowed / Divorced
12	Married during year
13	Profession, Occupation or Trade
14	Months unemployed this year
15	Currently ill? If so, specify.
	Health
16	Blind
17	Deaf & dumb
18	Idiotic
19	Insane
20	Disabled
21	School this year
22	Cannot read
23	Cannot write
24	Birthplace
25	Birthplace of Father
26	Birthplace of Mother

1880 Census

Local Community _____ County _____ State _____

Enumerator _____ Date Census Taken _____ Supervisor District # _____

[Official census day—1 June 1880] Enumerator District # _____

Written Page No.	Printed Page No.	Street Name	House Number	Dwelling Number	Family Number	Name of every person whose place of abode on 1 June 1880 was in this family	Description			Month born if during census year	Relationship to head of this household	Single	Married	Widowed / Divorced	Married during year	Profession, Occupation or Trade	Months unemployed this year	Currently ill? If so, specify.	Health					School this year	Cannot read	Cannot write	Birthplace	Birthplace of Father	Birthplace of Mother
							Color	Sex	Age										Blind	Deaf & dumb	Idiotic	Insane	Disabled						
				1	2	3	4	5	6	7	8	9	10	11	12	13	14	15	16	17	18	19	20	21	22	23	24	25	26

UNPUZZLING YOUR PAST WORKBOOK

1900 Census

Local Community _____ County _____ State _____

Ward _____ [Official census day—1 June 1900] Supervisor District # _____

Enumerator _____ Date Census Taken _____ Enumeration District # _____

Written Page No.	Printed Page No.	Street	House Number	Dwelling Number	Family Number	Name of every person whose place of abode on 1 June 1900 was in this family	Relationship to head of family	Color	Sex	Birth Date Month	Birth Date Year	Age	Marital status	# Years married	Mother of how many children?	# of these children living	Birthplace of This Person	Birthplace of This Person's Father	Birthplace of This Person's Mother	Year of Immigration	# Years in U.S.	Naturalized Citizen	Occupation of every person 10 & older	# months not employed	# months in school	Can read	Can write	Speaks English	Owned or rented	Owned free of mortgage	Farm or house	No. of farm schedule
			1	2		3	4	5	6	7		8	9	10	11	12	13	14	15	16	17	18	19	20	21	22	23	24	25	26	27	28

UNPUZZLING YOUR PAST WORKBOOK

1900 Census

UNPUZZLING YOUR PAST WORKBOOK

Local Community _____ County _____ State _____

Ward _____ [Official census day—1 June 1900] Supervisor District # _____

Enumerator _____ Date Census Taken _____ Enumeration District # _____

Written Page No.	Printed Page No.	Street	House Number	Dwelling Number	Family Number	Name of every person whose place of abode on 1 June 1900 was in this family	Relationship to head of family	Color	Sex	Birth Date		Age	Marital status	# Years married	Mother of how many children?	# of these children living	Birthplace of			Year of Immigration	# Years in U.S.	Naturalized Citizen	Occupation of every person 10 & older	# months not employed	Education				Owned or rented	Owned free of mortgage	Farm or house	No. of farm schedule
										Month	Year						This Person	This Person's Father	This Person's Mother						# months in school	Can read	Can write	Speaks English				
			1	2		3	4	5	6	7		8	9	10	11	12	13	14	15	16	17	18	19	20	21	22	23	24	25	26	27	28

1900 Census

Local Community _____ County _____ State _____

Ward _____ [Official census day—1 June 1900] Supervisor District # _____

Enumerator _____ Date Census Taken _____ Enumeration District # _____

UNPUZZLING YOUR PAST WORKBOOK

Written Page No.	Printed Page No.	Street	House Number	Dwelling Number	Family Number	Name of every person whose place of abode on 1 June 1900 was in this family	Relationship to head of family	Color	Sex	Birth Date Month	Birth Date Year	Age	Marital status	# Years married	Mother of how many children?	# of these children living	Birthplace of This Person	Birthplace of This Person's Father	Birthplace of This Person's Mother	Year of Immigration	# Years in U.S.	Naturalized Citizen	Occupation of every person 10 & older	# months not employed	# months in school	Can read	Can write	Speaks English	Owned or rented	Owned free of mortgage	Farm or house	No. of farm schedule
			1	2		3	4	5	6	7		8	9	10	11	12	13	14	15	16	17	18	19	20	21	22	23	24	25	26	27	28

1900 Census

UNPUZZLING YOUR PAST WORKBOOK

Local Community _____ County _____ State _____

Ward _____ [Official census day—1 June 1900] Supervisor District # _____

Enumerator _____ Date Census Taken _____ Enumeration District # _____

Written Page No.	Printed Page No.	Street	House Number	Dwelling Number	Family Number	Name of every person whose place of abode on 1 June 1900 was in this family	Relationship to head of family	Color	Sex	Birth Date		Age	Marital status	# Years married	Mother of how many children?	# of these children living	Birthplace of			Year of Immigration	# Years in U.S.	Naturalized Citizen	Occupation		# months in school	Can read	Can write	Speaks English	Owned or rented	Owned free of mortgage	Farm or house	No. of farm schedule
										Month	Year						This Person	This Person's Father	This Person's Mother				Occupation of every person 10 & older	# months not employed								
		1	2			3	4	5	6	7		8	9	10	11	12	13	14	15	16	17	18	19	20	21	22	23	24	25	26	27	28

1900 Census

Local Community _____
Ward _____
Enumerator _____

State _____
Supervisor District # _____
Enumeration District # _____

County _____
[Official census day—1 June 1900]
Date Census Taken _____

Written Page No.	Printed Page No.	Street	House Number	Dwelling Number 1	Family Number 2	Name of every person whose place of abode on 1 June 1900 was in this family 3	Relationship to head of family 4	Color 5	Sex 6	Birth Date Month 7	Birth Date Year 7	Age 8	Marital status 9	# Years married 10	Mother of how many children? 11	# of these children living 12	Birthplace of This Person 13	Birthplace of This Person's Father 14	Birthplace of This Person's Mother 15	Year of Immigration 16	# Years in U.S. 17	Naturalized Citizen 18	Occupation of every person 10 & older 19	# months not employed 20	# months in school 21	Can read 22	Can write 23	Speaks English 24	Owned or rented 25	Owned free or mortgage 26	Farm or house 27	No. of farm schedule 28

1910 Census

Local Community _____
Ward _____
Enumerator _____

County _____
[Official census day—15 April 1910]
Date Census Taken _____

State _____
Supervisor's District # _____
Enumeration District # _____

Col.	Heading
	Page No.
	Street
	House No.
1	Dwelling No.
2	Family No.
3	Name of each person whose place of abode on 15 April 1910 was in this family
4	Relationship
5	Sex
6	Color
7	Age
8	Marital status
9	# Years—Present Marriage
10	Mother of how many children?
11	# living children
12	Birthplace of — This Person
13	Birthplace of — Father
14	Birthplace of — Mother
15	Year of Immigration
16	Naturalized or alien?
17	Speaks English? If not, give name of language.
18 / 19	Profession or Occupation & nature of business
20	Employer or Wage Earner or Working on Own Account
21	Out of work 15 April 1910?
22	# weeks out of work in 1909
23	Can read
24	Can write
25	School since 1 September 1909
26	Owned/rented
27	Owned free or mortgaged
28	Farm or house
29	No. of farm schedule
30	Civil War Veteran
31	Blind
32	Deaf & dumb

1910 Census

Local Community _____ County _____ State _____

Ward _____ [Official census day—15 April 1910] Supervisor's District # _____

Enumerator _____ Date Census Taken _____ Enumeration District # _____

UNPUZZLING YOUR PAST WORKBOOK

Page No.	Street	House No.	Dwelling No.	Family No.	Name of each person whose place of abode on 15 April 1910 was in this family	Relationship	Sex	Color	Age	Marital status	# Years— Present Marriage	Mother of how many children?	# living children	Birthplace of — This Person	Birthplace of — Father	Birthplace of — Mother	Year of Immigration	Naturalized or alien?	Speaks English? If not, give name of language.	Profession or Occupation & nature of business		Employer or Wage Earner or Working on Own Account	Out of work 15 April 1910?	# weeks out of work in 1909	Can read	Can write	School since 1 September 1909	Owned/rented	Owned free or mortgaged	Farm or house	No. of farm schedule	Civil War Veteran	Blind	Deaf & dumb
		1	2		3	4	5	6	7	8	9	10	11	12	13	14	15	16	17	18	19	20	21	22	23	24	25	26	27	28	29	30	31	32

1910 Census

Local Community ——————— County ——————— State ———————

Ward ——————— [Official census day—15 April 1910] Supervisor's District # ———————

Enumerator ——————— Date Census Taken ——————— Enumeration District # ———————

	Column	Label
		Page No.
		Street
		House No.
	1	Dwelling No.
	2	Family No.
	3	Name of each person whose place of abode on 15 April 1910 was in this family
	4	Relationship
	5	Sex
	6	Color
	7	Age
	8	Marital status
	9	# Years—Present Marriage
	10	Mother of how many children?
	11	# living children
Birthplace of	12	This Person
	13	Father
	14	Mother
	15	Year of Immigration
	16	Naturalized or alien?
	17	Speaks English? If not, give name of language.
Profession or Occupation & nature of business	18	
	19	
	20	Employer or Wage Earner or Working on Own Account
	21	Out of work 15 April 1910?
	22	# weeks out of work in 1909
	23	Can read
	24	Can write
	25	School since 1 September 1909
	26	Owned/rented
	27	Owned free or mortgaged
	28	Farm or house
	29	No. of farm schedule
	30	Civil War Veteran
	31	Blind
	32	Deaf & dumb

1910 Census

Local Community ——————
Ward ——————
Enumerator ——————

County ——————
[Official census day—15 April 1910]
Date Census Taken ——————

State ——————
Supervisor's District # ——————
Enumeration District # ——————

No.	Label
	Page No.
	Street
	House No.
1	Dwelling No.
2	Family No.
3	Name of each person whose place of abode on 15 April 1910 was in this family
4	Relationship
5	Sex
6	Color
7	Age
8	Marital status
9	# Years—Present Marriage
10	Mother of how many children?
11	# living children
12	Birthplace of: This Person
13	Father
14	Mother
15	Year of Immigration
16	Naturalized or alien?
17	Speaks English? If not, give name of language.
18	Profession or Occupation & nature of business
19	
20	Employer or Wage Earner or Working on Own Account
21	Out of work 15 April 1910?
22	# weeks out of work in 1909
23	Can read
24	Can write
25	School since 1 September 1909
26	Owned/rented
27	Owned free or mortgaged
28	Farm or house
29	No. of farm schedule
30	Civil War Veteran
31	Blind
32	Deaf & dumb

1910 Census

Local Community —————

Ward —————

Enumerator —————

County —————

[Official census day—15 April 1910]

Date Census Taken —————

State —————

Supervisor's District # —————

Enumeration District # —————

		Column
		Page No.
		Street
		House No.
	1	Dwelling No.
	2	Family No.
	3	Name of each person whose place of abode on 15 April 1910 was in this family
	4	Relationship
	5	Sex
	6	Color
	7	Age
	8	Marital status
	9	# Years—Present Marriage
	10	Mother of how many children?
	11	# living children
Birthplace of	12	This Person
	13	Father
	14	Mother
	15	Year of Immigration
	16	Naturalized or alien?
	17	Speaks English? If not, give name of language.
Profession or Occupation & nature of business	18	
	19	
	20	Employer or Wage Earner or Working on Own Account
	21	Out of work 15 April 1910?
	22	# weeks out of work in 1909
	23	Can read
	24	Can write
	25	School since 1 September 1909
	26	Owned/rented
	27	Owned free or mortgaged
	28	Farm or house
	29	No. of farm schedule
	30	Civil War Veteran
	31	Blind
	32	Deaf & dumb

1920 Census

Local Community _____ County _____ State _____

Ward _____ [Official census day—1 January 1920] Supervisor's District # _____

Enumerator _____ Date Census Taken _____ Enumeration District # _____

Page No.	Street	House No.	Dwelling No.	Family No.	Name of each person whose place of abode on 1 Jan 1920 was in this family	Relationship	Own or rent home	Owned free or mortgaged	Sex	Color or race	Age	Marital status	Immigration year	Naturalized or alien?	Naturalization year	School since 1 Sept 1919	Can read	Can write	Birthplace of						Speaks English?	Profession or Occupation & nature of business		Employer, wage earner, or self-employed	No. of farm schedule
																			This person	Mother tongue	Father	Mother tongue	Mother	Mother tongue					
1	2	3	4	5		6	7	8	9	10	11	12	13	14	15	16	17	18	19	20	21	22	23	24	25	26	27	28	29

UNPUZZLING YOUR PAST WORKBOOK

1920 Census

Local Community ———

Ward ———

Enumerator ———

County ———

[Official census day—1 January 1920]

Date Census Taken ———

State ———

Supervisor's District # ———

Enumeration District # ———

		Page No.											
1	Street												
2	House No.												
3	Dwelling No.												
4	Family No.												
5	Name of each person whose place of abode on 1 Jan 1920 was in this family												
6	Relationship												
7	Own or rent home												
8	Owned free or mortgaged												
9	Sex												
10	Color or race												
11	Age												
12	Marital status												
13	Immigration year												
14	Naturalized or alien?												
15	Naturalization year												
16	School since 1 Sept 1919												
17	Can read												
18	Can write												
19	This person (Birthplace of)												
20	Mother tongue												
21	Father (Birthplace of)												
22	Mother tongue												
23	Mother (Birthplace of)												
24	Mother tongue												
25	Speaks English?												
26	Profession or Occupation & nature of business												
27													
28	Employer, wage earner, or self-employed												
29	No. of farm schedule												

1920 Census

Local Community _____

Ward _____

Enumerator _____

County _____

State _____

Supervisor's District # _____

Enumeration District # _____

[Official census day—1 January 1920]

Date Census Taken _____

Page No.	1 Street	2 House No.	3 Dwelling No.	4 Family No.	5 Name of each person whose place of abode on 1 Jan 1920 was in this family	6 Relationship	7 Own or rent home	8 Owned free or mortgaged	9 Sex	10 Color or race	11 Age	12 Marital status	13 Immigration year	14 Naturalized or alien?	15 Naturalization year	16 School since 1 Sept 1919	17 Can read	18 Can write	Birthplace of						25 Speaks English?	26 / 27 Profession or Occupation & nature of business	28 Employer, wage earner, or self-employed	29 No. of farm schedule
																			19 This person	20 Mother tongue	21 Father	22 Mother tongue	23 Mother	24 Mother tongue				

1920 Census

Local Community _____
Ward _____
Enumerator _____

County _____
[Official census day—1 January 1920]
Date Census Taken _____

State _____
Supervisor's District # _____
Enumeration District # _____

1	2	3	4	5	6	7	8	9	10	11	12	13	14	15	16	17	18	19	20	21	22	23	24	25	26 27	28	29
Street	House No.	Dwelling No.	Family No.	Name of each person whose place of abode on 1 Jan 1920 was in this family	Relationship	Own or rent home	Owned free or mortgaged	Sex	Color or race	Age	Marital status	Immigration year	Naturalized or alien?	Naturalization year	School since 1 Sept 1919	Can read	Can write	Birthplace of — This person	Mother tongue	Father	Mother tongue	Mother	Mother tongue	Speaks English?	Profession or Occupation & nature of business	Employer, wage earner, or self-employed	No. of farm schedule

Page No. _____

1920 Census

U N P U Z Z L I N G   Y O U R   P A S T   W O R K B O O K

Local Community _____ County _____ State _____

Ward _____ [Official census day—1 January 1920] Supervisor's District # _____

Enumerator _____ Date Census Taken _____ Enumeration District # _____

Page No.	Street	House No.	Dwelling No.	Family No.	Name of each person whose place of abode on 1 Jan 1920 was in this family	Relationship	Own or rent home	Owned free or mortgaged	Sex	Color or race	Age	Marital status	Immigration year	Naturalized or alien?	Naturalization year	School since 1 Sept 1919	Can read	Can write	Birthplace of						Speaks English?	Profession or Occupation & nature of business		Employer, wage earner, or self-employed	No. of farm schedule
																			This person	Mother tongue	Father	Mother tongue	Mother	Mother tongue					
1	2	3	4	5		6	7	8	9	10	11	12	13	14	15	16	17	18	19	20	21	22	23	24	25	26	27	28	29

Pre-1930 Period

Interview with _____

Interviewer, date, place _____

Your age in 1930 _____ or circle as appropriate: child   teenager   young adult   adult

Size of your family in the 1920s: _____. Names of persons in the household & relationship to you:

Residence(s) before 1930, with dates, street, town, state _____

When did the family get any of these "modern conveniences"? Telephone _____ Car _____ Electricity _____
Indoor plumbing _____ Running water in the house _____ Vacuum cleaner _____ Electric fans _____
Washing machine _____ Other?

What kind of cooking stove did you or your mother use before 1930? What kind of refrigeration for food?

How was your house heated in the winter? _____

Did your family own its home? _____ Rent? _____ How much was rent? _____
What can you tell me about your house(s) before 1930? Rooms? Size? One, two or more stories? Wood, brick, etc.?

Did your family ever experience a house fire? _____ flood? _____ other natural disaster? _____ Elaborate.

Were you a student before 1930? _____ How far in school did you go? _____
How far from home was your school? _____
Did you have to buy your books or did the school provide them? _____
What can you tell me about your elementary or high school experiences?

What jobs did family members hold in the 1920s or before? (Did any of the women work outside the home?)

Did you work in the 1920s? Doing what?

How did you decide "what you wanted to be when you grew up"?

What did you do for entertainment in the 1920s or before?

When did you or your family get a radio for the first time? _____ a phonograph? _____
Did anyone in the family play a musical instrument? Who? What?

How often did you go to movies? Favorites?

Did the family have pets? Explain.

What part did sports or games play in your life in this period?

During childhood, what is your earliest memory of home and family? How old were you?

What is your earliest memory of events outside the family? How old were you?

During childhood, what were your favorite toys and games? Did you make any of your own toys?

To what extent were family gatherings part of your life before 1930? Explain.

To what extent were religious activities a part in your life before 1930? Explain.

What, if any, rules governed Sunday or the Sabbath in your home before 1930?

Was dancing allowed in your family? _____ Card playing? _____ Dating without a chaperone? _____
Were family members restricted in what they could read for pleasure?
What other rules or customs governed behavior?

How did your family celebrate or observe birthdays? Christmas or other religious holidays? July 4?

What wedding or funeral customs do you remember in your family or community in this period?

Do you remember when you or your family got a camera for the first time? _____

What kind of transportation did you use most? _____

How did you get to school or work? _____

What did the family do at lunch time? Come home or eat elsewhere? What do you remember about school lunches?

Was the main meal at noon or in the evening? What did you call that meal?

If you lived on a farm, what crops did the family raise? What food?

Did any family members serve in the military in World War I? Who? Where?

How did the family celebrate the end of World War I?

Was this a good period in your life? _____ How did your experiences before 1930 affect your life thereafter?

Depression—1930s

Interview with _____

Interviewer, date, place _____

Your age in 1930 _____ or circle as appropriate: child   teenager   young adult   adult

Size of your family in the 30s _____. Names of persons in the household & relationship to you:

Your residence(s) in the 30s, with dates, street, town, state: _____

Did the family own its home? _____ Rent? _____ How much was rent? _____

Did the family have a telephone? _____ electricity? _____ electric appliances? _____ indoor plumbing and running water? _____

What kind of cook stove was used? _____

Which of these were acquired for the first time during the 1930s?

Were you in school any time in the 30s? _____ What level? _____ How did the Depression affect the students in the family?

How did you or they finance education? (jobs, scholarships, parents, etc.?) _____

Did elementary & high school students have to buy their own books or did the school provide them?

Did you or family members have to drop out of school to work? _____ Temporarily? _____ Permanently? _____

Who in the family held jobs during the 30s? Doing what? How many hours/day or days/week did you or they work?

Did you or family members have trouble finding a job? _____ How were you/they able to find work?

Were wages paid in cash, goods, scrip?

Was the family self-supporting? _____ Did you help support your family? Explain.

Was the family a "do-it-yourself" group? If so, explain. Sewing? Carpentry? Making toys? Etc.

How did you or the family "make ends meet"?

Were you or the family able to buy on credit? _____ What items?

Do you remember prices of any items?

What did you do for recreation or entertainment? _____

Did you go to movies? How often? _____ When did you see your first movie with sound? _____ Title?

     First movie in color? _____ Title? Favorite movies, stars?

Did your family own & listen to a radio? _____ Favorite programs?

What part did sports or games play in your life in the 1930s?

If you were a child, what were your favorite toys & games?

Did the family have pets? Explain.

What chores were the children and teenagers expected to do?

To what extent were you involved in religious activities in the 1930s? school activities?

Which social, civic, service, labor, or fraternal organizations were you involved in?

Did you or the family own a car? _____ More than one? _____ What make/model car? _____

Do you remember the price of the car or of gasoline? _____ If you had no car, what kind of transportation did you rely on?

Did you or family members travel? _____ By what means? _____
Were trips mostly for business or pleasure? (Comments are welcome.)

What is your earliest or most vivid memory of home and family? How old were you?

What is your earliest memory of events outside the family? How old were you?

In the 1930s, did the family raise, hunt, make, can, preserve any of its own food? If so, what items?

Which food items were most difficult to obtain? _____ easy to obtain? _____

Which commodities (clothes, appliances, tools, toys, etc.) were most difficult to obtain?

Which were easy to obtain?

Did the family have to sacrifice any luxuries or conveniences during the Depression? Explain.

Did you listen to President Roosevelt's Fireside Chats on the radio? _____ What did you think of him as President during the Depression?

Did you or family members work for any of the New Deal agencies (Works Progress Administration, Civilian Conservation Corps, etc.)? What kinds of jobs? Where?

Did you hear Orson Welles's *The War of the Worlds* on radio on 30 October 1939? _____ What did you think? Did you or family members believe it was true? Why or why not?

How have your experiences during the Depression affected your attitudes and life of the present?

World War II and the 1940s

Interview with _____

Interviewer, date, place _____

Your age in 1940 _____ or age group during the war: child   teenager   young adult   adult

Size of your family in the 40s _____. Names of persons in the household & relationship to you:

Residence(s) during the war _____

Residence(s) after the war (1945-1950) with dates, street, town, state: _____

In the 1940s, did you or your family own your home or rent? _____

Which "modern conveniences" did you or your family have before 1940: telephone; radio; electric toaster, mixer, or vacuum cleaner; washing machine; record player; attic or whole-house fan, etc.?

Did you acquire any of these for the first time after the war and before 1950? _____

Did you or your family acquire television or air conditioning before 1950? _____

After the war, what were some of the first major purchases you or your family made?

Were you or your family part of the "rush to the suburbs" after 1945? _____ When? _____ Where?

Were you a student during the 1940s? _____ What level? _____

Did you or family members pursue higher education during the war? _____ Who? Where?

How did the start of the war change your life or plans?

Your job(s) during the war: _____

What jobs did other family members have?

What kind of work schedule did you have? What were your wages?

Who in the family did wartime volunteer work and what kind? Please be specific.

What did you do for entertainment during the war years?

To what extent were you involved in social, civic, service, labor, or fraternal organizations in the 1940s? Which ones?

If you were a child, what were your favorite toys & games?

Did you or your family own a car? _____ More than one? _____ What make/model? _____

What difficulties did you have in keeping it (repairs, parts, tires, gasoline)?

Were you able to travel for pleasure? _____ By car, bus, train? Destination(s)?

What were you doing when you heard about the attack on Pearl Harbor, 7 December 1941? What was your reaction?

Did you hear Roosevelt's "Day of Infamy" speech on 8 December 1941? _____ What was your reaction?

Were you or family members in military service? Who? Which service? Rank(s)?

Were you or family members volunteers or draftees? _____ When did you or they enter service?

Where were you (they) stationed? Or where did you (they) fight? Please comment.

Did your family raise any of its own food during the war? If so, what items?
Did your family can or preserve any of its own food? If so, what items?

What food items were most difficult to obtain? _____ What food items were easiest to get?
What problems did you have in using ration stamps?

What commodities (clothes, toilet tissue, appliances, tires, toys, gasoline, etc.) were most difficult to get?

What items were not available at all?

Did your area experience blackouts? _____ brownouts? _____ Please comment.

Did you rely more on radio, newspapers, movie newsreels, or friends for news?

If you were a child, what is your earliest memory of home & family? How old were you?

What is your earliest memory of events outside the family? How old were you?

To what extent were you aware of the war?

What was your reaction (or your parents') to Roosevelt's decision to seek a fourth term in 1944?

What was your reaction (or your parents') at the time to dropping the two atomic bombs in Japan?

How did you celebrate the end of the war, either VE or VJ Day? If you were in the military, when did you get home?

After the war, did you or family members have difficulty finding work?

After the war, how was your life different from what it had been in 1940?

How have your World War II experiences affected your attitudes or your life?

Decade of the 1950s

Interview with _____

Interviewer, date, place _____

Your age in 1950 _____ or circle as appropriate:　　child　　teenager　　young adult　　adult

Size of your family in the 1950s _____. Names of persons in the family & relationship to you:

Residence(s) during the 1950s, with dates, street, town, state: _____

Did your family own its home? _____ How much did the home cost? _____

Did your family rent its home? _____ How much was rent? _____

In what ways was your home different in the 1950s from the 1930s or 1940s?

Did you live in a new house? an older house?

Which conveniences did you or your family get for the first time in the 1950s? When?　　washing machine _____, clothes dryer _____, dishwasher _____, electric or gas cook stove _____, vacuum cleaner _____, television _____, air conditioning _____, other?

If you were in school in this decade, what level? _____ Where?

What rules & regulations did your school(s) have?

What job(s) did you or family members have in the 1950s?

When did you get your first job? _____ What were your wages/salary? _____

Did you have any job(s) as a teenager? Elaborate.

What did you do for recreation and leisure activity in the 1950s?

To what extent were sports part of your life in this period? As participant or spectator?

What family rules or restrictions governed dating in the 1950s?

Was dancing allowed in your family or community? _____ If so, what dances did you enjoy?

If you were a child in the 1950s, what were your favorite toys and games?

Did you have and ride a bicycle?

If you had a TV, what rules or restrictions, if any, governed its use?

What were your favorite TV programs?

Favorite movies?

Did you listen to radio in the 1950s? _____ Favorite programs?

Did you buy phonograph records of popular music? _____ of other music? _____

Did you have favorite popular music stars? _____ If so, who? _____

Were you an Elvis Presley fan? _____ Did you go to drive-in movies? _____

What fads or fashions did you enjoy in the 1950s?

What organizations (social, civic, service, labor, or fraternal) were you involved in?

To what extent were religious activities part of your life in the 1950s? Explain.

When and why did you take your first airplane trip? (Even if before 1950) _____

If you were a child or teen, did you get an allowance? _____ How much, how often? _____

What chores, if any, were attached to the allowance? _____

What chores were you or children and teens in your home expected to do in the 1950s?

Do you remember prices of anything, including cars, education, appliances, food?

Which, if any, major news events did you watch on TV? (Eisenhower's inaugurations, Queen Elizabeth II's coronation, the McCarthy hearings, etc.)

Were you or family members in the military during the Korean War (1950-1953)? Elaborate: who, when, where, etc.

What was your reaction to the outbreak of the Korean War so soon after WWII?

Looking back, what differences, if any, do you see between life in the 1940s and the 1950s?

What "firsts" occurred in your life in the 1950s?

What significant events in your life occurred in the 1950s?

How would you characterize the 1950s in your life? How did this decade compare to ones before or after?

Decade of the 1960s

Interview with _____

Interviewer, date, place _____

Your age in 1960 _____ or circle as appropriate: child   teenager   young adult   adult

Size of your family in the 1960s _____. Names of persons in the family & relationship to you:

Residence(s) in the 1960s, with dates, street, town, state: _____

Did your family own its home? _____ When was the home purchased, at what price? _____

Did your family rent its home? _____ How much was rent? _____

Describe your main residence of the decade. What were its outstanding characteristics, features, amenities?

If you were a student during the 1960s, what level, where? _____

What level of schooling did you complete?

What school rules governed dress and behavior for students in your family in the 1960s?

To what extent did your schooling prepare you for your career?

How did you decide what career you would pursue?

What job(s) did you or family members have in the 1960s? Do you remember the level of wages?

If you were a teenager during the 1960s, did you hold any job(s)? Elaborate.

What did you enjoy most for recreation and entertainment in the 1960s?

If you were a child in the 1960s, what were your favorite toys, games, pastimes?

To what extent was television part of your life in the 1960s?

What family rules, if any, governed the use of television in your home?

To what extent were movies, popular music, and radio part of your life in the 1960s?

To what extent were sports part of your life, as participant or as spectator?

What *family* rules, if any, governed dating and teen activities in the 1960s? (use of car, curfew, dress code, etc.)

What fads and fashions did you enjoy in the 1960s?

Were there fads, fashions, or aspects of popular culture you avoided in the 1960s?

Were you or family members considered "hippies" or "flower children"? Explain.

As a child or teen, did you get an allowance? _____ How much, how often? _____

Were chores attached to the allowance? _____ What chores were you or children in your home expected to do in the 1960s?

To what extent were religious activities part of your life in the 1960s?

Which social, civic, service, labor, or fraternal organizations did you participate in?

Did you watch on television or listen on radio to any of these news events? What was your reaction?
   (a) First US manned space flight, May, 1961

   (b) Cuban missile crisis, October, 1962

   (c) US military build-up in Vietnam from 1963 forward

   (d) President John F. Kennedy's death and funeral, November 1963

   (e) Assassination of Dr. Martin Luther King, April, 1968

   (f) Apollo 11 landing on the moon, 20 July 1969

   (g) Other?

Were you or any family members involved in anti-war, feminist, or civil rights demonstrations during the 1960s? Who? Where? Elaborate.

Were you or any family member in the military during the Vietnam war? Who? When? Where? Drafted or volunteer?

Comments?

What "firsts" occurred in your life during the 1960s? (first car, first time to vote, first job, first child, etc.)

What significant events occurred in your own life in the 1960s?

How would you characterize the 1960s in the life of the country? in your personal life?

How did this decade compare to those before or after, in your life?

Family Group Sheet of the _____ Family, continued

Father _____ Mother _____

Children of this marriage	Birth date & place	Death date, place, & burial place	Marriage date, place & spouse
Source #s			
Source #s			
Source #s			
Source #s			
Source #s			
Source #s			
Source #s			
Source #s			

Notes

Family Group Sheet of the _____ Family

Full name of husband	Birth date
His father	Birth place
	Death date
	Death place
His mother with maiden name	Burial place

Full maiden name of wife	Birth date
Her father	Birth place
	Death date
	Death place
Her mother with maiden name	Burial place

| Other Spouses | Marriage date, place, etc. |
| Source #s | Source #s |

Children of this marriage	Birth date & place	Death date, place, & burial place	Marriage date, place & spouse
Source #s			
Source #s			
Source #s			
Source #s			
Source #s			
Source #s			

Family Group Sheet of the _____ Family, continued

Father _____ Mother _____

Children of this marriage	Birth date & place	Death date, place, & burial place	Marriage date, place & spouse
Source #s			
Source #s			
Source #s			
Source #s			
Source #s			
Source #s			
Source #s			
Source #s			

Notes

Source #   Sources (Documentation)

Family Group Sheet of the _____ Family

Full name of husband	Birth date
His father	Birth place
	Death date
	Death place
His mother with maiden name	Burial place

Full maiden name of wife	Birth date
Her father	Birth place
	Death date
	Death place
Her mother with maiden name	Burial place

| Other Spouses | Marriage date, place, etc. |
| Source #s | Source #s |

Children of this marriage	Birth date & place	Death date, place, & burial place	Marriage date, place & spouse
Source #s			
Source #s			
Source #s			
Source #s			
Source #s			
Source #s			

Source #	Sources (Documentation)

Family Group Sheet of the _____ Family, continued

Father _____ Mother _____

Children of this marriage	Birth date & place	Death date, place, & burial place	Marriage date, place & spouse
Source #s			
Source #s			
Source #s			
Source #s			
Source #s			
Source #s			
Source #s			
Source #s			
Source #s			

Notes

Family Group Sheet of the _____ Family

Full name of husband	Birth date
His father	Birth place
	Death date
	Death place
His mother with maiden name	Burial place

Full maiden name of wife	Birth date
Her father	Birth place
	Death date
	Death place
Her mother with maiden name	Burial place

| Other Spouses | Marriage date, place, etc. |
| Source #s | Source #s |

Children of this marriage	Birth date & place	Death date, place, & burial place	Marriage date, place & spouse
Source #s			
Source #s			
Source #s			
Source #s			
Source #s			
Source #s			

Source #   Sources (Documentation)

Family Group Sheet of the _____ Family, continued

Father _____ Mother _____

Children of this marriage	Birth date & place	Death date, place, & burial place	Marriage date, place & spouse
Source #s			
Source #s			
Source #s			
Source #s			
Source #s			
Source #s			
Source #s			
Source #s			
Source #s			

Notes

Source #	Sources (Documentation)

Family Group Sheet of the _____ Family

		Source #
Full name of husband	Birth date	
	Birth place	
	Death date	
His father	Death place	
	Burial place	
His mother with maiden name		

Full maiden name of wife	Birth date	
	Birth place	
	Death date	
Her father	Death place	
	Burial place	
Her mother with maiden name		

Other Spouses	Marriage date, place, etc.
Source #s	Source #s

Children of this marriage	Birth date & place	Death date, place, & burial place	Marriage date, place & spouse
Source #s			
Source #s			
Source #s			
Source #s			
Source #s			
Source #s			

Source #	Sources (Documentation)

Family Group Sheet of the _____ Family, continued

Father _____ Mother _____

Children of this marriage	Birth date & place	Death date, place, & burial place	Marriage date, place & spouse
Source #s			
Source #s			
Source #s			
Source #s			
Source #s			
Source #s			
Source #s			
Source #s			
Source #s			

Notes

Source #   Sources (Documentation)

Family Group Sheet of the _____ Family

Full name of husband	Birth date
	Birth place
	Death date
His father	Death place
	Burial place
His mother with maiden name	

Full maiden name of wife	Birth date
	Birth place
	Death date
Her father	Death place
	Burial place
Her mother with maiden name	

| Other Spouses | Marriage date, place, etc. |
| Source #s | Source #s |

Children of this marriage	Birth date & place	Death date, place, & burial place	Marriage date, place & spouse
Source #s			
Source #s			
Source #s			
Source #s			
Source #s			
Source #s			

Source #	Sources (Documentation)

Family Group Sheet of the _____ Family, continued

Father _____ Mother _____

Children of this marriage	Birth date & place	Death date, place, & burial place	Marriage date, place & spouse
Source #s			
Source #s			
Source #s			
Source #s			
Source #s			
Source #s			
Source #s			
Source #s			
Source #s			

Notes

Source #	Sources (Documentation)

Family Group Sheet of the _____ Family

Full name of husband	Birth date
	Birth place
His father	Death date
	Death place
His mother with maiden name	Burial place

Full maiden name of wife	Birth date
	Birth place
Her father	Death date
	Death place
Her mother with maiden name	Burial place

Other Spouses	Marriage date, place, etc.
Source #s	Source #s

Children of this marriage	Birth date & place	Death date, place, & burial place	Marriage date, place & spouse
Source #s			
Source #s			
Source #s			
Source #s			
Source #s			
Source #s			

Source #   Sources (Documentation)

Family Group Sheet of the _____ Family, continued

Father _____ Mother _____

Children of this marriage	Birth date & place	Death date, place, & burial place	Marriage date, place & spouse
Source #s			
Source #s			
Source #s			
Source #s			
Source #s			
Source #s			
Source #s			
Source #s			
Source #s			

Notes

Source #	Sources (Documentation)

Family Group Sheet of the _____ Family

Full name of husband	Birth date
His father	Birth place
	Death date
	Death place
His mother with maiden name	Burial place

Full maiden name of wife	Birth date
Her father	Birth place
	Death date
	Death place
Her mother with maiden name	Burial place

| Other Spouses | Marriage date, place, etc. |

Source #s   Source #s

Children of this marriage	Birth date & place	Death date, place, & burial place	Marriage date, place & spouse
Source #s			
Source #s			
Source #s			
Source #s			
Source #s			
Source #s			

Source #	Sources (Documentation)

Family Group Sheet of the _____ Family, continued

Father _____ Mother _____

Children of this marriage	Birth date & place	Death date, place, & burial place	Marriage date, place & spouse
Source #s			
Source #s			
Source #s			
Source #s			
Source #s			
Source #s			
Source #s			
Source #s			
Source #s			

Notes

Source #   Sources (Documentation)

Family Group Sheet of the _____ Family

	Source #		Source #
Full name of husband His father His mother with maiden name	Birth date Birth place Death date Death place Burial place		
Full maiden name of wife Her father Her mother with maiden name	Birth date Birth place Death date Death place Burial place		
Other Spouses Source #s	Marriage date, place, etc. Source #s		

Children of this marriage	Birth date & place	Death date, place, & burial place	Marriage date, place & spouse
  Source #s			
  Source #s			
  Source #s			
  Source #s			
  Source #s			
  Source #s			

Source #	Sources (Documentation)

Family Group Sheet of the _____ Family, continued

Father _____ Mother _____

Children of this marriage	Birth date & place	Death date, place, & burial place	Marriage date, place & spouse
Source #s			
Source #s			
Source #s			
Source #s			
Source #s			
Source #s			
Source #s			
Source #s			
Source #s			

Notes

Family Group Sheet of the _____ Family

Source #

Full name of husband	Birth date
	Birth place
His father	Death date
	Death place
His mother with maiden name	Burial place

Full maiden name of wife	Birth date
	Birth place
Her father	Death date
	Death place
Her mother with maiden name	Burial place

| Other Spouses | Marriage date, place, etc. |
| Source #s | Source #s |

Children of this marriage	Birth date & place	Death date, place, & burial place	Marriage date, place & spouse
Source #s			
Source #s			
Source #s			
Source #s			
Source #s			
Source #s			

Source #	Sources (Documentation)

Family Group Sheet of the _____ Family, continued

Father _____ Mother _____

Children of this marriage	Birth date & place	Death date, place, & burial place	Marriage date, place & spouse
Source #s			
Source #s			
Source #s			
Source #s			
Source #s			
Source #s			
Source #s			
Source #s			
Source #s			

Notes

Source #   Sources (Documentation)

Ahnentafel Table for No. 1 _____

Double a person's number to find the father. Double the number and add 1 to find the mother.

Paternal Line	Maternal Line
Parents	
2	3
Grandparents	
4	6
5	7
Great-Grandparents	
8	12
9	13
10	14
11	15
Great-Great-Grandparents	
16	24
17	25
18	26
19	27
20	28
21	29
22	30
23	31
Great-Great-Great-Grandparents	
32	48
33	49
34	50
35	51
36	52
37	53
38	54
39	55
40	56
41	57
42	58
43	59
44	60
45	61
46	62
47	63

Ahnentafel Chart for No. 1 _____ continued

Paternal Line	Maternal Line
Great-Great-Great-Great-Grandparents	
64	96
65	97
66	98
67	99
68	100
69	101
70	102
71	103
72	104
73	105
74	106
75	107
76	108
77	109
78	110
79	111
80	112
81	113
82	114
83	115
84	116
85	117
86	118
87	119
88	120
89	121
90	122
91	123
92	124
93	125
94	126
95	127

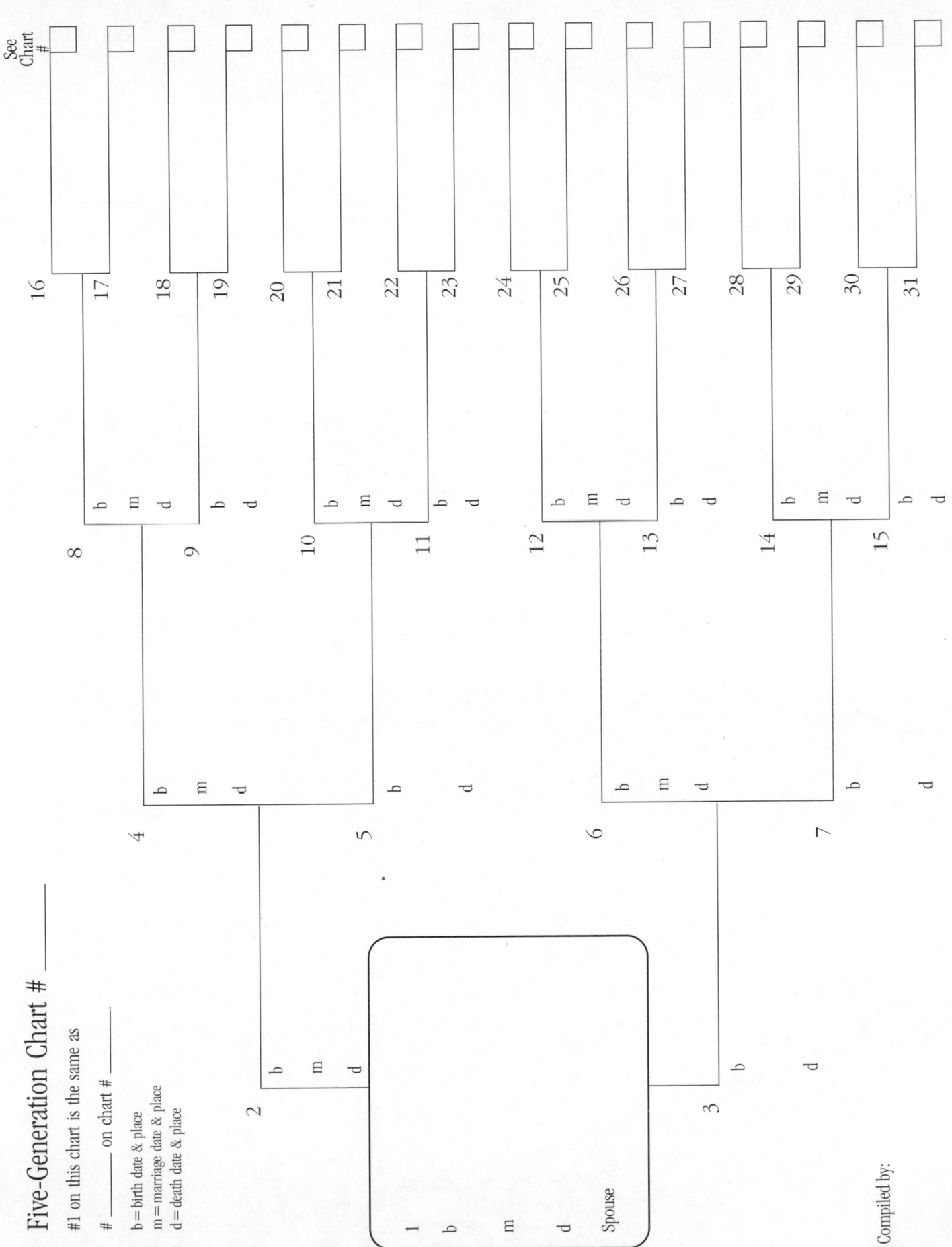

Five-Generation Chart # _____

#1 on this chart is the same as

_____ on chart # _____

b = birth date & place
m = marriage date & place
d = death date & place

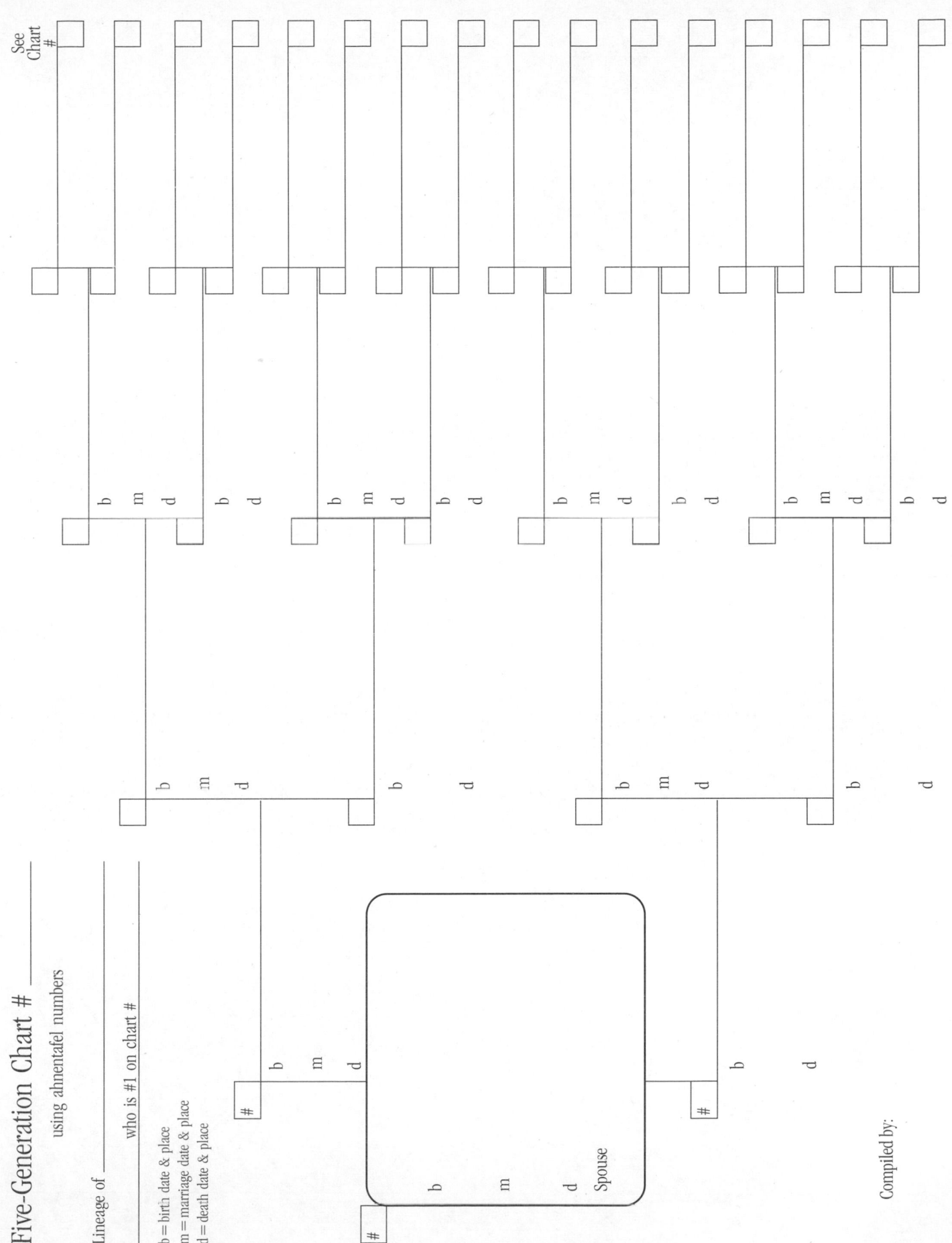

Five-Generation Chart # _____

using ahnentafel numbers

Lineage of _____

_____ who is #1 on chart #

b = birth date & place
m = marriage date & place
d = death date & place

See Chart #

Spouse

Compiled by:

Biographical Outline of the Life of _____
(Name of person)

With information on education, military service, marriage(s), children, illnesses, religious milestones, migrations, residences, jobs, family events, land purchases, court appearances, death & burial, etc.

Date	Age	Event and Place	Documentation
Birth		Place	

Date	Age	Event and Place	Documentation
Death		Place	
Burial		Place	
Probate		Place	

Biographical Outline of the Life of _____

(Name of person)

With information on education, military service, marriage(s), children, illnesses, religious milestones, migrations, residences, jobs, family events, land purchases, court appearances, death & burial, etc.

Date	Age	Event and Place	Documentation
Birth		Place	

Date	Age	Event and Place	Documentation
Death		Place	
Burial		Place	
Probate		Place	

Biographical Outline of the Life of _____

(Name of person)

With information on education, military service, marriage(s), children, illnesses, religious milestones, migrations, residences, jobs, family events, land purchases, court appearances, death & burial, etc.

Date	Age	Event and Place	Documentation
Birth		Place	

Date	Age	Event and Place	Documentation
Death		Place	
Burial		Place	
Probate		Place	

Biographical Outline of the Life of _____

(Name of person)

With information on education, military service, marriage(s), children, illnesses, religious milestones, migrations, residences, jobs, family events, land purchases, court appearances, death & burial, etc.

Date	Age	Event and Place	Documentation
Birth		Place	

Date	Age	Event and Place	Documentation
Death		Place	
Burial		Place	
Probate		Place	

Gaylord Stickle Company, Houston Texas

Gaylord Stickle Company, Houston Texas

UNPUZZLING YOUR PAST WORKBOOK

Timeline 1600-1800

Family or Surname _____

1600									

—1607 Jamestown VA founded

—1620 Pilgrims land at Plymouth MA

1625

—1630 Massachusetts Bay Colony

—1634 First settlers to Maryland

—1642-1649 English Civil War

—1649 Charles I beheaded. Cromwell
    & Parliament rule England.

1650

—1660 Restoration of established 1660 church & monarchy.
    Charles II crowned.

—1670 First permanent English settlement in South Carolina

1675

—1682 Pennsylvania colony begins.

1700

—1709-1710 First large German immigration (Palatine)

—1717 Large Scotch-Irish immigration begins, first wave.

1725

—1733 First settlers to Georgia

1750

—1754-1763 French & Indian War

—1763 Treaty of Paris—
    Britain gets Canada & most land east of Mississippi River

1775

—1775-1783 American Revolution

—1788 US Constitution adopted
—1790 First US federal census

1800

Timeline 1750-1950

Family or Surname _____

1750

—1754-1763 French & Indian War

—1763 Treaty of Paris—
    Britain gets Canada & most land east of Mississippi River

1775

—1776 Declaration of Independence—

—1783 Treaty of Paris ending American Revolution

—1788 US Constitution adopted
—1790 First US federal census

1800

—1803 Louisiana Purchase

—1812-1815 War with Britain

—1821 US acquires Florida

1825

—1836-1845 Republic of Texas

—1846 Great Irish potato famine begins
—1849 California gold rush begins

1850

—1858-1859 Colorado gold rush
—1861-1865 Civil War

—1869 Completion of first transcontinental railroad

1875

Between Civil War and WWI—
Westward migration

Urbanization

Industrialization

Immigration, especially from southern &
eastern Europe

—1898-1899 Spanish-American War

1900

—1917-1918 US involvement in WWI

1925

—1929 Great Depression begins

—1941-1945 US involvement in WWII

1950

—1950-1953 Korean War